AN UN G OF *U S*

NORMAL JOYCE FOR NORMAL PEOPLE

By

Russell Raphael

∞

I fear those big words, Stephen said, which make us so unhappy.

LOUGHTON
THE ALDERTON PRESS
2021

First published in 2021 by The Alderton Press (an LDHS imprint)

ISBN 978–1–905269–36–5

A CIP catalogue record for this title is available from the British Library.

Cover design: Sonia Ostrovsky
Cover by Artform, Little Tew, Oxon
Text design, typesetting in Linotype Palatino and production by Ted Martin

Printed in Great Britain by
Blackwell Print
Great Yarmouth

Contents

Acknowledgements ~ 6
Preface ~ 7

Lecture 1, 23 September 2020: Introduction ~ 9

PART I – THE TELEMECHIAD

Lecture 2, 7 October 2020: Episode 1, Telemachus and the Shan Van Vocht ~ 24
Lecture 3, 21 October 2020: Episode 2, Ancient Nestor and the Disappointed Bridge ~ 36
Lecture 4, 4 November 2020: Episode 3, Proteus and the Third Eye ~ 47

PART II – THE WANDERINGS OF ULYSSES

Lecture 5, 18 November 2020: Episode 4, Calypso and the Dude ~ 60
Lecture 6, 2 December 2020: Episode 5, Lotus Eaters and the High Grade Ha ~ 73
Lecture 7, 16 December 2020: Episode 6, Hades and the Dignified Send-off ~ 85
Lecture 8, 6 January 2021: Episode 7, Aeolus in the Windy City ~ 99
Lecture 9, 20 January 2021: Episode 8, Lestrygonians and the Bottomless Buffet ~ 112
Lecture 10, 2 February 2021: Episode 9, Scylla, Charybdis and the Cuckolded Bard ~ 123
Lecture 11, 16 February 2021: Episode 10, Wandering Rocks Gather No Moss ~ 141
Lecture 12, 3 March 2021: Episode 11, Sirens Turn Up, Tune In and Drop Out ~ 157
Lecture 13, 17 March 2021: Episode 12, One in the Eye for the Cyclops ~ 171
Lecture 14, 31 March 2021: Episode 13, Nausicaa and the Coming of Elijah ~ 185
Lecture 15, 21 April 2021: Episode 14, Oxen, Suns and Mothers ~ 196

Lecture 16, 5 May 2021: Episode 15, Circe, Part One – the Witching Hour ~ 212
Lecture 17, 19 May 2021: Episode 15, Circe, Part Two – Potatoes and Chandeliers ~ 226

PART III – THE HOMECOMING

Lecture 18, 2 June 2021: Episode 16, Trust Me, I'm Eumaeus ~ 241
Lecture 19, 16 June 2021: Episode 17, Ithaca Part One, A Heaventree of Stars ~ 253
Lecture 20, 7 July 2021: Episode 17, Ithaca Part Two, Crumbs and Comfort ~ 267
Lecture 21, 21 July 2021: Episode 18, Lady Penelope and the Word Known to All ~ 278
Lecture 22, 4 August 2021: Epilogue, In Our Ends are Our Beginnings ~297
Notes ~ 310
Appendix 1: Gilbert Schema ~ 325
Appendix 2: Music Playlist ~ 327
Bibliography ~ 328

For Claire, Tamar, Beth, Ella and Aidan

Acknowledgements

My thanks to Chris Pond and Ted Martin at The Alderton Press for guiding me through the hitherto unknown mysteries of book publishing; to Sonia Ostrovsky for the lovely watercolour cover artwork; to Marianna Popova for looking over and stylising my initial manuscript; to Anne, Catherine, Sally, Sergei and Sonia with whom I have waded through the book for well over a year; to my wife Claire for indulging me in my latest obsession – most of all, to the little band of hardy and extraordinary folks who to my constant surprise turned up to the lectures for nearly a year.

Preface

Should any of my lovely children ever produce grandchildren and should any of them ask their grandfather what he did in the UK lockdown of 2020, I shall be able to say that alongside the day job, keeping food on the table and applauding outside on summer Thursday evenings, I gave, for reasons I cannot explain, a series of free online lectures on the novel *Ulysses* by James Joyce. I had never done anything like that before; I had never critiqued a book before. But it was a crazy time, so I was a little crazy. They were received quite well and people that had thought *Ulysses* to be a book beyond them finished it and with a sense of achievement; including my mother albeit she still maintains that she doesn't like it. Crazy or otherwise I'm publishing the lectures in this little book. It is refined a little because the spoken word especially mine, can clang somewhat in written form and also but only very occasionally, where a significant thought subsequently occurred. Generally though, they are pretty much as I gave them.

I've taken a slight liberty and tweaked the title. The lecture series was called 'Understanding Ulysses', but it was obvious all too soon that I could not justify so bold a claim. There is no single understanding and, even if there was, I was not so brave as to assert it. So it's an understanding and more to the point, mine.

For ease, reference to 'chapters' usually means Lectures or chapters in this book; chapters in *Ulysses* (indulging that they exist) tend to be labelled 'Episodes'. All Ulysses quotations are from the Penguin 2000 edition.

The first lecture, delivered on 23 September 2020, was an introduction to the series and so serves as an introduction to this book.

RUSSELL RAPHAEL

Fortis Green–East Finchley–Muswell Hill.

2020 to 2021.

LECTURE 1, 23 SEPTEMBER 2020

Introduction

Music: 'To Cut a Long Story Short' – Spandau Ballet

It begins.

> Stately, plump Buck Mulligan came from the stair-head, bearing a bowl of lather on which a mirror and a razor lay crossed.[1]

I'm intrigued by the first lines of novels; how the author must in that instant, draw the reader in and not let go. Here we are intrigued but also learn so much from so little.

A man is about to have a shave. Why would he need to be stately? Who is stately for a shave? As the very first word, it must be an emphatic characteristic and it suggests to me at least, some sort of performance, an Act, which implies an audience. The bowl, and the laid crossed utensils hint of the chalice used in a Catholic mass and that is confirmed by his first words:

> *Introibo ad altare Dei.*[2]

The opening words of the mass – 'I go unto the altar of God'.

From these few words, what do we glean? We have a man, we know his name and that he's plump; a visual, presumably he doesn't go short of food. He comes from the stair-head, so that visual is of a man ascending as though approaching an altar.

What do we think? He is something of a mimic, a joker, a showman. And a blasphemer. It is 1904 Ireland, rigidly Catholic; yet he reduces the sacred act of the mass to his morning shave. His audience will be confirmed in the next few lines but from these initial words, we have identified, correctly, as it turns out, the character of Buck Mulligan and are entitled even at this embryonic stage, to make a far from hazardous guess that the book before us will be comical, a little base, will deal with big issues and be symbolic by virtue of linking matters of mythical magnitude to supposedly innocuous everyday acts.

Such is Joyce and his amazing economy. Every word is precisely right.

—

Welcome to this series of lectures, entitled An Understanding of *Ulysses*. My name is Russell Raphael, and I'll do my best to guide you through what might be considered a challenging novel. A suitable epithet might have been 'normal Joyce for normal people' because I do not intend this to be at PhD geeky level. There's enough of that out there and if that's your thing, it's fantastic, but it's not this thing. Nor though is it an idiot's guide: for there are certain issues to which, if we do not do justice, we miss too much.

This is a book with a reputation, stigma even. Accusations abound of difficulty, vulgarity and obscenity; often from those that have not read it. Some parts are challenging. So what? Not everything in life is easy. If you want a superficial page-turner there are plenty out there. Vulgar? Yes, it's real life, so it gets down and dirty but also scales the heights. Obscene? Well, not in the sense of what we are used to these days. It's not going to titillate but even a hundred years on, it's capable of shocking which I'd say is a good thing. So yes, there are passages that might raise pulses and all the better for that.

In this introduction I'll cover five areas:

1. Some general background.
2. The link to Homer's *The Odyssey*.
3. A little on structure style and content.
4. An overview of two central themes, and
5, I'll finish with an introduction to the main three characters.

Some general background to begin

Ulysses was published in Paris on Joyce's 40th birthday, 2 February 1922. His then published prose works were *Dubliners* a collection of short stories in 1914 and a semi-autobiographical novel *A Portrait of the Artist as a Young Man* in 1916. *Finnegans Wake* would follow in 1939.

Ulysses has been banned, burned, trashed and loved in equal measure. It's a bloody great something of a novel. What that something is, I couldn't say; for it so brims over with laughter and pathos, and song and dance and flesh and blood, pain and joy, blasphemy and reverence, envy and generosity, body, and oh so complex mind, no, and yes, death and life . . . as to defy category. All life is within. It's crammed packed with life; more life than you could shake a stick at or more appropriately, an ashplant.

A novel in which to get lost, drowned, journey, no matter how far, one never quite arrives because there is always a secret garden down an undiscovered lane. To approach it as a challenge is fruitless because it cannot be conquered. If the search for secrets is the compulsive aim, the joy of the ride will be missed. Just let it ooze over you and get what you get; next time there will be more. Don't lose the phosphorescence of the prose in the search for pearls way beneath. Rejoice in the language, celebrate the ordinary. A Day in a life, a Life in a day.

These lectures are primarily directed towards those new to the book, or who have previously struggled with it which, let's face it, catches pretty much everyone.

I'm no academic: simply someone that read, enjoyed, read some more, and was inspired to delve deeper and get under the skin of the thing. I shall try to provide a taster per chapter, to enable you to then read the corresponding episode with some confidence and finish it, satisfied that you understood its essence, even several of the nuances. Of course, technically there are no episodes/chapters but don't worry, we'll get to that. I doubt very much I will say anything original. There cannot be any aspect of *Ulysses*, that has not in these ninety-nine years been stripped bare and had investigative tubes plunged into every orifice for some book or thesis. I will, though, try to give a lively even occasionally jocular overview, so that you may know your Sandymount from Glasnevin, Parnell from Griffiths, Sceptre from Throwaway and The Ormond Hotel from Barney Kiernan's. You may even venture some thoughts on the man in the Macintosh.

The link with Homer

Part two of this introduction is the link with Homer. One will hear that the book is a retelling of Homer's *The Odyssey*. The title is the Latin name for Odysseus, hero of *The Odyssey*, so there's a clue. But were it not for that one maybe forgiven for missing any link between it and Joyce's *Ulysses*. After all, what could Leopold Bloom, a middle aged cuckolded Dubliner of Hungarian Jewish descent, an advertising salesman by trade and pacifist by nature have in common with Odysseus, the warrior king from Ithaca? He of many turns and adventures, usually involving bloody battles and sexual conquests. One survives countless shipwrecks, the other loses control of a rowing boat.[3] One story spans a familial absence of twenty years, in the other hubby pops out, completes some errands, comes home. For this book is set on a single day in Dublin: 16 June 1904.

And yet, Joyce indeed intended Leopold Bloom to be his Ulysses, reincarnated if not intact then in essence. Just as he cast Bloom's wife, the adulterous Molly, as the faithful Penelope and Stephen Dedalus as Telemachus, son of Odysseus and Penelope. Not only are Bloom and Molly not Stephen's parents – his mother has recently died and his father, Simon, appears throughout the novel, alive and very much kicking – but Stephen and Bloom barely know each other. So what's going on? Well it's analogous and analogy does not always walk straight. In this book it does a bit of a jig, staggers about and spills its beer. If it is analogous, then, to what? That, we shall revisit as we go along.

We shall not get too hung up on *The Odyssey*. A phrase one reads is that the book is strung across the loom of the epic; that it's a jumping-off point but not more. That seems to me to strike the right note, as well as chiming with a nice Odyssean theme of weaving. I will refer to it as necessary. For now, suffice to say, Homer's classic is an epic story of usurpation and revenge with lots of adventure (bloody and sexual) along the way. While Odysseus is struggling to return from the Trojan wars, his home is invaded by potential suitors for the hand of his wife, Queen Penelope, who against all odds, maintains dignity and fidelity. Odysseus eventually returns and kills them all.

Joyce read it or a distilled a version of it, at school in Dublin. He had a Jesuit education which is to say, as well as being steeped in religion – Old and New Testaments, was also a superb classical training.

Years later, living in Zurich, he befriended an English artist, Frank Budgen, who Joyce asked, who did he think was the complete human being in literary history; complete, as in whole, three-dimensional, as a sculptor would see a person. Joyce answers his own question:

> Ulysses is son to Laertes, but he's father to Telemachus, husband to Penelope, lover of Calypso, companion in arms of the Greek warriors around Troy and King of Ithaca. He was subjected to many trials, but with wisdom and courage came through them all. Don't forget that he was a war dodger who tried to evade military service by simulating madness . . . But once at the war the conscientious objector became a jusqu'auboutist. When the others wanted to abandon the siege he insisted on staying till Troy should fall.[4]

It's apparent that Joyce reaching forward from as he sometimes saw it, two-dimensional Victorian literature, contemplated a novel featuring fully rounded, real people observed from all directions. A parallax, a word with which Leopold Bloom will grapple, is the difference revealed when viewing something from different perspectives. Joyce intended a study of Dublin humanity but through the prism of that complete human being, the mythical Odysseus. One ought not to forget the feverish excitement that engulfed Victorian and early Edwardian intellectual society following the discovery of the ruins of ancient Troy in the late nineteenth century.[5]

Let's take a minute to run through a potted synopsis of a book that's been described as having both too much and too little plot.

It starts at 8am on a pleasant summer morning in a rather odd fortification tower, south of Dublin. It's called a Martello tower and several of these were built a century or so earlier in concerned anticipation of a French invasion. Three men, in their twenties, have spent the night because it's very cheap accommodation. Two Dubliners, Stephen Dedalus and Malachi 'Buck' Mulligan and an Englishman, Haines.

After breakfasting they part and arrange to meet in a pub at 12.30pm. From Stephen's internal thoughts we know he resents the other two, in particular his so-called friend Buck Mulligan and he wishes to sleep there no more. He sets off for his place of employment, a school in leafy Dalkey, a mile or so away, where he's a part-time teacher and we sit in on lessons until mid-morning. We note that Stephen, dressed in black, is grieving for his mother who died a few months earlier. That day, Thursday, 16 June, is a half-holiday and work stops at lunchtime and for Stephen, it is also monthly pay-day.

We then flash across town to number 7 Eccles Street in the northwest of the city and rewind to 8am. Thirty-eight-year-old Leopold Bloom has made breakfast in bed for his wife Molly. They discuss that later that day, around 4pm, Molly will be visited by local theatre impresario Blazes Boylan, ostensibly to discuss the programme for a touring show the following week which is to feature soprano Molly. What is left unsaid, but well known to both, is that any discussion between Molly and Boylan will take place in the matrimonial bed. Bloom leaves the house and for our introductory purposes, will not return until the small hours. His day will focus on practicalities. For example, attending the funeral of an acquaintance and therefore he, too, is dressed in black and also in trying to earn some money by placing a newspaper advertisement for a customer. But really, he's just keeping out of the way and to mentally cope with the strong expectation that his wife of nearly twenty years will be unfaithful that afternoon; whether this is a regular occurrence, or one off, we know not until very near the end.

We shall learn that Bloom will struggle to maintain the moral high ground. He will conduct a clandestine affair of his own, albeit only via correspondence and will harbour lustful thoughts for other women. Molly and Bloom have not had sex for over ten years, since the death of their son Rudy who lived only eleven days, which provides context to Molly's infidelity and Bloom's bawdy reverie. They have a daughter Milly, aged fifteen, who has recently moved away to take a job and which adds to her father's angst.

As the story unfolds we gradually sense that Stephen and Bloom have some sort of connection but are only peripherally aware of each other's existence and do not really meet until around 10.30 that night at a maternity hospital. Neither has an obvious reason to be there so it is somewhat serendipitous. Meantime, we follow them separately around Dublin, more Bloom than Stephen, which is a blessing because Stephen, like his *alter ego* the young James Joyce, has a deep brooding nature with tendency to over intellectualise and condescend. Whereas Bloom, in spite, or because of personal peccadilloes and fallibilities, is more in chime with the normal reader. Bloom episodes are a lot easier than Stephen episodes. Day gives way to night and Bloom develops paternal feelings for Stephen. He is aware of Stephen's mother's recent death and that his boozy father seems intent on driving the family to the poorhouse. Beyond midnight, he follows the by now very drunk Stephen to the red light area and when Stephen gets into a fight, rescues him from prosecution. They return to Bloom's house for a cup of cocoa before Stephen departs. In the final episode, Molly gives her version of events.

And that's it. We are not dealing here with drama on an epic scale or anything close but put a microscope to ordinary life and properly observed, we have drama, pathos, and comedy nonetheless. We may say, we have the inspiration for the soap opera.

Structure style and content

A word now on structure style and content. Taking its cue from Homer, the book splits into three parts; the first three episodes constitute the Telemachiad. In *The Odyssey*, this is where Telemachus sets out to find his father and in *Ulysses*, these centre on Stephen Dedalus. The next twelve episodes are the Wanderings of Ulysses in which we observe Bloom's various trips around Dublin. This is the heart and great bulk of the story. The final three episodes correspond to the Homecoming or nostos in *The Odyssey*, and depict Stephen and Bloom returning from Nighttown, for a cup of cocoa at Bloom's house. The book could end there but thank goodness it does not for, in the final episode, Penelope, we have the inner thoughts of Molly Bloom as she lies in bed with her sleeping husband. A *tour de force* of world literature.

It's a book of many styles and after initial orthodoxy, style fluctuates per episode. But the narrator, sometimes reliable, sometimes not, is generally in charge. More of a technique is the use of *le monologue interieur;* stream of consciousness. The inner thoughts of a character set out on the page. Joyce is far from unique in its use, even then; but what makes him sometimes so difficult is that he hops from narrative to dialogue to *monologue interieur* and back; mid-sentence, interchanging characters, interchanging language. Sometimes the person talking or thinking maybe an inanimate object! All without a 'by your leave' to the reader.

Taking a cue from Nabokov's *Lectures on Literature,* let's look at an early example.

It's right at the beginning back up on that roof of the Martello tower where Buck Mulligan is shaving. He's talking to or rather at Stephen in the typically mocking and crude manner which we'll come to expect of the Buck. They both look out over Dublin Bay. Pertinent background here is that Stephen was bedside when his mother died a few months earlier. A devout Catholic, she asks him to pray for redemption of her soul, but Stephen, following Joyce in vaguely comparable circumstances in 1903, has renounced religion and does not. Mulligan having snatched Stephen's handkerchief to clean his razor, makes crude remarks about the 'dirty noserag'. He looks out over circular Dublin Bay (he calls it the snotgreen sea, the scrotum-tightening sea) and recalls how the poet Algernon Swinburne described the sea as the grey sweet mother. He admonishes Stephen: why could he not have just done the decent thing and prayed for his mother, like a normal person?

All this feeds into Stephen's thought. The circular bay, the snotgreen sea, the sweet mother and in his head, he's back at her deathbed. The ring of bay and skyline encircling the snotgreen sea reminds him of the ceramic bowl at his mother's bedside, into which she vomited the green bile retched from her rotting kidneys. The sweet mother resonates the bitter memory of his (or her) bitter tears.

This, all in a millisecond as the conversation ping-pongs. It also serves to contrast the characters: Buck Mulligan for whom life is generally a crude joke and Stephen for whom trivia is serious business, so we can only imagine how the death of his mother and his own part in that, must be torturing him.

Turning from style to content, like Forrest Gump's box of chocolates, there's something for everyone, so broad is Joyce's grasp. Really, no matter the background, a particular reader might appreciate nuances that most scholars do not. If you know Dublin you have, even after one hundred years, an advantage in being able to better visualise what the rest of us can only imagine. If you were raised Catholic or Jewish; if you know some Irish history, or some Latin or the classics; if you've studied philosophy, Shakespeare or understand the pub industry or newspapers, or are musical, etc, etc., any and more might reveal nuggets that sail over other heads, even clever heads.

Before introducing the main three characters, I'd like to discuss some themes or undercurrents that run throughout. These are myriad: compassion, Irish nationalism, racism, animal rights, many more. But I highlight just two to be able to drill down a little. The first is somewhat whacky and esoteric but hang on in there – we are on steadier ground with the second.

Overview of two central themes

Souls in time and space

The first one is Souls in time and space.

It is a book about time. While uncertainty might generally abound, we tend to know the time of day. Yet, time concertinas. At one point, Stephen has a real or imagined time-shift to mediaeval Dublin whereas in the crazy, magical and very funny episode 'Circe', Bloom experiences visionary sequences running several pages but which in real time last a millisecond.

We first meet the Blooms in episode four. Molly, reading in bed, asks Bloom the meaning of a word she has read in her novel:

> Met him what? he asked.
>
> Here, she said. What does that mean?
>
> . . .
>
> Metempsychosis?
>
> Yes. Who's he when he's at home?
>
> Metempsychosis, he said, frowning. It's Greek: from the Greek. That means the transmigration of souls.
>
> Oh rocks! She said. Tell us in plain words.[6]

We may be more familiar with the word reincarnation – that our souls transport across the ages, residing awhile in various receptacles. The question is asked in episode fourteen: 'What is the age of the soul of man?'[7]

Odysseus and Bloom may be separated by thousands of years and are superficially at least, so different but nevertheless as the story unfolds, we wonder if their souls are connected and that if time between them might evaporate. Intertwined in this is the notion that history is a constant cycle of repetition. Giambattista Vico, a philosopher born in 1668 in Naples, not only considered there to be nothing new under the sun, but that the repeating historical cycles beat to a certain rhythm. Tapping through autocracy, aristocracy, democracy, chaos before a great convulsion or thunderclap, say a pandemic for instance, resets the circuits and the pattern restarts.

Stephen in typically offhand way, says that 'History . . . is a nightmare from which I am trying to awake'. [8]

Remember Joyce wrote *Ulysses* living in Italy, France and Switzerland and for a large part during World War One. The pointless loss of life, repeating the pattern of so many previous wars, and as per usual, it was the young and the poor that bore the brunt. The pacifism of Bloom, notably in the Cyclops and Circe episodes, echoes that of Odysseus from time long gone.

So we have souls marching across time. How about if they also move across space?

Consubstantiation: For those that don't know, this is the idea that the three hypostatic pillars of Christianity: the Father, the Son and the Holy Spirit, might in a sense be notionally separate but, in another, are one and the same. And for the greater part of the last two thousand years, challengers to that were deemed heretics which likely meant excommunication at best and often a swift passage to the afterlife. This introduces the Father/Son relationship, a theme that will develop throughout. Look out for Stephen's circle (the Son) and Bloom's circle (the Father) orbiting each other and eventually partially eclipsing in a sort of mystical inter-galactic Venn diagram of the soul. The autobiographical Joyce starts out obviously Stephen but by the end, maybe he's more than a little Bloom.

At one point, Bloom passes along the sunny side of the street and ruminates on the headpiece (or logo) of a newspaper, the *Freeman's Journal*. A real newspaper at the time, and one in support of Home Rule for Ireland. The headpiece shows the sun rising over the Bank of Ireland which means it will rise in the Northwest. Of course, this can never happen because the sun rises in the east and Bloom wonders if this has put the mockers on Home Rule ever occurring. Yet, allowing for the pun of sun (the planet) and son (the child), the sun will rise in the Northwest because Stephen Dedalus, actual son of Simon and arguably surrogate son of Bloom, will rise that night from Bloom's house in northwest Dublin and the same might be said of Bloom if he can be seen as a spiritual successor to Parnell. Bloom of course is blissfully unaware of such machinations of the gods as he meanders down the street. We sense that minor acts of seeming inconsequence somehow have galactic reverberations and *vice-versa.*

That's enough time, space and inter-Galactics. You'll be relieved to know the other theme I'd like to talk about is more normal and readily understood.

Usurpation

At its end, the book is signed off: 'Trieste-Zurich-Paris, 1914–1921'.[9]

So the book that has come to embody Dublin, and perhaps the Irish, more than any other, was written in voluntary exile. Joyce left Ireland in 1904 and died in 1941 without having meaningfully returned beyond brief sojourns and felt usurped both from his land and people. Yet somehow collectively *with* his people, for Joyce the young creative artist perceived the collective suffering of the Irish, particularly the working class, just as Telemachus and Penelope felt usurped from their home and Hamlet a constant undercurrent, felt his birthright denied.

By the end of *A Portrait of the Artist as a Young Man*, Stephen Dedalus (the young Joyce/Dedalus personae are at this point one and the same – a risky statement but there, it's said) is desperate to flee Ireland. He bemoans that every soul born in Ireland, is caught up in nets and that it's the very act of hemming in that is the push to leave. Yet, once geographically free, Joyce spends the rest of his life thinking and writing about Dublin. Can't live with her, can't live without her, expresses the conflicted love/hate sentiment many Dubliners had for their city and country at that time. Or as the newspaper headline in episode seven Aeolus puts it: 'Dear Dirty Dublin'.[10]

I'd like to consider what I think might be four nets.

First, imperialism. 1904 Dublin; the second city of the British Isles and a significant if provincial trading post in the Empire, was ruled by London. The Viceroy's residence was in Phoenix Park, the civil service was centred in Dublin Castle and various military barracks throughout the city underlined who was in charge. Not everyone was against this. The spectrum of opinion ranged from not insignificant support for the British, with the majority, generally ambivalent but, if pressed, likely favoured some form of home rule, through to nationalist armed resistance.

The second net was the rigid constraints of the Catholic Church, with over 80% of the population in tow. As Stephen explains in episode one to the Englishman Haines, he has two masters: one British, one Italian. The ineffectiveness and stagnating effect of both, Britain and Vatican – Caesar and Christ – is beautifully demonstrated in the Wandering Rocks episode.

The third net? – the acquiescence of the Irish middle class. Some Catholic, such as Buck Mulligan, but mostly Protestant, economically vested in the *status quo* and like the church, had no desire for change.

As for the lower middle and working classes, overwhelmingly Catholic, these have perhaps the most interesting net. One that Joyce/Stephen considered to be sucking out the life and retarding the progress of his people: sentimentality. Stoked on one flank by romantic poets led by W B Yeats and the Irish Literary Revival and on the other by nationalist Republicanism, there was a harking back to a mythical golden age of the Irish: over the rainbow and into the mists of time, the sons and daughters of Erin were a plucky warrior nation of passion and poetry. Whereas, and forgive the generalisation, the reality Stephen saw, starting with his father around his own table, were men that gambled and drunk away the weekly wage, leaving women to keep body, soul, countless children and the family home intact. This sentimentality as Joyce saw it, soaked in booze, led to a general inertia and an inability in particular among the working class, to deal with the very real problems they faced. In episode three, look out for the empty bottle of stout, 'stogged' to its waist in the sand.

Bloom meanwhile, is being supplanted by another man in his own bed. How's that for usurpation. What does he do? He goes out! No one has driven him from his home. He goes willingly; he keeps out of the way and allows it to happen. What kind of latter-day hero he? What would Odysseus or Siegfried or Cuchulainn have done? Does he not want to fight for his marriage? He does. Desperately, in fact. That he does not, may speak to cowardice or subtlety of tactics or that he gets a masochistic thrill from the cuckolding – there's some truth in that. Whatever the reason, he resigns himself to what will be, will be; what, he seems to think, is the point in fighting the inevitable? He rationalises it in his mind and takes comfort that in the long run, he is her husband, and Molly will come around.

The three protagonists

The final part of this introduction is a few words on the three protagonists. Stephen, Bloom and Molly. I've already talked quite a bit of Stephen and Bloom but let's embellish that a little.

Stephen Dedalus

We know Stephen Dedalus to be very, very clever but not as clever as he thinks he is. A brooding poet and budding Bohemian, having just spent three months in Paris where he was scraping around for every centime. Back home, it's for every penny. He thought he was gone for good; that he'd escaped the nets, but his mother's terminal illness drew him back. His Hamlet persona is genuine and suits his personality but also suits the mysterious intellectual persona he wishes to cultivate. His borrowed and frayed black hand-me-downs reflect not only his grieving and his poverty but also the aspirational aura of the artist, pained by the universe. He has relinquished religion but once took it so seriously as to contemplate Holy Orders and retains respect and reverence for certain Jesuit priests and educators. His renouncement of the clergy was in no small part due to his heartfelt resignation that he would learn life's lessons as a sinner.

From *A Portrait*:

> . . . the snares of the world were its ways of sin. He would fall. He had not yet fallen but he would fall silently, in an instant. Not to fall was too hard, too hard: and he felt the silent lapse of his soul, as it would be at some instance to come, falling, falling but not yet fallen, still unfallen but about to fall.[11]

Going by his name, he did fall. Dedalus. What an odd name for an Irishman! After Daedalus: the great inventor of ancient Greece. The creator of the great maze of Crete and of waxen wings so that he and his son Icarus could escape. But Icarus, flies too close to the sun, the wax melts and he crashed to a watery death. I'm not sure why he flew too high; was he trying to outdo his father or simply to strive for the sake of striving? We shall think about this. Look out for Stephen's various allusions to flying, fear of water and drowning.

Look out, too, for the portrayal of Simon Dedalus, Stephen's literary father and the conflation with Deadalus: 'as the great artificer whose name he bore'.[12]

If Stephen is prone to falling, it may be due to his difficulty in seeing where he's going. His myopia is terrible and we learn late in the book that he has broken his glasses, reminding us of the Father Dolan injustice in *A Portrait*.

Leopold Bloom

Our second protagonist is Leopold Bloom. What a joy! Bloom blooms. If Stephen is the inner world, Bloom is the outer. His lot in life is fair to middling. At a superficial level, he's okay. He's sufficiently above the poverty line, knows where the next meal is coming from and even has some savings. This puts him comfortably above many of his associates largely because his life does not revolve around the pub. He's suffered some of the hardest knocks life can throw. The marriage is complex and his wife plays around, though maybe not as much as Bloom fears. Although not technically Jewish, he is at best treated as an outsider by most people and, at worst, the victim of regular and horrible racial slurs, both to his face and more often behind his back. His father committed suicide eighteen years earlier and Rudy, his only son, died eleven years ago, aged just eleven days.

Yet he remains optimistic and life-affirming. He has a lovely daughter Milly and, despite all, he adores his wife. He enjoys his food and, in moderation, wine, cider and an occasional cigar. If not dapper man about town, he's comfortable in his body. He likes to read and has an enquiring mind. He also likes to help people. Not because he thinks it's the right thing to do, rather, it's the natural thing to do.

Contrast with Stephen. One, a Jesuit-educated Catholic from generations of Irish, yet feels an outsider. The other entitled to feel an outsider in every respect is, ignoring some lapses, sanguine and pretty much at home. Bloom has several neuroses but whereas Stephen allows his own to pervade, Bloom rationalises for Bloom is a rational man, a graduate of the University of Life. Take the renunciation of faith. Like Stephen and Catholicism, Bloom has renounced Judaism or, more accurately, he carries the guilt of his father having done so, who, like many immigrant Jews in the mid-nineteenth century, converted to Christianity either for marriage or in order to earn a living. Bloom the son compounds this by being baptised for both Protestants and Catholics. It is a similar guilt yet somehow it weighs so much heavier with Steven. Time spent inside Stephen's head descends so far down dark holes, we wonder if he, and we, will cope. Time spent inside Bloom's head also reveals a thinker but at a far more practical level. We may be a little shocked at the full gamut of his peccadilloes but at the same time, are assured. Bloom will be all right. Because of Bloom, we feel Stephen will be all right and because of Bloom, somehow, we will all be all right.

Tempting though it is to leave Bloom on such a note, I can't help but fear I have grossly simplified such a complex, three-dimensional character. Like Odysseus, indeed a man of many turns.

Marion (Molly) Bloom

Of the many people that try to read the book a considerable proportion turn to the very last episode and read Molly's soliloquy. If we dare to place it in time and space, it's around three in the morning. She's lying in bed with her sleeping husband's feet in her face, because the weirdo likes to sleep top to toe, his face in her buttocks. A person can't even fart in bed, she laments[13] while she reflects on her day, her marriage, her life.

By this time in the book we've heard lots about her. She may already be judged but now that judgement is held to account in a full-blooded, ribald stream of thought that runs some fifty pages, almost without pausing for breath. Molly is 'parallaxed'; when considered from a different perspective, her own, she is seen anew. She expects no favours nor does she intend to dish them out – a free spirit in both a patriarchal world and an inadequate marriage. She gets on with life. Bloom drives her mad in several respects and we sympathise with her as to much of it.

She relives in lurid detail the afternoon spent with her lover Blazes Boylan. She aches for Monday when Boylan has promised to return and then for the following week and Boylan's touring ensemble, which seems likely to star Molly in every respect. It will tour Belfast and then perhaps Liverpool. She doesn't know how she will get through the three days until then – longing again to be serviced by 'that tremendous big brute of thing his has'.[14] However, as her thoughts spin out, something unexpected percolates, almost unnoticed until upon us: an undeniable fondness for . . . Bloom, infuriating Bloom. Finally, her thoughts turn to the afternoon on Howth Head, many years before, where she and Bloom first made love. This echoes Bloom's own recollection, earlier that day of the same scene. He was alone in a café, watching two flies on the window, stuck amid drying paint.

We do not know how 17 June and beyond will pan out. But despite the water that has flown under so many bridges since that sunny afternoon atop Howth Head, they both recall that time with such fondness that, yes, let's be optimistic.

Those are the main actors in our play. There are of course many others including Dublin itself. The book teems with life, mainly from the drinking lower-middle and working classes, but also the intelligentsia as befits Stephen Dedalus. The bad guys, the obvious usurpers, Buck Mulligan and Blazes Boylan, light up the pages when they appear. The Buck gets most of the best lines as bad guys tend to. Boylan is denied that and much else by way of serious character development. Joyce bestows upon him a total of three words of interior monologue and he generally stews in the juices of his two-dimensional nastiness.

I dare not offer any conclusions for we are at the start of our journey. In a book of journeys, the task of reading *Ulysses* is another. Perhaps not of epic struggle, but you'll know you've been in a fight. There's no roadmap but that's the fun of the best journeys. How boring to have every turn and undulation clearly signposted kilometres in advance. I lower the flag and declare this journey underway.

PART I – THE TELEMECHIAD

LECTURE 2, 7 OCTOBER 2020: EPISODE 1

Telemachus and the Shan Van Vocht

Music: The Shan Van Vocht – Ron Kavana & The Alias Acoustic Band

After our gentle introduction last time, we take a closer look at each episode, starting not unnaturally with episode one.

In its original 1922 form *Ulysses* had no episode headings or numbers and even now, the vast majority of editions follow suit. Prior to publication, Joyce sent his friend Carlo Linati, a chart explaining the fundamental aspects of the book.[1] He pointed out eighteen natural breaks in the story and how each might correspond to books in *The Odyssey*. Hence chapters or episodes, such as they are, have adopted the names they commonly go by today. The schema also attributed a time, colour and science or art to each episode. Joyce expanded on this in a second schema sent to Valery Larbaud to assist his preparation of a lecture and that added a symbol for each episode as well as stylistic technique and even, lord preserve us, a bodily organ. This is better known as the Gilbert schema[2] as it was published in a book by that author in 1930. We can for now ignore references to organs because these do not kick in until Episode 4.

These schemata are useful clues to Joyce's thought process and, based upon them, we call the first episode 'Telemachus'. That's our Homeric link. Its Art, or underlying theme, is 'Theology' and its colour, yellow and white. Having established the link, let's take a look at Book One of *The Odyssey*.

Penelope and her 22-year-old son Telemachus, on their estate in Ithaca, are becoming increasingly distraught. They have been invaded by male Suitors. (I'd assumed around thirty of them but later to be confirmed at over a hundred.) Each invites Penelope to choose him as the new king of Ithaca for they say Odysseus must be dead by now otherwise, after all of these years, he would have made contact or someone would have heard something. It had been twenty years since he left for Troy Meantime, the Suitors, the most vocal of which is Antinous (translation: anti-mind), are eating, drinking and abusing the servants, all at Penelope's expense.

But we are privy to what has happened to our hero. Following victory at Troy, Odysseus tried to return home with the other warriors. But he angered the gods, in particular Poseidon, god of the sea, whose son he blinded. And so, he was blighted with all manner of trouble. However, for Zeus, king of the gods, enough was enough; he admired Odysseus – his cunning, his bravery – and, moreover, was concerned with what was happening back home in Ithaca. Whilst reluctant to undermine Poseidon, it was time for Odysseus to return home and save his innocent and faithful wife and son.

Zeus sends his daughter, Pallas-Athena, to Ithaca, disguised as an old man, Odysseus' old friend Mentes. He/she tells Telemachus not only that is father is alive and trying to return but also reminds him he is no more a child and must set off to find his father and also somehow deal with the Suitors. Telemachus embarks on the well-trodden path of a son seeking his father or, as Jung and Freud might have it, a youth discovering the world and their role in it. His first steps are to consult with two of his father's fellow warriors, Nestor and Menelaus, to see if they have news or suggestions as to what he might do. These trips feature in Episodes 2 and 3 of *Ulysses*. Episode 1 is really about setting the scene and Pallas-Athena delivering her message.

Based on what we now know, for what shall we look out for in this episode?

- A message from the gods - and what is it?
- Where and who is Pallas-Athena?
- We know Stephen is Telemachus. Is he searching for a father?
- What references are there to Yellow, White and Theology?

and based on our general themes as we saw in the Introductory lecture, let's look out for

- Usurpation; and
- Consubstantiation – this coagulation of father, son and Holy Spirit.

You will recall, we begin in a Martello tower; one of a series of similar structures built around the British Isles in the eighteenth century to protect against French invasion. Thus Stephen Dedalus, who resents the imperialism of the British usurper, is living in a building with walls several feet thick, that symbolises maybe as much as Dublin Castle, the British Empire, its impenetrability and indestructibility. It is surrounded by sea, the life-blood of the Empire, for Britain, as we know, rules the waves. Plus he lives there with two great usurpers. Haines is English and though his love of all things Irish may be genuine – it is the love of a hobbyist and bestowed from the lofty perch of conqueror. Buck Mulligan, middle-class medical student, is the gay betrayer,[3] the joker for whom the *status quo* in Ireland is pretty good and, at whose invitation, Haines has arrived from Oxford University.

For Mulligan, life is no more serious than getting drunk and writing heretical and semi-pornographic poetry. Mulligan calls the tower the *Omphalos* which is Greek for navel and which, if one has a protruding navel, an outie, one may see the resemblance. As relevant, though, is the notion that the navel is the centre of the body, the source, the original life force and, like the Omphalos in classical Delphi, Mulligan wanted to make this Martello tower a centre of Greek culture in Ireland. We should Hellenise Ireland he says, displaying his utter disconnect with real Irish problems. We note his Homeric reference to the *Epi oinopa ponton*,[4] the wine-dark sea, as he looks out over Dublin Bay.

Like many characters in *Ulysses*, Haines and Mulligan were based on real people: respectively, Richard Trench and Oliver St John Gogarty, who both spent a while with Joyce, in this very Martello tower. The more interesting of those is the template for 'Buck' Mulligan. Joyce met Gogarty in a queue at the Library of Ireland in December 1902,[5] and, based on common interests in poetry, literature and Classical Greece, they became friends. But it was unequal. Gogarty was a few years older, more confident, worldly, with family money and blessed with rapier-sharp wit. He also had a sadistic streak and took pleasure at Joyce's misfortune, often instigating it. He publicly humiliated Joyce at most given opportunities: for example, as much as Joyce enjoyed his drink, he couldn't hold it and, egged on by Gogarty,[6] got into fights, which Joyce invariably lost. The resentment Stephen has for Buck Mulligan in the early episodes, reflects this real-life relationship and, via the novel, Joyce sought revenge and won it in spades. So effectively, that once the book gained traction in Ireland, Gogarty, by this time a respected surgeon and published poet, claimed his life was ruined and emigrated to America.[7] Buck Mulligan's poetry, as recorded in *Ulysses*, wickedly blasphemous and blushingly rude, is generally snippets of real Gogarty and in fact, toned down. We note, with some irony, that the Martello tower, which Gogarty dreamed would be this great cultural centre, is in fact nowadays an homage to his dogsbody. It is the James Joyce Museum.[8]

In the opening episode, Joyce introduces many of the important themes and establishes significant characters. Haines is peripheral throughout the book but Stephen and Mulligan are crucial and their characters, as introduced and established here, remain generally consistent and reliable, ignoring here any transformation of Stephen's character that may become a central theme, some fourteen episodes hence.[9] Let's be patient.

The introductory lecture provided some insight into Stephen's character, lets now delve a little deeper into that of Malachi 'the Buck' Mulligan. He's having that shave up on the roof. His mimicry of the priest, his flippancy as to transubstantiation – likening shaving foam to white corpuscles transforming into the body of Christ – undermines the possibility of him being a real priest and father figure. Instead it suggests a joker and blasphemer. Our wariness of a false or unreliable father figure is cemented because the mass has the feel of a black mass, the blood not of Christ but rather the sacrificial Christine. Indeed Mulligan, with his unbridled yellow dressing gown, cord flowing akimbo, has a hint of the devil with his tail.

Parenthetically, there is a school of thought,[10] that Joyce's body of work, here I mean the novels, echoes that of Dante's. *A Portrait of the Artist* is *La Vita Nuova, Ulysses* is *Inferno, Finnegan's Wake, Purgatorio* with the book Joyce planned but did not live to write, corresponding to *Paradiso*. So if *Ulysses* is *Inferno*, Buck Mulligan as devil/tempter/serpent fits the profile. This all gets quite deep and as it relates to books beyond these lectures, you can safely ignore, if you wish and still very much appreciate the book. But for those that want to investigate further and are familiar with the other works, I may issue some pointers as we go along. There is no doubt that Joyce draws on *The Divine Comedia* in the writing of *Ulysses*.

To re-cap, Mulligan accuses Stephen of killing his mother by refusing to pray for her at her deathbed. He does this not because he believes it to be true – as a medical student, he knows that cancer was the killer [11] – but rather he understands Stephen's guilt and Mulligan, the artful Buck, knows precisely which buttons to press to most upset Stephen. Here he hits three bullseyes with one shot. The dredging-up of the death of his mother, the guilt (though not regret) which Stephen feels for not praying at her deathbed and, lastly, his guilt (again without regret) of having rejected religion. You can take Stephen out of the Church but only a priest can exorcise the Catholicism out of Stephen. And Mulligan ain't no priest.

I spoke last time of the stream of consciousness technique. The inner thought of a character and I picked an example from this very scene, concerning the sea as grey and then great sweet mother and that allusion to Stephen's dying mother. No need to repeat. In fact the book's first example of the technique is a single word. '*Chrysostomos*',[12] says Stephen to himself in internal accusation of Mulligan. He is referring to the Ancient Greek rhetorician who was referred to as golden mouth on account of his oratory skills. In this context Stephen thinks that Mulligan talks hot air, but also has in mind wealthy Buck's gold-capped teeth, sparkling in the sun; in contrast to his own decaying dentures.

Conversation turns to Haines, the Oxford student. Stephen wonders when he'll be leaving in light of events the previous night. It transpires that Haines, asleep on a hammock near Stephen, had a nightmare involving a black panther, this is a sub-conscious allusion to Leopold Bloom whom Haines does not know; Bloom as panther and other cats is a theme that will develop. In the dream, Haines tries to shoot the panther. Unfortunately, the sleepwalker was up brandishing a real gun and scared Stephen witless. Buck Mulligan sides with Stephen and, well out of Haines' earshot, calls Haines a ponderous Saxon and says Stephen should dupe him for money. Haines, it transpires, is in Ireland researching for a book concerning all of those sentimental Irish legends and quaint Celtic sayings that, even to this day, the tourists love. Buck cajoles Stephen that he must know loads of those and Haines will pay for them. Besides, he goes on, if he gives more trouble, he'll get a ragging like Clive Kempthorpe. From Stephen's head we have a vision of an Oxford college where a group of male students are ragging one of their number (apparently a Mr Clive Kempthorpe) and playing semi-violent pranks. There are effeminate and homosexual overtones. It is interesting for two reasons. One, Stephen has never been to Oxford nor does he know these people, let alone to give one a ragging. This detailed vision in his head arises only from snippets he's heard from Mulligan. Secondly, instead of feeling part of the jovial hullabaloo, Stephen retreats to the image of the deaf college gardener who, outside of the immediate scene, mows the lawn and pays scant attention to silly students. .This suggests that Stephen, insular at best of times, is withdrawing from any hint of alliance with Mulligan, against Haines. They both may be usurpers but Haines is a comparative irrelevance; the enemy is Mulligan.

As well as reminding of Homer's Antinous, we also think of that other artful, usurping and duplicitous character, Claudius, in Shakespeare's *Hamlet*. He's King Hamlet's brother whom he kills, and marries the widow, Queen Gertrude. So, in one murderous most foul swoop, usurps kingdom, wife and mother. A basic scan of Hamlet will not be wasted in understanding this book. In further echoes of Claudius, Mulligan tries to ingratiate himself with Stephen whilst blurring his true agenda; he suggests Stephen may be mad (GPI that fellow says you had: 'general paralysis of the insane!').[13] This was also a colloquialism for syphilis – so a twin-dig at Stephen visiting prostitutes. Continuing in Claudius vein, taking Stephen's arm, Mulligan implores of him, 'why don't you trust me more?'[14] – Stephen is sceptical. It reminds him of Cranley's arm, his university pal in whom he bestowed too much trust.[15] Mulligan tells Stephen to stop brooding over a dead parent and, finally, as this Claudius replicant, Mulligan is after the key to the tower, when it is Stephen that has been paying the rent.[16] *Hamlet* the play, is a pet subject of Stephen's. It's implications gnaw at his sense of well-being; the haunting of the dead parent; the tower reminds him (and Haines) of the Elsinore battlements and Dublin Bay might be the tempting flood into which, one may beetle o'er the base.[17] This will be explored in detail in episode nine.

After those insights into the character of Buck Mulligan, let's get back to the episode. There's an interesting phrase, which might be narrative or Stephen's thought; often with Joyce we are not sure. I think it's Stephen: 'We ourselves . . . New paganism . . . Omphalos.'[18]

At the end of *A Portrait*, only some months earlier, Stephen self-declared an aim: ' . . . to forge in the smithy of my soul, the uncreated conscience of my race . . . [19]

The words 'Sinn Fein' in English mean: 'We Ourselves'. New Paganism may refer to theosophy that as we shall see, is much beloved by certain influential figures in the Irish Literary Revival and Gaelic League and Omphalos might refer to Mulligan's middle-class absurdity that all Ireland's problems would be solved if people were only more familiar with classical Greece. Stephen considers all three to be blind alleys down which he will not be forging his people's conscience. It's true that Joyce/Stephen has nationalist sympathy, he's no West Brit,[20] he is or at least was Parnellian [21] and more of that to come.

Now a word on Stephen's mother: we have discussed Stephen's remorse and its circumstances. May Dedalus, replicating Joyce's mother, Mary Jane, was bearer and rearer of many children (some 15 pregnancies of which 10 survived),[22] which, as one can imagine, pretty much preoccupied her whole life until cancer clipped her energy and finally claimed her. Months after her death, the bedside trauma continues to haunt Stephen and rears its head throughout this episode and beyond. We have the prayer for the dead – *Liliata rutilantium*,[23] the

Yeats poem, 'Who Goes With Fergus'[24]which his mother liked Stephen to sing for her and which line 'And no More Turn Aside and Brood', manages to combine, Yeats, Telemachus, Hamlet as well as Buck Mulligan and Stephen.

She appears to Stephen in a dream:

> Pain, that was not yet the pain of love, fretted his heart. Silently, in a dream she had come to him after her death, her wasted body within its loose brown grave-clothes giving off an odour of wax and rosewood, her breath, that had bent upon him, mute, reproachful, a faint odour of wetted ashes.25

Reproachful yet also suffocating. It was she that foiled his escape; her illness that reeled him back into the restraining nets of Ireland; guilt, tinged with resentment. Amid reverie of her from child to deathbed, we hear echoes of Hamlet and Telemachus: 'No mother. Let me be and let me live.'[26]

Premature loss of parent, as well as child, will interweave Stephen with Hamlet, Shakespeare, Telemachus and Leopold Bloom. Also significant for that cast list, is image of mother and we shall see how Molly fits that mould.

The episode continues with the reinforcement of Buck Mulligan's character by his offering Stephen more cast-off clothes. Apparent generosity barely disguising the insulting reality that Stephen relies on Mulligan, among others, for the second-hand clothes on his back and the boots on his feet. Stephen observes his own sub-standard appearance in the cracked shaving mirror and we get a play on Oscar Wilde's commentary on Victorian society and on Irish art.[27] Despite Stephen's poverty and Mulligan's family money, it is Stephen that appears to have paid the rent on the tower.[28] But worry not, help is at hand, it's Stephen's monthly payday! Mulligan celebrates with the exclamation: 'Four shiny sovereigns!'[29] And bursts into song in faux cockney accent about Coronation Day. Why celebrate a British King?[30] Well his face is on the coins, coins buy beer and beer makes for a happy Buck, happy to serve the British master. He skips downstairs to breakfast.

Back up on the roof, Stephen lingers; staring blankly at Mulligan's dirty abandoned shaving bowl. Should he clear it up? Like at Clongowes School, where as an altar boy, he'd tidy the chalice after the mass. If Mulligan is servant to Haines, as Ireland is to England, he is clearing up after Mulligan. A servant to a servant. A further play on words: one of the Pope's titles being *servus, servorum Dei*, servant of the servants of God. Stephen descends to join the others. We mark in passing the reference to dead animals. Stephen's mother is beastly dead, Stephen is a dogsbody, Haines was shooting at the panther. Animal cruelty is a permeating theme.

To breakfast. Our Holy Trinity of three men eat in this episode of Theology,[31] three yellow and white fried eggs. Yellow and white being the colours of The Vatican and yellow representing purity if not the absolute purity of white. But yellow, the colour of Mulligan's robe and, when dressed, his waistcoat, might also represent cowardice . As the eggs are served, the mock theological ambience is maintained by Mulligan: '*In nomine Patris et Filii et Spiritus Sancti.*'[32]

Tea is poured, Mulligan parodies for Haines' amusement and potential payment, rude tales from rural Ireland, reminding the reader of the net of sentimentality. It involves two hags, Mother Grogan and Mrs Cahill and how they mustn't mix their water (meaning urine) and tea in the same pot. But hang on, where's the milk? No milk! Can't have tea without lovely local Sandycove milk! Stephen's suggestion of drinking it black with lemon is swatted away by the Buck as one of Stephen's Parisian fads. Mulligan slumps into a funk, fortunately, a real old hag, the milk woman, arrives to save the day. Mulligan furthering his ruse to tempt Haines to pay for stories, asks Stephen's opinion on Mary-Anne, another young lady of questionable west-of-Ireland folklore who, apparently, lifts up her petticoats and urinates like a man. Mulligan, equal opportunities blasphemer, queries mischievously, if the story of Mary-Anne is to be found in the *Upanishads* – the Sanskrit texts of historical and religious significance. This opens an enormous can of worms that percolates through *Ulysses* with inferences to Hindu gods, Buddhism, kabbalah and mystic theosophy. This book contrasts orient and occident and leans, for those with eyes to see, distinctly east.

Back to our decrepit milk woman: Haines speaks to her but she does not understand and asks if he's speaking French. He, an Englishman, is speaking . . . Irish. By comparison to English, Irish is rarely spoken in Ireland and little known beyond the rural west and academics such as Haines, W B Yeats and 'A E'.[33] None of whom will be spared Joyce's ire as we progress through the book.

Stephen feels slighted as he senses that she fawns to Haines, the British conqueror, and to Mulligan, the middle class medic, whilst ignoring him, the poor artist. Here folks lies the message from the goddess Pallas-Athena and crux of the episode: Ireland, or the essence of Ireland, had among poets and minstrels become known by various *nom de plumes*, often to avoid a charge of sedition. Let's take, for example, a poem intended to rouse the Irish peasantry to action. To slip it by the British censor, 'Ireland' might be the 'pretty young maid' or, more commonly, the 'silk of the kine' (which means the best of the cattle herd) or, and in this case, the 'poor old women' which in Gaelic is the 'shan van vocht'. Therefore, the milk woman epitomises an Ireland barely recovered from the famine some 60 years before. Old, worn-out, her breasts, long redundant, she nourishes her masters with the milk of another. She is well past resistance and servile to her twin usurpers.

The message conveyed to Stephen is that, like Telemachus, he needs to get up off of his backside and seek his father in order to save his homeland because what's left of the indigenous people [34] is making a pretty poor job of changing the *status quo*. There's no need to search for his birth father, Stephen knows where he is and he's hopeless. What Stephen seeks is a spiritual father, a guide in life and role model. This has a number of interesting aspects and possible interpretations but, of most interest, is that it concerns the role of and challenge for the artist in society. Not any old artist, the artist that would elevate society by turning a modernist literary mirror on itself.

To rise to such a challenge, Stephen must change. He must break out of his insulated silo, his self-centred, over-intellectual, egoistic existence. This day is 16 June 1904. Not 17, not 15. It can only be 16 June for that was the day that Joyce first dated Nora Barnacle,[35] his significant other, his life-partner and soulmate. This is the day of the epiphany of James Joyce. The day he, and so Stephen, realised he is not the centre of the universe and must venture out, he must engage other, he must join the human race. He must begin to contribute, he must give as well as receive. This also sounds like he needs to engage his feminine side and that, as we shall see, may be right. It's early, both in the day and in the book and Stephen does not yet perceive this challenge, let alone understand how and what he needs to do. Bloom will reveal that to him far later that evening. What he does realise at this point is that his life cannot continue as is. He needs to get up off his backside.

So the milk woman was Pallas-Athena? Who would have thought! Well, maybe yes, maybe no. Don't forget Buck Mulligan's real name is Malachi, named not only for the legendary Celtic hero, but also the Old Testament prophet and whose name means Messenger of God. Joyce doesn't provide one right answer when he can offer several.

Back to our three heroes. Mulligan, cajoled by Haines, grudgingly pays but short-changes the milk woman.[36] They finish breakfast and set off for the Forty Foot, a safe bathing area of Dublin Bay. On the way out, Mulligan establishes the whereabouts of the key to the tower, flings open the main door and, as opposed to Matthew 26:75: 'and he went out and wept bitterly', he blasphemes: 'And going forth he met Butterly',[37] in reference to the Butterlys, a Dublin family of that time.

As they walk, Haines introduces the subject of Shakespeare's play, *Hamlet*. He's noticed the resemblance of the tower to Elsinore and he understands from Mulligan that Stephen has a theory about the play. Mulligan cuts that conversation off at its knees. Either ironically or ignorantly he confuses Thomas Aquinas with Aristotle but says he can't possibly listen to Stephen on *Hamlet* without a few pints inside him. Further, to stifle any further debate for now, he paraphrases Stephen's theory as follows:

> 'It's quite simple. He proves by algebra that Hamlet's grandson is Shakespeare's grandfather and that he himself is the ghost of his own father.'
>
> 'What? . . . He himself?!'[38] exclaims Haines, decidedly confused.

Confusion abounds and we are all in good company but fortunately we don't need to worry too much about Shakespeare just yet. This is an episode for establishing themes, not resolving them. Plenty of time for that. Here, though, we have, via *Hamlet*, the blurring of the lines between father, grandfather and son.

Mulligan is more at home with his ribald poetry and in this episode of theology, launches the 'Ballad of Joking Jesus':

> "I'm the queerest young fellow that ever you heard.
> My mother's a Jew; my father's a bird
> With Joseph the Joiner I cannot agree,
> So here's to Disciples and Calvary.
> . . .
> If anyone thinks that I amn't divine,
> He'll get no free drinks when I'm making the wine
> But have to drink water and wish it were plain
> That I make when the wine becomes water again.[39, 40]

This could hardly be more offensive to Catholics if it tried (and Gogarty was trying). Starting with a self-mockery of Jesus as a queer young fellow before reminding that the Virgin Mary was a Jewess, something Catholic hierarchy have, for a thousand years been at pains to suppress. Then reference to the divine essence that impregnated

Mary, as a bird. Well, fair enough, the Holy Spirit is traditionally represented as a dove. Or was it Joseph? Note the word 'Joiner' referring to a carpenter of course or, maybe this Jewish mortal is the Holy Spirit that conjoins father and son consubstantially. That would be desperately heretical: not simply questioning the divine parentage of the Messiah but replacing deity with a Jew, no less. Jesus then suggests that his disciples are only there for the free wine! Finally, Mulligan twists the knife by inverting the water to wine miracle. Instead, Jesus offers non-believers the prosaic metamorphosis of wine back to water: that is, they can drink his pee. Amusing and offensive in equal measure, which sums up Buck Mulligan. More seriously, like Mrs Grogan earlier, we have urination as the creative process, something that resonates with both Stephen and Bloom later that day.[41]

They arrive at the Forty Foot, where amid more vulgarity, Mulligan undresses and dives in. Haines will not swim until his breakfast is digested and meantime engages Stephen in conversation on religion and Ireland. Stephen, intellectually superior, dangles Haines along as Hamlet did Polonius[42] whilst internally musing on heretics who, like Buck and his ballad, have tested the belief of consubstantiality. Then, feeling slightly impolite, engages with Haines and accepts a cigarette from the silver case with the emerald jewel in the crown, so to speak. Haines's trinket.

As to Britain's treatment of its trinket, Ireland, Haines opts out of any personal or national responsibility and foreshadows the theme of episode two: 'It seems, history is to blame.'[43]

He also throws in some casual anti-Semitism, no history to blame there, just the Jews. More foreshadowing. We then have a slightly left-field but important brief distraction. Within earshot two men discuss that a man has drowned nine days earlier, just off of that coast. The ninth day, legend has it, being the day that bodies, where they have not been recovered, tend to surface of their own accord. Stephen, modern day Icarus, digests this and will muse upon it in a few hours a mile or so along the coast. Stephen, like Icarus, prefers not to swim. Not even, as Mulligan acerbically points out, for his monthly wash. Actually that's generous. Stephen much later that day[44] admits to having not bathed for over a year. Like Joyce, he's hydrophobic and we again sense Icarus from time long gone. Mulligan not only swims but socialises. He speaks to a chap who knows both Mulligan's brother and a mutual acquaintance, Alec Banham, who has a new sweetheart in Mullingar. Watch this space.

The episode draws to a close. Stephen, observing a priest emerge dripping from the sea, is again beset with guilt for his mother. He resolves not to return to the Martello tower. His family home also not a viable option, he is rendered homeless. Mulligan shouts from the sea to meet them in The Ship pub at 12.30 and as a *coup de grace,* asks/tells Stephen to leave the key (its big and heavy) on Mulligan's pile of clothes, just to stop them blowing away, he explains. Oh, and a bit of change for a pint.

Themes have been established: Usurpation, fathers and sons. We have a feel for the characters of Stephen and the Buck. And the gods have delivered their message. We finish as we started: A single-worded sentence of interior monologue: Usurper.[45]

LECTURE 3, 21 OCTOBER 2020: EPISODE 2

Ancient Nestor and the Disappointed Bridge

Music: I Am the Very Model of a Modern Major General– D'Oyly Carte Opera Company

Episode one eased us in, episode two moves us on. We accompany Stephen, like Telemachus, on further travel. Now to Dalkey, next episode, to the beach. Last time, a taster of his interior thoughts, this time, a little more, next time, life full-blown inside his head. But we then relax in the calmer episode four waters of the Bloom household.

Back to now. It's 10 am and Stephen is at work teaching at a school in Dalkey, a village a mile or so south of the Forty Foot, the bathing area where Stephen Dedalus left Buck Mulligan and Haines at the end of episode one. Our schematic theme is History, our colour is Brown and our symbol, a Horse.

The Homeric parallel is that Telemachus has been told to seek out his father but poor kid, he doesn't know where to start. All he can think is to consult his father's co-warrior, Nestor, who lives on the coast at Pylos, to see if he has any ideas. Nestor is an old, wise and revered warrior: an accomplished horseman, charioteer and breeder of fine cattle. Hospitable Nestor warmly welcomes his old friend's son. A sturdy heifer is sacrificed and another served in a fine feast at which Nestor, surrounded by his children, regales all with his adventures at Troy and elsewhere. He's entertaining, if a little long-winded, and is not sure what happened to Odysseus. He suggests Telemachus speak to King Menelaus over at Sparta. Not such fertile ground for our episode but let's see.

It's a comparatively short episode and dare one say, comparatively easy but don't be fooled – there's a lot going on. These first three episodes plant the seeds out of which the story grows.

Falling neatly into thirds, the first two are set in a classroom where we find Stephen initially teaching classical history but segues into English literature with some Milton poetry. At the bell, the boys rush off for hockey but one boy, Cyril Sargent, must remain behind for some extra algebra tuition with Stephen. Algebra. Remember Mulligan's comic summation of Stephen's *Hamlet* theory: 'he proves by algebra'?[1] The conversation between Stephen and Cyril Sargent is our second third. The last segment occurs in the headmaster's study, wood-panelled and leather-bound, where Stephen will be paid his monthly wage by the headmaster, Mr Deasy, an elderly gentleman with a lot to say to the young teacher. In so far as anything in this book is clear, it would seem that Mr Deasy represents Nestor.

We know Stephen to be complex: he is, one tentatively claims after all, autobiographically, the author of the book with which we grapple. Time spent inside his head is not easy, but it may help to bear in mind his disposition on this bright June morning. His immediate emotion, one expects, is anger at Mulligan for effectively having thrown him out of his home. Just a little further back are thoughts of his family situation. His father, Simon, purveyor of the perfect witticism and fabulous drinking partner, is not so good as provider for his ten surviving children. He's pretty much abandoned them to care for themselves. So Stephen is angry at him. Then, seeping and gnawing from even further back, the grieving for his dead mother, his resentment at being back in Ireland and that his status as genius remains unrecognised. Finally, a faint but constant hum: his disgruntlement at the state of his country and his people. So, all in all, an unhappy and homeless chappy. Bearing in mind the book only lasts a day, we should not expect this mood to change any time soon, though it might be ameliorated with a little alcohol.

It.s Thursday, half-day. Not much teaching and added to which, it's Hockey up next, so a quick bit of History and English Lit and he's done for the day. The episodic theme of history parades before us three generations. The boys: it is a boys only private school, all are around 14 or 15; Stephen is 22 and Mr Deasy we expect is at least 70. The episode opens mid-lesson, mid-sentence. A boy is struggling to answer a question about Pyrrhus. King Pyrrhus was a gun-for-hire warrior who raged battles against Romans on others' behalf. This battle at Asculum at 279BC was won but at great cost. One boy recalls the date and Pyrrhus's famous quote: 'Another victory like that and we are done for.'[2]

Hence, 'pyrrhic victory', a phrase now so embedded in our mindset, it has lost the eponymous connection. Another boy, Armstrong, drawing a blank on Pyrrhus, wonders if Stephen is asking him what he knows about a pier: 'A pier sir, . . . A thing out in the waves. A kind of bridge. Kingstown pier, sir.'[3]

A bridge, chuckles Stephen to himself. A pier is a disappointed bridge. No point saying that out loud to this lot, only confuse them. Maybe it's the sort of cute Irishism that Mulligan would have Haines pay for. Stephen may chuckle but he thought he had a bridge across to France[4] and freedom from drudgery, but, no, it turned out to be only a pier and here he is again, trapped. He muses upon his class before him, generally privileged and, so we assume, Protestant boys who make him feel inadequate: 'All laughed. Mirthless high malicious laughter.'[5]

These lads are not particularly relying on an education because, one way or another, it is they and others like them that will be running the country in fifteen or twenty years' time. And, even though much younger than he, he noted their cavalier and comfortable attitude to sex:

> With envy he watched their faces. Edith, Ethel, Gerty, Lily. Their likes: their breaths, too, sweetened with tea and jam, their bracelets tittering in the struggle.[6]

In Stephen's fertile mind, these are the girls with whom he imagines the boys are not only at ease but unfettered by Catholic angst, have most likely already conquered.

Stephen, being Stephen, his thoughts become complex. What is history? He muses on William Blake, who thought the traditional version of history as not only boring but a skewed reality.[7] I'm conscious at this point that I tendered 'normal Joyce for normal people', but a little brainwork here may be well invested. There are alternate ways to look at, and teach, history. First, traditional: one plodding event after another. This followed that, followed this, followed that. One can feel a schoolboy rhythm: And then the Greeks beat the Byzantines (or whomever ran the show before the Greeks), then the Romans or the Persians beat the Greeks and then the Turks beat the Romans and then the British beat the Turks and on . . . and history as we know is written by the victors, so what actually happened is anyone's guess. But it is the job of every good schoolboy and schoolgirl to learn these historical 'facts' – something with which this class struggles. Talking of class struggle, this is not to make a political point, Marxists, too, subscribe to this linear process and would hate how Stephen will query this thinking every bit as much as reactionary Tories like Garrett Deasy.[8]

Another way to look at the 'progression' of humanity, and here's where we get a little wacky, is contemplated by those a little off-piste, as it were, such as the poet William Blake or perhaps James Joyce, various hermetic theosophists, some eastern religions and maybe also you: if you've freed your mind with some substance or other. Such a point of view is that each moment is an end in itself. That is to say, history or reality is not a path along which we plod in a given direction – it is a collective of moments that are each self-sufficient, permanent and heading nowhere. This you may think is likely unsupported by the Abrahamic religions: Judaism, Christianity, Islam which encourage obedience in this life for reward in the hereafter, though, no doubt, the matter is not that simple. The alternative is not to say there is no hereafter, it may well exist; but it's already here not after, which has awkward moral consequences for if crime is not followed by punishment, why not do the crime? Perhaps because good is an absolute. One should just be good for its sake and as an end in itself, without the need for reward in the afterlife. Whilst you may understandably be thinking this is a load of rubbish and whilst philosophical detail is well beyond these lectures, there is suggestion that both Plato and his student Aristotle conjured with similar ideas and so, it would seem, did Joyce. Forgive just a smidgeon more of Aristotle.

Thinking of events concerning Pyrrhus and Julius Caesar, Stephen muses:

> They are not to be thought away. Time has branded them and fettered they are lodged in the room of the infinite possibilities they have ousted.[9]

What's that about?

What we do in the moment is *actuality*. One has an array of choice as to what to do in the next moment and all of these, *potentiality*. Only when we make our choice and act on it does it move from potential to actual and ousts the other infinite possibilities that are consigned to the 'room of never were'. What if the roof tile didn't hit Pyrrhus on the head? What if Julius Caesar wasn't killed by his courtiers? How would history have been different? What if West Ham didn't win 3–0 at Leicester City? The world would be different and my weekend would have been duller. The film *Sliding Doors*[10] from some 20 years ago pondered these thoughts of Aristotle. Joyce is grappling with destiny, chance, cause and effect.

As if by slip of time, the boys are reading an extract of John Milton's poem, 'Lycidas' written in 1638; it was a poem to commemorate Milton's friend Edward King, who had drowned. Why suddenly literature? And of all of literature, why this one? Possibly, an affinity of short-sighted Stephen with the blind poet? He heard in episode one about the man that has drowned and in episode three Stephen, hydrophobe, will dwell more on watery ends. But that, if we trust time, can't be why the boys are reading it, they are supposed to know it by heart (the boy hides the book with his satchel as he pretends to recite). It cannot be that they started it there and then because Stephen heard about a drowning two hours earlier; it must be on the curriculum. But Joyce, fiction-writer, is able to play with Aristotle's infinite possibilities of the next moment. There's more: the body of Milton's buddy was never recovered and, if there's no body, how do we know he drowned? A bit like that tree falling in the woods. And this may be Aristotle's point, or at least one of them. How can we trust what we are told occurred in history if we weren't there? How do we know how Pyrrhus died?

Enough confusing philosophy, hopefully we have laid sufficient groundwork to contrast Mr Deasy's conventional worldview with that which we shall shortly encounter.

Back in class, the lesson is nearly over. With hockey approaching Stephen maintains interest by offering a riddle. It seems, and is, nonsensical. Riddles often are and this one is based on a popular riddle of the time[11]:

> The cock crew,
> The sky was blue:
> The bells in heaven
> Were striking eleven.
> Tis time for this poor soul
> To go to heaven.[12]

What is that? The answer? A fox burying its grandmother under a hollybush. This does not impress the boys who run off for hockey. A fox? Jesus is sometimes represented as a fox – as is Parnell. Stephen imagines himself a hunted animal – a stag or a fox and later in the book the story of Actaeon and Diana is referred.[13] The fox of our riddle is burying its grandmother. The real riddle on which this is based says mother, not grandmother, but Stephen's guilt of having 'killed his mother' is too close for comfort and too painful for levity, so a generation is transposed for protection. Or we may read it as 'grand' mother, a mother that is grand. Anyway, the riddle is a bit of a riff to the next scene in the episode. A shout is heard outside and it's time for hockey. The boys gather their stuff and run off. Stephen has his pyrrhic victory; the lesson concluded for privileged boys with little interest in or especial need for education. One boy, Cyril Sargent, remains. He approaches Stephen with the algebra he was told to copy out for extra tuition. He is dishevelled, bespectacled, with hands and face ink-smudged. Among his contemporaries, Sargent appears way down the food chain in terms of brains and family money.

He copied the algebra as tasked but doesn't understand it. It's a wonderful scene. Stephen sees in this boy himself at similar age. A boy only a mother could love. It's marvellous prose as Stephen contemplates mothers, Sargent's or in general, but most likely his own and that the only certainty in life . . . a mother's love. *Amor matris*. Or is it love of mother? You decide.

> She had saved him from being trampled underfoot and had gone, scarcely having been.[14]

The fox is back.

> . . . beneath winking stars a fox, red reek of rapine in his fur, with merciless bright eyes [Joyce's eyes were incredibly blue] scraped in the earth, listened, scraped up the earth, listened, scraped and scraped.[15]

Having buried its mother, is the fox is trying to bring her back to life? Scraping and listening, might she not be dead? But, no, one can't turn back the clock. She's history. Stephen looks back at the algebra in the book and we are treated to the sort of paragraph that has sane people on the verge of tears.

> Across the page the symbols moved in grave morrice, in the mummery of their letters, wearing quaint caps of squares and cubes. Give hands, traverse, bow to partner: so: imps of fancy of the Moors. Gone too from the world, Averroes and Moses Maimonides, dark men in mien and movement, flashing in their mocking mirrors the obscure soul of the world, a darkness shining in brightness which brightness could not comprehend.[16]

Wonderful. We mentioned last time that this book looks east, in its general sense of orientalism which back then would include North Africa. Both Morris dancing and algebra were created by the Moors of North Africa and introduced to Europe via Spain. The very word algorithm comes from a gentleman, Al-Juarismi, considered to be an originator. Here Stephen imagines, the numbers moving across the page in Morris dance choreography as they resolve the algebraic formula. Their hats being the little 2s and 3s above algebraic figures. Interwoven are two great Semitic philosophers, one Muslim,[17] one Jewish,[18] both deemed heretics for trying to marry natural science and philosophy with their religion and before we know it, we have a third. With the words, 'soul of the world', we enter the territory of a James Joyce favourite, Giordano Bruno.[19] Another heretic, this one burned at the stake for what we might consider quite modern views.[20]

Having alluded to views on the nature of history from Aristotle, through William Blake, Averroes, Maimonides and Giordano Bruno, it is easy to miss that one of the boys lived on Vico Road (remember Giambattista Vico from Lecture One with history being a repetitive cycle?),[21] Vico Road happens to be a real road in Dalkey.

A far more conventional view of history is presented in our third segment by Mr Deasy, modern-day Nestor. He's the headmaster so should know what he's talking about. Despite his unsavoury views, its easy to form a favourable view of this character who has the air of a comical Colonel Blimp.[22]

Its payday and Mr Deasy asks Stephen to await him in his office while he sorts out the hockey teams. A traditional office: wood, leather; how one imagines a headmaster's room to be at a private school. It's described as stale and smoky, the leather abraded and scarred. Stephen takes in the scene, the pictures of the long-dead thoroughbred horses, the display of historic and so obsolete coins, Stuart coins no less, with those political connotations.[23] Trays of seashells, long since empty of the life that once dwelt within and also reminiscent of money (shells, clams etc) and power. A mollusc was the source of the purple dye of which royalty and the church were so fond. One is whirled like an emir's turban, possibly that of Al-Juarismi of algebraic invention, or perhaps of Harun al Raschid, of whom, we will learn, both Stephen and Bloom dreamt last night.

Looming large is a picture of kilt-wearing Albert Edward, Prince of Wales, who, since 1901, had been Edward VII, King of the United Kingdom and Ireland and Emperor of India. So by 1904 this picture was an historic inaccuracy, another relic to go with the dead horses and empty shells. These are not the trappings of a radical Fenian republican: Mr Deasy is rather what is known as a West Briton – an Irishman very much in favour of rule from London. He might hail from the north; he refers to Ulster but equally could be Dublin-born and bred. In any event, the Stuart coins suggest the ineffectiveness of a Catholic regime as well as the baseless value of dead money.[24] Stephen reminisces of the condescension received on his previous two visits to the study and, as per Vicoan history, he's expecting this meeting to be no different. Deasy though is quite well-meaning and pretty respectful. He seems to quite like Stephen but has the air of the elder generation talking at the younger. Another father figure? We tried Mulligan in episode one, how about Deasy?

To business. He pays Stephen's wages from a leather money contraption that he assiduously describes. It's not the four pounds as Mulligan expects but £3 12 shillings which doesn't seem much for a monthly wage but we don't know how part-time is part-time. Mr Deasy is concerned about and careful with money. He boasts that like any good Britisher he has paid his way. At his grand age he owes not a farthing.[25] Can Stephen say that? Stephen's various creditors run through his mind. No, he can't say that.

> Because you don't save, Mr Deasy said, pointing his finger. You don't know yet what money is. Money is power, when you have lived as long as I have. I know, I know. If youth but knew. But what does Shakespeare say? Put but money in thy purse.[26]

Stephen murmurs that was Shakespeare writing for Iago, one of the nastiest characters he created. Garrett Deasy though, like his ancient counterpart, is beyond hearing, he's in lecture mode. We shall store Deasy's cherishment of money and recall it when he blames the Jew merchants in a few minutes' time. Mr Deasy's lecturing moves from money to history, Irish history. *Per vias rectus* is his family motto – only the straight road, only the proper way. He then proceeds to be wrong in most aspects of his sermon, even assuming historic facts are absolute, and Stephen cannot get a word in edgeways of Deasy's inaccuracy, misogyny and racism. Then Mr Deasy remembers that Stephen can help him out. He is very concerned at an outbreak of foot and mouth disease which if left unresolved may decimate the Irish cattle industry. He'd like Stephen to use his journalist connections to have published in a newspaper a letter Deasy is in the throes of completing. Deasy has been campaigning to save the cattle but feels he's been thwarted by nefarious influence of unseen hands: Jews, merchants that eat up a nation's vital strength. Surely, observes Stephen, a merchant is one who buys cheap and sells dear, Jew or Gentile? But no, Mr Deasy explains, it's not just about how Jews are with money (not for a second spotting the irony of his lecture on money a few moments earlier), it's that they sinned against the light (note the word 'light') and so are condemned to forever wander the earth without a home. This obviously is a reference to the Wandering Jew motif.[27] He further explains that history is the way of God, a forward motion of constancy along a designated path, divinely designed and which excludes Jews and presumably other sinners. That is, it's all written down, learn your Bible, do not deviate, stay on the path and you will proceed inexorably into the light. This view also reflects the poem 'Lycidus', where Milton believes that provided his dying friend allowed Jesus into his life, they will all meet again in the afterlife. Which dilemma applies of course, to Stephen and his mother and to Bloom, his parents and son.

In possibly the most famous line in the book, Stephen says that history is a nightmare from which he's trying to awake,[28] subscribing possibly more to the Viconian pattern of repeating circles but with an occasional escape hatch. He's not so sure about God either and hearing the boys celebrating a hockey goal, says, that is God. 'What is God?' says Deasy. That, says Stephen (in arguably the second most famous line), God is 'a shout in the street'.[29] Deasy is perplexed, so, if nothing else, Stephen has momentarily shut him up.

Among the things this shout in the street might refer, let's posit the following:

- That God is not a light at the end of a pre-destined historical path, God is everywhere as Spinoza tried to explain and was excommunicated for his trouble.
- Socrates, and possibly Plato, wrote nothing down. His teaching was only audible. You walked with him and learned from what you heard. Peripatetic. A shout in the street.
- A shout. It could be the thunderclap in the Vicoan cycle as we shall hear at broadly the centre of the book in episode fourteen or to be seen in *Finnegans Wake* with Tim Finnegan falling off the scaffolding.

Without negating the other two, I'd probably go for the first one.

Let's return to the reference to light; those bloody Jews that sinned against the light. Consider this, in the context of earlier passages from Nestor:

- Back in Paris, at St Genevieve Library; in Stephen's 'mind's darkness a sloth of the underworld, reluctant, shy of brightness, . . .'[30]
- A corruption of the word of Jesus. Matthew 22:21:

  To Caesar what is Caesar's, to God what is God's. A long look from dark eyes, a riddling sentence to be woven and woven on the church's looms. Ay.[31]

This concerns money and tax, but note the look from dark eyes; that is, Jesus has dark eyes, which is not unlikely, he was, after all, a Jew from Nazareth. Leopold Bloom, too, will be characterised by dark heavy eyes.

- One thinks of Giordano Bruno's 'obscure soul of the world, a darkness shining in brightness which brightness could not comprehend'.[32]

This theme will endure, including in the context of the stars in the sky, always there, but obscured by light of day.

So, all in all, Stephen dressed in black (along with Bloom) gives an impression of favouring dark over light. Contrast Mulligan's primrose waistcoat and Blazes Boylan's serge blue tie. This is also a Schopenhauerian theme apparent in Wagner's opera *Tristan und Isolde*, in which the lovers seek the sanctuary of dark night over the harsh reality of day.[33] The discourses of Schopenhauer are relevant to our book in several respects and we will consider him in our lecture four, Proteus, episode three of *Ulysses*.

Considering Mr Deasy is so wedded to heading towards the light, it is ironic that it causes him a little jip on this fine sunny morning. It illuminates for our amusement his ill-dyed hair as he marches upon the hockey field. A shaft through the window monetarily blinds him, mid-speech and it flings imaginary spangled money at him in the final words of the episode. After clanging away on the typewriter, the old man gives Stephen the letter. Stephen scans it, silently noting an abundance of cliché. Nevertheless, it's a work environment and Stephen is polite, even a little overawed by his boss come paymaster. So again servant of a servant,[34] Stephen agrees to try to oblige by delivering copies to two newspaper editors. Besides, helping ill cattle must be a decent cause and he suspects Mulligan will have a new name for him: the Bullock Befriending Bard. Odysseus learned the hard way the consequences of irreverence to cattle[35] and so, amid much inaccurate bluster, Mr Deasy has, like Nestor, conveyed a useful message to Stephen.

Stephen leaves, passing concrete lions at slumber on the way. Toothless terrors. But his exit is parried by Mr Deasy who chases after him to levy a final damning, anti-Semitic slur that he seems to find amusing.

And so we come to the glorious final lines:

> On his wise shoulders through the checkerwork of leaves the sun flung spangles, dancing coins.[36]

Deasy, partially in shadow, is adorned by his precious light with ersatz currency; about as useful as the shells in his study. Thank you, Mr Deasy, you taught us well.

Let's review those original reference points from the schemata to see if we have covered them. History, of course. Remember that this was penned against a backdrop of World War One, pyrrhic victory *par excellence*. Brown? Well we've had brown dark eyes and Deasy's room, leather, wood-panelled, thoroughbred horses. A brown ambience, certainly. But horses? Aside from a very brief allusion to those pictures, has there been much? Especially when one compares Mr Deasy to Nestor, famed as a great horseman and it's not as if the history lesson concerned the Trojan horse as we might have expected. Wouldn't cows have been more relevant? King Pyrrhus was astride his horse when fatally hit by a thrown roof tile and Deasy reported his cousin Mr Blackwood-Price riding to Dublin to vote for the Union. Hardly smoking guns. Let's take a closer look at those pictures on the wall.

They are of winning horses, usually the Classics. These are the 1000 Guineas, the 2000 Guineas, The Oaks, The Derby and The St Ledger. All run in England but close to the heart of many Irishmen, adding to the servile feel. Lord Hastings' Repulse won the 1000 Guineas in 1866. Shotover won the 1882 Derby. We then have reference to a winner of a foreign race, the Grand Prix de Paris, also in 1866. This is Ceylon. These are not facts casually inserted, nothing is in this book. Who was born in 1882? James Joyce and, therefore, also, Stephen Dedalus. Which 38-year-old with foreign connections, was born in 1866? Mr Leopold Bloom, yet to be introduced. Suddenly these horses, corporeally long expired, become a little more interesting. We might apropos nothing, throw in eugenics, the science of purity of race; the Edwardian notion that Darwinism might be applied from animals to humans so that inferior races, such as Jews and gypsies, could be marginalised by the encouraged procreation of the superior races. Much as are thoroughbred horses.

Bloom, at just about this time in Dublin, has accidentally tipped a horse for the Gold Cup to be run later that day in Ascot, England. As that race is run, the fine filly Molly will run her own race in Eccles Street.

These early episodes plant seeds from which great oaks grow.

LECTURE 4, 4 NOVEMBER 2020: EPISODE 3

Proteus and the Third Eye

Music: Those Lovely Seaside Girls – Kevin McDermott & Ralph Richey

Proteus. The notorious episode three.

This is a passage of the book that has readers running for the hills wondering why they are bothering with this unintelligible nonsense, particularly as it comes so early and lends a daunting feel to the weight of the book. But it's just a walk along a beach and who doesn't like a walk on the beach? There's a dog, a couple of cockle-pickers, no problem. Well there are problems and the first one is that the episode lives almost entirely inside Stephen's mind. That visit to his Aunt Sara, the time in Paris – forget it. It's all Stephen daydreaming, he doesn't leave the beach. The second difficulty is the logic-defying concepts to be faced. In the interest of mental equilibria, if you are really struggling, don't read it. Clearly Joyce intended us to read and digest the book in the presented order, but the book won't be offended if you do not. The following five episodes are so much easier; they read normally and are fun. Please don't ditch the whole book for this episode. But naturally it's better to bear with it if you can and hopefully this guidance will help, it will divulge treasure that enhances the rest of the book.

Let's start on solid ground at a little before 11 am. Stephen has two errands: The delivery of Mr Deasy's letter to a newspaper editor and to meet Mulligan and Haines in a pub called The Ship at 12.30. To pass the time, he's left the tram a few stops early and will walk the last half-mile or so into Dublin City centre. This takes him along a beach called Sandymount Strand. He's still feeling pretty miserable for the reasons we mentioned last time.[1] On the plus side, he has got some cash – £3.12s give or take his tram fare and he's in creative mood. He's toying with the composition of a poem and with a Vampiric theme that is likely to feature. Another Dublin resident published *Dracula* a few years earlier[2] and, even though pretty low-brow for Stephen, it remains in vogue. And he's thinking, thinking, thinking. Continuing his musing on the nature of history from last time, which leads him to ponder time, space, cause, effect, perception, reality; the usual stuff we all fill our heads with. And he's alone. At breakfast, he was dogsbody to Mulligan, at school, at the beck and call of Deasy; indeed his short-term future revolves around obligations to them both. But for half an hour, in quiet contemplation on the beach, he will be his own master. This is the Stephen Dedalus show. Remember, too, his poor eyesight and that he's broken his glasses.[3] So what he sees is not necessarily what is.

For this episode, we need all the help we can get, starting with Homer.

Nestor's longwinded advice to Telemachus amounted to 'go see Menelaus. He may know something'. So, off he trots to Sparta to visit King Menelaus and Queen Helen. Menelaus hasn't a clue about Odysseus but tells of his own travel woes.[4] Lack of wind to fill his sails left Menelaus stuck in the Nile Delta at Pharos for wind and waves are at the whim of the local god Proteus. Unless he stirs up a breeze, one could be stuck for good. Proteus is a tricky blighter. A shape shifter that alters guise at will. It's almost impossible to pin him down but if one can, he will help. Further, he has a weak spot, he is shepherd to a flock of seals which, once a day at noon, bask on the rocks to rest. Proteus lies among them. Apparently one must hold one's nose (the seals are seriously pongy), tip-toe between them and then jump on Proteus. He will struggle like fury and transform into all sorts to escape. Not just animal life: this chap is elemental – earth, wind, fire, water. But control him and he'll eventually submit and do one's bidding. The plan worked and Menelaus continued his journey home.

What do we glean from this?

- Protean . The word comes from Proteus and means to change, to be versatile, to adapt.
- It's an apt word for tidal flow which is constantly changing and constantly changing its neighbour, the beach. Never the same two moments running. Flotsam and jetsam, real and as imagined by Stephen will wash up and we shall look out for constant transformation, dare we say transubstantiation.[5]
- Proteus doesn't imitate the different persona, he actually becomes them. Remember this when we consider Perception and Reality.
- Will there be seals? Any connection to Egypt? Who or what is supposed to be Proteus and what is changing?

Joyce's schemata inform as follows. Organ: none; Colour: green; Symbol: tide; Art: philology which is the study of the structure of language. It will be of no comfort at all that the confusion and challenge may not simply be to cope with Joyce's self-indulgence. It may also be that but, primarily the reader must engage in a personal struggle with Proteus. And struggle we shall with some of the ideas mulled over by

Stephen; humanity has done so forever and they are here presented, squirming and wriggling inside Stephen's head and trying to avoid being pinned down and understood.

Finally, before launching in, it's important to remember that this is the last episode of Part One of the book, called 'The Telemachiad'. Whilst technically there are no chapters, the book is formally split into parts 1, 2 and 3. Part 1 is about the Son, Telemachus, who in *The Odyssey* leaves his home and mother in search of his father. Like Telemachus, Stephen must learn to accept two realities:

- Life without his mother; and
- Life beyond his insular self. His home, his Ithaca, is inside his head. He must break out artistically (to forge in the smithy of his soul etc[6]) and also personally because Joyce at Stephen's age (and on this day) first dated Nora Barnacle[7] and is at the point in life where one engages other.

Stephen will not learn these lessons so early in the day, but now is germination; crystallisation comes later.

It may help to set out two themes and apply them to skim through the episode hoping to make some sense along the way. They entail some mental gyration but, with these safely stored, the episode might flow easier and, if of comfort, remember that this is one of the toughest chunks of the book.

Let's call the first theme PERCEPTION and it is perfectly illustrated in the impossible opening paragraph:

> Ineluctable modality of the visible: at least that if no more, thought through my eyes. Signatures of all things I am here to read, seaspawn and seawrack, the nearing tide, that rusty boot. Snotgreen, bluesilver, rust: coloured signs. Limits of the diaphane. But he adds: in bodies. Then he was aware of them bodies before of them coloured. How? By knocking his sconce against them, sure. Go easy. Bald he was and a millionaire, maestro di color che sanno. Limit of the diaphane in. Why in? Diaphane, adiaphane. If you can put your five fingers through it, it is a gate, if not, a door. Shut your eyes and see.[8]

Ineluctable modality of the visible: this simply means that if you have your eyes open you can't help but interpret the world by what you see. It's ineluctable, unavoidable. Why couldn't he have just said 'unavoidable'? It's the first word in the episode so it must be important. We recall the significance of the word 'Stately', the first word in the book and the knowledge gleaned from its utterance.[9] Recall also that the Art of the episode is philology. Say 'ineluctable', roll the word around your mouth. Then 'unavoidable'. The former has more going on; more fun, more tactile, more sensual. Four proper engagements of the tongue, whereas, with the latter, the tongue limply lolls. For those in a *Finnegans Wake* frame of mind, at the heart of ineluctable there's luck, whereas in unavoidable, a void.

Stephen walks and sees: seaspawn, seawrack, the tide, a rusty boot. But are they real? Can he trust their modality? Can any of us, but particularly him with his poor eyesight? Philosophers from Plato onwards have grappled with the question 'how do we know what we see is real?' Our human equipment is limited to five fallible senses capable only of sending signals to our brain which absorbs and interprets, based on experience and which experience might be flawed. Transcendental Idealism[10] is, one understands, the school of thought that suggests that there is a reality out there and it may and probably does coincide with what we see, hear, smell, touch and taste: but only probably. Subscribers to this, following Plato, include George Berkeley, the Irish Bishop of Cloyne[11] and, to whom Stephen regularly refers, Immanuel Kant[12] and Arthur Schopenhauer.[13] It postulates whether material objects are actual or merely actual ideas. Sounds daft you may think: why not bash your head on that wall over there if in any doubt or, as Stephen puts it in the first paragraph, knock his sconce against them.[14] But we have a nagging concern that, if we can't trust what we perceive, where are we?

Against such an odd backdrop, we might translate that first paragraph as follows:

> I can't but help to see things. My eyes send a message to my brain which labels objects. As an artist I'm here to read these signals written by someone/something – who/what has written them? The sea? Nature? God? I can differentiate objects by their colour; snotgreen of the sea, silver blue, rust. But colour is just a light wave interpreted by my brain and differently by different brains. Aristotle knew this, that colour was an outer sheen of an underlying reality. How? By knocking his stick against it? But isn't touch as unreliable as sight? What if I couldn't see, could I tell the difference between a door and a gate by touching it? Sure, you can stick your fingers through a gate. Maybe perceived reality is the door blocking out (adiaphane) the real reality; whereas a gate allows a glimpse beyond the veil (diaphane) into true reality.

Stephen experiments: he closes his eyes to see if the world disappears simply because he can't see it. This is the reality for the blind (a blind character will enter our story[15]) and Stephen uses his ashplant,[16] his stick, to tap as he walks along, sea shells crackling under his step. This ashplant will, at various times, correspond to his walking stick, his cane, his sword and his crucifix. He opens his eyes; it was there all the time without him, unless it all re-animated that instant for, can an object exist without a subject to perceive it? It makes one a little dizzy thinking of it.

The second theme flowing out of the first is COMPASSION. This is a huge theme in the book, perhaps the pre-eminent theme. We approach it in a careful roundabout way as Menelaus approached Proteus and, in doing so, must navigate a little more tricky philosophy. In the next paragraph of the episode, Joyce introduces two German words: *nacheinander* and *nebeneinander*.[17] Important words. The first means one thing after another, i.e., time; the second, one thing alongside each other, i.e., space. These words smack of the philosopher, Arthur Schopenhauer. Time might be one's inner world because one marks it with eyes shut; Stephen counts his steps, one after the other, crackling shells. The ineluctable modality of the audible. Space is the outer world, things we see, objects and the space in between objects. One demarcated from the other by a reliable or unreliable outline or different colour. Time and space: are both real or just markers created by our brains because we cannot cope with the void that would otherwise exist? If a void can be said to exist. Schopenhauer built upon Berkeley, Kant and the others. He labelled our world, as perceived, the Phenomena, and, as unperceived, but nevertheless the true underlying reality, as the Noumena. Dare one say he might have called it Proteus?

Noumena is all matter: everything. We cannot comprehend it because we only have the sensory equipment for the superficial phenomena which, by definition, must also be part of the Noumena. Because Noumena is unbound by time and space it can only be one unified mass of everything that ever was, is and will be. Therefore, if divisions between humans, animals, plants, rocks, water, etc, are all artificial, then divisions and arguments between human beings are ludicrous. Such divisions, says Schopenhauer, are simply perceptions created by millions of years of conditioning (by god knows what to who knows whom?) that has instilled a fundamental human condition – self-preservation. But, he says, it is false because there is no true self to preserve.

Another German word, *Mitleid*, means compassion. This says Arthur is a rare portal, a glimpse through the adiaphanous veil to the Noumena, our genuine reality. A recognition that competition against other people, animals, vegetation and the planet is futile because we are all one. This is a central theme of several Wagnerian operas as it is of the book before us. An essential difference being that one can love both Ulysses and its author, whereas with Wagner, one can love the art but not the man.

So as we proceed through the episode we shall bear in mind both PERCEPTION AND COMPASSION and also let's not forget our friend, Consubstantiation, the coagulation of Father, Son and Holy Spirit.

This is why we and Stephen staring at the beach are so interested in the concept of 'change'. How can father and son be both separate and as one? If the Son is there to read the signs on the beach written by the Father, then the Holy Spirit is the modality. It is simultaneously both the divine essence that unites them and yet also the medium for expressing differentiation, that is, individual shape or form. No wonder the Holy Trinity is central to our book. It may sound incomprehensible but we have absorbed much of this as second nature. A table is a table, no denying that, but only because its Wednesday. On Tuesday it was a tree and on Thursday it became firewood. So, why not humans? Our molecules constantly reproduce so that after every five months or so we are entirely re-constituted: 'Shattered glass and toppling masonry.'[18]

Further, what is the demarcation between life and death? When does sperm become a separate life from the man that produced it and the women that gestated it? What is death? The molecules simply do inside the coffin what they have done a thousand times during the previous three score years and ten. Makes no difference to them.

With such easy notions tucked away, we attack the rest of the episode with some swagger. Ready for anything.

Stephen sees a couple of older women scrambling unsteadily along the stones towards the water's edge. One has a decent size bag; the other an umbrella. Stephen's poor eyes transmit an unreliable signal to his brain which labels them midwives on a mission to cast a still born baby into the sea. What else to do with the tiny poor dears? They've not been baptised so denied a Catholic burial and with no place in heaven, they are consigned to a state of limbo. 'A misbirth . . . hushed in ruddy wool.'[19]

Note allusion to Rudy, Bloom's son who lived only eleven days and who would have been eleven years by this day. We will observe a host of premonitions concerning Bloom whom Stephen does not yet know. For example, Stephen will muse on the missing bit of Eve, her navel.[20] This will be the portal a little later that day, in episode nine, through which he will meet Bloom outside the National Library where, to Mulligan's mischievous delight, Bloom will be surreptitiously checking if the statues of Greek goddesses have been sculptured with anuses. If not, missing anatomy.

Midwives, deliverers of life and, in this instance also, final dispatchers. Birth, life, death, re-birth. This cycle will re-cycle and reincarnate throughout the book, here chiming via Rudy and subsequently with number eleven. Each generation connected via umbilical cord telephone lines back to Eve, back to the original sin in which we are born and to Lucifer that tempted her. Eve had no navel, belly without blemish, for the obvious reason that she was made not born. Stephen muses on his own creation, also made, not begotten. To beget implies a holy deed whereas, although his parents did as the Lord commanded, going forth and multiplying, his creation, he thinks, was a little more prosaic. He compares the holy trinity with the son and his own consubstantial father with whom he feels a physical connection but little more and fears transubstantiating into him as another Dublin drunk. The Stephen/Simon similarity is no accident.

We then have a lovely long and made-up word. These are a rarity in *Ulysses* but proliferate in *Finnegans Wake*:

'contransmagnificandjewbangtantiality.'[21]

Joseph Campbell,[22] contemporary of Joyce, felt that this word summed up the whole shooting match, so let's have a stab at figuring it out.

Con + tiality (at the end) must refer to consubstantiation.

Trans = Transubstantiation. Bread and wine become body and blood of Christ. (Remember Mulligan, observing the white shaving foam in the bowl and remarking on his difficulty with the white corpuscles?)

Magnificat – the Canticle of the Virgin Mary,[23] which stating 'My soul doth magnify the Lord', implies that God is present within each of our souls. Note, Mary – Marion – Molly.

Jew – Jesus's earthly father Joseph, was a Jew, as was Mary, therefore also Jesus. This is a transparent allusion to Bloom, who, in his way, might be the saviour to come, at least of his marriage and/or the heralder of Stephen, saviour of Irish literature.

Bang. Could this be the moment of conception, immaculate or otherwise? The Big Bang? The Vico thunderclap? The shout in the street? Or, maybe, knocking one's sconce against something to test its reality.

So a take on this word might be the creation of souls at the moment of conception, the merging of such souls and the saving of souls. And that we are all able to take control because God (for want of a better word) is within all of us and all things and, as we are thereby indivisible, we may as well be decent to each other (tips cap to good old Arthur Schop).

Moving on.

Stephen approaches that part of the beach where he could divert to his Aunt Sara in Strasbourg Terrace. This would not merely be a social call. He needs a bed for the night and this is an obvious consideration. At first reading, a difficult passage but not so once one has worked through to figure who says what; reading aloud helps. Stephen imagines his father Simon asking his other children if they know where Stephen has been sleeping these nights and then Simon mimics his (that is Simon's) brother-in-law, Richie. To Stephen, this is Uncle Richie.

Richie, gives himself the airs of a lawyer but he's actually only a clerk that prepares court trial costs schedules. Then, Stephen imagines that he indeed visited his aunt and uncle and there's Uncle Richie sat up in bed working at home, ostensibly because a bad back prevents him attending the office, though it's more likely due to a heavy drinking session the previous night. This is all in Stephen's imagination.

This passage begins with Stephen's mimicry of his father:

> 'Did you see anything of your artist brother Stephen lately? No? Sure he's not down in Strasburg Terrace with his aunt Sally? Couldn't he fly a bit higher than that, eh?
>
> And and and and tell us Stephen, how is uncle Si? O weeping God, the things I married into. De boys up in de hayloft. The drunken little costdrawer and his brother, the cornet player. Highly respectable gondoliers. And skeweyed Walter sirring his father, no less. Sir. Yes, sir. No, sir. Jesus wept: and no wonder, by Christ.'[24]

And the point? It's creating a picture of family decline and decay. In debt, but always money for booze. Note his uncle and cousin are on the look-out for debt collectors when Stephen knocks (imaginary knocks) on the door.

The wind picks up. It stirs Stephen from that particular reverie and we move to another. The Transubstantiation theme is continued in the 'dringadring' paragraph.[25] Stephen imagines several (well-fed) priests administering the Eucharist to (less well-fed) congregants and then tidying away the ritualistic candlesticks, vessels and what not. Lots of little bells are rung. This is happening in churches across Dublin at the same or very near the same time. *Nebeneinander*. Alluding not only to the quotidian control and power of the Catholic Church but also questioning how the body of Christ can literally (and we are told it is literal) be in all these different biscuits in different churches and then in all of us at the same time. Is it Jesus's whole body or is he in bits? Joyce is here challenging most of the pillars of Catholicism: Consubstantiation, Transubstantiation, the Magnificat and let's throw in secular orderly *nebeneinander* as well.

Also worthy of note are the paragraphs where Stephen speaks with two voices. The relevance of Schizophrenia to the whole book is worthy of wider study and no doubt many have.[26] Twenty-two-year-old Stephen mocks his teenage self for his highfalutin literary aims and the series of books he was to write, with each title, simply a letter: 'Have you read his F? O yes but I prefer Q. Yes but W is wonderful. O yes, W.'[27]

You will note the self-deprecation. He admonishes his younger self's pretension whilst doing the same with the current self for not achieving those lofty ambitions. Again, playing with time and transformation.

Back in reality, he sees the two large chimneys as the docks come into view. It's a building called the Pigeon House, after the family name of the owner some hundred years earlier. That reminds him of a book called *The Life of Jesus* by the Frenchman Leo Taxil.[28] He paraphrases in French and as broadly translated:

> "Joseph (on observing the pregnant Mary): But how did you get in this position?
> Mary (in reply): I don't know Joseph, I think it was the pigeon!"29

Thus we are back to consubstantiality. The pigeon (more commonly a dove) is the representation of the Holy Spirit, the divine essence that facilitates the oneness of father and son. Leo Taxil was something of a mischief maker, a blaspheming anarchist of whom Joyce seems to have been very fond. Reference to France and Taxil's book links Stephen to Patrice Egan to whom it was lent. Patrice is the son of Kevin Egan, Fenian bomber, now exiled to France and distant relative of Stephen's father. Stephen shared absinth-fuelled sessions separately with both father and son in Paris just a few months earlier. Patrice the son is thoroughly French, atheist and socialist – his Irish heritage being little more than an interesting novelty. The father Kevin: republican, killer of military and civilians alike yet devoutly religious and oddly prim, cuts a sorry figure. His 'cause' remains vital but the steady hands that would light the fuse wire now shake as he struggles to light a cigarette in a dingy bar. Worse yet, the beloved cause has abandoned him, as has his wife. He's pitiful: daily marking his stations of the cross (a regular pub crawl) whilst trying to sing the Lord's song in a strange land,[30] that is, keep the cause alive. He can't even do that right and muddles two very different songs – the romantic and sentimental 'The Boys from Kilkenny' and the more rousing and radical Napper Tandy tribute, 'The Wearing of the Green'.

Stephen's French sojourn (the real one not his reverie) is cut short; the telegram telling him of his dying mother pulls him back to the sucking sands of Ireland. Not Isle of Saints, rather Isle of dreadful thirst.

Note hereabouts: the wreaking of sewage breath and also noon slumbers.[31] In those days this part of the beach was an outlet for metropolitan effluent, discharging directly into Dublin Bay. For our purposes: noon, smelly – Proteus and the seals are slumbering. A notion confirmed as we time switch to beached whales in medieval Dublin. The message for Stephen is that the true artist, the people's prophet, must get down and dirty and mix with smelly real life, like Jonah, into the belly of the beast. This is difficult, for his insulated arrogance notwithstanding, Stephen is timid. But it's a challenge to which he must rise.

A bad smell foreshadows the coming Bloom, though in a good way. He is the outer world to Stephen's sterile inner. His world is the physical and practical, comfortable in the smelly detail of real life. Stephen, slightly later in the episode (but it illustrates here), recalls a snippet of a dream the previous night, set somewhere oriental. Street of Harlots. He can't quite remember, as happens with dreams. He's 'almosting'[32] it. A great Joycean verb. One is trying to grasp fragments of a dream as it slips away. A perfect transubstantiating word. There's a brothel keeper, it might be Harun al Raschid,[33] who coaxes him inside by holding a melon to Stephen's face so he may smell the creamy fruit. The man says that the answer will be inside. We shall discover that Bloom, same night, had a similar dream.

Which brings us back to smelly real life and the belly of the beast. A dog: actually two dogs – one alive, one dead. The live one, runs towards Stephen and probably belongs to a pair of cockle-pickers at the water's edge. Stephen, scared of dogs as well as water, is startled. The dog, however, is distracted by the carcass of a dead dog. In the most obvious protean reference, the live dog metaphorically runs through several alternate persona (including, significantly, a panther or pard) before empathy brings it home.[34] It is again a dog sniffing its dead brother. Compassion. For Stephen still well short of this level of consciousness, the carcass is simply dirty, smelly, repulsive and above all, separate. He imagines the drowned man to be washed up on this, the ninth day. Still in water, allusions abound as tiny fish swim through his open fly to bring life to a dead placid sex organ. Stephen cannot be that dog, who not only sticks his nose in to sniff his dead brother but also roars defiantly at the waves and takes a piss, there and then, on the beach without a care in the world. Stephen is not yet there with nature or 'other'.

Could he as did Mulligan, save a drowning man? He likes to think he would (we recall he did not pray for the life of his own mother), but not so as to risk his own life: 'I would want his life to be his, mine to be mine.'[35]

Joyce screams Schopenhauer. Stephen is not at the point where he would risk his life for another. He does not have that compassion. Bloom will show him this, before the day is out, and Stephen will improve. For now, though, his observations remain of a world reflecting and revolving around Stephen. Not only has he not yet defeated ego, the battle has not really commenced.

The last few paragraphs concern the sense touch. We've had sight, sound, smell. Do we have taste? Maybe not, but Mr Bloom will more than compensate. Touch is arguably the most important sense, so fittingly left to last. Might the unscientific amateur argue that all senses rely initially on touch? In order to smell, air particles must touch our nasal receptors. Light waves and airwaves are received somewhere before being processed. Touch is about sex and sex represents creativity. Stephen imagines the female cockle-pickers to be gypsies, which is a very short walk from Egyptian. Gypsies, a people that trudge, traipse and shlep[36] through space and across time, possibly further foreshadowing of the Wandering Jew motif that will gather strength. He imagines the female gypsy is a prostitute. Cockle-picker by night as well as day and that her man is her pimp. This leads to erotic reverie but then, good Jesuit boy, he fears the onset of thunder and lightning to punish him.

Not for the first time this episode: Stephen conflates sex with menstrual blood, the tide and the moon. He mulls over the emergence of a line for his poem – vampires, kissing mouths, the moon – but has nothing on which to write and, if he doesn't pin down the creativity, it will be lost. He's 'almosting' it when, just in time, he finds Deasy's letter in his pocket. He tears off the blank portion at the end and, resting on a flat rock, records his creativity. He rolls words and sounds around his mouth to find the right ones, just as we did with 'ineluctable'. Leaning over that flat rock at noon, he observes his shadow and contemplates the sun, universe and perspective. Turning, he reclines on the rock, his mood ever more erotic. Kissing, touching, women unable to resist the vampire.

The cockle-pickers pass and he imagines that the gypsy whore shoots him an amorous glance. She's his erotic fantasy; but not only her, also the pretty woman at the bookshop window the previous Monday. He dredges her up through the adiaphane into the diaphane before remonstrating with himself for using, what he supposes to be, an innocent virgin as his erotic aid. He's aroused and secluded among the rocks:

> Touch me. Soft eyes. Soft soft soft hand. I am lonely here. O, touch me soon, now. What is that word known to all men? I am quiet here alone. Sad too. Touch, touch me.[37]

Does he, doesn't he? Who can say? Stephen being Stephen, masturbation on a public beach seems pretty unlikely. He lies there gazing at the sky with Giordano Bruno stars obscured in the noon brightness,[38] as he mulls the perspective of Kant and Berkeley. He rises and urinates. He also picks his nose and, realising his handkerchief was appropriated by Mulligan, smears the creative product of his excavation on the same flat rock. He walks on as we approach the end of this dense episode. We have covered much but disappointingly omitted more; one hopes we have pinned down the gist.

What have we learned from Stephen's coastal contemplation of the universe? For now, it remains a universe revolving around the Sun named Stephen, including that Delta of Cassiopeia upon which he just brooded. But he has managed to take a pee, right there and then, out in the open, like the dog. Is that a sign? Unlikely, as drunken Stephen would have pissed up many a wall but maybe it's a start.

He feels a presence behind him and turns to look. A schooner approaches the docks. A three-master. The Holy Trinity? Crucifixes? Whatever other depths to this image, as we close The Telemachiad, here is the father, the sailor, the pilgrim returning to Ithaca. Here comes Leopold Bloom.

PART II – THE WANDERINGS OF ULYSSES

LECTURE 5, 18 NOVEMBER 2020: EPISODE 4

Calypso and the Dude

Music: La Ci Darem la Mano – Don Giovani Act One (Mozart)

This lecture might have been entitled 'Calypso and the Vitruvian Man'. Calypso, of course, because Joyce explained its relationship with book five of *The Odyssey* where Calypso enslaves Odysseus for several years. Vitruvian though, for all its aural appeal and classical magnificence, would have been wrong. Leonardo Da Vinci painted his Vitruvian Man as an image of the ideal man. The chap we meet in this episode and accompany for eleven more, wandering around Dublin, is far from ideal. Leopold Bloom, a flawed man, just ask his wife.

'Calypso and the Dude' is also an imperfect title but does present the opportunity to parallel a cherished film, *The Big Lebowski*.[1] Jeffrey Lebowski, known only as the Dude, lives in suburban Los Angeles, goes bowling, drinks white Russians and smokes splifs. Beyond this he seeks to leave as small a footprint on life as he reasonably can. Yet it's such qualities or vices, depending on perspective, that endears and imbues him, inexplicably, with heroic status. He's described by the cowboy narrator Sam Elliott as a man for his time and place, that he fits right in for he's, well, he's the Dude.

Bloom, fitting right in, specific time and place? This doesn't sound right. As said, an imperfect title but there is something about Bloom, a quotidian man for his time and all time. A man that will wander through the day, bestowing help and wisdom as he goes, sometimes unselfishly, usually unknowingly. A truly unremarkable hero and they are the best sort.

Episode three presented two huge problems. One, it was really hard to understand what Joyce was saying and, two, to the extent we worked that out, it was even harder to get to grips with the deep issues with which he grappled. So the good news is that in episode four at least one of those problems subsides, the episode reads much easier. Unfortunately, the other problem hasn't ebbed away. As with Nestor, episodes that superficially appear easier disguise serious issues lurking not far beneath. In this episode and, for most of part two of the book (this and the ensuing eleven episodes), we will accompany Leopold

Bloom and his Wanderings of Ulysses. We shall be permitted to glimpse inside his head and shall observe that, like Odysseus, Bloom, too, is trapped. Stranded for years and, like Odysseus, he needs to break free and get home. In contrast with Stephen, whose issues tend toward the intellectual, for Bloom, trouble lies with affairs of the heart.

We left Stephen at around 12.15 on Sandymount Strand. We now go back in time some 4 hours to 8 o'clock, the same time we first met Stephen and enabling us to parallel our two protagonists. *Nebeneinander*. No need for obsessive comparison but we'll keep both on the radar, in case anything should crop up. We are in 7 Eccles Street in the north-western part of central Dublin. A terraced house sloping down towards the street so that the kitchen is at basement level and the same floor leads to the ground level garden at the rear. It is rented by the Blooms (Leopold and Molly). Their parlour and bedroom are on the floor above where there is an inside toilet but, we think, no separate bathroom. The second floor is empty, with rooms for rent. Outside to the rear is a small and partially planted yard and an outside toilet, or 'jakes', which apparently is shared with other houses.[2]

Just why Joyce selected this house out of all Dublin may be of interest. In August 1909, Joyce, made a rare return to Ireland from Trieste in another disheartening attempt to progress the publication of *Dubliners*. A friend, or so-called friend, Cosgrave, took the opportunity to disclose to Joyce that, back in 1904, Nora was two-timing Joyce with him. Joyce, emotionally, was a fragile man. Capable of immense highs and abyss-like lows. He was distraught and wrote a terrible letter to Nora[3] which, fortunately, took several days to arrive. (Nora at this time was either in Trieste or had possibly journeyed with the children to her family in Galway.) In the meantime, Joyce sought solace in and counsel from another friend, Byrne. Byrne assured him that Cosgrave had told a pack of lies, fuelled by a long-held grievance that Nora had rebuffed him. Of the two men, Joyce had regard and trust for Byrne way beyond that of Cosgrave and readily accepted this version of events. Incredibly relieved, he sorted matters out with Nora and forewarned of the letter in the post. So delighted and so grateful was he to Byrne, that he used Bryne's house, 7 Eccles Street, as his hero's location.[4] As for Cosgrave, he appears as Lynch, the medic who in episode fifteen will abandon Stephen in his time of need.

We meet Mr Leopold Bloom in the kitchen preparing breakfast and in conversation with the cat. In contrast with Stephen, startled by dogs and frankly, all of nature, Bloom is comfortable in the cat's company and strikes an empathetic note by yes, of course, wanting to feed it, but, less commonly, trying to see the world through the cat's eyes. Bloom will do this with other wildlife during the day. It's his Schopenhauer compassion and moreover sows the seed of Bloom as reincarnated cat/panther/pard/lion. But there's also a hint of psychological trouble as he wonders if cats can mouse after their whiskers have been clipped, for we will shortly learn that he and Molly have not had full penetrative sex since their baby son died a decade earlier. Conversely it casts Molly as cat toying with her mouse which almost enjoys the torture. Bloom is not naturally a resentful man, he is placid and generally accepting of the cards dealt, but the death of Rudy shook him to the core and eleven years on it remains a wedge driven between husband and wife.

Further character development in the kitchen with hints that Bloom is Jewish but clearly not kosher. One might associate religious ambivalence with the death of his child. Technically not Jewish, Bloom is baptised Christian[5] but that holds no emotional sway. In his heart, Bloom is no apostate. He feels Jewish and whilst the death of Rudy has tested this naturally optimistic man, this does not explain his lack of religious conviction. That we attribute to a lively logical and scientific outlook.[6] But the Rudy factor will be borne in mind.

There is an issue that possibly exposes the difference between an essay and an episode-by-episode guide for the reader. An essay would legitimately draw on future aspects of the book and other sources to make a point. But I try to limit borrowing from future episodes so as to enhance the 'real-time' reading experience. Bloom's religious convictions, positive or negative, are not established here. We know he can't be an observant Jew but that's about it. As an allied point, the book is littered with puzzles that are solved later but so subtly one assumes the mystery remains unanswered. For example, at one point in Lestrygonians, Bloom thinks of a man but struggles to recall his name.[7] Later on, apropos nothing, he blurts out a name, no context, just a name, and then moves on to his next thought. It would take a pretty good bridge player to recall the earlier quandary and connect the dots. Joyce simply presents life without any inclination to provide the reader with a helping hand. We shall follow a very real and so very flawed person for several hours. He thinks as we all do, with logic of sorts, but is no respecter of an ordered chronology. The unrecalled man? Penrose. A priestly looking chap who'd look into the Bloom house on Lombard Street West as he passed. Way off in episode seventeen we learn, in virtually the only other reference to him, that Bloom believes him to have had an affair with Molly and it's not until about 3 am, the next morning, that Molly confirms the answer to that.

Bloom decides on a pork kidney for his breakfast, for which he'll need to pop out to Dlugacz, the butcher around the corner on Dorset Street. Like Bloom's father, Dlugazc immigrated to Ireland from Hungary.

Bloom establishes courteous husband credentials by tip-toeing upstairs, so not to unnecessarily disturb his wife. He listens and, on hearing movement in the bed, gently knocks on the door. He's going around the corner, would she like anything?

The neutral reply comes: 'Mn'.[8] That could be yes, could be no. Could be in her semi-sleep she didn't really hear the question. Bloom construes: negative. Through the closed door, the bed creaks as the old brass quoits jingle in cry of attention under the womanly form. This jingling, to be heard throughout the day and the city, becomes a *leitmotif* for the adultery to be committed on these springs that afternoon. The bed was a wedding present from Molly's father, Major Tweedy, acquired so Bloom believes from the governor-general of Gibraltar. Molly's mother, the Gibraltarian Lunita Laredo, was long dead by the time the Blooms married and we'll take a closer look at Molly's antecedence as opportunity presents. Meantime, we register that Gibraltar was classically known as Calpe as it was thought to be Calypso's island.

It's no real spoiler to say that Molly speaks the very last word of this book and that the word is 'Yes'. It is spoken sometime in the wee hours of 17 June. Academic reputations have been staked upon explanation of that last word and so her first word must surely also be worthy of interest. A non-word: 'Mn'.

In his excellent guide, Harry Blamires[9] has some fun with this. If we insert Leo, L E O. inside M N and give it a stir, we have both Melon and Lemon. Melon, as we shall see, is Bloom's affectionate term for each of Molly's buttocks and he carries a bar of lemon-scented soap around with him all day which serves as a marker of an errand for Molly. One may say, and Blamires does, that at 8 am on 16 June, Leopold is in danger of ebbing out of the marital picture (or word) but if Molly can re-insert him (including in the physically intimate sense) and shuffle the letters around a bit, that is, shake him up, then maybe, just maybe, by the wee hours of the next morning, she may turn the negative-neutral into, at the very least, a hesitant 'Yes'.

Joyce may or may not have meant this, we cannot know. We do know he considered himself a master of words and that he could wage and win any war with them.

Bloom heads out for the butcher's. He closes the door to just as he realises he doesn't have the key. A creature of habit, they are in his regular work trousers but today he's donning a black suit for Paddy Dignam's funeral at 11 o' clock. Returning to fetch it would mean again disturbing Molly, so he pulls the door closed but leaves it unlocked. Oh, come on Leopold! Leaving the door unlocked is virtually inviting the usurpers!! What next, a red carpet? It does not escape notice that both Bloom and Stephen, have misplaced their door-keys.

He crosses to the sunny side of the street. We pondered in the introductory lecture his mulling over the *Freeman's Journal's* home rule sun, rising in the north-west and the pun on the word sun, as in planet and son as in boy.[10] Bloom thinks of sunnier climes in the orient. His reveries, wild and exotic as they may be, tend to be centred in logic. Not until episode seventeen is it revealed that, upon his parlour bookshelf sits an illustrated travel guide called *In the Track of the Sun*[11] and we then comprehend the genesis of Bloom's oriental mind pictures. 'Track of the Son' needs, of course, no explanation. Note similar oriental touch-points between Stephen and Bloom. Stephen's dream of the oriental bazaar and Bloom's semi-logical thought that, if one travels east, keeping an hour ahead of the sun, one may avoid ever getting older. He has an enquiring, if untrained, mind. The vision of the exotic eastern bazaar or the orient generally, is, in Bloom's and Stephen's heads, another *leitmotif*, this time, if not for sex, then, at least, sensuality and exotica. Not to be confused with other character usage of 'orient' or 'oriental', which tends to the derogatory, not to say, racist. For many, 'Oriental' simply meant foreign or outsider and so would, for pointed example, include Molly's birthplace, Gibraltar. Both Stephen and Bloom also reference the pantomime character Turko the Terrible (Bloom much later[12]) whom, Stephen reminisced, was a childhood favourite of his mother.[13]

On the corner of Eccles Street is the licensed grocery store, Larry O'Rourke's. And there, bright and early, is Larry. Morning pleasantries are exchanged which one may think unworthy of comment, but the commentator Frank Delaney [14] considers O'Rourke's abruptness typical of the cold-shoulder treatment that Bloom, the outsider, will face all day. Delaney goes as far as to call it anti-Semitic, which might be something of a stretch. The cameo also reveals Bloom considers that

Stephen's father Simon Dedalus to be a good mimic, Stephen having had the same thought in episode three and any thought nexus between Stephen and Bloom is noteworthy. Bloom considers Simon Dedalus to be a friend. We shall see in due course if that feeling is mutual.

The Art of this episode is Economics and, as he approaches Larry O'Rourke's, Bloom ponders small businesses generally and the economics of the pub business. We had the art of home economics back in the kitchen and Bloom will shortly consider investing in a cooperative farm in early Zionist Palestine and, in a few short years, these collective farms would be heavily influenced by Marxist economics.[15] There are hints at various points in this early part of the book of the link between Jews and economics – the Jewish home, Deasy's Jew merchants, the Zionist settlements. Here, though, it is the pub business under scrutiny and Bloom, uncharitably, considers that many publicans must be operating scams because one moment they are curates (lowly bar-hands) arrived from some rural backwater and the next, they own the pub. He thinks the economics are implausible unless someone is fiddling someone somewhere. Thus Bloom is not above the sort of general stereotyping which is but a short step from the racist myopia of the citizen whom we shall meet later. Even decent people, for example, Martin Cunningham, are guilty. Lazy stereotyping is an easy trap into which we all sometimes fall.

Arriving at the butchers, Bloom is concerned. There's only one lonely pork kidney on display and he fears that the women ahead of him in the queue will buy it. Fortunately, she goes for some sausages. Upon closer attention, Bloom realises she is next door's scullery maid whom he's noticed in their garden whacking carpets. A sturdy young woman who really swings her hips as she gives the rugs a good whacking. Now we wonder if Bloom's breakfast duty was less chivalry and maybe more hen-pecked husband who quietly enjoys the pecking; even a good whacking when he's been naughty.

There is an array of leaflets in the butchers. The two that catch Bloom's eye concern Zionist pioneer ventures in Palestine, then, some forty years before the establishment of Israel, part of the Ottoman Empire. The first one concerns a collective cattle farm in the north, in Galilee, the other he will read as he walks home. He buys the kidney.

An interesting phrase: 'A speck of eager eyes from foxeyes thanked him. He withdrew his gaze after an instant. No: better not: another time.'[16]

Foxeyes is how Bloom has just now described the butcher's eyes as a bit like those of a fox. But it's not that nor the Parnellian hunted fox connotations. It's the bit after: withdrawing his gaze. Delaney thought this might have been Bloom contemplating selling the butcher an advert and electing not to do so but, more interesting, might be this pair of Jewish immigrants (or in Bloom's case, son of) shooting each other a knowing glance of comradely acknowledgment. If it is so, Bloom's assimilated Irishness takes over and he doesn't go through with it. To commit would be tantamount to rebutting the assimilation. Outsiders the world over may give this shy, half-signal when meeting a fellow traveller. Nabokov hints at this pretty astute observation on Joyce's part.[17]

Back on the street, Bloom reads the other Zionist pamphlet. There are in *Ulysses*, various letters, pamphlets and fliers. They tend to be significant. Deasy's letter, those we shall see soon from Blazes Boylan and Milly Bloom, a letter from Martha Clifford in episode five, newspapers, the Christian evangelist flier in episode eight, the hangman's letter in episode twelve, Hester Stanhope's and no doubt others unrecalled.

So this one also warrants a close look:

> Agendath Netaim: planters' company. To purchase waste sandy tracks from Turkish government and plant with eucalyptus trees. Excellent for shade fuel and construction. Orange groves and immense melon fields north of Jaffa. You pay eight marks and they plant a dunum of land for you with olives, oranges, almonds or citrons. Olives cheaper: oranges need artificial irrigation. Every year you get a sending of the crop. Your name entered for life as owner in the book of the Union. Can pay ten down and the balance in yearly instalments. Bleibtreustrasse 34, Berlin, W. 15.[18]

At first glance, a prospectus to invest in a Zionist farm and the economics would intrigue Bloom's business brain but, wary of first glances, let's look deeper. For Bloom as per Odysseus, the prime driver is to return home. To Ithaca. Is Bloom's Ithaca a Zionist Palestine? The Promised Land? This shouldn't be ruled out and Joyce in the schema casts Dlugacz as the call to return but nothing we know so far of Bloom's character or action suggests it to be the case. Bloom has barely left Ireland: has been baptised both Catholic and Protestant, married a Catholic girl and eats pork kidneys. To restrict Zionism to the religious is naïve but, even so, Israel is not Bloom's Ithaca. His Promised Land is much closer: it's that jingly marriage bed in 7 Eccles Street wherein lies his Penelope. He may already be nominally present there but emotionally he's been absent for ten years. He needs to figure out how to get back home.

The leaflet reveals more. It's a call for investment in fecundity. To plant seeds in barren wasteland. Trees will bloom, immense melon fields will blossom and we shall see that Bloom likes an immense melon. For over ten years his seed has spilled unproductively. This must be put right. His name must be re-entered in the book of the union, the marriage union. German speakers will note that this real address in Berlin means 'Stay True Street'. And that Molly is 34 and Milly 15.

During this time, as he walks in the sun, Bloom's mood is relatively light and he visualises a Jewish utopia being created in the Holy Land. But as he approaches his house a cloud casts him in shadow, the very same hypostatic cloud that put Stephen in a funk atop the Martello tower, and with it Bloom's view of the Promised Land sours. Now it is grey wilderness, desolate and barren, where no seed shall find purchase. Dark thoughts: Epicentre of sin, Sodom and Gomorrah. The Dead Sea whose heavy metallic waves no wind could lift.[19] This is Bloom's personal Ithaca and the psychological baggage trailing in its wake with which he has struggled for years. Furthermore, it's a foreboding premonition of imminent bad news. On this day, a decade of stored trauma will come to a head.

He enters his house and three items of post lie in wait, a letter for him and a card and a letter for Molly. The postcard is from their daughter Milly, just turned fifteen and living away in Mullingar for her first job. The letter addressed to him is in the same familiar teenage hand but it is the other letter that has his attention. It's addressed to Mrs Marion Bloom: 'His quick heart slowed at once. Bold hand. Mrs Marion.'[20]

Why would this chill him? Why bold hand?

Let's return to the first words of the episode: Mr Leopold Bloom. It's 1904 and that is how a male person would be addressed. The male person's wife would be properly addressed as Mrs Leopold Bloom. To write to her as Mrs Marion Bloom is indeed a bold move – signalling an author that is either rude or making a point to husband, wife or both. The owner of such a bold hand will be confirmed shortly. Bloom brings the mail to Molly and while he's opening the window blind, notices that she slides the letter under her pillow for subsequent private reading.

She sends him down to make the tea and bring up breakfast. And then shouts after him: 'Poldy! . . . Scald the teapot.'[21]

Now, Poldy may be a term of endearment but could also be the de-lionising of the man – that is Leo removed. And does the command to scald link obedience with pain? He leaves his kidney cooking while he runs up with her breakfast. 'What a time you were,'[22] she says, neither of them realising we are dealing with a time traveller. Nor Dlugacz earlier, with his parting salutation: 'Thank you, sir. Another time.'[23]

Against his better judgement, Bloom enquires as to whom the letter was from. Molly nonchalantly replies it is just Boylan confirming that he's visiting that afternoon at 4 o'clock to run through the forthcoming tour programme. Blazes Boylan, local impresario, promoter, bookie and general cad about town, is arranging a tour of Ulster the week after next starring the soprano Molly. This confirms Bloom's worst fear: it's gone beyond mutual flirtation, there's a real prospect of consummation in this very bed, this very day. The letter explains that Molly is scheduled to perform two songs: 'La Ci Darem la Mano' from Mozart's *Don Giovanni* and 'Love's Old Sweet Song'. 'La Ci Darem La Mano' fits the bill. Boylan is Don Giovanni, imploring the naïve Zerlina to ditch her fiancé and nip around the corner with him. Zerlina equivocates: 'I'd like but I would not like.'

Bloom, psychologically traumatised, mis-recalls the words; he thinks it's '*voglio*' not '*vorei*': a Freudian slip. I 'want' but I would not like. Either way, it's a worryingly sexy duet. The other song, an Irish ballad, is not about sex: worse yet, it's about love. Glass half-full, the love interest continues to be Bloom; half-empty and, oh my gosh, her feelings for Boylan are far more serious than he feared.

We then have some wonderful prose and the nub of the episode. Molly, mouth full of breakfast, gesticulates that she wants something from the edge of the bed. It turns out to be a book that has fallen underneath. She requires an explanation of a word she read: metempsychosis. The scene is set out in the Introductory lecture[24] so no need to repeat. Bloom explains that it means reincarnation and gives an example by reference to the framed picture of the nymph hanging above their bed. Depicted in Ancient Greece, her soul may have hopped into many folk over the centuries. Indeed, Bloom mentally notes that the nymph looks a bit like a slimmer Molly. More to follow on this Calypso nymph.

And the book? Ruby: *Pride of the Ring* by Paul de Kock. Or Poldy Cock. Or Pol de-Cocked, whichever way one wishes to take it. Anyway,

Molly's taste in books seems to head in the low-brow, nice-but-smutty direction. She'd like another by same author: 'Nice name he has.'[25]

Not that she understood all of it. 'Is she in love the first fellow all the time?',[26] she asks, wisdom innocently tripping from her lips.

Literary enquiry ends abruptly as Molly smells burning and Bloom runs down to his kidney in panic. Thus both Bloom and Stephen have partially burnt breakfasts, hinting at Homeric Calypso's burnt offering. The kidney rescued, Bloom settles down to eat while reading the letter from his daughter, Milly. It's clear that she is Photo girl of whom the friendly swimmer spoke to Buck Mulligan at the Forty Foot.[27] She innocently mentions Blazes Boylan which deepens Bloom's mood. It's bad enough that the man plays hanky-panky with the mother but god forbid he is also somehow also mixed up with the budding sexuality of the daughter. Bloom sits, paralysed, powerless to protect either wife or, some fifty miles away, daughter.

Back to the nymph who represents the fundamental theme of reincarnation but, more significantly at this juncture, sex. That natural zesty enterprise as Julianna Moore may say in *The Big Lebowski*. With apologies to Leo, we need to delve a little deeper into his sex life and his attitude over some years towards the physical act of love. Actually for ten years. His wife is 34 years old, after sixteen years of marriage,[28] maybe she's not quite as gorgeous as she once was but, we will hear from various third-party accounts and indeed from Bloom, that Molly remains vivacious and desirable. Curvy, with Spanish almond eyes and 'waveyaveyheavyavey' hair.[29] Many are envious of Bloom. Then, in the other corner of the marriage bed, we have Leopold. By all accounts a decent if ordinary guy. His aspect is quite optimistic, gregarious, happy to engage with other – quite the opposite of Stephen, in fact. Well, Bloom engaged with other, he married, he started a family, he was enjoying life and what happened?

In the last days of December 1893, to Mr and Mrs Leopold Bloom, a son, Rudolph (Rudy). Named, by Jewish tradition, for the father's late father. A brother for Millicent. But with the Christmas lights barely down, in early 1894, gone. Dead. Bloom's son was taken at just eleven days old. The pain endures even eleven years later. Bloom blames himself; he seems to recall and believes, a Jewish old wives tale that the baby's health comes from the father.[30] So Bloom, the murderer, retreats to play it safe. He's outwardly still gregarious but inside his head things are different and, behind bedroom curtains, there's no way he's risking another pregnancy. Calypso; beautiful immortal nymph, held Odysseus prisoner on her island for seven years. The Nymph over the marriage bed has held Bloom for even longer. She's the safe option; pretend, immortal fantasy, forever young, forever beautiful, forever a goddess. And she can't get pregnant.

Bloom's sexual experiences are revealed in snippets at various points in the book. Mid-teens, he lost his virginity, we think, to the teenage Bridie Kelly. He has almost certainly engaged with prostitutes including whilst married, 'engaged' being the word. A safe business transaction. Under the pseudonym Henry Flower, he has conducted semi-erotic pen-pal correspondence with a lady named Martha Clifford of which, more next episode. Again, it is safe, they have not even met. He will even send her money, in his mind, keeping matters on a business footing. He plays fast and loose with public decency, as we shall see. All this just concerns this day; one expects there have been other 'pen-pals' and there is a suggestion that he may have tried it on with a former house girl. Intimacy with Molly avoids penetration. She remains fertile, he remains capable. But his fear of another pregnancy has him trapped. He will not risk the guilt of killing another living thing and repeating the pain of ten years before. Molly: a seed-field that lies fallow for want of a ploughshare.[31] That's what comes of engaging with other. Better play safe, keep oneself to oneself.

Episode One carried the phrase: 'Pain, that was not yet the pain of love, . . .'[32]

It preceded Stephen's recollection of the dream of his dead mother. His pain inflicted by her death was so all-consuming, it left no room for other emotion. So endures the void Rudy has left in Bloom's life. It prevents him progressing other relationships and, vitally, his marital one. Now all this says little of Molly. Pain is not a male preserve and it's a tantalising feature of the book that Molly's feelings on numerous matters are saved for the very end. Though, in context, we may look upon her forthcoming extra-marital dalliance with broader understanding.

We anticipated Bloom to be the opposite of neurotic Stephen: the antidote, but we see that Leo can hold his own in this regard. Stephen is wary of proper adulthood responsibility. Bloom was not but he's been scarred by its actuality. The reader may question this whole line of commentary, for sex and Rudy barely appear in the episode. This is true. It is a conclusion formed by a re-reading of it, armed with information gleaned from later in the book, which, as this is a guide to real-time reading, may or may not be fair. But in his schema, Joyce calls this episode, Calypso, linking to that episode of *The Odyssey* and moreover he tells us[33] that Calypso is represented by the pictorial nymph and not, as one might assume, by Gibraltar-born Molly. So it's not only legitimate but obligatory to figure out why. We must make sense of how Bloom, like Odysseus, is trapped and there's enough right here in the episode – Bloom's links with Zion and his drastic mood change, on approaching the house, to make the point.

After breakfast, Bloom feels a heaviness. To repeat a thousand previous observations, this is probably the first literary depiction of a man taking a crap. And nicely descriptive it is, too. Underlining that Bloom is as comfortable with bodily function as Stephen is not. He enjoys eating animal organs and, it transpires, is just as at ease allowing his own to process them. Perhaps 'allow' is the wrong verb for that implies passivity on the part of the 'allower'. Bloom exercises a degree of control over the process which may entitle Freudians to consider him anally retentive. Selecting a back copy of *Titbits*,[34] a weekly journal of little eroticism to speak of, despite the name, he heads into the back yard for the jakes[35] and settles down upon the toilet. He looks through cracks in the faltering wooden structure in the hope of glimpsing some carpet whacking in the next door yard. Alas, nothing doing. Dealing manfully with this setback, Bloom settles down to his business while reading a short story by a Mr Philip Beaufort.[36] Joyce provides sufficient *double entendre* to cover both tasks at hand as befits the quality of the writing he scans.

The magazine explains that it pays by the column for short stories submitted by the public and Bloom calculates that Beaufort would have received £3 13s 6d for his story 'Matcham's Masterstroke' and he ponders if he might do likewise with material potentially supplied by Mrs Bloom. However, it's a short train of thought from this to the dance two weeks earlier when Molly first met Boylan. Try as he might, he cannot get the forthcoming tryst out of his head. His masterstroke is to tear out the page for use as toilet paper.

Note, a few minutes earlier his meander around the unkempt garden en-route to the toilet. He observes stubborn weeds and ponders that, properly fertilised, the area might be transformed into various flower beds and vegetable patches. Fast-forward to him flushing his own natural fertiliser down the toilet. Preposterous though it is to suggest he should have evacuated in the corner of the yard: one simply observes another missed target of fecundity to go with the Bloom ejaculate of the past ten years.

It's time the Dude cocked his pistol and got back in the saddle. Question is, will he?

LECTURE 6, 2 DECEMBER 2020: EPISODE 5

Lotus Eaters and the High Grade Ha

Music: The Last Rose of Summer – Martha, Act Two (Flotow)

Let's re-join Mr Bloom as he walks along Sir John Rogerson's quay near the docks on the east side of Dublin. It's 10 o'clock in the morning and quite far from Eccles Street. How he arrived, we know not. Why he's here, we shall discover. He's headed west towards the heart of the city. Earlier he popped around the corner to the butchers, which is hardly the Wanderings of Ulysses, but has now embarked upon a longer, dare one say, epic journey, and will not return to Eccles Street until the small hours. Some consider his wandering to arc in the shape of an infinity symbol[1] and check out the maps if you wish.

The eaters of the fruit of the lotus plant barely appear in *The Odyssey*[2]: just a few lines. Bedraggled from the latest disaster, the fleet bobs towards an island. Odysseus is wary, he must ascertain whether the natives are hostile but can't risk further casualties, so many have already been lost. So he sends scouts. Fortunately the natives turn out to be hospitable and all are invited to the *prix-fixe* lunch, the fruit of the lotus flower. Tasty, nutritious but intoxicating, it induces a pleasant euphoric lethargy so that the sailors are inclined to think they might be better off forever in the happy kingdom of the lotus eaters. Odysseus has to forcibly remove them for, whilst even he in a weaker moment, contemplates temptation, after all he's gone through, return to Ithaca remains the only goal. So, in a general mood of disgruntlement and disappointment, all return to the ships.

Fast forward to Dublin and an ambience of lethargic stupefaction as fumes of various herbs, perfumes and other euphoric temptations distract Dubliners from tasks at hand. Our modern Odysseus takes note. He is not immune and succumbs more than his ancient counterpart but let's see if and how he is able to stay on course. From the off, Bloom is cognisant of intoxicants or other conductors of momentary euphoria; the boy smoking a cigarette, the listless little girl with her hula hoop. Bloom, too, is lethargic. He imagines these kids later lingering outside a pub imploring their drunk, senseless father to call time: 'Come home to ma, da.'[3]

One may wonder why Joyce placed the lotus eaters parable this early in the day. It's 10 am, a time one might suppose of energetic eagerness.

People have plans for the day and a determination to carry them out. Surely a pleasant June morning such as this cannot be so hot at this hour as to incapacitate? It might be better suited to later in the afternoon. But Bloom is wearing a heavy black suit for the funeral and so he is hotter than he need be and has had a heavy cooked breakfast. We will also learn that this is the final day of a seemingly endless drought and perhaps these factors tend to sap energy. Or Joyce might be making the point that, in Dublin, the stultifying stupefaction settles in early on a working day. Anyway, there it is.

Consider Bloom's state of mind. He is, as he should be, in shock. Reeling from the letter of Mr Bold-Hand-Blazes-Boylan and compounded by Milly's news that now fifteen years, and beyond his protection, she has a boyfriend. Prior to reading the letters he had a daunting premonition. Remember his deteriorating mood as he approached the house? The Promised Land transformed from land flowing with milk, honey and enormous melons to a bone-dry infertile abyss. Thus distressed, he yearns for intoxicating numbness. Contrast with Odysseus who saw the narcotic effect on his men and resisted so as not to distract from the task. Bloom is conflicted: his natural inclination is to resist artificial distraction, for example, we shall see his detached observations shortly in church but on the other hand, Bloom needs it and Bloom seeks it. If his mood cannot be improved, it would be nice to at least anaesthetise by way of temporary euphoria. If we accept that Bloom's Ithaca is his marriage and his symbolic return home to be the improvement of marital relations, then he calculates that the best he can do for the time being, at least, is to keep out of the way while his wife commits adultery. At least until he can think of a better strategy.

He turns into Westland Row and lingers at the Belfast and Oriental Tea Company. Blankly his eyes follow the variously labelled teas from further east than his earlier reverie. This time to Ceylon. He removes his hat and wipes through his slightly sweaty hair. The scene seems to be in slow motion, as though his arm moves of its own accord, brain detached. On the inside of his hat, he absently reads the partially worn leather band: Plasto's High Grade Ha; the T of Hat has, over time, smudged to invisibility. Not so absently, he removes a card from under the band and pockets it in his waistcoat.

Intoxicating reverie continues: native Sri Lankan's, lolling in the sun. Nominally working but generally lazing around. He drifts back to Palestine, now a positive image. A man, happily stupefied, floats in the Dead Sea beneath the shade of a parasol. Bizarrely the barely moving waves support the floating figure. Bloom tries to ponder the science behind gravity, recalling from school something about 32 feet per second, per second, but, uncomfortably warm, he gives up. He's apparently on the right scientific lines and this is the speed of a falling body.[4] The significance of the number eleven has been briefly mentioned. The first after ten, so indicating the beginning of a new cycle and renewal. Number 32 is its counterpart. The number of the fall, so we might think. Original Sin. Thirty-two and eleven. Fall and resurrection: continue *ad infinitum* in Vicoan tradition. We'll look out for occurrences.

Lethargy must cease, Paddy Dignam's funeral is at eleven o'clock and Bloom has tasks to complete beforehand. There, eleven! He walks, unfolding a *Freeman's Journal* as he goes and furls it into a baton, with which to tap his leg. His sword? Is battle to commence? Perhaps a phallus, revealing the more ribald direction of his thoughts and steps? The bodily organ of this episode is the genitals. He arrives at the post office in Westland Row, furtively glances inside and notes it is empty. He acts strangely, something is on his mind, perhaps a mission and it arouses our suspicion. He approaches the counter: 'anything for me?' Note he mentions no name but simply hands over the card. While the postmistress checks, Bloom is interested in an army recruitment poster featuring soldiers of diverse regiments. He seeks out his father-in-law's uniform making us wonder if he'd rather Major Tweedy knew nothing of Bloom's mission. Yet, at same time, the vacant stares of the soldiers suggest hypnosis, as maybe befits not only lotus eating lethargy but also the many Irish poor that signed up to fight for the British.

The postmistress returns card through the grill with a letter addressed to Mr Henry Flower, c/o Westland Row post office. Ha! A High Grade Ha! Evidence of Bloom's duplicity. What else could it be? He accepts mail addressed to another man, surname Flower, his is Bloom. Prior to change by deed poll his father's name was Virag, Hungarian for flower. Clandestine activity confirmed. Collection of a letter from an out-of-the-way post office,[5] so reducing the chance of discovery. Unfortunately, an associate, McCoy, greets Bloom as Bloom emerges from the post office and wants to chat. Bloom attempts to fend him off with as little small talk as possible in order to quietly and privately read the letter squirrelled away in his pocket. He feels it as he talks and senses something inside the envelope. McCoy. We met him in the *Dubliners* story 'Grace'.[6] Pretty unimpressive and generally on the make with some con or other, a favourite being to borrow a valise on the spurious ground that his wife, the soprano Madame Grace McCoy, needs it for an upcoming touring engagement. She doesn't. He will pawn the portmanteau for booze money. Bloom alert to the ruse does not fall for it.

Two men, both on the periphery of the advertising/newspaper business, having had a variety of jobs, though McCoy now works in the Coroner's Office. Both are outsiders of sorts and tenuously familiar with each other via their wives. Neither are what you'd call idiots and McCoy has a tender side as we'll see later in conversation with Lenehan.[7] McCoy, a little older and beset with life's burden. Bloom recognises some commonality and thinks, 'You and me, don't you know? In the same boat.'[8]

McCoy is Bloom's glimpse into his own future; a somewhat pathetic man which Bloom might easily become if he doesn't improve himself and his marriage. So it is no surprise that Richard Ellman tells us[9] that C P McCoy was based on a chap, Charles Chance, who also served as a partial template for Bloom. One might also see the influence of Dante whose visit to hell during his lifetime provided a unique opportunity to observe what lay in store and divert his direction of travel. So Bloom here glimpses his prospective future

McCoy chatters away with meagre reciprocity. He's an annoying distraction from agenda item one: the reading of the letter. But the distractor is himself usurped as Bloom spies a fine looking woman across the road exiting the Grosvenor Hotel and about to board a cab. She's dressed for travel and, as Bloom imagines, country pursuits. This unknown woman underlines the dominant woman fantasy begun by serving Molly breakfast in bed and continued with carpet-beater-girl in the butchers. Now, enhanced with class superiority. McCoy drones on; they small talk about the funeral and how, if McCoy can't make it, Bloom should mention to the reporter that he was there. It was apparently common then for even ordinary folk such as Dignam – and we shall see he was truly ordinary – to get a modest newspaper obituary[10] including a record of the mourners in attendance.

Conversation ensues. McCoy references Bob Doran and Bantam Lyons, both of whom we recall from *Dubliners*.[11] A feature of our book will be the plethora of minor characters in cameo role each with their own personality and backstory, reminiscent in style of Damon Runyon's New York. As well as flavour they provide a vital take on the major characters. Our understanding of Stephen, Leo and Molly is gleaned from a blend of their own *monologue interieur* and, in substantial measure, how they are seen by others.

Meanwhile, across the road, luggage is loaded. The tension mounts as does Bloom's concealed excitement (precise angle of furled *Freeman's Journal*, unknown) as the woman prepares to raise a stockinged leg to board the cab. To add piquancy, she spots Bloom looking. It is a taster to the unabashed voyeurism of 8.30 that evening. What delights can he expect? A flash of calf – no doubt; a knee? Dare he hope for thigh and garter? Here we go . . . here we go . . . when, dash it all, a passing tram obscures the moment. Bold hand, that tram driver, coming between Bloom and his woman. It's a cameo of the episode. A prospect of a little light relief, then thwarted. Bloom can't read his letter because McCoy engages him, McCoy gets no valise money because Bloom is wise to it, Bloom is hoping to catch a flash of flesh but is thwarted by the untimely tramcar blocking his view. These drug-induced highs might be great but they don't last and one returns to earth with a bump. We do not write off McCoy, he may yet get false credit for attending the funeral, and we'll await the evening edition of the newspaper. But still he lingers, bragging of his wife's singing talents which Bloom trumps with news of Molly's forthcoming tour. Bloom is irritated that McCoy should mention Madam McCoy's virtuosity in the same breath as Molly. A further recurring theme is that, as much as Bloom wants to banish Molly's activities from his mind, he cannot. Thoughts, often proud and adoring thoughts, pulse in but often then sour with reminder of reality. Here, when Bloom mentions the tour of Ulster: 'Glad to hear that, old man', says McCoy, and innocently enquires: 'Who's getting it up?'[12]

Bloom and all of us know the answer. He unfurls the newspaper to check on the funeral time but this, too, reminds of his cuckold status. Beneath the death announcements appears an advertisement for a jar of meat: 'What is home without Plumtree's Potted Meat? Incomplete. With it an abode of bliss.'[13]

There's been no potting of Bloom's meat at home for several years. That afternoon, potting there will be, but, alas, not by hubby. Distraction again backfiring.

Bloom eventually moves on from McCoy and seeks a discreet place to read the letter. It's his second letter that morning, the first was from Milly and Bloom seeks relief from the pain that caused. En-route to a quiet spot he observes the billboards. Bloom always pays critical attention to adverts. One is of particular interest. The actress, Mrs Bandman Palmer is appearing in a play called *Leah*. Bloom also notes that she appeared in *Hamlet*, the previous night and as the prince, no less, so we have a connection with Stephen. But of greater significance here is the link between the play *Leah* and Bloom's father. Gifford[14] notes that the actual play, *Leah the Forsaken*, was a translation and adaptation of the 1850 German play *Deborah* and concerns anti-Semitism in 18th-century Austria. The villain, Nathan, has converted to Christianity to protect his position in the village and forsakes his relatives. Bloom, when a young boy, was taken by his parents to see it in London and it clearly resonated with his father, who also converted to Christianity: 'Every word is so deep, Leopold.'[15]

This and the Ophelia suicide reference[16] is how we come to learn that Bloom's father, Rudolph Virag (by then Bloom), committed suicide when Bloom was twenty[17] and shortly following the death of Bloom's mother.[18] Indeed the week after next will be the anniversary of his death. Bloom, of course, is saddened by his father's death but no longer (if he ever was) haunted by it in the way Stephen is by the death of his mother. That is to be expected, one event is much more recent than the other and inevitably raw. But the death of Virag eighteen years earlier still affects Bloom's psyche especially as that tragedy is compounded by the loss of Rudy.

Walking on, he passes a cabman's shelter and notes the gelded horses enjoying their drugs with their noses stuck in nosebags. Like him, emasculated and seeking euphoria elsewhere. As he walks he feels with excitement and curiosity the letter in his pocket. What is that bumpy thing? A badge? A lock of hair? At last in a nook beneath the railway arches, he opens the envelope and discovers that it's a little flower pinned to the letter.

He reads it:

> Dear Henry,
> I got your last letter to me and thank you very much for it. I am sorry you did not like my last letter. Why did you enclose the stamps? I'm awfully angry with you. I do wish I could punish you for that. I called you naughty boy because I do not like that other world. Please tell me what is the real meaning of that word. Are you not happy in your home you poor little naughty boy? I do wish I could do something for you. Please tell me what you think of poor me. I often think of the beautiful name you have. Dear Henry, when will we meet? I think of you so often you have no idea. I have never felt myself so much drawn to a man as you. I feel so bad about. Please write me a long letter and tell me more. Remember if you do not I will punish you. So now you know what I will do to you, you naughty boy, if

you do not write. O how I long to meet you. Henry dear, do not deny my request before my patience are exhausted. Then I will tell you all. Goodbye now, naughty darling. I have such a bad headache today and write by return to your longing

MARTHA

PS. do tell me what kind of perfume does your wife use. I want to know.[19]

In no particular order of thought, we observe that this is neither Martha's first letter to Henry nor his to her. It does not reveal why or when the correspondence commenced and it is suggestive, though not definitive, that the pair have not met. Bloom's choice of name, Flower; Virag means flower in Hungarian: Flower, Bloom, Flower, suggestive of rejuvenation. The name Martha Clifford may also be false. The grammatical errors – 'world' when surely she means 'word'; 'patience are exhausted' instead of 'is' may suggest poor education and a lower class. It's the second time that day Bloom has been asked to explain a word by a women in his life. We note the sado-masochistic theme with associated banter spanning several letters. Henry submissive; Martha, motherly. Martha wants to meet; this is indicated not only by stated intention which may be bluster but cogently because she is tackling practicalities such as Mrs Flower's perfume. We will learn that she has previously suggested an assignation after church. More practicalities as she tries to cling to respectability while dallying with another women's husband.

Last, but not least, the name Martha. Contrast with Mary (Mrs Marion Bloom). Bloom recalls the story of Jesus, Martha and Mary from a painting he has seen.[20] Martha is busying in the background with housework practicalities whilst it is the inert Mary, sat at the foot of Jesus, who commands the attention and favour of the Saviour. So Bloom's thoughts, even in duplicity, possibly especially so, return to Molly. Inert Molly, still at home and perhaps still in bed. Such casting of Bloom as Jesus is more likely to be in Bloom's head rather than Joyce's serious contention, though he playfully tempts us and will continue to do so.

We might compare this to Milly's letter read only an hour or so apart before. They are of a similar length, a single paragraph and each with a short postscript. Despite fifteen year old Milly begging forgiveness for bad writing, the content (never mind the penmanship) of Milly's letter is pretty clear, whereas Martha's is all over the place. Both have sexual connotations: in Milly's; her suggestion of burgeoning sexuality is unintended but for Bloom it is shocking and paralysing. In Martha's: it is intended to be titillating, but is it? On the contrary, the impression given is of a man wondering how to get rid of this problem he perhaps created. This Martha Clifford is unlikely to be worth the hassle. There's the risk of being caught, not to mention the drain on his emotions that he already suspects she will become, with her various demands. Our man of considered practicalities is not going overboard with Martha. Whoever she is.

If Milly's letter had a surprising sting, Martha's should have been the uplifting antidote. But it falls short.

Bloom muses on how the pretty and intoxicating flower of the affair will disguise the sharp pin-prick behind it and that he should be wary of meeting up. Perhaps we should think of Parnell at such point, the dead political leader and the affair with a married woman that led to his downfall. Parnell, a true hero in the Joyce household and so, one suspects, with both Bloom and Stephen, is another Christ-like Saviour/sufferer and we will consider him further in due course. Back to Bloom, whilst wary of meeting up, he is tempted to continue the correspondence. It's safe, like the nymph fantasy in the last episode. Here, it's words only, no touching. Fast-forward to the beach at 8.30 pm, where it will be looking but no touching. Bloom only has incomplete relationships. No abode of bliss. Today, only Blazes Boylan gets the real thing.

Many flowers are referenced, accompanied by much *double entendre* with phallic shapes, erect stalks and touch-me-nots. Bloom is reminded of the naughty rhyme in which Mary has lost the pin of her knickers so they keep falling down. Mary in this book usually alludes to Marion whose undergarments will be dropping a little later (and a pair of grey hose will be on display for Stephen). He pockets the letter but cautiously tears up the envelope referring to Henry Flower. Wouldn't want Molly finding that and, God forbid, the card. Finding the letter would also be a nightmare but at least it just says 'Dear Henry'. He throws away the hundred pieces and also the pin.

Let's follow his next train of thought for a moment. He worries: did he tear up only the envelope or also the letter. No, got the letter. Easy mistake, just as one might unintentionally tear up a cheque. This reminds him that, apocryphally, Lord Iveagh of the Guinness family, once cashed a cheque for a million pounds. Bloom tries to calculate out how many bottles of Guinness would need to be sold for such a sum. As a train roars over his head, he imagines untold amounts of Guinness being transported throughout Ireland and, like a torrent, escaping and bathing the whole country in intoxicating paralysing drowsiness. Which in fact, it practically does.

He arrives at the back of a church. It's St Andrew's Roman Catholic Church on Westland Row. He enters. This is a passive part of the episode as Bloom rests after much walking. He observes a sodality ceremony. This is a type of Catholic guild to encourage devotion and mutual support, examples being the Sacred Heart of Jesus or the Sodality of Our Lady. Bloom's religious observations are of interest. His perspective is that of the detached observer rather than a co-religionist. He had to study at Sunday school for his baptisms and benefits from that dangerous drug, a little knowledge. For example, he believes Molly when she tells him that INRI on the priest's cassock stands not for Jesus of Nazareth, King of the Jews, but for Iron Nails Ran In. But that's Bloom all over. He's a bright fellow who picks up scraps of knowledge on many subjects as he meanders through life but is a real authority on precious little. He's cynical of that old drug, religion, to which he considers much of Dublin and indeed much of Ireland is addicted. Echoing, perhaps with less grandiosity, much of the sentiment we heard from Stephen in the Telemachiad.

But we are getting ahead of ourselves. He enters the church. We're not sure why. Is it more hypnotic temptation? Does he just fancy a sit down? 'The cold smell of sacred stone called him in.'[21]

More likely it's because, as we shall discover, Martha Clifford suggested they meet after church and he sub-consciously and then consciously associates church with clandestine sexual frivolity. To wit: sitting snuggly next to an unknown pretty women last midnight mass.

From the off, he considers the church in business terms. Whether it's the Protestants trying to convert the Catholics or the Jews, or the missionaries in Africa, it's a selling game just like the advertising business.

We note phrases: 'Clever idea St Patrick the shamrock.'[22]

And later: 'Good idea the Latin.'[23]

And further on: 'Squareheaded chaps they must be in Rome: they work the whole show. And don't they rake in the money too?'[24]

And it is an actual business. He ponders inaccurately, monks making and selling Green Chartreuse and Benedictine as well as the money that pours in from bequests left in wills. A cynical business, too, as Bloom suspects the church plays fast and loose with delicate information learned in confession: 'Great weapon in their hands. More than doctor or solicitor.'[25]

Bloom has a tawdry impression of religion. Conceptually it's a drug; its institutions are drug-pushers and that the Catholic Church, in particular, uses drugs to induce the addiction. For example, he watches the congregants in a line for communion. Trance-like, awaiting their fix. Eating the communion wafer (like the lotus flower) and drinking the wine as the body and blood of Christ. Note his thoughts: 'Stupefies them first', 'Makes them feel happy', 'Lulls all pain'. Even the use of Latin obscures the reality with mystic chanting. And, back to business, Bloom notes how they cleverly use a wine substitute, otherwise they'd get a queue of alcoholics lining up for their nip. Actually, we shall see later in the 'Nausicaa' episode, how the church tries to keep alcoholic men within the fold.

Note, he likens the wafer to matzoth, suggesting that while his body is in church, his soul remains Jewish: 'Every word is so deep, Leopold.'[26]

Yet, without here implying the same cynicism to Jewish institutions, though, we will see that later in the day.

Note also that this is the second mass that we have seen. We had Buck Mulligan's parody Black Mass earlier in episode one. You may think that Bloom to be equally blasphemous but maybe not. Dante in the *Inferno* tells us that almost the greatest sin is Simony: using the church as a business. Sinful, because it deviates the church away from its proper purpose. So Bloom as unlikely as it seems, might be cast as a Christ figure, ruefully reflecting, like Stephen earlier with his 'dringadrings', upon what the church has become.

He kneels to pray (in his case, pretend prayer) with the other congregants. It hurts, though he tries, without success, to protect his knee with a newspaper. He will kneel again in worship later that night and in greater discomfort. It shall be at a different altar: the foot (or hoof) of the brothel madam, Bella Cohen.

Molly again intrudes and compels him to leave. He's tasked with buying her face cream from the chemist and barely has time to do so if he is also to squeeze in a bath at the public baths before joining Dignam's funeral cortège. In Sweny's the chemist he is surrounded by perfumes and drugs. And, fittingly, has forgotten the recipe for Molly's face cream (it's in his other trousers with the key) and so the pharmacist has to guess based on a previous order. Bloom takes a bar of lemon soap for which he is told he can pay later when he returning for the face cream. Bloom forgets to do so.

Outside on the street, he's greeted by another *Dubliners* hangover, a man called Bantam Lyons. So commences a cameo piece that will resonate to great effect later in the day. Lyons wants a quick look at Bloom's paper so he can check runners and riders for the Ascot Gold Cup that afternoon. As mentioned this is one of the five English horse racing Classics run every year during the summer. Bloom wants rid of him and tells him to keep the paper as he was about to throw it away. Bantam Lyons' attention is piqued and looks intently again at the paper. He had intended to back one of the favourites but now wonders if Bloom, possibly a Freemason, has inside knowledge on the rank outsider, the 20 to 1 shot, 'Throwaway'. Bloom doesn't, it was simply an innocent remark: a throwaway remark. Bloom knows nothing of what Bantam Lyons is thinking. Well wouldn't you just know it, on 16 June 1904, the Gold Cup was indeed won by the 20-1 no hoper, 'Throwaway'. Bloom in Wandering Jew mode, has bestowed a gift on someone without the first notion that he has done so and boy, will it land him in trouble later that afternoon.

Let's think a little deeper about this horse race: The Gold Cup. The prize is chalice-shaped, vagina-shaped. It may represent both the Holy Grail and Molly herself, which at the end of the day for Bloom, is the same thing. It's a race with Molly as the prize. Bantam Lyons initially fancied a French horse, 'Maximilian' the second. But the favourite is 'Sceptre'. You know what a sceptre is: a symbol of power, a flashy, golden, thrusting phallus expected to break through the finish line to the Holy Grail at 4 pm. We shall hear from Molly later how such an image bears a striking resemblance to Mr Boylan's appendage. But wait . . . is there a dark horse? A rank outsider that against the odds may yet prevail? We'll have to wait and see.

The episode is closing and we don't find out here, if Bloom made it in time to the public baths. But he visualises himself there and it is a vision replete with oriental overtones. The baths have Moorish architecture and ambience. A feel of a *hammam*. Bloom lies in the protective warm bath. 'A womb of warmth', he thinks. Further possible Christ references – this is my body – as he observes his naked, slightly flabby self, lying in the perfumed bath. He may or may not have masturbated. While in the chemist the thought of doing so at the baths crossed his mind: 'Also I think I. Yes I. Do it in the bath. Curious longing I. Water to water. Combine business with pleasure.'[27]

He is now as limp and useless as the gelded horses he passed earlier.

We started with the Homeric reference. That, for Odysseus, the only goal was to return home to Ithaca – to his wife Penelope, his son Telemachus, his father Laertes and even his dog, Argos. To do so he must resist the temptation of the Lotus Flower. Intellectually, Bloom attempts the opposite. His home, his abode of bliss, is Plumtree's Potted Meat but he ain't doing the potting and he's desperate to banish that from his mind. Yet, despite his many attempts at transient relief, it's all *ersatz*. Molly and her forthcoming dalliance constantly intrude. Even his Eastern day-dreaming links to Molly, for Bloom's knowledge of the 'Orient' is derived primarily from Molly's tales of an exotic Spanish/African upbringing, which Bloom intermixes with his own Eastern European antecedence and so, emotionally, the Orient is where his heart lies. Thus, Bloom's desire for escape is thwarted. Wherever he seeks brief euphoria, he finds only Molly. Just a few examples: the glimpse of the thigh outside the Grosvenor Hotel; and McCoy asks whose getting it up? Behind the erotic letter is a painful pin. Worse yet, in church, big pins, iron nails are run in. And lost pins mean Molly's drawers fall down. Finally when he hopes for a bit of me time, to masturbate in the bath, he is reminded (whether before, after or instead of sexual gratification) by his own manhood, there, floating in the bath, like the pond plant, Mother of Thousands, that he and his limp ironic father of thousands, has done no fathering for many a year.

There we leave him. Poor Bloom. He's not in a great place. But what better pick-me-up than next time in Hades, kingdom of the dead. And maybe not as depressing as one might think.

LECTURE 7, 16 DECEMBER 2020: EPISODE 6

Hades and the Dignified Send-Off

Music: Staying Alive – The Bee Gees

Joyce indicated in his schemata that this episode might be called Hades, which is the land of the dead in *The Odyssey*. It's an episode revealing and entertaining in equal measure and so it is fitting that it falls neatly into two halves. In the first, a funeral cortège makes its dignified way though the city, towards the Hades of Dublin, Prospect Cemetery in the north-western suburb of Glasnevin. The second half depicts a burial. An obvious contrast between Life and Death, though, by the end of the episode, the gimmicky question might be . . . which is which? Indeed, an episode of life and death. Constant references to both and to the heart, the pump of life and bodily organ of this episode.

Bloom continues to wander; now at a gentle carriage pace and this time in company. A new dynamic. More dialogue, less interior monologue. We observe our hero's social skills and how, in turn, he is treated by others. By now we have settled into Bloom as Odysseus and are therefore entitled to ask: why would Odysseus interrupt his journey by going far out of the way to miserable Hades? In excavating that answer, we realise that Joyce does not synchronise with Homeric sequence. Odysseus is advised by the witch Circe to go there to meet the blind prophet Tiresias because he has things to say that will assist his journey to Ithaca. Bloom will not meet our latter-day Circe until much later that night, well after Hades.

As a youth, Tiresias spied on a naked goddess who, as punishment, curses him with blindness. But she later reflects and bestows him with the inner sight of future events. This voyeuristic incident is not reflected in this episode but it may remind one of the epiphanic incident in *A Portrait of the Artist*, where Stephen is transfixed by the partially undressed teenage girl on the beach. Joyce, too, feared he would go blind in one eye and Stephen likewise. So whilst Tiresias is not obviously featured in our episode, he triggers a number of synapses. He was also destined to become a woman for several years, feeding into the androgenous aspect of our story to come.

This is the information Tiresias conveys:

1. Odysseus has angered Poseidon, god of the sea, by blinding his son, Polyphemus and consequently Poseidon will make life very difficult. (Note this blinding incident is not depicted in our book until about 6 pm.)
2. Odysseus might be advised to head towards the island ruled by Helios, god of the sun; but not to disembark or, if he must, on no account should he or his crew disturb the sacred cattle and other livestock. Follow this advice and he may yet safely arrive in Ithaca. But, if not, disaster will strike: the entire fleet and crew will be lost and, though Odysseus might eventually limp home, he will find his estate overrun with usurpers. We shall examine the cattle aspect in the Oxen of the Sun episode at 10.30 pm and, subsequently, his return to Ithaca.

We recall that, to introduce Bloom, Joyce took the trouble to re-set the clock to 8 am so that we can observe the parallel journeys of Bloom and Stephen. That links this episode timewise to Proteus which, in the Telemachiad, followed two comedic episodes summed up in the wit of Buck Mulligan and the cartoon Colonel Blimpness[1] of Garrett Deasy. Stephen then gets down to serious business in Proteus. Our first two Bloom episodes also had several light-hearted aspects that, which RM Adams[2] points out, highlight Bloom's more Charlie Chaplin-esque tints and so we might expect a more adult, darker, richer timbre, this episode. We shall see.

Patrick (Paddy) Dignam has died. Suddenly. He leaves a widow, five school-age children and slim pickings by way of a financial estate. A slight, inoffensive chap, he had a variety of clerkship positions, the last being at the office of the solicitor John Henry Menton, a job he was compelled to vacate for alcohol-related reasons. Whether he vacated the mortal coil in similarly undignified fashion, is debatable, though Bloom seems convinced. It's fair to say that he arrived and departed this life leaving little by way of footprint. Were it not for his fictional immortality bestowed by James Joyce, very few would have noticed at all.

The episode begins outside Dignam's house at 9 Newbridge Avenue, Sandymount, in south Dublin. It's around twenty minutes to eleven. Four men enter a small horse-drawn carriage, part of the funeral cortège: Martin Cunningham, Jack Power, Simon Dedalus (who is Stephen's father) and Leopold Bloom. What evidence there is suggests that Cunningham and Power are rear-facing and Dedalus and Bloom look ahead.

There's some beguiling descriptive prose to describe the journey's start:

> All waited. Then wheels were heard from in front turning: then nearer: then horses' hoofs. A jolt. Their carriage began to move, creaking and swaying. Other hooves and creaking wheels started behind. The blinds of the avenue passed and number nine with its crate knocker, door ajar. At walking pace.
>
> They waited still, their knees jogging, till they had turned and we're passing along the tramtracks. Tritonville road. Quicker. The wheels rattled rolling over the cobbled causeway and the crazy glasses shook rattling in the doorframes.[3]

This is smashing. We're right there in that carriage, though there's no room. The journey to Glasnevin cemetery will reflect the reading of the trip, around half an hour and because it's mainly conversation, we might assume a quiet background, akin to a modern city trip. But this passage reminds that our backdrop is horse hooves, creaking springs, creaking wood, creaking leather. Glasses rattling in the windows and a constant bump of wheels over cobblestones. Even quite main roads have no tarmac; the cobbled Tritonville Road is quite a substantial thoroughfare. Noise aside, bodies are snuggly cramped, knees clanging amid a constant and sometimes quite violent swaying.

Characterisation begins immediately. Martin Cunningham, whom we will see is a generally decent man, addresses Simon Dedalus, as Simon. Leopold Bloom. however, is Bloom. Outsider from the get-go. Four men: Bloom we know. Cunningham and Power are civil servants at Dublin Castle; lower middle-class men of the establishment – representatives of the British Crown. Both Stephen and Bloom have mentioned Stephen's father, Simon, and now we meet him. Recently widowed and father of ten. Of no regular employment, beyond the pub. Lover of song and the witty one-liner but, as his children will tell you, that fills no bellies.

Last chapter we covered a goodly proportion of the incidents but still skipped much. There's even more going on this time but let's see what we can do by way of concise summary.

Part One – Dublin, the living

The cab heads north through Irishtown near Sandymount Strand. Bloom sees a slim young man walking on the beach, it is Stephen for this is also real-time Proteus. He alerts the father to the son who despite straining across Bloom (so we know Bloom is sat on the right-hand-side) he does not see. Simon talks in amusing and robust fashion of the bad company Stephen has been keeping, particularly Buck Mulligan. Bloom is receptive to Simon's pride in his son and internally muses on his own dead son, Rudy; how Molly suffered when he died and how he, Leo, could have shaped his son's character. If twenty-two year old Stephen needs a father figure and guide which is a big 'If'; and, if so, then for what? which is an even bigger 'If', but, if he does, then in such moment and without anyone realising, the baton may be passing from birth father to surrogate father.

There's then an amusing little passage about biscuit crumbs on the seats which shall resonate many chapters hence. Have, it is enquired, previous occupants had a picnic? The phrase used is 'picnic party'.[4] Closer, but one hopes circumspect inspection revises consensus suspicion to flakes of dried ejaculate; picnic party indeed. Bloom upon first reading, was troubled by Milly's letter, and its reference to 'picnic' will not help to allay concern. Back to the carriage: sperm, the beginning of life, the most natural thing in the world says Simon Dedalus, father of ten. Fast forward to the end of the book[5] when Bloom, at long last, gets into bed and feels remnants of Plumtree's Potted Meat, evidence of combined picnic and party. In this book of time, Joyce is no respecter of it; for whilst each episode marks time, the resonances, inferences and synapses constantly swing back and forth all over the place. This life essence reminds Bloom of when Rudy was conceived in the house in Raymond Terrace opposite a military barracks then displaying the Isaiah motto: 'cease to do evil, learn to do good',[6] which emanated from its former prison status. This is an internal musing: he says relatively little out loud on the trip.

> Must have been that morning in Raymond terrace she was at the window, watching the two dogs at it by the wall of the cease to do evil. And the sergeant grinning up. She had that cream gown on with the rip she never stitched. Give us a touch Poldy. God, I'm dying for it. How life begins.[7]

A delightful little passage. Revealing, we are shocked, that a woman might not just talk openly about sex but may actually instigate it and do so, oh my goodness, in the daytime no less and, heaven forbid, that she could be titillated by observing the rutting of dogs in the street. Heady stuff. Little wonder the book was banned. But look at what it tells us about Bloom. You'd think that any thought of Rudy would be shrouded in the misery of tragedy. Yet he reminisces fondly on the moment of conception. For whilst he will undulate emotionally he is, by nature, life-affirming. But, to repeat, he undulates and, in one dip of this more serious episode, muses philosophically and strangely on Rudy's death: 'Our. Little. Beggar. Baby. Meant nothing. Mistake of nature. If it's healthy it's from the mother. If not the man. Better luck next time.'[8]

Bloom harks back to apocryphal Jewish 'wisdom' and blames himself for the poor health and thence the death of his son.

The sky spits a little rain. Bloom feels it because at that moment he happens to have poked his head outside the window. An innocuous vignette. Or is it?

> A raindrop spat on his hat. He drew back and saw an instant of shower spray dots over the grey flags. Apart. Curious. Like through a colander. I thought it would.[9]

In our consideration of episode five we questioned whether the weather was sufficiently warm at 10 am to bring on the lethargy that characterised that episode. It was unlikely to be hot but the atmosphere was increasingly close and humid. In Calypso, Bloom was shadowed by a small cloud, as was Stephen at the same time, as it passed across the sun. It altered both of their moods. Little clouds tend to be a foreshadowing, literally, of bigger clouds to come and so Bloom suspected rain later. There has been a drought for several weeks and one may recall that Bloom rejected a boiled egg for breakfast due to insufficient fresh water.

The significance? In short, the prophet Elijah and his connection to Bloom. This and its impact will emerge on and from episode eight but here, at the fruition of Bloom's earlier prophecy of rain, we have an early, or perhaps the first, connection. The Bible (in the first book of Kings) records[10] that Israel is in drought, a barren land, just as Bloom visualised **?it** in episode four. Elijah the prophet, from atop Mount Carmel, sees a little cloud and tells King Ahab to prepare for heavy rain storms. More on this in due course. Apropos nothing or everything, 'A Little Cloud' is the title of a story in *Dubliners*. And rain through a colander? Might this echo those Ancient Greek sisters[11] sentenced to carry water in a sieve? Maybe.

They pass the Queens Theatre and Bloom thinks of vaudeville which turns his mind depressingly to Blazes Boylan, the impresario. Barely minutes later, a dapper chap outside the Red Bank seafood restaurant, tips a straw boater to salute the cortège and Martin Cunningham responds in kind. Why it's Blazes Boylan! Martin, Simon and Jack

Power all wave in hearty greeting. Bloom, fortunately, sat on the opposite side is paralysed in embarrassment and can only stare at his fingernails whilst registering the coincidence of Boylan's appearance just after he thought of him. One of many to be registered in the Akashic records for that day. We tangibly feel Bloom's acute isolation and suffering which will intensify with the subsequent discussion of Boylan and of the forthcoming tour starring Madame Bloom.

They cross the River Liffey and pass beneath the foreboding Daniel O'Connell statue. There is the hunched figure of Reuben J Dodd a Jewish moneylender in pain as he walks with a bad back, and to whom at least two of the occupants, Martin Cunningham and Simon Dedalus, are in debt. Simon Dedalus is openly rude and anti-Semitic but even the decent and humane Martin Cunningham is acerbic and one feels an air of three gentiles versus Bloom. What is perhaps even sadder, the understandable but unforgivable tactic of the outsider, Bloom eager for dissociation with victim, tries to join the racist bandwagon. He fails. Between them, they tell a story about the son of Reuben J Dodd, who, in an apparent suicide attempt following a love affair gone bad, jumps into the Liffey but is saved from drowning by a passing boatman. Reuben J Dodd financially rewards the hero and Simon Dedalus cracks a witticism to general amusement. It's a resounding Homeric echo of paying the boatman Acheron to ferry the dead across the River Styx to Hades.

Reuben J Dodd was a real moneylender to whom Joyce's father was in serious debt[12] and there are elements of truth regarding the son and reward. The fictional element, however, was him being Jewish for he was actually Catholic but it's a good story that Joyce wished to include so he made him a Jew and it thereby tied in with Bloom.

We pass Dublin's tallest landmark, Nelson's Pillar. The one handled adulterer (as he shall be described) is atop and a fruit seller afoot: 'Eight plums a penny! Eight for a penny![13]

The men discuss Dignam's death. Whilst internally noting that he died in an alcoholic stupor. Bloom toes the official, more socially acceptable, line of apoplexy which seems to cover all manner of malady. He remarks that the death was, at least, instant and comparatively peaceful. Jack Power weighs in that the worst death is suicide because of the shame brought on the family. He's apparently ignorant of Bloom's father's suicide so, as it seems suspiciously, is Simon, who compounds the insult. Martin Cunningham though, is alive to the sensitivity and tries tactfully to change the subject. Bloom looks on him kindly, observing that he's a decent man but goodness, how he suffers with that alcoholic wife who pawns household goods to feed her addiction. Cunningham works hard to rebuild the home only for the pattern to depressingly repeat. The allusion, of course, is to Sisyphus whom Odysseus meets in Hades and who is trapped in a cycle of pushing a rock up a mountain, only for it to topple down again. A little like carrying water in a sieve.

Bloom's thoughts naturally and sadly turn to his father and specifically the coroner's inquest eighteen years ago, out in Ennis, County Clare. Bloom is due to return there the week after next on the anniversary of the death and, tellingly, if that means he misses Molly's tour of Ulster, it rather leaves the coast clear for Blazes Boylan.

Continuing north-westerly through north Dublin, they cross a junction with Eccles Street, passing the large Mater Misericordiae hospital and hospice. My house down there thinks Bloom. Music is heard from a street organ: 'Has Anybody Here Seen Kelly?' and the Death March from Saul: one missing, the other, dead. And an Irish/Jewish connection, underlying the affinity Joyce felt and spelled out to his Italian friend Linati that lay between the twin tribes of Israel and Ireland.[14] The morbid theme continues as the cortège is halted. Cattle drove to slaughter: Friday tomorrow, killing day and Bloom would know, he used to attend the slaughterhouse in the employ of the cattle trader Joseph Cuffe. All the best beef is exported to Liverpool. Let's pocket this abuse of sacred livestock and its symbolism of life blood draining from Ireland. We shall need it later.[15]

Further waterways are crossed, rivers of Hades. In the vicinity of Finglas Road, they pass the scene of an infamous 1889 murder case,[16] in which a Mr Samuel Childs was charged with the murder of his brother Thomas but escapes justice through lack of evidence and the artful oratory of his counsel, the sniggeringly named Seymour Bushe, KC. Joyce attended the trial and we shall hear more of this in the next episode. The *double entendre* extends beyond the lawyer's name for Bloom, we know, in deep subconscious, considers himself a child murderer. His own son.

Glasnevin cemetery looms. White sepulchres and headstones rear up in the stone-cutting yard outskirts and behind passing hedgerows. They resemble the shades and ghosts residing in Hades. Life as we know it, is over as we approach the city of the dead. All are welcome but none may leave.

Part Two – Prospect Cemetery, Glasnevin, the Dead

The cemetery is overseen by the superintendent, John O'Connell, we self-indulge and assume a descendent of the Liberator himself, Daniel O'Connell[17] but undoubted descendent of King Hades for this is Mr O'Connell's kingdom. Bloom will wonder how in such a morbid profession O'Connell manages to attract women or whether, in fact, love among the tombstones, dicing with death, is actually something of a turn-on. His thoughts chime with Stephen's poetical vampire creation, possibly at this precise moment. O'Connell's namesake from one hundred years earlier, Daniel O'Connell, Irish hero and Hercules, was a notorious womaniser, apparently with legions of offspring all over the place. His body is also all over the place, for while most of it is buried in the O'Connell mausoleum at the heart of the cemetery, his heart, as per his last wishes, rests in Rome. Another fallen hero, Parnell, is also here (some will disagree), a modern Agamemnon,[18] both adored leaders of men and both, in different circumstances, killed off by marital affair.

The cemetery is vast, the largest in Dublin. But this day, only sparsely populated, above ground at least, to mark the end and give the thanks for the life of Paddy Dignam: an inglorious man getting a less than dignified send-off – Bloom, Cunningham, Power and Dedalus from our coach. The widow Dignam, one of her sons, Patrick, and her brother-in-law and, from another coach, Ned Lambert, Tom Kernan, Joe Hynes and John Henry Menton, solicitor and Dignam's erstwhile employer. There is another mystery man. Therefore, we may summarise the mourners as some of the immediate family (younger kids are absent) and a few others who, if they described themselves as friends of the departed, it would be out of generous respect. The assembled snake their way towards the Chapel. Simon Dedalus and Ned Lambert swap pleasantries of the old days back in Cork but Simon deftly changes the subject when he senses the conversation heading towards a donation to a support fund for the Dignam children. The irony is not lost, when we learn[19] that Bloom, the Jew, has not only pledged five shillings but paid up on the spot.

The memorial service: Father Coffee presiding. One of those muscular Christians, Bloom observes. A phrase then in vogue to describe enthusiastic evangelists who value purity of body alongside purity of soul, albeit in this case, the muscle seems concentrated around the mid-driff. He may be word-associating 'Muscular Jew', a phrase also in vogue in early Zionist literature and with which we know Bloom is at least partially familiar. A rebellion against typical anti-Semitic tropes depicting the Jew as weak as well as effeminate. A muscular Jew is the Jew for the twentieth century no more to be kicked around and we shall explore this further in episode seventeen.[20] Continuing his observation of the priest, Bloom thinks, 'bully about the muzzle', large mouth. What with this and the Simnel cakes being sold at the cemetery gates resembling dog biscuits and we suspect that this bulldog like priest is our Cerberus, the multi-headed canine, guardian of Hades. Not to mention that Joyce tells us so in the schema. And, hang on, didn't Stephen think about Lambert Simnel on the beach?[21]

Bloom's knees still throb sorely from the stone floor at Westland Row church so now he takes the precaution of adding on top of the newspaper, the padding of his apparently uncrushable felt hat beneath his knee. No joy; still hurts. Further rehearsal for his worship at the altar of sado-masochism later that night. We note, moreover, that his religious observations have not improved since St Andrew's in Westland Row:

> The priest took a stick with a knob at the end of it out of the boy's bucket and shook it over the coffin. Then he walked to the other end and shook it again. Then he came back and put it back in the bucket. As you were before you rested. It's all written down: he has to do it.[22]

One suspects that stick, knob and bucket may not be the technical terms for these ceremonial artefacts but this is how Bloom sees it. He surmises that the water being shaken over the head of the coffin is symbolic of throwing water on the face of the deceased to see if he doesn't wake up. And who's to say he's wrong? Furthermore, we understand his cynicism as the priest plods mechanically and formulaically through the service. Little wonder, thinks Bloom, he does the same service multi times a day. The cemetery is a factory, thousands dying every day, millions around the world every moment. It's a wonder for all the over-crowding, that they're not popping up again all over the place. Birth, death, burial, re-birth. A constant Sisyphus cycle. Water carried in a sieve. And he wonders, to what end?

Service over, the mourners follow the coffin to its final resting place. Simon Dedalus thinks of his wife's fresh grave over yonder and breaking down, calls on his maker to take him any time. Very laudable; though one may uncharitably recall his ten children who could do with his support in this life. Contrast with Bloom who's earthly account reads: one dead son, two dead parents, one live but absent daughter, one virtually broken marriage and yet who feels, as we shall see, very much alive and with so much to live for and for which to be grateful. Men pair off. The two *ersatz* Catholics, Bloom, well, we know his history, and Tom Kernan, a reluctant convert from Church of Ireland, are walking together. Kernan is critical of the Catholic service; he prefers the Protestant version but still, he takes comfort in the whole resurrection idea and that we shall be reunited come the day of judgement. For Bloom, pragmatist, dead is dead just as soon as the rusty pump of the heart gives out. It's then the turn of the rats and termites to run the subterranean show and make use of our bodies in the creation of new life. Ever practical, Bloom comically pictures all these patched together bodies on that resurrection day of judgement, looking for various organs and limbs as they frantically try to piece themselves together.

Up ahead, the solicitor John Henry Menton walks with Ned Lambert and looking back at Bloom, asks him, who is that chap? Familiar but he can't quite place him. Ned Lambert explains Bloom by reference to Molly, Marion Tweedy as was. The penny drops. Menton, it transpires, had his own designs on Molly years ago and can't believe that she went and married that 'coon', as he delicately puts it. Jealousy and racism; a heady cocktail. Bloom doesn't overhear this but he recognises Menton and recalls his character, defined by a decided lack of manners. They crossed swords when Bloom, with beginner's luck, beat Menton in a game of bowls sixteen years earlier. And Bloom will get one over on this chap, this modern day Ajax, before we leave Glasnevin.[23]

At graveside. Paddy Dignam is as it were, centre stage. When Odysseus enters Hades, he is surprised to see the ghost of Elpenor, one of his men. Odysseus is staggered; he had no idea he was dead. It turns out that Elpenor had got very drunk at Circe's palace and on a lovely night fell asleep up on the roof. Awaking in the dark and forgetting where he is, the poor chap falls off the roof to an untimely death. He was left behind on Circe's island, unburied, and Odysseus now promises him a proper burial upon return to Ithaca. We are pretty sure that Dignam's death was also alcohol-related but we cannot say for sure if it involved a fall. We must venture to Joyce's final novel for that and we are not going there now. We surmise that Dignam is a family man, a heavy drinker and is cut down in his prime with no-one to blame but himself. These days someone would have Circe up for breach of health and safety or that it was a societal problem but in 1904 and, far less, ancient Greece, no such complications. Molly will later observe that, for all his faults at least Bloom is not married to the pub, which it seems is quite a rarity round these parts.

As we consign Dignam to his resting place Bloom ponders diverse matters spanning life, death, the universe just as, simultaneously, in episode three, Stephen does on the beach in intellectually opaque style. Bloom's musings skip through the macabre to the hilarious. Questions like: why aren't people buried vertically to fit more in? Observations that coffins are such a waste of good wood and how fertile the soil must be: simply teeming with life. This synchronising with Stephen's thoughts of molecules temporarily inhabiting a corpse: 'God becomes man becomes fish becomes barnacle goose becomes featherbed mountain.'[24]

Bloom ponders the nightmare of being buried alive. He takes comfort that Dignam died three days earlier so if anything were capable of stirring, it would, by now, have stirred. But surely in these civilised times one must guard against even the faint possibility. Various bizarre solutions meander through his mind: a personal favourite, the installation of little telephones inside coffins. Another link to Stephen whom we recall thought about a telephone wire of umbilical cords linking us all through the generations, right back to Adam and Eve.[25]

We encounter one of the book's more famous passages. Bloom counts the mourners, which doesn't take long: there are so few. It seems Dignam didn't make much of a mark on life. But there's an unknown man, tallish and slimish, or as Bloom puts it, the 'lanky looking galoot over there in the mackintosh'. Theories abound as to the identity of the chap because Mr Joyce does not divulge. Bold suggestions abound; from authorial Joyce to Jesus to the returning Parnell, the Wandering Jew, Odysseus, Athena, Tiresias. Insert your suggestion in the space provided. Some bright spark may discover the answer but now, ninety-nine years after publication, if we don't know we probably never will and that is Joyce's little game. But man-in-mackintosh adds colour and depth as well as mystery – for instance, Bloom's surprise at not recognising a mourner. In 1904, Dublin was the second city of the British Empire and whilst barely three miles top to tail had a population of well over a third of a million inhabitants.[26] One might think that would be ample for Dignam to know someone beyond Bloom's circle. Yet surprised he was and one can only conclude that the city had the colloquial feel of a village. Bloom thinks that the man in the mackintosh brings the number of mourners to an unlucky thirteen and, of passing interest here, might be the vague resemblance to the Jewish minyan.[27]

Personal calculation reveals only twelve but Joyce says thirteen and he should know. Maybe there's another Dignam child or perhaps Bloom counts Corny Kelleher there in a professional capacity.

Joe Hynes, who is definitely counted, is also semi-pro because he's charged with writing an obituary for the *Evening Telegraph* and must record the attending mourners. He approaches Bloom to ask, ignorantly and insensitively, for his Christian name. And this the man that has not only worked with Bloom but knows him well enough to have borrowed three shillings, three weeks ago. Apparently though, not so well as to know his first name or to repay the money. Bloom honours his earlier assurance and asks Hynes to record McCoy's attendance. Hynes enquires of the mystery stranger: 'You mean him in the mackintosh?' Bloom asks, but slapdash Hynes has already assumed his name is Mackintosh and has moved on. Bloom it seems is not a man with whom he needs to linger.

The burial done, the mourners slowly and with dignity, disperse. Bloom looks over headstones, how we soon forget the dead, even superstars like Parnell fade from memory. Maybe headstones should display more memorable and interesting information: 'So and so, wheelwright. I travelled for cork Lino. I paid five shillings in the pound . . . I cooked a good Irish stew.'[28]

A rustling attracts his attention: a large rat, shuffling behind a headstone and beneath a structure. It's emblematic of the Hades kingdom that assumes control once human funereal formalities are complete. A headstone marks the spot of one Robert Emery which is close enough to make Bloom think of Robert Emmet,[29] the Irish patriot that Bloom understands to be buried somewhere thereabouts. The irony being that the location of his butchered and disassembled carcass remains a matter of ongoing conjecture. What is certain, to follow Bloom's train of thought, is that some rat or other will make short work of him, wherever he is.

But not of Bloom, for Bloom is infused with the stuff of life. He's not ready to go; 'they won't get me this innings'. Blooming Bloom, life-affirming Bloom.

The episode ends with John Henry Menton, that disagreeable and racist solicitor, we met earlier. A man, we think, used to demanding and getting the respect as befits his position but reciprocity perhaps not his strong point. Bloom, reaching out for peace, as Odysseus to Ajax, draws Menton's attention to a crease in his hat. It's a delicious moment and there follows a wonderful frozen pause as Menton stares intently at

Bloom, mindful of the age-old jealousy over Molly of which he's only just been reminded. His aspect radiates resentment, ill-will and racial superiority but nonplussed by a random act of kindness that he struggles to process, he cannot produce a suitable response. Jilted into action by Martin Cunningham he forces a steely 'Thank you'.

Bloom, assuming Menton will not recall him, takes mischievous pleasure that it will dawn on him later and he will be upset. Bloom is no saint, either, it's the stuff of life. We leave Bloom relieved to exit the Hades gates having escaped death's icy grip this time around. He has no time for death: too much left to do, too many gifts to bestow upon humanity before his time is up. And Bloom seems to be one of those blessed people for whom the joy is in the giving not receiving.

We revisit the question posed at the outset: City of Life; City of Death, which is which? It may seem a bizarre question but Bloom was in mortal agony on that coach ride. Sat on the bar of lemon soap and too squashed to move, he was physically uncomfortable but also made to feel quite miserable. Brazenly so by mean Simon Dedalus, diluted and sugar-coated by Martin Cunningham. Even generously allowing for Jack Power's ignorance, his talk of suicide and Molly's tour will have been daggers to Bloom, nonetheless. In company, Bloom was more alone and inhibited than in either Calypso or Lotus Eaters. Some of the silences echoed around the carriage and festered in Bloom's head. The cameos with Simon Dedalus were telling, particularly as Bloom regards Simon as a friend. This is especially sad.

On the pavements, people have stopped dead in their tracks in respectful and dignified salutation that the Dignam name demands, more so it seems in death than in life. Others, like Reuben J Dodd hobble rather than walk. A tramp sits transfixed on the pavement; statues are, well, statues. Is the city's heart rate dropping? Is it more than the paralysis of the previous episode? More dead than alive? That's not really a sustainable argument in the context of what's to come especially in the Aeolus episode where energy and bluster is much in evidence but to no meaningful effect.

Yet somehow the feeling lingers that, pulses rise somewhat inside the City of the Dead. Bloom, generally alone with just his thoughts for company, returns by and large to good humour and the *joie de vivre* that deserted him on the journey. No sooner was he in, he's thinking, the dirty devil, about sex among the tombstones. This is not to say he's comfortable there, a cemetery is no place for Bloom, for he sees the pointless ritual for what it is and, triggered by Martha Clifford, he does not like that other world.[30] But it provides the time and space for him to focus on the practical help, that is surely necessary back in the land of the living: the five shillings donation for the Dignam kids and sorting out the widow Dignam's endowment policy. One may consider both to be distractions from his own very real domestic issues. Death does not phase Bloom. Like Odysseus, it helps him on his journey; he's very much alive and very much out of there.

If as surmised, it is appropriate to pair Telemachus and Nestor with Calypso and Lotus Eaters, (and otherwise why did Joyce re-set the clock to 8 am?) then, what do we learn by comparing Proteus with Hades.? Detailed analysis is beyond this short précis but we might say is that Stephen, like Bloom in this episode, considered many aspects of the universe but all in the context of his own personal realm. By the end of the episode it was still about him; how all that he could see, hear, touch, etc, might serve him and his art. Bloom's contemplation of universal truths is from a perspective of his place in something much bigger than he. How he fits into it and what he can do to help the whole. Bloom feels a responsibility to give; Stephen assumes an entitlement to receive. Their planetary Venn diagrams need to orbit a little closer.

LECTURE 8, 6 JANUARY 2021: EPISODE 7

Aeolus in the Windy City

Music: The Air that I Breathe – (The Hollies)

Can't talk; things to do, people to see. Places to go, money to make.

It's fitting that Aeolus is the first lecture of this New Year 2021. It has resolve. Where the lethargy of episode five? Gone. These people haven't time to sit around eating the fruit of the lotus flower, they mean business! No time either for Homeric parallel, that will have to wait. This episode seven is an episode of action and here we go!

We start with a bird's eye view of the frantic economic activity at the heart of the Hibernian metropolis. Dublin's tram system had been transporting people around the city for decades but not like this. For now it is electric powered! Ultra-modern and infallible as befits the second city of the Empire and it runs on time or drivers will feel the icy wind of the Inspector timekeeper. The Royal Mail, resplendent under the regal vermillion legend of the British crown, delivering invoices, legal documents, letters of credit; keeping the wheels of business turning as well as, of course, conveying personal correspondence. Barrels of Guinness's porter are lowered into cellars as contemporaneously, empty brothers are dull-thudded up ramps. Hard work fires a thirst and this rhythmical undulation ensures pubs don't run dry. God forbid! A seamless cacophony, nay, symphony of industrious harmony keeps the city ticking like clockwork.

We zoom in a little closer. A newspaper office where the frenzied activity continues, now against a clanging backdrop of modern electric printing presses, noisily bashing out the latest editions. Sister papers; the *Freeman's Journal* and *Evening Telegraph*. A newspaper is a business, of course it is, and journalism a fine and noble profession. The Gentlemen of the Press. People need to know who said what to whom, how Russia and Japan are bashing each other[1] and sporting odds and obituaries and that Lady Such and Such is joining some hunt at the such and such on Saturday. Dubliners part with good money to read these nuggets and, therefore, businesses pay to advertise in such august journals.

It's a little breezy outside but more so in ambience. Stories blow in from all over Ireland and beyond. Doors blow open, people breeze in, breeze out; tissue leaves of newspaper glide the thermals. There's a whiff of lack of control; dare one say, a touch chaotic? The presses are unrelenting in their clanging and, we wonder, are humans running the machines or vice-versa? For the machines, eerily, do seem to breathe as they rhythmically rattle along. All in all, one may be reminded of that very funny novelette, *The Diary of a Nobody*,[2] where the neighbours rejoice in surnames the Cummings and the Goings and the Cummings are forever coming and the Goings always going. Save when it's the other way around.

Amidst the kerfuffle, a little Aeolus explanation. The fleet has rested a few weeks on the island of Aeola, where Aeolus, father of the winds dwells, appropriately, in the cave of the winds.[3] A generous sort, he offers to help Odysseus by giving him a bag of winds fastened with a silver cord. It contains all the unfavourable winds and so, provided it remains shut fast, the way is left clear for helpful zephyrs and Odysseus will be back home in Ithaca before he knows it. What could possibly go wrong? Occasionally, Odysseus, crafty and suspicious, is too clever for his own good and keeps this good news to himself and so, when within sight of Ithaca, he falls asleep holding the closely guarded bag, his men assume he has been closely guarding treasure and open the bag. All hell breaks loose. The bad winds rush out and the fleet is blown hither and thither, all the way back to Aeola where, having had his altruism thrown in his face, Father Aeolus is far less receptive and refuses to help. Our Aeolus is Myles Crawford editor of the *Evening Telegraph*.

This is a different sort of episode. Neither Stephen nor Bloom are centre stage, though they have walk-on parts and, one breathlessly reports, are in the same building at same time but that's as close as it gets. The narrative is driven by other characters or, worryingly, even the machines. We notice a change of style. Prose is broken up by block capital loud sentences, one is tempted to say, newspaper headlines, except very few would be fit for purpose. Some read more like picture captions, others simply confuse. It all adds to the chaotic, staccato feel. From this point on in the book, the style of writing will increasingly reflect content; as though the book itself is trying to wrestle control from the author, just as the machines might be doing at the newspaper. Our bodily organ this time is the lungs and our art; rhetoric. So a newspaper makes for a fitting location; opinionated journalists with bloated egos and out-puffed cheeks, shouting above noisy printing presses and all the while, persuading. Or not.

Let's think about wind, the rushing of air. One is tempted, dare one say, especially with the Press, to think windbags, opinionated men full of hot air (and then it was all men). Negative connotations are understandable, especially being a fly on the wall in this office. But surely air can only be neutral? One recalls a funny scene in the Mel Brooks' Petrovian parody, *The 12 Chairs,*[4] involving a scam whereby someone pretends to collapse in the street, hoping for donations from passers-by. In trying to 'revive' his collapsed friend, the partner in crime, possibly Ron Moody or Dom de Louise, is pushing up and down on his friend's chest and saying, 'Out goes the bad air, in goes the good air'. The scam may be later repeated massaging a woman's bosom, as her suspicious husband unexpectedly approaches. Excuse the digression, for the point is, air is neutral. Sometimes, bad, say flatulence or a cold ill-wind, other times refreshing and inspirational as in '*animas*' or a Hebrew word for wind, '*ruach*'. This is different altogether; a rush of air to nourish the soul, our spirit, our *animas*. All of which unites us with our old friend, consubstantiation. The Father, Son and Holy Spirit: the Holy Spirit being the wind; the active agent that impregnates the Virgin Mary to create the son and conjoins father and son into the inseparable whole. In poetic terms, the divine *afflatus*, the other-worldly breath of inspiration, that brings the page to life.

In the act of speaking, air fuels our words, good and bad. Our rhetoric may be persuasive and inspiring, the wind beneath our wings, or it may be boring, ill-informed nonsense, stoked by smoky stale breath. In this chapter we examine rhetoric: good and bad.

Bloom and Stephen will be in the same building and although they do not speak it is the closest their planetary Venn diagrams have orbited so far. Bloom is there to negotiate the placement of an advert for his client Mr Keyes, owner of several grocery stores. Earlier both protagonists have misplaced keys and now keys draw them closer. Stephen, bullock-befriending bard, intends to deliver Mr Deasy's foot and mouth letter to the editor of the *Evening Telegraph*, Myles Crawford, and also to spend a little time in the company of writers. The interrupted, jolting nature of the episode puts one on alert. The pinball machine prose of colliding people, colliding conversation and colliding objectives is further disrupted by these newspaper headlines, or whatever they are, interposing every few lines or paragraphs, chopping the piece into sixty-four short articles. Quality and accuracy is patchy but they made it to the printing press by the deadline and that, in this episode, is what counts. Getting the story, any story, out there, is more important than accuracy, style or relevance.

Let's get into it.

Bloom goes to see the foreman Mr, I beg pardon, Councillor, Joseph Nannetti,[5] to discuss terms for the advert. They barely hear each other over the noise of the printing presses and so mis-communicate. Bloom tries to explain his artistic objectives for the ad design, which entail a play on the word Keyes, also symbol of the Manx parliament, the House of Keys, which might appeal to tourists from the Isle of Man. Possible significance is the local god of the sea, Manannan Mac Lir after whom the Isle of Man is named. He was in the protean thoughts of Stephen and will play a pivotal role in Circe, not to say the entire novel. One might say, Mac Lir holds the key. In the last episode, a street organ played 'Has Anybody Here Seen Kelly'? A song apparently as Irish as they come. Yet as originally composed, Kelly is not Irish at all but rather from the Isle of Man and was 'shamrocked' for a Broadway musical.[6] Nannetti is of Italian heritage and Bloom, with 'La Ce Darem' on his mind, is about to ask him a question of pronunciation of an Italian lyric but wisely reconsiders. Nannetti, second generation immigrant, future Mayor of Dublin, is as solidly Irish as Kelly is not. This muddling of true 'Irishness' has greater significance in episodes eleven and twelve.

That Bloom cannot properly explain the crossed keys design over the sound of the presses is important because it propels Bloom to the National Library at 2 pm to copy the design that was used in a previous edition of the *Kilkenny People*. With design details to follow, Nannetti offers terms which Bloom shall discuss with his client. Mr. Keyes lives a good tram ride away and may not even be in but the Editor Myles Crawford has a telephone, so Bloom will call him instead. Bloom is, apparently, on sufficiently good terms with the editor to presume to be able to do this – indicating either their personal relationship or the financial importance to the newspaper of placing adverts.

So he heads from the offices of the *Freeman's Journal*, through the same building to its sister newspaper, the *Evening Telegraph* and specifically, the office of the Editor. This takes him past gigantic printing presses. One is being populated with blocks of page type. Before internet-fuelled computers there were electronic word processors and before that, each word had to be physically assembled in the presses and, no less, in backward mirror image. It reminds Bloom of his father reading to him from the *Haggadah*, the prayer book for the Jewish festival of Passover. Written in Hebrew, naturally it reads right to left just like the type blocks in the printing presses. An important passage for several reasons: one, it suggests and even establishes that Rudolph Bloom may have converted but is no apostate; he continues to raise his son, the Baptised Catholic, as a Jew. For another, Passover tells the story of the exodus of the Israelites from bondage in Egypt to freedom in Israel, in parallel with the Irish struggle against the British and so establishing a Moses equals Parnell motif that will reverberate beyond this episode, as well, of course, marking the parallels between the Exodus journey and the wanderings of Odysseus, Dante and Bloom.

In the *Telegraph* office, under the headline ERIN, GREEN GEM OF THE SILVER SEA, three men, Ned Lambert, Simon Dedalus and Professor McHugh, sit in an anteroom beyond the Editor's office. They discuss a speech given the previous evening by local politician, Dan Dawson, extracts of which are in the paper. Simon and Ned have hot-footed it from the funeral for that fine journalistic tradition, the lunchtime trip to the boozer. Dawson's speech is verbose unwieldy and full of over flowery language. Simon Dedalus sums it up in inimitable style: 'Agonising Christ, wouldn't it give you a heartburn on your arse?'[7]

We'll see more of Ned Lambert, but Professor McHugh only in this episode. He's a teacher, Latin and Classics but probably no actual professor.[8] He considers himself an erudite knowledgeable sort and so the ironic soubriquet suits. Also a freelance writer, he's there hoping to earn a few bob with a commission from Editor Myles Crawford.

Dawson's rococo-rhetoric provides the first of three contrasting oratory displays that we shall see this episode. The hyper-flamboyance does not go down well with the local crowd. Bloom arrives mid-discussion and asks a pertinent question but, before an answer is delivered (one of many truncated conversations this episode), the door bursts open and Bloom is bashed in the small of his back with the doorknob, which incidentally puts him around five foot nine inches in height. In walks J J O'Molloy. Let's blame the building with its swinging doors and talking printing presses, it seems to have a soul and a voice of its own. Humans aided or thwarted by machinery. Bloom silently acknowledges that O'Molloy is a clever barrister but whose talents are blunted by a gambling addiction. A nearly man, one of many in the book. We learn that he hopes to secure a loan from Myles Crawford.

On cue, the Editor. Enter Aeolus, Father of the Winds. Ushered in by the headline, WHAT WETHERUP SAID, with barely a mention. A subtle insight into how the book, gaining a life of its own, elects to treat him.

Ned and Simon's thirst waits for no man and they head for the pub. Crawford will follow shortly. Staccato choreography ensues; two in, two out. Continuing the bedroom farce, make that three in, three out, for Bloom also leaves to make his phone call but Lenehan, the horseracing oracle, enters offering a dead cert for the Gold Cup. As a reliable constant, if there's free beer or cigarettes, Lenehan will be around and about. Lenehan will also fall prey to the merciless swing doors and is bashed as Bloom re-enters. He, Bloom, is rushing having learned that Mr Keyes happens to be in a nearby auction house. Our Aeolus, Editor Myles Crawford, is initially helpful to Bloom by letting him use his telephone, after all, advertising revenue propels the paper. Furthermore, when Bloom says he must rush out to find Mr Keyes, Crawford encourages with: 'Begone! He said. The world is before you.'[9]

Despite use of the word 'Begone', which echoes Aeolus's subsequent admonition, this probably represents the helpful wind. But when Bloom returns, initially by phone, Crawford is not so receptive: he's in the midst of a good yarn and will not be interrupted. On his actual return, Bloom tells him Keyes is likely to renew and possibly for a two- or three-month repeat but only if Keyes receives a par or a puff. This is a short advertorial paragraph in which the newspaper sings the praises of the grocery stores. This time Bloom gets a proper blow-out, never mind a puff. He is told to tell Keyes that he can kiss Crawford's arse. And, when pushed, that he can kiss Crawford's royal Irish arse.

But this is to jump ahead. First, we have more rhetoric to consider and next up is the art of journalism. Stephen Dedalus has joined the crowd, having arrived with Mr O' Madden Burke. He's tasked with delivery of Deasy's poorly crafted foot and mouth letter and to try to get it published. The group has a bit of mirth at Deasy's expense whose wife, it transpires, has left him which goes some way to explain, if not excuse, his misogyny in episode two. We also note Crawford's fawning demeanour towards Stephen which contrasts interestingly with his short-tempered treatment of Bloom – though it's an unfair contest, one a writer, the other a jobbing ad man. In the paragraph headed YOU CAN DO IT, Crawford accepts the letter for publication, and encourages Stephen to write for the paper. He's hoping for something different and modern: 'Something with a bite in it. You can do it. I see it in your face.'[10]

J J O'Molloy in an aside warns Stephen: 'He wants you for the press gang . . .'[11]

Crawford laments the decline of oratory skills. Neither politicians, journalists nor barristers are as they were in the golden age of Crawford's living memory and, without irony, Mr Editor provides his example of supreme journalism. The Phoenix Park murders occurred in

1882 (Joyce and Stephen's birth year) and scandalised the world. Lord Frederick Cavendish, appointed Chief Secretary for Ireland just the previous week and Thomas Henry Burke, the most senior civil servant were pounced upon and stabbed to death as they left the Viceroy's Lodge in Phoenix Park. The assassins were members of the Invincibles, a spin-off from the Irish Republican Brotherhood,[12] itself a precursor to the IRA. Iron-clad British censorship starved the world's press of detail but Ignatius Gallagher,[13] a young journalist on this very paper, transmitted the essential facts to New York in code by way of an innocuous advertisement. Thus he cemented his reputation as a legendary journalist. **CLEVER, VERY,** it no doubt was, but good writing it ain't. Quite the opposite, as Stephen mutely noted, the story was conveyed by a few secreted consonants.

J J O'Molloy, playfully resentful of Crawford's harking back to the good old days, presents his nomination of modern rhetoric on behalf of the legal profession. Though he says he holds no brief for the third profession (classically law is a poor third after divinity and medicine) and he's right, he can hold no brief for he's disbarred due to gambling addiction. He tells, as he looks at Stephen, of the superb forensic cross-examination by Seymour Bush, King's Counsel, in the 1889 Childs fratricide murder case; we recall the funeral cortège passed the scene of the crime, last chapter: 'And in the porches of mine ear did pour.'[14]

Stephen thinks, reminding us of 'fratricided' King Hamlet.

The learned counsel contrasted Roman Law and the earlier Mosaic Law of strict liability, an eye for an eye. Moses, as sculptured, unites both; Michelangelo's statue in San Pietro, Rome with reproduction in the Dublin central criminal court, where O'Molloy, Seymour Bush and, in the public gallery, James Joyce, would have seen it. Moses shall intrude and influence this episode with increasing regularity and vigour just as his statue has a beguiling vital quality. It's almost alive.

Then, a fascinating passage. Cigarettes are passed around and matches struck to ignite:

> Messenger took out his matchbox thoughtfully and lit his cigar.
>
> I have often thought since on looking back on that strange time that it was that small act, trivial in itself, that striking of that match, that determined the whole aftercourse of both our lives.15

Two ways of looking at this piece, perhaps more, but here's an initial two. We assume it to be Stephen's internal monologue. The first possible explanation is that Stephen, apropos nothing, parodies the anticipated oratory of J J O'Molloy in clichéd Dickensian style and in character of a Mr Messenger. That there's nothing more to it.[16, 17]

However, another way:

O'Molloy is cast as a messenger and, if of God, so collaborating Malachi, Moses, Athena, Hermes, Elijah. But what is the message? The striking of the match will be seismic in terms of two lives. Whose lives? Surely the book's main two protagonists, Stephen and Bloom, otherwise why would Joyce distract us so? But what life-altering seismic event have we witnessed? It can't be simply the firing of the match? Are we supposed to glean that Bloom, a man he barely knows, from this moment on, begins to nudge into Stephen's conscience? A few minutes later, Bloom will observe Stephen from afar, paternally pleased to see him in sturdier footwear and wonders if he is the 'moving spirit': a Manannan Mac Lir.

Are we helped by what happens next? J J O'Molloy, quotes more of Seymour Bush as he refers to this statue of Moses:

> He said of it: that stony effigy in frozen music, horned and terrible, of the human form divine, that eternal symbol of wisdom and prophecy which if aught that the imagination or the hand of sculptor has wrought in marble of soultransfigured and of soultransfiguring deserves to live, deserves to live.[18]

And, after reciting, looks specifically to Stephen for his approval. Stephen blushes.

Moses, messenger of the omniscient, lawgiver, regulator of society, soul-transfiguring Jew, metempsychosis, here in the form of a very life-like statue, deserves to live. Is this referring to Bloom, the would-be regulator of society and his increasing influence on Stephen? We don't yet know but it's an interesting thought. Let's throw in another, equally intriguing. We have three protagonists, not to forget Molly. In Proteus, Stephen thinks of evolution or reincarnation and thinks Barnacle goose, featherbed mountain. In the final episode, Molly will soliloquise from her bed, her mountain of Nora Barnacle goose feathers. There will be more than one suggestion that something may develop between Stephen and Molly, that it may even be encouraged by the Oedipal Bloom. So one should not rule out that the two lives that may be forever changed are Stephen and Molly, the catalyst being the increasing influence of Bloom, the Mosaic figure. Neither of these explanations is conclusive and the most persuasive answer (to a question that may have no basis) is secreted in a far-off episode where Stephen, fittingly as this lecture is delivered 6 January, will, at the spark of a struck match, have an epiphany.[19] This last theorem would also conveniently detach the Moses from Messenger, which is much better as it leaves 'deserves to live' as a stand-alone comment, meaning that he (Moses) deserved to enter the promised land – In Bloomian terms, that Bloom deserves another chance at saving his marriage. Cut a long story short, we'll await Lecture Seventeen for the most likely answer.

Back to the oratory sweepstakes where Professor McHugh may well take the prize. We preface his candidate with an undercurrent of an underlying conversation that ricochets around the room in this episode of conversations begun, cut short and deflected off. McHugh the Classics teacher, posits that the Irish have traditionally backed the lost cause – the Greeks versus the Romans; the Irish against the British. Just as Pyrrhus, as we saw in episode two, tilted a pointless lance towards the Romans, so the Irish are pretty inadequate in escaping the yoke of the British. Culturally, however, he feels that both the Irish and the Greeks were superior to the conquering imperialists in all respects save the cloacal, as apparently both Romans and British built excellent toilets with associated drainage. All of which is a short hop to the continuing thread of the Israelites held in bondage by the Egyptians which has run from Bloom's Passover memory at the printing press, flowing through the statue of Moses to now, our next oration.

The best speech McHugh ever heard was given by John F.Taylor[20] at a Trinity College debate concerning the revival of the Irish language. Some context is important there. Back in episode one we recall the old milk lady ashamed at neither speaking or understanding Irish. The Irish Literary Revival was a loose cultural group that sought to promote all things culturally Gaelic, pivotal to which was the revival of the language, otherwise in danger of being obliterated by colonial English. Several Irish literary titans, W B Yeats, John Millington Synge, George Russell, Lady Gregory, Fred Ryan, George Moore were involved. It was the nice genteel cultural end of more robust anti-British action favoured by the likes of Maud Gonne and Arthur Griffiths. This is no doubt a gross simplification for expertise in this area or the republican struggle generally is way beyond the scope of these lectures.

Joyce, despite nationalistic sympathies, was no fan. We know from *A Portrait* that he considered himself a master of words and was a great linguist yet knew only scraps of Gaelic and wrote in English; he hardly wished to blunt the tools of his trade. Beyond this myopia, he wished to modernise his people, to calibrate the Irish so as to look towards Europe for inspiration (which was prophetic) and not languish back in what he considered to be misguided myth: tales of Leprechauns, giants and nymphs plucking harps and righting wrongs. Joyce considered this dangerous sentimentality and charts its course, particularly in the Sirens and Cyclops episodes.

Back to McHugh. His account of fine oratory comes from this debate on the revival of the Irish language. Taylor speaks in favour of Gaelic revival and it is worth setting out in full, for, if nothing else, it represents one of the few surviving examples of Joyce's own reading from the book.[21]

> Mr Chairman, ladies and gentlemen: Great, was my admiration in listening to the remarks addressed to the youth of Ireland a moment since by my learned friend. It seemed to me that I had been transported into a country far away from this country, into an age remote from this age, that I stood in ancient Egypt and that I was listening to the speech of some high priest of that land addressed to the youthful Moses . . . And it seemed to me that I heard the voice of that Egyptian High Priest raised in a tone of like haughtiness and like pride. I heard his words and their meaning was revealed to me.
>
> Why will you Jews not accept our culture, our religion and our language? You are a tribe of nomad herdsmen; we are a mighty people. You have no cities nor no wealth: our cities are hives of humanity and our galleys, trireme and quadrireme, laden with all manner merchandise furrow the waters of the new globe. You have but emerged from primitive conditions: we have a literature, a priesthood, an age long history and a polity . . .
>
> You pray to a local and obscure idol: our temples, majestic and mysterious, are the abodes of Isis and Osiris, of Horus and Ammon Ra. Yours serfdom, awe and humbleness: ours thunder and the seas. Israel is weak and few are her children: Egypt is an host and terrible are her arms. Vagrants and day labourers are you called: the world trembles at our name . . .
>
> But, ladies and gentlemen, had the youthful Moses listened to and accepted that view of life, had he bowed his head and bowed his will and bowed his spirit before that arrogant admonition he would never have brought the chosen people out of their house of bondage nor followed the pillar of the cloud by day. He would never have spoken with the Eternal amid lightnings on Sinai's mountaintop nor ever have come down with the light of inspiration shining in his countenance and bearing in his arms the tables of the law, graven in the language of the outlaw.[22]

An important piece. In the biblical exodus, the story of liberation, we have a clear example of the parallel between the down-trodden Irish and the Israelites. But note also, were it not for the plucky young Moses insisting on Hebrew liberation, mankind would not have received the Ten Commandments, the bedrock of civilisation. Has Joyce got his loyalties reversed? He has been pushing the Irish/Jewish connection from the outset, but this speech favours the Gaelic revival and Joyce is decidedly not, or so we thought, in that camp. The lesson here might be that it's dangerous to pigeonhole Joyce and a bigger picture may be the impression that the telling of the story made upon the listening Stephen, deepened by the perceptive O'Molloy's quip, that Moses may have led his people to the Promised Land but was denied entry himself.

Stephen suggests adjournment to the pub. All head for Mooney's across Sackville Street (now O'Connell Street) but Myles Crawford has forgotten his keys (not the best day for keys) and returns to the office. J J O'Molloy takes this opportunity to catch him for a quiet word. Stephen crosses Sackville Street and with Prof McHugh, heads towards the pub. They pass Nelson's Pillar, Dublin's tallest landmark, and Stephen takes that opportunity to tell a story of two old spinsters that want to see Dublin from atop this vantage point. They buy plums from the fruit seller at its entrance, we heard the merchant's holler last episode as the funeral cortège rumbled past[23]; and they start the climb. But it's hard going being higher and harder than expected. They tire and suffer vertigo and, upon finally reaching the top, all they can do is sit back against the plinth, eat plums and spit the stones through the railings and onto the street below. It's not much of a story. Crawford and O'Molloy have caught up and hear most of it.

Crawford claims to like it but he's been fawning to Stephen anyhow. To Crawford it's a harmless public interest story of a day out. He wanted a story with some bite in it; well, they bit into the plums. The most insightful question he can muster is, from where do they get the plums? This, with the fruit seller at the foot of the Pillar, barely yards from where he stands. McHugh, the faux classical professor, struggles to remain on Stephen's intellectual plane. Only J J O'Molloy, the sharp but down-at-heel barrister, sees, we think, the true meaning. When asked what he will call the story, Stephen answers, the 'Parable of the Plums' or the 'Pisgah Sight of Palestine', thus revealing we are into cryptic biblical territory.

Translation as follows:

The two elderly spinsters, Shan Van Vocht, like the milk woman back in episode one, Telemachus, represent the Irish. They want to view Dublin, parochial city of the Empire, to observe it from upon high, to reclaim it, one might say. So what's their plan? They go to the most obvious representation of the British Empire in the city, Nelson's Pillar. This might yet be an act of rebellion, after all the imposing erection was blown up by the IRA in 1966, but we do not have that impression. They are subservient; they struggle to climb, are overcome with vertigo and, when they finally summit, they have a quick look at some steeples, argue over which is which and lie back exhausted. A representation one may think of Ireland's fragmented, disorganised and ineffective opposition to British rule at the time. Their remaining energy is consumed by titillation, as they stare up at the phallic, womanising glory of Nelson, British Lord, ruler of the waves. They eat plums, a biblical symbol of fertility, but the stones that they spit through the railings, will get no purchase from the barren paving stones below.

To sum up: it's an episode of hustle and bustle; of much rushing about but to little effect. Thwarted aims. Bloom tries to place the ad, he fails. Nor does he succeed in getting Hynes to repay him the three shillings owed, despite the third hint. Prof McHugh hopes for a commission but no sign of that. J J O'Molloy needs a loan; Miles Crawford is hard up, himself. Seymour Bush doesn't become a judge. The Vestal Virgins want to see the view from atop Nelson's Pillar but are too timid and too knackered to look once they get there. Moses wanted to lead his people into the Promised Land and, tantalisingly, God reveals it to him from Mount Pisgah, but like Odysseus, within sight of Ithaca, is denied entry. The Irish want rid of the British; nothing doing. Parnell it seemed was the great leader but, like Moses, was destined to fall short. The City itself, at the outset electrically charged, is stranded and becalmed amid an electricity power cut.

Readers are also frustrated. After three Stephen episodes and three Bloom episodes, here we have both together. We anxiously await a meet and greet but, alas, join the ranks of the disappointed. Further, although Bloom wasn't there to hear Stephen's parable, we heard it on his behalf and are on alert at any reference to the Promised Land, for we know that Bloom's Promised Land is Molly whom he left in their marriage bed awaiting the arrival of another.

And what of Aeolus: Myles Crawford? He wants Stephen for his pressgang but will be left wanting: for this episode sees the crystallisation, no, not crystallisation, not yet, but at least a maturation of Stephen's artistic ambitions. He reads the papers and has heard today the journalist view of good oratory and that the pinnacle of journalism was a code hidden in an advert. The daily churn of inaccurate articles under silly headlines is not for him. It may be Clever, Very, just as are Joyce's references to the sexual allusions of the Plumtree's Potted Meat advert are clever, but wit alone is not beautiful writing. Not on Stephen's aesthetic terms. [24]

Stephen peripatetically recites his story as he walks to the pub, it's a shout in the street[25] which at first blanch says little. Yet upon close analysis contains an abundance of hidden truth for those with ears to hear. It is beyond both the hackneyed pomposity of Prof McHugh and the 'make the deadline' pragmatism of Myles Crawford.

It has been said that Aeolus is a weaker episode; that if any episode could be dropped – and why have such a debate? – it might be Aeolus. This is preposterous in a novel that thrusts consubstantiation from the get-go, surely the episode of the wind, the Holy Spirit, the energising Ruach, is pivotal?

LECTURE 9, 20 JANUARY 2021: EPISODE 8

Lestrygonians and the Bottomless Buffet

Music: Food For Thought – UB40

It's about 1 pm. Bloom has physical needs. We've seen his mind turn to matters sexual, and will again this episode, but at this hour, such thoughts will battle but lose on points, to matters culinary. It's lunchtime and Bloom is hungry. He had a decent breakfast but that was at 8 am. Since then he's been to a funeral, walked a fair few miles and, by the time he gets his lunch, he'll have walked a couple more. Food is on his mind and also Joyce's for, in all its grammatical variants, it will seep through the very pores of the episode: Food. It's elemental, obviously. But not just what we eat, it's when we eat, where we eat, how we eat, how often and with whom we eat. All feeds into who we are. One is, apparently, what one eats. The very first thing we learned about Bloom was his favourite food. Let's see how, if at all, that was instructive.

Bloom's interior monologue is the episode's driving force. His Proteus. There's a fair bit of dialogue but Bloom's thinking constantly intrudes, so much so that our narrator struggles to keep up. Last episode we felt a creeping suspicion that the book might be taking over. The narrator does its best but sometimes lacks command and on occasion makes a complete pig's ear of it.

For instance: 'Wine soaked and softened rolled pith of breath mustard a moment mawkish cheese.'[1, 2]

It tries to help but seems as sickly as the mawkish cheese. Bloom gets us back on track but he finds the hour before he eats a little bilious and unpleasant; the narrator seems similarly afflicted.

We will watch for Homeric harpoons thrust down from towering cliffs by cannibal Lestrygonians onto unsuspecting sailors in the harbour below[3] and shall find them in the sea gulls swooping down to the Liffey for food and also in the pigeons using the folks below as bird-poo target practice. We will look out for cannibals consuming their prey and that will be all too obvious. We will watch for the caution of Odysseus, who held back his own boat and anchored outside the harbour. Turned out to be a good move.

Despite the brush-off last time from Myles Crawford, Bloom remains hopeful of placing the Keyes ad, broadly in line with the terms discussed with Councillor Nannetti. He needs to check a back copy of the *Kilkenny People* for the ad artwork to show Nannetti and, for this, he will go the National Library on Kildare Street. But first, lunch. He ponders what to eat and, while so doing, a man thrusts a leaflet into his hand. Bloom reads 'Bloo' on the folded page and momentarily thinks 'me?' But the leaflet unfolded reveals *Blood of the Lamb.* It's a flier advertising a forthcoming tour by an American evangelist preacher, Dr John Alexander Dowie, restorer of the church in Zion. Bloom briefly scans: it ends by prophesying a prophet: 'Elijah is coming, Elijah is coming.' And thus we meet a new character: not Dr Dowie, not Elijah, though both will feature, but the flyer itself and we shall follow its crumpled journey through much of the book. We shall mark, again, Elijah mixed up as Bloom and recall that Elijah appears not only in the Book of Elijah but again in almost the last words of the Old Testament, to prophesy the imminent arrival of the Messiah. We shall wonder if this is Bloom's task. As said, the flier says 'Blood of the Lamb' so its intended thrust is that it is the sacrifice of this lamb that will wash away all of our sins, just as believers believe Jesus died for our sins. The link to Bloom? Aside from 'Bloo' let's look at blood sacrifice. The first thing we learn of Bloom is that he eats offal; with relish, no less. He cooks his pork kidney and will eat it and thereby commits a sin as per the *kashrut* laws of the Book of Leviticus. But you may also recall that he burns it, so, albeit unintentionally, washes his sin in that fiery sacrifice. The flier is a throwaway which like the horse of same name and like our Pilgrim, will make its way through the course to the finishing line. Finally, we have seen Bloom's affinity with animals and the sacrifice of the lamb might represent animal cruelty, a theme already there and one that will develop further, possibly reflecting the pointless sacrifice of so many animals in World War One.

Standing at O'Connell Bridge, Bloom observes the seagulls. He empathises with them; sees the world through their eyes underlining the quality he displayed with his cat. He crumples up the Evangelist throwaway and launches it into the river. The gulls swoop towards the Liffey but, quickly realising it isn't a meal, curve upward again. Thirty-two feet per second, per second, reminds us, if not Bloom, of the Fall, original sin, and that perhaps we need Dr Dowie. Bloom is sceptical, the last of these American evangelist chaps to visit fell flat on his face tying to justify polygamy in this deeply Catholic town. Bloom, kindly Bloom, Schopenhauerian, empathetic Bloom buys two oat cakes and throws chunks into the river where they are quickly scoffed by the gulls. We note here, the reversal of the Elijah story who, living as a hermit, survived on cakes of food delivered by ravens[4] and to ensure the Bible is on our radar, Bloom assumes the gulls must think the food is manna from heaven,[5] Elijah being a messenger of god and Bloom, in this sense, being God of the gulls. The humanisation of the birds continues as Bloom bemoans their lack of gratitude. Not so much as a caw of thanks.[6]

It's no surprise that Bloom will critically review adverts within his scope. Standing there by the bridge, he notices with some pleasure and respect, that the clothes shop Kino's have placed an advert (trousers, 11/-) on an A-board tethered in a rowing boat. Not only has it claimed a prime position in the city centre he wonders if they even pay for it; after all, who owns water? A little downstream is the likely answer for someone, presumably the municipality, has billeted a sign that says 'Post No Bills'. Squinting, Bloom thinks it might say 'Post 110 Pills'. The two ads combine to remind Bloom that a clever doctor (Dr Hy Franks) stuck up posters in men's toilets to drum up business for his venereal disease clinic. Bloom is impressed with that, too; it not being an easy service to promote. But his mood lurches when, as if Molly's imminent sexual encounter wasn't awful enough, he ponders the dreadful possibility of Boylan having a venereal disease. No, too horrific to contemplate. Cad, as he is, surely even Boylan wouldn't stoop so low.

Moving on, Bloom bumps into Josie Breen. We learn that when single she was Josie Powell and either an actual or desired old flame of Bloom's. Either way there's a pang in his heart and a little electricity in the air, though he notes that she's not aged so well. Not as well as Molly, anyhow. Always the comparison to Molly and, as per usual, the compared falling short. Maybe he thinks, it's the stress of putting up with her husband Dennis, a local character with an increasingly tenuous grasp on sanity. We have a couple of pages of lovely dialogue and learn that a mutual acquaintance, Mrs Mina Purefoy, is having an awful labour with her tenth child. It's her third day at the maternity hospital in Holles Street and sets up an episode we encounter at 10.30 that evening.[7] Further, that Josie's husband, Dennis, has been tipped over the edge upon receipt of an anonymous postcard that simply says 'UP: up'. Hard to know what this may mean[8] but Mr Breen considers it a grave insult and he's determined to bring a libel action for £10,000; is roaming from lawyer to lawyer, trying to find a gun for hire. Aside from deciphering what the message actually means and never mind whether it is libellous, his challenge might be just who to sue; seeing it has been sent anonymously. Apparently this does not concern him.

Dennis might be bested in the crazy stakes by the man now approaching: Cashell Boyle O'Connor Fitzmaurice Tisdall Farrell. Bloom advises Josie Powell to move out of the way; good advice for as we shall see, this chap takes no prisoners as he zig-zags along, refusing to walk on the pavement side of a lamppost.

Beneath the dialogue, Bloom's interior monologue constantly babbles – always food-related; smells wafting from a nearby café, pastry crumbs on Josie's collar. Mrs Breen spots her husband busying across the street nursing two law books against his chest and she rushes to meet him, as a shepherd would a stray lamb. A line of five sandwich boarded men snake past. Each wears a hat displaying a letter, so that together they spell out 'HELY'S',[9] the stationery shop, one of Bloom's former employers. The power of this particular advert relies on the discipline of the line and loses impact as one of them, trying to scoff some lunch on the go, fails to keep pace. Bloom reminisces on the fantastic advertising opportunities he used to suggest to Mr Wisdom Hely who would reject them in favour of his own rubbish ideas.

Sympathetic Bloom passes by Trinity College. He's concerned for Mina Purefoy, suffering hard labour. Surely, he thinks, in these scientific times women shouldn't suffer so. It's a foreshadowing in counterpoint of the beginning of episode fourteen, set in the maternity hospital, where the narrator is congratulatory of wonderful modern Irish maternity facilities. Bloom contemplates the futility of it all. Poor women: suffer in labour and then birth, risking the life of mother or infant. Then, for many women with ten or so children, there ensues a constant of pregnancy and breastfeeding before, and often all too soon, death: either for child or exhausted mother. It's the same flow of churning thoughts he had at Dignam's grave. Humanity: in one end, out the other. He will later in the episode consider the body as a microcosm of same. Food in one end, out the other and, on a universal level, where our little lives are barely noticeable, the same repeating pattern; planets, balls of gas, spinning, clashing, burning up, dying and, in the process, creating and perpetuating. Bloom's mood depresses in line with his hunger and all the time, there's time – moving inexorably towards 4 pm.

He looks up at the sun and wonders if, as he's read, he can eclipse it with his little finger. He can. Bloom's observation of anything planetary is worth noting and storing in our mind banks for Part Three of the book, The Homecoming.

Further interesting incidents occur en-route. Two coincidences. First, Bloom sees John Howard Parnell,[10] Provost of the City of Dublin, as he walks towards the DBC: Dublin Bakery Company or, as Mulligan will observe in episode ten, 'Damn Bad Cakes'. John Howard is brother of the great and late Charles Stuart Parnell, of whom Bloom was just thinking. John Howard did not particularly seek the exalted position of Provost, he had, as it were, greatness thrust upon him by virtue of his brother. Then, another coincidence. Out of nowhere, Bloom hears:

> Of the twoheaded octopus, one of whose heads is the head upon which the ends of the world have forgotten to come while the other speaks with a Scotch accent. The tentacles . . . [11]

and it fades away.

What on earth is going on? One gradually realises, that Bloom has overheard a snippet of conversation. A bearded man, pushing a bicycle, is talking to his female escort as they pass the ambling Bloom. Bloom notes it is George Russell.[12] The woman, whose lazily fallen stockings indicate to Bloom a lack of concern with personal appearance, Bloom imagines to be Lizzie Twigg, from whom Bloom has recently received a letter. From this narrative we assemble the genesis of the Martha Clifford correspondence. It transpires that Bloom placed an ad in the *Irish Times*, possibly in the local hearts or even, perhaps, the situations vacant section (we learn that the distinction is immaterial for those with eyes to see).[13] Words to the effect that an assistant is sought to aid a literary gentleman: RSVP Mr Henry Flower. Of the many replies he received, one was from a Lizzie Twigg who cites experience as an assistant to the eminent essayist, Mr George Russell. Bloom was only just thinking of them both and notes the further coincidence. A third would be the earlier sight of Blazes Boylan outside the Red Bank Seafood Restaurant. Coincidences are significant for Joyce.

George Russell is of interest. An editor and essayist often writing under the pseudonym AE, he was then, and remains, a respected and influential figure in Irish literary and philosophical circles. We will properly engage him next episode via Stephen but Joyce clearly thinks we need some Bloom prep. A man of diverse interests, but of relevance here is Theosophy; an interesting coagulation of eastern mysticism, Hinduism, Christianity and a *soupçon* of Jewish *Kabbalah*. It was in vogue in *fin de siècle* Ireland and elsewhere in Europe. Russell was a proponent for the cause but the leading stalwart was a London-based Russian lady, Mrs Helena Petrovna Blavatsky.[14] Beware, 'Normal

People seeking Normal Joyce'! This is a foxhole from which we may struggle to emerge but, if it intrigues, further research on theosophy will not go unrewarded in understanding some of the book's inner mysteries. We shall do it a little justice but, for now, it is relegated beneath Bloom's competing emotions of sex and food. The imagined Lizzy Twigg and her wrinkled stockings are not to Bloom's taste; actually quite off-putting sexually. And she was way too compliant, even with docile George Russell and his gentle mansplaining. Bloom prefers his women in tight jodhpurs, in charge and ready for country pursuits. He's also sceptical of Theosophist occultism and unconvinced by the linked vegetarianism: though he's no fan of needless killing of animals either. Eat beef and the cows' eyes will follow you to eternity.[15] And he recalls awful experiences when working for the cattle trader Cuffe he attended the slaughterhouse. But he's tried those nut steaks, pretending to be beef; no taste and gave him a lot of wind. Bloom here tries to align his sympathetic nature with his immediate hunger and his stomach wins out.

He passes clocks: time ticking on towards four pm. It was at a dance about a month ago that he suspects Molly started the fling with Boylan. He recalls that the band played Ponchielli's 'Dance of the Hours'.[16] Strolling home afterwards along the River Tolker, he and her, walking ahead, she sings a line, he completes it.[17] Their hands brush against each other's in secret signal; he asks with his finger, her finger stealthily answers . . . 'yes'. So it begins. Yet despite this unsavoury memory, as he looks in the windows of the upmarket shops on Grafton Street,[18] his thoughts are only for what nice pretty thing he could buy for Molly, if he can only place the Keyes ad.

Bloom arrives at the Burton restaurant in Duke Street and peers inside from the doorway. Cautious Odysseus. The graphic sight that greets him deserves a full airing:

> His heart astir he pushed in the door of the Burton restaurant. Stink gripped his trembling breath: pungent meatjuice, slop of greens. See the animals feed.
>
> Men, men, men.
>
> Perched on high stools by the bar, hats shoved back, at the tables calling for more bread no charge, swilling, wolfing gobfuls of sloppy food, their eyes bulging, wiping wetted moustaches. A pallid suetfaced young man polished his tumbler knife fork and spoon with his napkin. New set of microbes. A man with an infant's saucestained napkin tucked round him shovelled gurgling soup down his gullet. A man spitting back on his plate:

halfmasticated gristle: no teeth to chewchewchew it. Chump chop from the grill. Bolting to get it over. Sad booser's eyes. Bitten off more than he can chew. Am I like that? See ourselves as others see us. Hungry man is an angry man. Working tooth and jaw. Don't! O! A bone! That last pagan king of Ireland Cormac in the schoolpoem choked himself at Sletty southward of the Boyne. Wonder what he was eating. Something galoptious. Saint Patrick converted him to Christianity. Couldn't swallow it all however.

—Roast beef and cabbage.

—One stew.

Smells of men. His gorge rose. Spaton sawdust, sweetish warmish cigarette smoke, reek of plug, spilt beer, men's beery piss, the stale of ferment.

Couldn't eat a morsel here. Fellow sharpening knife and fork, to eat all before him, old chap picking his tootles. Slight spasm, full, chewing the cud. Before and after. Grace after meals. Look on this picture then on that. Scoffing up stewgravy with sopping sippets of bread. Lick it off the plate, man! Get out of this.

He gazed round the stooled and tabled eaters, tightening the wings of his nose.

—Two stouts here.

—One corned and cabbage.

That fellow ramming a knifeful of cabbage down as if his life depended on it. Good stroke. Give me the fidgets to look. Safer to eat from his three hands. Tear it limb from limb. Second nature to him. Born with a silver knife in his mouth. That's witty, I think. Or no. Silver means born rich. Born with a knife. But then the allusion is lost.

An illgirt server gathered sticky clattering plates. Rock, the bailiff, standing at the bar blew the foamy crown from his tankard. Well up: it splashed yellow near his boot. A diner, knife and fork upright, elbows on table, ready for a second helping stared towards the foodlift across his stained square of newspaper. Other chap telling him something with his mouth full. Sympathetic listener. Table talk. I munched hum un thu Unchster Bunk un Munchday. Ha? Did you, faith?

Mr Bloom raised two fingers doubtfully to his lips. His eyes said.

—Not here. Don't see him.

Out. I hate dirty eaters.

He backed towards the door. Get a light snack in Davy Byrne's. Stopgap. Keep me going. Had a good breakfast.

—Roast and mashed here.

—Pint of stout.

Every fellow for his own, tooth and nail. Gulp. Grub. Gulp. Gobstuff.

He came out into clearer air and turned back towards Grafton street. Eat or be eaten. Kill! Kill![19]

We have just witnessed the Lestrygonian cannibals. Bloom enjoys his meat as much as anyone but he's not a messy eater and detests that as much as a messy stocking. It's not what but how one eats.

So he moves on to Davy Byrne's a quieter pub. Bloom calls it a moral pub, which is an interesting adjective. He respects Mr Byrne whom, Bloom observes, doesn't chat much to patrons but leaves them to enjoy their refreshment. What we will observe is that Davy Byrne is actually quite the chatterbox, just not with Bloom. It's a famous scene, not least because the pub is still there[20] and each Bloomsday Edwardian replicants flock there for Gorgonzola and mustard sandwiches, washed down with a glass of burgundy. After those thoughts of theosophy and the repulsion of the Burton, a vegetarian snack – the grape, the grain, the cheese. Well almost vegetarian, not meat, anyway. Again cautious Odysseus not jumping wholeheartedly into vegetarianism, hanging back outside the harbour to see what will unfold. Bloom steering his own course a temperate middle ground, between flesh and vegetable,.

Nosey Flynn, a throwback to *Dubliners*,[21] is there in his usual seat. Not a handsome man in the traditionally accepted sense; jug ears, protruding duck lips and an unfortunate and distracting dew drop that intermittently droops from his nose before, in defiance of gravity, is snuffled up. Amidst snuffles, he engages Bloom. Further dagger reminders of Molly's tour next week coinciding with the heat of the mustard hitting the back of his throat. The pub clock, by tradition, five minutes fast, says 2 o'clock. Bloom settles into a seat by the widow a safe distance from Nosey Flynn and with his thoughts for company. Food, sex, sex, food, time, misery. He's muddled and the narrative mentioned earlier doesn't help:

Wine soaked and softened rolled pith of bread mustard a moment mawkish cheese.[22]

But then... better:

Mild fire of wine kindled his veins. I wanted that badly. Felt so off colour.[23]

Spirits raised, the pendulum swings from food to sex and back. He notes the womanly curves of the sensually smoothed wood forming the bar. He contemplates all sorts of weird and potentially dangerous food and the brave first person to have tried them, risking life: jugged hare, fifty-year-old Chinese eggs. And oysters! God only knows how they became food. Impossible to open and, even if one manages to do so, the inside looks like a lump of phlegm. Who would eat them? Pondering on their apparent aphrodisiac properties, he shivers as his mood darkens. He saw Boylan outside the Red Bank Seafood Restaurant. Eating oysters for virility? Oh God, no! Ah, no R in June. Luckily.

Stomach sated and thoughts of Boylan receding, the pendulum swings again towards romance with a beautiful and sensuous foreshadowing of Molly's famous longer version of similar events. Years ago, atop Howth Head, amidst the rhododendrons, he and Molly lay together. As they kiss, bits of half-eaten seed cake, pass mouth to lover mouth. Mouth to mouth's kiss. They make love for the first time. There's a rustle nearby but it's just a mountain goat evacuating little currents of effluent. A delightful time, before they were married. Considering the timing of Milly's birth, it's why they married. 'Me. And me now',[24] Bloom ruminates, as two flies buzz on the window, stuck in drying paint.

More nihilistic thoughts, Stephen-like, as to the pointlessness of it all. Humans as meaningless consumers. Born, eat, nourish, defecate, reproduce, deteriorate, die, nourish the earth. The happy memory of Howth Head seems a long, long time ago. He thinks of Classical Greek gods. No mundane existence for them. No eight penny lunch at the Burton for them, they eat ambrosia. Wow! Must be like eating electricity. But, he wonders, as they are gods, what happens to the consumed food? He's never heard of a god going to the lavatory. Do they have anuses? Are they bottomless? He's never thought about it before but intends to sneak a look at the statues of Venus and Juno when he goes to the National Library. For, if they do not have anuses, if they are indeed bottomless, then they are not like the rest of us, mere food processors. It gives hope that somewhere, in a godly realm, life is lived on a higher plane, that maybe has a point beyond perpetual repetition.

Human Bloom receives a message from nature that he must urinate; he heads for the facilities. He is discussed in his absence by Davy Byrne and Nosey Flynn. Enter Paddy Leonard, Tom Rochford and Bantam Lyons, the latter being the chap that received the innocent 'Throwaway' tip from Bloom earlier that morning and, indeed, they discuss the Gold Cup. Bloom returns after his toilet, greets all, hello and goodbye, and continues his journey. Cue general disbelief when Bantam Lyons identifies Bloom as the mysterious pundit of this no-hope horse. Not that anyone takes it seriously: it hasn't a chance, despite their suspicion that Bloom is a Freemason and may have secret information.

Bloom heads for Kildare Street.[25] He's about to cross Dawson Street when he sees a slim young man hesitating on the curb and realises that he is blind. Bloom's offer to help is accepted. Guiding the blind stripling amid vans and cabs, he thinks: pass in front of the horse not behind. This is another example of the very subtle ways in which Bloom is connecting with Stephen. Back in episode one, Stephen looks at the smiling Englishman Haines and thinks not to trust him. He mis-recalls the Irish proverb: 'Beware the horns of a bull, the heels of a horse and the smile of a Saxon'.[26] Here, the same proverb runs through Bloom's head. Pass behind a bull, it can't gore you if it can't see you and in front of a horse because he believes that horse anatomy prevents it kicking forward. Leaving aside the accuracy or otherwise of the proverb, an amazing quality of this book is that innocuous sentences, barely noticeable at the time, are gears calibrating to propel the book forward in the most subtle of ways, in this case several episodes later. Moreover, one can't but help to parallel Bloom's pondering upon how the blind perceive colour, shape and form, with Stephen's more intellectual but similar exercise in Proteus. Next episode we will contrast the whirlpool of Plato's whimsical abstract notions, with the practical solid frameworks established by his student, Aristotle. Stephen's mental gyrations in episode three were barely comprehensible but Bloom's clandestine unbuttoning of his waistcoat to try to understand how a yellow-white, smooth stomach is construed by the congenitally blind, brings it to life.

They part. Bloom hums the music of the 'Commendatore' dream sequence from *Don Giovanni*.[27] More food and sex. Blazes Boylan is a fitting Don Giovanni and the song concerns a dinner invite at which there will be retribution. And, of course, by way of further coincidence, there's Blazes Boylan. It's an awful moment for Bloom. One of those unbearable 'he knows that he knows that he knows moments', all of which would have to be suffered by Bloom in a brief handshake greeting to observe the social nicety. That would be intolerably horrible. Bloom makes a run for it and hopes Boylan has not seen him. He thinks the sun over which he has control (he eclipsed it with his little finger before lunch), may have shone directly into Boylan's eyes, obscuring his vision. Bloom runs for the portico of the National Library, he's flustered, his heart booming within his ribcage. He attempts to regain some dignity by raking though his pockets as though looking for something and believes the ruse may have worked.

Safe!

He cannot stop time; it ticks relentlessly towards 4 o'clock but for now he has avoided the immediate confrontation of that reality. He is safe at least from that and can take refuge in the National Library. From what we've seen so far, people amble through the day in this city without doing much of anything. Bloom's next distraction from Molly and Boylan is to try to do something constructive, copy that advert from the *Kilkenny People*. This, he believes, will secure the ad for Mr Keyes which in turn will entitle his commission payment and enable him to buy something pretty for Molly from one of those smart shops in Grafton Street.

LECTURE 10, 2 FEBRUARY 2021: EPISODE 9

Scylla, Charybdis and the Cuckolded Bard

Music: Sigh No More Ladies – David Snell

In Aeolus, Stephen checked out but rejected journalism, his creative writing was to veer in an altogether different direction. This episode he will meet more writers but these, at least in their opinion, are a rung or two higher up the intellectual ladder. Indeed these mix in high-falutin literary circles right into the rarefied atmosphere of the finest in Ireland or at least, again, so they like to think.

The bodily organ for this episode is the brain. Please engage it for it is needed in this among the densest episodes in the book. If only to scaremonger, Gifford devotes twenty-two pages of reference explanations to Proteus, our most challenging episode so far. For Scylla, there are sixty-six pages. This is, of course, a silly and arbitrary point and easily explained by this episode being replete with literary references: almost every line and mainly but not exclusively, Shakespearean. To follow even a few of them will knock this brief overview off kilter and brevity demands we must ignore the vast majority. But where does that leave us? What help is a lecture that ignores most of the episode? Particularly as not a single word is dispensable. 'Every word is so deep, Leopold'.[1] But it's not so difficult once worked through, our problem being that one might spend fifteen minutes per sentence.

Hence, a different approach. We shall alight upon selected aspects and in doing so hope to shine some light in this dark corner of the library. In the hope that it's not too flippant an approach, we shall boil down Scylla and Charybdis to certain lifestyle choices and see what these bring to bear upon Stephen's writing and where it otherwise leads us. It's a challenging episode and we use that as excuse for further liberties whereby we do not proceed chronologically but hop around as is convenient to make the point.

Homer is not always that helpful to our task but this time is on the money.[2] Circe advises Odysseus to avoid the way-too-dangerous Wandering Rocks which means, unfortunately, that he must run the narrow gauntlet between Scylla and Charybdis. Scholars think that this corresponds to the narrowest part of the Straights of Messina, barely an arrow flight wide so one must veer either too close to Scylla, a tall cliff, or to Charybdis, a small rock on which grows a single fig tree. Scylla looks ominous. High up in a cave on the cliff, too high to kill, lives a dragon. She has six long necks and, at the end of each, a head full of razor-sharp teeth. Sail too close and she will reach down and eat six of the crew. She can't be fought, loss of men is inevitable. So, the Charybdis fig tree it is; how bad can a fig tree be? Well, unfortunately, it's pretty bad. At irregular times a day, a whirlpool deep beneath sucks down anything sailing by the rock and, if caught in that, the whole fleet will be lost for it consumes everything in its wake.

There's the choice: inevitable loss of six or probable loss of all. The devil and the deep blue sea, rock and a hard place, etc, etc.

We'll consider some choices but for now let's establish our bearings. We are in the Assistant Librarian's office in the National Library of Ireland, then, as now, 7–9 Kildare Street, quite near Trinity College. Stephen's task is to deliver the remaining copy of Deasy's letter to another newspaper editor, George Russell, editor of the *Irish Homestead*[3] who is there meeting the Head Librarian. But this disguises Stephen's real purpose, which is to impress or simply lock horns with some of Dublin's literati.

Bloom will also come to the library. At the end of the last episode he arrived at the library portico, heart panic-pumping after a near-miss with Blazes Boylan. He needs to find the Keys advert, with its crossed Keys design, in a back edition of the *Kilkenny People* and copy it out for Counsellor Nannetti. And while he's there, will rectum-check that statue of Venus.[4]

Now, Stephen has his theory concerning Hamlet and you may recall Mulligan provocatively summarised it for Haines, in episode one:

> It's quite simple. He proves by algebra that Hamlet's grandson is Shakespeare's grandfather and that he himself is the ghost of his own father.[5]

The assembled dignitaries have heard about it and while sounding preposterous, it intrigues them. Whether it's a real theory is neither here nor there. There is a race to be run as a prelude to the Ascot Gold Cup in an hour or so and it is called the Stephen Dedalus Handicap. Has he got what it takes to become Ireland's new literary genius? Can he, and, if so, how, achieve his aim to forge in the smithy of his soul, the conscience of his race. Whether he regards the three sat around that library table as equipped to arbitrate we shall see, but they are the hurdle to be faced. One may ask; what has Shakespeare and Hamlet in particular, got to do with that: our story and the Homeric legend that underpins it? The answer may lay in usurpation, dead parents and guilt-ridden offspring; these might be golden threads that guide through Odysseus, Shakespeare, Hamlet, Leopold Bloom and Stephen Dedalus.

The episode features just five people, excluding Mulligan who enters later, and Bloom, with a cameo. Let's meet them: they are all real people, save Stephen, and you know who he is.

Presenting the cast for this evening's performance:

Mr Thomas W Lyster, referred to by Joyce throughout as, the 'Quaker Librarian' and was top-dog at Ireland's National Library from 1895–1920.

Mr William K Magee, Assistant Director of the Library. He also edited the literary periodical *Dana* and was an essayist, under the pseudonym John Eglington; an older, slightly stuffy, figure. Notably, *Dana* rejected some of Joyce's work,[6] not that Joyce was one to bear a grudge.

Mr George Russell.[7] We met him last time as he walked past Bloom pushing a bicycle and talking about an octopus. Editor of the *Irish Homestead,* which is an interesting periodical concerning practical, homespun agricultural issues, vegetarianism and local self-sufficiency. But, especially under AE's helm, there was always room for cultural issues. A proponent of the Irish Literary Revival, he moved in mystic and theosophist circles. He was and remains, an influential cultural figure.

Mr Richard Best. Not arrived as we begin the episode, but will join shortly. Assistant Director of the Library and, like Magee, a future top-dog. A younger man and cuts a more dashing figure than Magee. Joyce plays on his Ulster accent and rather unfairly hints at a slower wit,[8] whereas the real Richard Best was a respected academic with a fertile mind.

Mr Stephen Dedalus, who needs no introduction.

We sit in the high-domed private office of the Assistant Director. *Dramatis personae* orbit the table, sitting, save the Quaker Librarian who hovers as he pops in and out. What light there is, is provided by green semi-translucent desk lamps that cast the protagonists in murky *aurora borealis* shadow. Whilst it's a normal discussion of highly intellectual issues, there is a hint of a séance. One expects dialogue in this mini theatre and, by and large, one can work out who says what. Interior monologue is all Stephen and the narrator, much like through the

Telemachiad, are in the Stephen camp. The lay-out of the episode falls into two, split by the entry of Buck Mulligan.

Let's consider those choices to which we alluded at the outset. As we peruse the episode we might note at least twenty fairly binary choices to be made, generally by Stephen. We examine just the following few and hope thereby to achieve some understanding.

Plato versus Aristotle;
Journalism versus Irish Literary Revival;
Married versus Single;
Conjugal Love versus Scortatory Love;
London/Paris versus Stratford/Dublin,
Father versus Mother, and, finally,
Mooney's versus The Ship.

Brevity precludes consideration of:

Alcoholism versus Temperance;
Homosexuality versus Heterosexuality;
Swimming versus Drowning;
Simon Dedalus father versus Leopold Bloom father;
Real Name versus Pseudonym;
Sinning versus Holy Vows;
Classical Style versus Romantic Style.

Some of these, like the Quaker Librarian, may pop in and out and the lines between all of them are blurred.

Let's start with:

Plato versus Aristotle

We, the reader, enter the episode as a fly on the wall, mid-sentence. The Quaker Librarian is talking about Goethe but the context is Stephen's Shakespeare theory and discussion is well underway; we the reader need to catch up. The Librarian is standing, hovering may be the better adjective; creaking his leather shoes as he rocks back and forth, he wants to stay and participate but must not neglect his other duties – the choreography of a polite man and dedicated professional.

He says:

> The beautiful ineffectual dreamer who comes to grief against hard facts. One always feels that Goethe's judgements are so true. True in the larger analysis.[9]

Our first choice. We want to dream but life's realities intrude. But what is real? We were prepped in Proteus, episode three, as Stephen strolled along the beach, noting the signs he the artist was there to read but unsure if he could trust what he saw. Was any of it real? Let's remind ourselves of the gist of Plato's world of ideas, distilled through Bishop Berkeley, Immanuel Kant and Arthur Schopenhauer. All that pain we endured in Proteus. There is a reality out there but beyond our ability to comprehend for our understanding is limited by the sensory equipment we have and, from which, signals are dispatched to and interpreted by our limited brains. Take, for example, a red book placed on a table. Our brain interprets the image. Whether it really is a book of whatever colour is unknown, what we have is our idea of a red book. We only exist and can only exist in a world of ideas. Aristotle was a student of Plato and he takes this point but considers it unacceptable. We have to make some practical sense of our world if only to preserve sanity, so he defined, categorised, reconciled and codified. He created a sturdy framework of principles upon which we can rely, if not utterly, then sufficiently to exist within this ephemeral cloud of Plato's ideas.

Thus we have our allegorical parameters. Scylla, the imposing sturdy cliff, is the Aristotelean rock of hard facts; Charybdis, the whirlpool of dreamy platonic ideals and ideas.

Our next choice is:

Journalism versus Irish Literary Revival

Newspapers deal in hard facts, with scant room for aesthetics and creative writing. Deadlines must be met and articles, whether accurate, well-written or otherwise, will all be tomorrow's fish wrapping. It is undoubtedly Scylla, hard-rock of hard-hitting headlines. Myles Crawford virtually draws a picture of the dragon when he says to Stephen: 'I want you to write something for me . . . Something with a bite in it. You can do it . . .'[10]

The Irish Literary Revival is not a style of writing, so there's no direct comparison. It, as we briefly considered earlier,[11] is rather more a general embodiment of the promotion of all that is culturally Gaelic and may be said to be the genteel cultural end of anti-British sentiment; and sentiment being the word, as Joyce felt that its proponents tended toward the sentimental – the folklore, the glorious Celtic myth of yore. Its central tenet was the promotion of the Gaelic language which was quite a task for its usage in the early twentieth century had fast diminished as previously considered with the Shan Van Voch and elsewhere.[12] Richard Best will disclose that Haines has gone to seek the book *Lovesongs of Connacht* by Douglas Hyde,[13] poet, President of the Gaelic League and, indeed, would in due course be the first President of Ireland. His poetry might be said to typify the said sentimentality and is, we presume, why Joyce introduces him at this point and via Haines.

We can see that the promotion, indeed glorification, of mythical stories and ideas in a language that relatively few could understand as quite platonic/Charybdian. Hence, the revival movement, that may have grown out of well-meaning anti-imperialist ideals, was paradoxically but inevitably (as it entailed study of a language), elitist and exclusivist. We shall see in episode twelve that the idea of an ancient and powerful Irish race has broader appeal at a certain level but, as far as language and literature go, it was generally the preserve of foreign scholars like Haines (one of the few in the book, perhaps the only one, to speak Gaelic)[14] and the Irish aristocracy and academia or their immediate circles such as Lady Gregory and W B Yeats.

Think back to the flowery, overblown prose of Dan Dawson as laughed at by Simon Dedalus and Ned Lambert in Aeolus.[15] W B Yeats was particularly helpful to Joyce as he struggled to make his name, yet Joyce, in quite typical fashion, accepted the help and rubbished the helper, nonetheless. He acknowledged the beautiful craftsmanship of Yeats' poetry but considered much of the subject-matter – Irish legends, mysticism and the occult – at best, irrelevant, stagnating and away with the fairies, but also as potentially dangerous and we shall consider this danger in episode twelve. In 1905 Joyce published a poem called 'The Holy Office'[16] which, without naming names, was scathingly critical of the main ILR protagonists.

Around our table, the ILR is represented, primarily but not exclusively, by George Russell. There has clearly been some discussion of Hamlet which Stephen has placed in the context of Shakespeare's personal life experience:

> All these questions are purely academic, Russell oracled out of his shadow. I mean, whether Hamlet is Shakespeare or James I or Essex. Clergymen's discussions of the historicity of Jesus. Art has to reveal to us ideas formless spiritual essences. The supreme question about a work of art is out of how deep a life does it spring. The painting of Gustave Moreau is the painting of ideas. The deepest poetry of Shelley, the words of Hamlet bring our mind into contact with the eternal wisdom, Plato's world of ideas. All the rest is the speculation of schoolboys for schoolboys.[17]

And a little later, he continues:

> Interesting only to the parish clerk. I mean, we have the plays. I mean when we read the poetry of King Lear what is it to us how the poet lived? . . . Peeping and prying into greenroom gossip of the day, the poet's drinking, the poet's debts. We have King Lear: and it is immortal.[18]

More Platonic/Charybdian sentiment. Who cares about real life detail when we have the ideas of the plays? To contextualise, we must consider the point Stephen has been trying to make and that entails getting into his Hamlet theory. Let us preface that, with this. *Hamlet* is considered one of if not the finest of the Shakespearean plays and the general school of thought is that, if Shakespeare, actor as well as author, would personally have played any character it would surely have been the star-turn, Prince Hamlet: the brooding, moody young man who dominates almost every scene and whose birthright has been stolen by his evil uncle, Claudius. However, Stephen's contrary point is that Shakespeare identifies not with Hamlet, the son and Prince, but with Hamlet, the dead father and ex-King, the ghost of Act One, Scene Five: he that was cuckolded by Queen Gertrude and murdered by her lover, and his brother, Claudius, who by murder most foul, usurped both throne and queen. The ghost appears before his son to report the ghastly news and implores him to avenge. Stephen expands upon his theory: more than mere identification with the ghost, Stephen suggests that Shakespeare wrote the play, indeed all of his plays, to express and even exorcise the personal angst arising out of his own circumstances – either intentionally or sub-consciously.

Stuffy Eglinton nails his colours to the mast early doors. Stephen will have a stern task persuading him that Shakespeare associated with the ghostly ex-King, a minor walk-on part, rather than the Prince of Denmark, the central character. On such matters his opinion is as firm as a rock – which neatly returns us to the rock, Scylla. Let's consider Stephen's theory from the solid Aristotelean perspective which is that Shakespeare, a writer of international renown, translated into French, German and a host of other languages, did not create the plays out of a Platonic, whimsical whirlpool: he drew on his own real-life experiences. And, with all respect to George Russell, Stephen's point is that the plays alone are insufficient; they can only be properly understood in the context of the poet's drinking and the poet's debts. So, and this is Stephen formulating what are still muddled thoughts: if there is someone sufficiently talented to write the definitive book of the Irish (one wonders, who he has in mind?) such author must surely draw on real-life, everyday experience and not hark back to mythical Celtic warriors who rescue nymphs and maidens in Erin, the land beyond the rainbow. But his theory, so far, is half-baked. Why would Shakespeare, alive, kicking and doing pretty damn well in London, identify with a murdered man whose kingdom had been usurped? He was a successful playwright; his wife and family, whom he left voluntarily, were back in Stratford while he was living it up in London.

Stephen has won the attention of his audience and grows in confidence to make his point by providing further detail of Shakespeare's personal life. This brings us to our next choice.

Married versus Single

It's a very well-worn point that 16 June 1904 was personally significant for Joyce it being his first date with Nora. As suggested in Proteus, an aspect of this fictional day is that it shall, later in the evening, mark the emergence of Stephen, guided unknowingly by Bloom, from the chrysalis of self-absorption to the path of mature life, as enriched by the opening up to and sharing with others. In other words, the single man realises it's time to take a wife. Stephen, this day, will only take the first tentative steps along such a path but we need to keep it in mind and it is relevant here. In the summer of 1582 William Shakespeare and Anne Hathaway had sex in a cornfield. It may, as pedantic Richard Best points out, have been a rye-field. She was 26, he 18 and technically a minor. They were shotgun married in the November prior to the birth of Susanna. Some years later, Will spends most of his time in London having become the enormously successful playwright and businessman that we know. He returns periodically and, in fruition of which, Ann gives birth to twins in 1585: a daughter Judith and Hamnet, a son. Hamnet tragically dies aged eleven, in 1596, probably plague-related. The play *Hamlet* premiered in 1609 and the names Hamlet and Hamnet are used interchangeably during Shakespeare's life. Stephen's point is that Shakespeare was deprived of any real choice as to marriage and of the opportunity to sow his wild oats and, therefore, the ability to sexually mature as a young man might. He parallels Shakespeare's poem, 'Venus and Adonis',[19] in which the goddess of love attempts to seduce the young man, barely a man, Adonis. But he prefers to go boar hunting and is killed, gorged with ironic symmetry, on a boar's tusk. Stephen's contention is that, notwithstanding Will's infidelity in London, it was the premature taking of his virginity and trapping him in marriage that emasculated him. His confidence with women was shot, poor lamb, and this haunted him all his days. Yes: wild oats were sown and plenty of them but way too late.

He says:

> That memory, Venus and Adonis, lay in the bedchamber of every light-of-love in London . . . Do you think the writer of Antony and Cleopatra, a passionate pilgrim, had his eyes in the back of his head that he chose the ugliest doxy in all Warwickshire to lie withal? . . . He chose badly? He was chosen, it seems to me. If others have their will, Ann hath a way. By cock, she was to blame. She put the comether on him, sweet and twenty-six. The grey eyed goddess who bends over the boy Adonis, stooping to conquer, as prologue to the swelling act, is a boldfaced Stratford wench who tumbles in a cornfield a lover younger than herself.[20]

And later, after his sceptical detractors look askew, being asked to believe that the writer of *Romeo and Juliet*, a playboy, was emotionally, a crippled wreck of a man . . .

> Why? Belief in himself has been untimely killed. He was overborn in a cornfield first (ryefield, I should say) and he will never be a victor in his own eyes after nor play victoriously the game of laugh and lie down. Assumed dongiovannism will not save him. No later undoing will undo the first undoing. The tusk of the boar has wounded him there where love lies ableeding.[21]

Thus we have a killing: a killing of Shakespeare's sexual and perhaps broader self-confidence. And the killer has been identified – Ann Hathaway. Hence Shakespeare's (and Stephen's) affinity to the ghost, of whom, by the way, Leopold Bloom was thinking around the same time.[22] Further, whilst Stephen acknowledges that among the characteristics of a ghost, death ranks pretty high, it is not exclusive. A ghost might be also someone alive but long-departed geographically, say, to London from Stratford. For emphasis, he sets the scene at the Globe Theatre on the south bank of the Thames. It's the day of the premier of *Hamlet* and, in this imaginary version, the ghost played by Shakespeare, speaks to Prince Hamlet, played by Richard Burbage[23]:

> Hamlet, I am thy father's spirit - bidding him to list. To a son he speaks, the son of his soul, the prince, young Hamlet and to the son of his body, Hamnet Shakespeare, who has died in Stratford that his namesake may live for ever.[24]

Thus, the analogy is partially clarified. Character ghost speaks to character Hamlet, whilst, simultaneously, author Shakespeare speaks to his dead son Hamnet ,who, had he lived, would have been, give or take, Hamlet's age (and thereby also Stephen's). In both cases (perhaps all three cases), the message is the same: the ghost was killed and the son denied his birthright. In both cases, the queen is guilty. Gertrude we know is guilty of infidelity with the dead king's brother. The charge against Ann Hathaway, as we will shortly learn, is strikingly similar.

Let's pause for breath.

Stephen has a dual purpose here, leaving aside, for now, the Deasy letter. On the one hand he's trying to impress his audience in the room. He'll shortly be asked by Eglington if he believes his theory (as yet unresolved) and Stephen replies that he does not. But he's displaying his immense breadth of knowledge and mental agility to make a rational case out of an outlandish claim. At the same time, Stephen is trying to work things out in his mind and playing with broader concepts which support his theory, such concepts animate several significant themes in the book. What is he trying to work through? His guilt over his mother; his resentment of perceived usurpation, his attitude toward women and, in particular, a life partner? Other giants, such as Catholicism and politics, are already nearer resolution. And why is he trying to work these things out? For art's sake: to be a better forger in the smithy of his soul.[25]

Thirty-something Joyce (at the time of writing the episode) is returning to his 22-year-old self to resolve what were then, the unresolved aspects. On the very day Joyce meaningfully meets Nora, Stephen reflects on Shakespeare, the Saxon, his literary Virgil.[26] He observes his guide's aspect to women and to marriage and it ain't turning out so good with Ann Hathaway. Against such a backdrop, as yet unknown to Stephen but apparent to the reader, a similar story is being played out between Leopold and Molly Bloom. We know by now that Bloom will be some sort of guide for Stephen and, significantly, at the conclusion of episode fifteen, while Stephen lies a-bleeding in the road, Bloom, his carer, will see an apparition of eleven-year-old Rudy. At the age of Hamnet's death, Rudy will resurrect in apparition and, at the age of Hamlet's death, Stephen will arise from the road: multiples of eleven, the number of re-birth.

Eglinton's comment on marriage is to say that Shakespeare's finest creation was the bachelor Falstaff.[27] Mulligan will, later in the episode, observe that Eglington, Best and Russell are all unmarried. He banters homosexuality and, with typical vulgarity, that their sex lives are confined close at hand, their own. Which neatly brings us to scortatory or sinful love?

Marital Love versus Scortatory Love

Stephen presses on, as does Shakespeare. His literary creations reveal inner rage and sexual violence; the rape of Lucrecia,[28] the attempted rape of Imogen.[29] Numb to his own sexual gorging and revealing his true self only in his plays. This links to a further significant point. Ghostly ex-King Hamlet tells his son he was murdered in his sleep by his brother Claudius pouring hemlock into his ear. How can he know this, if he was asleep at the vital moment? Only, Stephen avers, by permission of a superior power, his creator. Thus Shakespeare is creator. Son, he may no longer be; his father has died.[30] Father to his son he may no longer be; his son has died. Yet father to world literature he is. Creator of all characters reaching back in time and so he is indeed, in this sense, father of the grandfather; the son, consubstantial with the father. And Stephen maintains that his plays continue to reveal his life. Ann, the overbearing woman, is revealed in *Anthony and Cleopatra,* as Katherine in the *Taming of the Shrew*, among others.

And her infidelity?

In later life, with Will still, by and large, absent, Ann turns to religion and accommodates religious lodgers, though quite where they slept, Stephen mischievously posits, is conjecture. But back in her prime, what else was going on? This Stephen says is revealed by further analysis of the plays. Shakespeare had three brothers Richard, Edmund and Gilbert.[31] The latter does not appear in the *oeuvre* but Richard and Edmond are two of the three worst villains he created, the third being Iago. Richard: the only King in all of Shakespeare's plays not cast in a flattering light. Stephen's point is that, while Will was away in London, Ann did the dirty, the beast with two backs,[32] with one or both of them. Ann Hathaway as Gertrude, adulteress, fornicating with the King's brother; killer of the King. Shakespeare is telling the world via the play *Hamlet,* whilst, at the same stroke, bestowing immortality upon his dead son. Hamnet died but finds immortality in *Hamlet*.

Stephen continues: why should *Hamlet* not be this secret conveyer of truth? Look how his other plays are also drawn from reality. Take for example, *The Merchant of Venice*: why would Shakespeare, himself a moneylender, draw Shylock in such an unfavourable light? Why? Because he was pandering to the mob. Queen Elizabeth's personal physician was a man called Lopez, a Spanish Jew. He fell under the spotlight once war was declared with Spain and was accused, on trumped-up charges, of plotting to kill her. Amidst an anti-Jewish furore, the Queen had him hung, drawn and quartered.[33] Stephen cites *Macbeth, Love's Labour's Lost* and *The Merry Wives of Windsor* as further examples of topical reality providing structure to the narrative..

He bolsters his case with the further claim that betrayal and usurpation features in most of the plays:

> Why? Steven answered himself. Because the theme of the false or the usurping or the adulterous brother or all three in one is to Shakespeare, what the poor is not, always with him. The note of banishment, banishment from the heart, banishment from home, sounds uninterruptedly from The Two Gentlemen of Verona onward till Prospero breaks his staff, buries it certain fathoms in the earth and drowns his book.[34]

Yet, his later plays, the Quaker Librarian, good man, faithful man, believer in marriage, points out, are actually less violent. Does this suggest Shakespeare reconciled with Ann? Perhaps, says Stephen, but to have a reconciliation, there must first have been a sundering and, if there was reconciliation, one must find out why. His daughter Susanna presents a grandchild. Shakespeare returns to Stratford to enjoy his family and his indulged granddaughter (a Richie Goulding little lump of love[35]), revealed in the later plays as Perdita, Miranda and Marina.[36]

We then have quite an illuminating line: 'There can be no reconciliation, Stephen said, if there has not been a sundering. Said that.'[37]

Breaking that down, the first five words are dialogue. Then narration 'Stephen said', then seven more words to complete Stephen's dialogue. Finally, two words of inner monologue – 'Said that'; Stephen thinks to himself that he's committed a *faux pas*. It's a really good line but he said the same thing just a few moments earlier. Why would Joyce write him not only doing so but then emphasising to the reader that he did it? The answer might lie in an earlier claim about Shakespeare's regretful marriage to Ann. Eglinton says Shakespeare erred but at least then made the best of a bad job by living apart from her in London.

Stephen then replied: 'Bosh! Stephen said rudely. A man of genius makes no mistakes. His errors are volitional and are the portals of discovery.'[38] Joyce makes Stephen repeat a line not in error but because he really wants us to take the point: because it is a portal of discovery. So just what is the point?

To find out, we seamlessly proceed under the subheading:

London/Paris versus Stratford/Dublin

Stephen's been in Paris; Shakespeare's been in London. Both are bastions of literary refinement and from which both men return to comparative backwaters. Stephen returned to Dublin a ghost of his former ambitious self. An Icarus with clipped wings, now a low-flying or, in his case, no flying Lapwing, having returned steerage to Newhaven; his only Bohemian souvenirs, a couple of secreted French erotic magazines. But Dublin, it transpires, was his destiny and thence to be a father of literature. All and any of these cities could be either Scylla or Charybdis. What we might think about is a middle path – two opposites drawing closer, cities merging. The philosopher Giordano Bruno,[39] quite an influence upon Joyce and particularly noticeable in *Finnegans Wake*, writes of the coincidence of opposites. After being cast asunder, bodies naturally and inevitably, reconcile. A universal truth from atoms to the expanding universe is that opposites repel and then harmonise. In the last Lecture we considered coincidences and their significance for Joyce, here is further construction of the word, of things coinciding, coming together.

Now, enter Mr Bloom . . .

Not into the domed office itself but his dark shadow can be seen through opaque glass in the corridor beyond, where the Quaker Librarian treats him so decently in guiding him to the section housing back issues of domestic newspapers. It's an incident all the more striking because, thus far, we have only seen Bloom dealt with in off-hand manner. Lyster resembles George Fox[40] the founder of the Quaker movement, a man who remained true to his moral principles despite a hunted existence. Fox, hunted. Bloom arrived at the library as a hunted animal. We won't see him again, and the middle-way he might represent, until Stephen departs the building. Stephen meanwhile, presses on with his theory and, stirred by Eglington, moves to a serious point on the notion of fatherhood.

Father versus Mother

Eglington agrees with George Russell; the Bard's family circumstances are inconsequential. In his opinion, one need only look to the Bard's finest character, Falstaff, a single man. Stephen thinks this speaks more to Eglington's own circumstances as not only a confirmed bachelor but a man embarrassed by his country bumpkin of a father.

At the beginning of *The Odyssey*, Athena asks Telemachus if he is the son of Odysseus. The youth replies: 'I'm told I am but who can really know their own father?'[41] Fatherhood, says Stephen, is a mystical state, created in a moment's rutting, as Stephen may potentially have done in the brothels of Paris. Fatherhood inevitably leans Oedipal; the growth of the son contrasts the demise of the father as they vie for the love of the mother. He thinks of his own father. A man blessed, like the original Daedalus, with wit and creativity but is drowning and has allowed himself to drown in alcoholism and gambling debt to the extent that he cannot support his family. Stephen fears that, unless he is very careful he will be re-cycled Simon, just as Bloom saw his future self in McCoy when they met outside the post office in Westland Row. No; it's a mother's love, *amor matris*, that is the only reliable truth. Cranley told him so in *A Portrait*[42] and Stephen thought-spoke it to Cyril Sargent in episode two.

And, continues Stephen, Rome underlined this premise. The Vatican powers that be, concerned that the Father/Son notion in the Holy Trinity of Consubstantiation was too difficult a concept for the mob, cynically elevated the importance of the Virgin Mary: The Mother. And this, hundreds of years after heretics were burned at the stake for questioning consubstantiality, suddenly it was all about the mother.[43]

Stephen is not only working though his guilt, again, he is framing a new consubstantiality, a father in literature. Shakespeare, god, creator of all the plays, is father, grandfather and son, all at once. And Stephen, if he can find a Virgil and follow the right path, can be, too. What are we saying: that we no longer need fathers or that the sexes are opposites that inevitably will merge? That is to stretch a point too far but men accessing their feminine sides will do no harm and feature in the second half of the book.

In the midst of all this, Mulligan walks in and announces: '*entr'acte!*'[44]: entitling an expectation of a new tone in the second half of the episode.

Stephen was in mid-flow and, knowing that he's trying very hard to impress, Mulligan sets to deflate him, such is the small-minded nastiness of the Buck. First off, he calls him Kinch, meaning child; apart from condescension, it casts Stephen as son and no father. Lyster returns after attending upon Bloom. The ad-canvasser gave him a business card which the Quaker Librarian leaves on the table when called away again. We know it says L Bloom not H Flower because Mulligan exclaims 'the sheeny!',[45] a derogatory word for a Jew and he tells how he observed Bloom sniffing about the backside of the statue Venus.

Mulligan reaches into his pocket and withdraws a folded telegram. It is from Stephen and he reads it with a flourish. We recall that Stephen had an arrangement to meet Mulligan and Haines in The Ship pub at 12.30. He went instead to Mooney's with the journalists but sent a telegram to explain his absence.

Our final choice:

Mooney's versus The Ship

Stephen had already decided journalism was not for him, so, electing to have a liquid lunch with Prof McHugh, Myles Crawford and J J O'Molloy, was no career move and can only be seen as a rejection of Mulligan. Mulligan is Stephen's usurper just as Boylan is Bloom's, Claudius to Hamlet and Richard and Edmund were to Shakespeare. Remember it was Mulligan who, via his aunt, accuses Stephen of killing his mother.[46]

Mulligan proffers an amusing pastiche in the style of John Millington Singe (notably in the Irish Literary Revival camp) as to how he and Haines were waiting in the pub when Stephen's telegram arrived. He assumed it was sent from the Kips, a red light district, further belittling Stephen in front of everyone. Amidst various other slights, Mulligan accuses Stephen of urinating on Singe's doorstep, when in fact the culprit was the drunken Mulligan. All a pretty childish attempt to undermine Stephen but in doing so Mulligan unintentionally assists his enemy. We mentioned that Lady Gregory was a leading light of the Irish Literary Revival. W B Yeats arranged for Stephen, a bright young poet to review her latest book which would really propel his career. This reflects reality with Joyce. However, Stephen's review is as scathing as was Joyce's in real life.[47] Mulligan asks why Stephen couldn't have reviewed it like Yeats would have done and proceeds to parody in the creepiest sycophantic style that Joyce suggests would have been adopted by Yeats: 'The most beautiful book that has come out of our country in my time. One thinks of Homer.'[48]

Joyce has it in for a number of unfortunate souls and in many ways *Ulysses* is a book of revenge. But, even so, he really seems to have it in for Yeats and here enlists Mulligan to undermine W B Yeats and bolster Stephen as the Irish Homer. The serious take on all this is that Stephen rejects the writers of the Irish Literary Revival as he rejected journalism. Its sentimentality and potential ensuing dangers will be considered in episodes eleven and twelve. Allowing ancient myth to frame one's cultural and political outlook can lurch all too quickly towards fascism as prescient Joyce would see in the next decade in Europe.

George Russell has to leave for a meeting at *The Homestead*. Eglington hopes to see him at George Moore's[49] party that evening. The Irish Literary Revival crowd will be there and even Mulligan and Haines are invited. Stephen is not and it is a little indelicate of Eglington to mention this in front of him. Worse still, it becomes apparent that Russell is creating an anthology of works by Ireland's new young poets. Nothing for Stephen here either, reflecting actuality for Joyce.[50] This personal resentment feeds in to Joyce's treatment of the respected George Russell and also Yeats, Gregory, Millington-Singe and the ILR crowd generally.

Stephen wins a victory of sorts. Eglinton, who started firmly in the Shakespeare as the Prince camp, concedes, that the Bard is father of all. He is after all, consubstantial: The Prince and the King. He is all one.

Exactly says Stephen: 'The boy of act one is the mature man of act five.'[51]

Thus, we see Giordano Bruno's coinciding of opposites gain traction. What start off as opposites, over time attract. The immaturity and radical views of youth are tempered with age. Howsoever we set out to change or reinvent ourselves it is simply new experience building upon and embroidering the same soul.

Whatever we do, or wherever we go in life, we meet ourselves:

> If Socrates leaves his house today he will find the sage seated on his doorstep. If Judas goes forth tonight it is to Judas his steps will tend . . . We walk through ourselves, meeting robbers, ghosts, giants, old men, young men, wives, widows, brothers-in-love. But always ourselves.[52]

Which is a double-edged sword for Stephen because he thinks, despite molecules completely changing every five months, the Stephen that borrowed one pound from George Russell (known as AE) several months ago, might be a different one to him now. But the soul remains the same, so AE, IOU.

Mulligan takes the point. He mimics Zeus who grew the goddess Athena out of his own brain: this subjugation of male/female into a single androgynous self-sufficient state. Mulligan has heard Eglinton's earlier comment on Falstaff and support for the single life, since when he has been surreptitiously scrawling a note. Discussion has drawn to a close and Stephen and Mulligan leave the library. On the way out,

Mulligan shows Stephen the notes. It's the introduction for a play and the vulgar theme is sexual self-sufficiency . . . masturbation.

He calls it:

Everyman his own Wife
or
A Honeymoon in the Hand
(A national immorality in three orgasms)
By
Ballocky Mulligan.[53]

Enough of Mulligan; let's get back to Bloom. We hinted that he may become Stephen's Virgil and a guide along a new path between polar extremes.

As they leave the building, Stephen, for a second time that day, feels a presence behind him. He felt it as he was leaving Sandymount Strand when the presence was a silent three-master schooner out at sea but heading towards Dublin docks. We wondered if it might carry the Odyssean pilgrim returning as Bloom, and indeed we met Bloom a few lines later. This time, it actually is Bloom. Joyce refers to the step of a pard. Dressed in black, we have our black panther, Haines' worst nightmare. Bloom also dreamed the previous night but his dream, with similarities to Stephen's, was a Molly figure dressed in exotic oriental garb. Haines was afraid of the stranger; Stephen, subconsciously and tentatively, seems willing to embrace.

Stephen moves aside to let Bloom through. Mulligan calls him the Wandering Jew which by now we know that, despite the intended slight, might also be an unknowing compliment, alluding to the stranger bearing gifts. Bloom looks at Stephen paternalistically as he passes. Mulligan compounds anti-Semitism with homophobia, suggesting Bloom's glance was an homosexual come-on. Ironic, as Stephen suspects the same of Mulligan, in whom he senses a touch of Cranley from *A Portrait*.[54]

But what has really occurred? Mulligan and Stephen part like Scylla and Charybdis, and Bloom charts the middle course between them: the mesial groove[55] – the middle line, not only of Venus's backside but also in life. It is Bloom, he of the University of Life, leading the way to inclusiveness: personal growth through life experience. To working with and harmonising both Scylla and Charybdis in Consubstantiation; he is in my father, I am within my son. Stephen will not be a journalist but that does not mean rejection of the hard facts of life. He must learn to use real experiences all around him. They must go into the smithy of his soul. Yes, Irish mythology is sentimental but it, too, led by Mananaan MacLir, will go into the mix. And, as Mulligan confides to Stephen his personal disgust of Bloom, Stephen is processing his personal disgust of Mulligan and this new strange empathy towards Bloom. In this book, that begins with a view of the sea and which looks back to the Odyssean sea journey, we may have just had a sea-change.

Back on Kildare Street, the air feels soft and kind as though we have resolution, even if Stephen does not yet appreciate it. There is barely any wind now and smoke from the altar-like chimneys opposite rises undisturbed. The sky is empty of birds, to whom Stephen – Icarus, Aengus of the Birds[56] – has earlier used for augury. He must, in the words of the witch Circe, cease to strive and learn that he does not need to fight the world; he cannot kill Scylla the dragon. All life should be his friend; all is grist to the mill in the smithy of his soul, if he, the part-time algebra teacher, is to be the literary father of his grandfather and of all Ireland.

LECTURE 11, 16 FEBRUARY 2021: EPISODE 10

Wandering Rocks Gather No Moss

Music: The Wanderer – Dion & The Belmonts

This is a clever and informative episode. A totally different style to the preceding but by now we expect no less. The episode falls into nineteen segments: each a bitesize snapshot of an event in Dublin between three and four in the afternoon. Several occur at the same time or near enough. First and last are longer and these bookend the intervening vignettes. Each invites us to listen to its story but none complete and to that end, confuse. As Daedalus created the labyrinth in ancient Crete, so Joyce creates it in Dublin. Many commentators consider this the central episode: it has that feel to it, the very different style with narrator dominant and the suppression of both Stephen and Bloom for the better exploration of minor characters including the city itself. It's the tenth of eighteen episodes and the seventh of the twelve Wanderings of Ulysses, so an off-centre centre. But we reside on a planet that revolves on an off-centre axis and Joyce himself calls it an *entr'acte*, so let's not split hairs. It feels halfway.

Bloom, who features dead centre of the nineteen snapshots, begins to change from that pivot. His demeanour towards Blazes Boylan was totally flustered in Lestrygonians but there's a sense of the worm turning in Sirens. It is also, in a sense, a pause for breath. An escape we think from the intensity of the Stephen and Bloom episodes. But be careful, the clue is in the name that Joyce suggested for the episode: 'The Wandering Rocks'. Accepting Circe's advice, Odysseus does not sail by the wandering rocks, which are thought to be somewhere around the Bosporus, and goes instead via Scylla and Charybdis. Joyce expects his readers to be more intrepid and do both. One can visualise the danger: rocks that appear to be of a certain shape and certain distance until receding waves reveal danger that has surreptitiously wandered way too close. Sailors were very lucky to escape the peril. So, shipmates, be on the lookout! There's likely trouble ahead.

Before we set sail, some safety announcements:

1. Our bodily organ is blood suggesting the city may be a living organism, with arteries for streets and real people with real blood coursing through their veins. Indeed, several characters are based on real people, sometimes under real names. The book gained a

little traction in Dublin in the 1920s, not much as the vast majority of booksellers refused to stock it but, as is the nature of contraband, there was some clamour to clap eyes on it and in particular by those who feared they were in it. Some readers come to this book straight off of the bat, without having previously read Joyce, others move chronologically through *Dubliners* and *A Portrait of the Artist*. The latter approach has the advantage of providing bedrock. The likes of Martin Cunningham, Tom Kernan, Mrs Sinico, Cranley, Lynch, Lenehan, Nosey Flynn, Bantam Lyons, to mention only the tip of the iceberg, all appear in the earlier stories which provide much depth, colour and a sturdiness for *Ulysses*. Several of these and others will appear in this episode and they, and especially the city itself, relegate Stephen and Bloom to the periphery which, after all we've read to now, is a little unsettling.

2. We have an aspect of the weird philosophy Stephen negotiated in Proteus. This is an episode of phenomena: bricks, saucepans, horses, hedges, carriages, books and deep-cut silk blouses. The world as it exists outside of Stephen and Bloom's heads. Can it be trusted?
3. Space not time. Up to now, aside from the re-set at episode 4, the book has progressed chronologically with each episode moving us through the day. By the end of this one, we will be as close to Bloom's feared 4 pm as any other, save the one in which the bell tolls. But, in this episode, time is of lesser consequence than space for we have a bird's eye view of several events in the land that time forgot. They occur, give or take, simultaneously: *Nebeneinander* not *nacheinander*. Time, we now know, is not to be trusted for it might simply be an artificial marker between events; an Aristotelean framework to help maintain sanity in the timeless, spaceless void of Platonic ideals – necessary but unreliable. Dublin runs on Dunsink time which is linked to Greenwich Mean Time, but the parallax allowing for curvature of the earth between the two, retards Dublin time by several minutes. We shall see in this episode if space fares any better within the labyrinth of clashing rocks and clashing people.
4. Father Conmee SJ in No 1 will head to the northern extremity of the city. The Earl of Dudley in No 19 ventures deep south. This contrasts with our longest journey yet; the funeral cortège which travelled opposite: south/north. One thinks again of the Rocks'

historic location on the Bosporus straddling, as it does, Europe and Asia, East and West. Are we supposed to construe our bookending of Church and State also in terms of Europe and Asia, Occident and Orient? That may be to stretch whatever point might exist.

5. We have gear shifts: little devices that seem to re-calibrate the narrative and propel it tangentially. To explain: lurking within many of the vignettes is an alien sentence which simply does not belong. We should not be lulled into thinking these are challenging Joyce poison pills that we do not understand and so overlook, these genuinely do not belong and serve to illustrate *nebeneinander*: different things happening at same time in different parts of the city. They seem unconnected but that may be illusory; they may illuminate rather than shroud. Why does Joyce select that particular gear shift? And why then? Do they fortify the labyrinth or guide a path through it? Many fascinating studies seek to explain them which are beyond this brief overview, but it is worth delving into if time allows, and, if not, at least hovering a while to consider. No doubt Joyce also intended them to mimic the way blood is squeezed upstream through veins and back to the heart, because our bodies have no pump for that return trip, we need our muscles to rhythmically contract and massage the blood back home. That is how we might see these 'gear shifts'.

No 1

Let's not hit a rock just as we start. Father 'Conmee', irrespective of one's views of organised religion, is not setting out to con anyone, never mind you, it's just his name. Very influential in the life of the young Joyce, Father Conmee was a teacher at Clongowes Wood (a well-respected Catholic school in County Kildare) and it was he that was so sorry to learn that seven-year-old Jimmy Joyce was forced to leave due to financial constraints, he pulled strings for enrolment at Belvedere College the far cheaper but still Jesuit alternative in the centre of Dublin. Indeed, recognising the kid's potential, he arranged for Joyce (and maybe Stanislaus, too) to receive a full bursary. He's on a similarly altruistic and well-meaning mission here: headed to see Brother Swann, the Father Provincial in Artane, to discuss a possible bursary for one of the Dignam children. But don't think Joyce will give him a free ride, Father Conmee, after all, represents the Catholic hierarchy, which, as we know, is near the top of the JJ hit-list. We are warned by the language in the first two lines that all may not be plain sailing. Words like 'superior', 'reset' and 'smooth' are all apt to confuse or trap the unwary.

We are treated to considerable interior monologue as the priest makes his way north. It is a welcome change to be inside someone else's head. But something's off, it's a little strange. For example, when he greets the young Belvedere schoolboys:

> And were they good boys at school? Oh that was very good now. And what was his name? Jack Sohan. And his name? Ger. Gallagher. And the other little man? His name was Brunny Lynam. Oh, that was a very nice name to have.[1]

Use of 'his' and 'was' suggests this is not all dialogue. Some dialogue seems mixed with narrative reflection upon the dialogue that occurred; yet it has a feel of a live recording and one inside Fr Conmee's head – if not his voice, then whose? We are not sure and although it provides an appealing warmth, we should take care. The narrator is in charge and as unreliable as the shifting rocks.[2]

Conmee walks. He greets and blesses various people, young children, the wife of David Sheehy, MP. The one-legged sailor, begging for cash, may feel aggrieved with only a blessing for his trouble but, before we lambast Fr.Conmee, SJ, Jesuit priests may only carry the money strictly needed for their day, in this case, tram fare, so we might give the benefit of the doubt. Though hang on, he does, in that opening paragraph, mention walking to Artane so this may be a mild rebuke at elevating his own personal comfort over the needs of the beggar.

He walks towards the Malahide Road from whereabouts he will get a tram to Artane. The stage performer Mr Eugene Stratton[3] gives a gleaming Negro smile from a large billboard poster as the tram passes. This is a white man, blacked up, vaudeville-style, which was acceptable in 1904 and which, to our collective shame, continued to be so up to around the time of the 'Black and White Minstrels' in the 1970s, when thankfully, it sank without trace. It makes Fr Conmee think of the millions of Africans condemned to a fiery hell for lack of a baptism. This depresses Fr Conmee but he takes consolation in an article by a Belgian Jesuit that put the numbers at acceptable levels. This is one of several examples of Conmee overlooking unfortunate events and proceeding in his cheerful way, content that a church-dominated, Catholic-ordered world is how it should be and thank goodness for that. Perhaps he is, after all, conning someone, himself. The most striking example is having disembarked from the tram and walking past a newsagent, he observes the headline of an awful tragedy that happened the previous day. A ferry, the *General Slocum*,[4] sank in the Hudson River, New York, with the loss of over 600 souls including many children. Well these things happen, thinks Fr Conmee and the main thing is that they had opportunity for perfect contrition. Well if perfect contrition is a peculiarly Catholic doctrine they're in a pickle because the victims were almost exclusively German Lutheran on a church picnic. Another instance, as he observes a canal boat lugging turf, might be his reflection upon the wonder of God, who created turf to lie in the bogs of rural Ireland so that men may have the back-breaking pleasure of digging it out so as to eke a meagre living.

This, rightly or wrongly, is Joyce's general dig: that the cream of the organised church in Ireland is the many Fr Conmees. Well-meaning men, relied upon by many people but, when push comes to shove, of little practical help. The worst is that too many priests and church administrators fall short of Father Conmee's benevolent standards and use the hierarchy for career advancement or other simonaic opportunity. One may or may not consider this ironic in the context of Fr Conmee's very real help to the Joyce family[5] and, without which, there would be no *Ulysses*. Yet, in any event, there it is.

Fr Conmee disembarks the tram in bucolic environ. Walking down a country lane he catches up on his Breviary, reading as he goes. The Breviary is the liturgical set of prayers priests must read every day. A young couple emerge from a gap in the hedge and, having obviously been up to some canoodling, are embarrassed to be face to face with a priest, the girl removes a clinging twig from her skirt. Kindly Fr Conmee blesses them but thinks 'Sin'.[6] Perhaps an expected priestly comment: but be careful, we may have clashed into a Wandering Rock. He may well have thought they had sinned and probably did. But there's subtler and more significant interpretation. The Breviary is divided into sections, each headed by a letter of the Hebrew alphabet, the penultimate one being '*Shin*', which can be pronounced with hard or soft 'S'. We know from the Res (or *Resh*) section that he just read, that this Sin is precisely the point he has reached as the young lovers emerge from the hedge. The Hebrew letter also suggests the mystical *Kabbalah* to which Joyce was increasingly drawn, attracted one expects both by the almost magical power of words and their derivative parts and also the power of coincidence. This is to touch upon a topic of real significance to an understanding of the book and of genuine fascination but is, regrettably, probably beyond Normal Joyce for Normal People. For further reading one might try *Joyce's Cities* by Jackson L Cope.

His story ends before he meets Father Provincial so whether he arrives and/or helps the Dignam child remains a mystery.

Gear shift: Possibly Mr Denis J Maginni at the corner of Dignam's Court. We are not sure of the location of 1904 Dignam's Court but Mr Maginni appears shortly in another part of town, crossing O'Connell Bridge, so this might be a gear shift or a wandering red herring or neither.

From now until No 19 the vignettes are shorter.

No 2

A police constable approaches O'Neil's undertakers near Newcomen Bridge. We expect it is the same constable who just saluted Fr Conmee, SJ, and was blessed. He speaks to Corny Kelleher standing outside. We know Kelleher as the man that organised the Dignam funeral and that he's rumoured, at least as per Bloom's inner confiding, to be a police informer. The conversation that takes place is another dangerous rock that neither confirms nor quashes the rumour.

Gear shift: No obvious candidates.

No 3

Corny Kelleher, who has the virtually unique privilege of spanning vignettes, spits a chewed remnant of hay in a graceful arc out over the pavement. The one-legged beggar, earlier blessed and no-changed by Fr Conmee, has better luck as he reaches Eccles Street where an arm extends from a window to drop a coin. It, the arm, knocks a small advertising card from the window sill. Face unseen but we assume it is Molly at home and preening for a visitor in an hour or so. It's all informative, we can, should we be so inclined, plot the beggar's route in time from Mountjoy Square where he was blessed by Fr Conmee and so may deduce, for the first time with near certainty, that different incidents are observed by us in bird's eye fashion and that they occur in different parts of the city and broadly at same time. This is because O'Neil's undertakers is some way from Eccles Street.

The coin dropped by Molly falls; thirty-two feet per second, per second: The Fall, original sin, which may or may not be an indication of Molly's nearing infidelity? On the other hand, the piece of hay, spat by Kelleher, propels in a graceful arc, suggestive of Kelleher's more ambiguous sin of informing. Did he, didn't he? Moreover, the bit of hay, like the Vestal Virgin's plum stones in Stephen's 'Parable of the Plums',[7] falls onto stony ground, whereas passing lads place Molly's coin in the beggar's cap. This may suggest that her infidelity will have a broader purpose, perhaps leading to a greater good.

Rabaiotti's ice cream van is mentioned, the first of several sightings this day.

The card advertising unfurnished apartments is no doubt doing just that, for the top floor of the Bloom house is vacant. But, as it is replaced a few minutes later, it may also serve as a signal to Boylan that the coast is clear.

Gear shift: The entire passage: Eccles Street is nowhere near Newcomen Bridge and J J O'Molloy is at St Mary's Abbey which is distanced from both locations.

No 4

Three Dedalus children, Katy, Boody and Maggy, are in the kitchen cooking. Its meagre pickings: some insufficient watery soup collected from the Sisters at a food bank. They are resentful of their father, who should be putting food on the table and also of a pawn broker who declined to take some of Stephen's books.

Gear shift: the lackey rang his bell. This is at Dillon's auction rooms where another sister, Dilly, is speaking with her father, Simon Dedalus, in vignette No 11.

No 5

Blazes Boylan is in Thornton's fruit shop and general store. We are close up and personal with him for the first time, even very briefly, inside his head. Our initial impression does not augur well. Nothing to rebut the Don Giovanni we take him to be. A smooth-talking creep, who takes the opportunity to peer down the blouse of the young assistant and presumes to take, without payment, a red carnation for his button-hole. The fruit that he selects for Molly, plump fresh and oozing juice, compares in a revealing way with Bloom's gift in Vignette No 10.

Gear shift: Bloom, under Merchants' Arch at the bookseller.

No 6

Near Trinity College, Stephen bumps into his old singing teacher Almidano Artifoni.[8] Stephen the linguist is a fluent Italian speaker; Joyce, writer of actuality does not spare the non-Italian reader and narrates their conversation entirely in Italian. After general greeting,

Artifoni reflects that it is a shame Stephen gave up his singing because he is talented and could make a nice living as a tenor. Stephen's horizons do not extend in a commercial direction and so 'a nice living' is no temptation, as we have seen and will see more.

This is likely a reflection on Joyce's father, John Joyce. The son had an accomplished voice but the father's was apparently really something special, a gift he seemed determined to waste beyond entertaining the troops in the pub. Joyce's relationship with his father is an undercurrent that deserves exploration including the son's likelihood to repeat the pattern and we shall see more of Simon Dedalus in Sirens, the next Lecture.

Gear shift: Possibly none. The statues of Oliver Goldsmith and Henry Grattan are both in proximity of College Green.

No 7

Miss Dunne is Blazes Boylan's secretary. She sits at her typewriter and types the date onto a letter. It's one of only a few instances in the book that pins the day to 16 June 1904. She reads the Wilkie Collins novel *The Woman in White*, in which the heroine, Marian Halcombe, may be linked to our Marion Bloom. She takes a call from Boylan which we know he makes from Thornton's in vignette No 5 and from this we learn that, of the several tickets to be booked for the tour to Belfast on Monday week, only two are to be booked for onward travel to Liverpool. Tantalisingly, which two is not revealed.

She tells him that Lenehan wanted a word and will be in The Ormond at 4 pm, when, of course, Boylan is due at Molly's.

Gear shift: Tom Rochford's machine described in vignette No 9. Possibly also H.E.L.Y'.S near Moneypeny's corner but the location of Boylan's office is uncertain.

No 8

Ned Lambert, whom we saw in Davy Byrne's and elsewhere, is in the crypt of St Mary's Abbey where he conducts historical tours. He guides a priest, Reverend Hugh Love, by candle in the gloomy half-light. We will soon learn that this priest is a local landlord. J J O'Molloy arrives, continuing his quest to borrow some money and wishes to try his luck with Ned Lambert. Ned handily sneezes to buy time while considering how to deflect the appeal and, typically for this episode, it is unresolved though J J O'Molloy appears in Barney Kiernan's pub at 5 pm so one presumes he struck lucky somewhere.

Gear shift: 1: John Howard Parnell playing chess at the Dublin Bakery Company. 2: The young woman removing the twig from her skirt whom we know from No 1 is way to the north of the city towards Malahide. We can, if so inclined, put a name to her face in episode fourteen.[9]

No 9

Tom Rochford was referred in Gear Shift No 7 and now we meet him. Not only is he a clever engineer, he is a local hero who, sometime before had rescued a man who fell into a drain. Here, he demonstrates to Lenehan, McCoy and Nosey Flynn a machine he has invented for use in vaudeville music halls. It has numbered disks that sequentially roll into place upon some mechanical activation. Audiences at variety shows come and go during performances and this invention will inform them which act is currently on stage, enabling them to work out where they are in the show. This prototype represents one of the few achievements by a Dubliner this day as recorded in the novel. Whether the vaudeville industry will be interested in using it, is unknown but Lenehan suggests that he will run it by Blazes Boylan when he sees him shortly at The Ormond

Lenehan and McCoy proceed towards The Ormond Hotel where Lenehan is due to meet Boylan. En-route Lenehan pops into a bookies and considers that he's done Bantam Lyons a good turn by dissuading him from backing the horse 'Throwaway'. They pass Merchant's Arch where they see Bloom perusing secondhand books. Lenehan tells a very amusing account of a drunken flirtation he once had with Molly. The story confirms Lenehan as the sort of scoundrel that would grope a woman in a snug carriage while her husband sits opposite. But it also hints, at least through his unreliable narration, that Molly was game. Further it reveals Bloom as not only a man with interest in and knowledge of astronomy and astrology but also, as a husband, blind or wilfully blind, to what is going on nearer earth and under his nose. McCoy turns out to be a surprising ally; we noticed in episode five some characteristics shared with Bloom and here Lenehan realises he may have misjudged his audience as his witty account backfires.

This account is placed immediately before Bloom's own appearance at the centre of this episode and so, give or take, the centre of the book. It adds to a sense, still only vague, that the worm might, just might be turning.

Gear shift: 1: the old lady and others including Richie Goulding at court. The old lady is reminiscent of Miss Flite in *Bleak House*.[2] The cavalcade leaves Phoenix Park. 3: In Eccles Street, Molly reinstates the 'Unfurnished Apartments' advert card back on the window sill.

No 10

Leopold Bloom is, fittingly, centre-stage in the central vignette suggestive perhaps that the Wanderings of Ulysses have reached their apex before waning. If so, it is noticeable that at the farthest metaphorical point from home he remains pre-occupied with Molly. That morning, over her breakfast in bed, she requested another book by Paul de Kock and Bloom is in an insalubrious bookshop, seeking one out. Apparently, he's a regular patron, so much so that the wretched proprietor, unsavoury king in an unsavoury castle, is aware of Bloom's literary taste. Unsolicited, he brings two books from the back of store both likely to appeal to the discerning gentleman with an interest in masochistic erotica. One is by the appropriately named James Lovebirch. But Bloom is not there on his own account: he seeks a gift for Molly, albeit, when he finds what he seeks, he rents rather than buys.

It's called *Sweets of Sin*. The wealthy husband lavishes his wife with expensive perfumes and silks but she wears them only for her lover, for Raul. This one, thinks Bloom, 'She'll like this'.

Boylan's gift was those plump peaches amid fat pears and alcohol. Despite the blush of their skin, their soft plump fruit flesh oozes with sensual sticky juice. He's nothing if not subtle. Bloom may be only renting but at least he's trying to accommodate what Molly said she wanted and not what Boylan wants her to want. Boylan focused on specific reward; Bloom having long since given up on physical reward, is simply trying to please his wife. Well that's the simplified version for, as we shall see in Circe, Bloom derives gratification in his own marriage from the cuckolded relationship played out in *Sweets of Sin*. In any event, we'll have to wait a bit to see which approach, Bloom's or Boylan's, fairs better with Molly.

Gear shift: Mr Denis J Maginni (again) on O'Connell Bridge. A possible wandering rock but gets the benefit of the doubt. O'Connell Bridge is just sufficiently far: Just.

No 11

Dilly Dedalus bumps into her father Simon outside Dillon's auction house. She asks him for money which he initially declines. We are more than a little disgusted at how he can cast his children adrift. His one-liners are very witty but insufficient to shift our concern. He eventually gives up a shilling. We are not sure if he's been in the auction room buying, selling or browsing. Maybe just passing but that's unlikely because Dilly has been loitering here in order to catch him. In a book that looks from oblique angles at consubstantiation, this pretty pathetic excuse for a man cannot be the father in the Trinity, even an oblique one.

Gear shift: The cyclists taking the corner at the College Library, Tom Kernan walking along James Street; the vice-regal cavalcade passes out of Parkgate.

No 12

We briefly met Tom Kernan at the funeral, chatting with Bloom, both converts to Catholicism and so both, to that extent, outsiders. We recall he criticised the service, preferring that of the Church of Ireland. We also recall him from *Dubliners* in which, as the central character in the story 'Grace', he collapses inebriated, down a pub staircase and bites off part of his tongue. Here, he is honoured: one of the very few, beyond Stephen and Bloom, in seventeen episodes on whom Joyce lavishes some serious interior monologue. He's a tea merchant and is pleased with himself, reliving, as he walks, his sales technique utilised in the recent clinching of a good sale. Such technique includes his easy-going repartee and his fine apparel which he admires in the reflection of a shop window.

Kernan is a 'West Brit', one who feels proud that Ireland is run from London and that these republicans are making a big mistake. He concedes, however, that Ben Dollard performs a very touching rendition of the nationalist song, 'The Croppy Boy', as we'll hear next episode. He almost catches, and is disappointed to miss, the vice-regal cavalcade.

Gear shift: 1: Simon Dedalus meets Fr Cowley. 2: The 'Elijah is Coming' leaflet that Bloom crumpled and threw in the River Liffey (in episode eight) has bobbed its way to Sir John Rogerson's quay. 3: Mr and Mrs Breen cross O'Connell Bridge.

No 13

In Bedford Row Stephen stares into a jeweller's window where an old lapidarist shapes and polishes semi-precious stones. He window-shops until alighting upon a bookseller. We assume it is a little more upmarket than that run by Bloom's onion-breathed purveyor but are not told. Stephen thumbs various books including a book of Jewish secrets which (be careful of wandering rocks) is written by a non-Jew, the abbot Peter Salanka. [10] The tips are wide-ranging – how to soften chapped hands, a recipe for white wine vinegar and how to win a woman's love. This last one raises an eyebrow. It seems that one repeats three times the following: '*Se el yilo nebrakada femininum! Amor me solo! Sanktus! Amen.*'[11]

This phrase catches the eye because, around midnight, it will be repeated by an apparition of Molly, dressed-up in Turkish garb and stood next to her camel. She appears in Bloom's waking dream: who could do worse than to learn how to win a woman's love. And, of course, both Stephen and Bloom dreamed of an oriental Turk the previous night. Joyce takes the opportunity, even in this brief glimpse of Stephen, to note how he moves, sub-consciously, ever-closer to Bloom.

Stephen's sister Dilly is also there contemplating using virtually her last penny to purchase a self-help French book. Stephen enquires after the family, whether his books have been pawned and whether Dilly can afford to spend money on books. He is not assured but, nevertheless, does not help. He is, in life as in literature, his father's son, give or take a little genius. He interior monologues that his family is drowning and so will he, if he gets sucked back in. Agenbite of inwit or more to the point, 'I want his life still to be his, mine to be mine'.[12]

Gear shift: 1: The 'midwife' cockle-pickers trudge through Irishtown. 2: Fr Conmee is in Donnycarney.

No 14

Father Bob Cowley is no man of the cloth, he has not been ordained. This may once have been an aspiration but, in any event, he holds the soubriquet. He's part of the crowd: he, Simon Dedalus, Ben Dollard and others. Each talented in their way but are so in the thrall of booze, gambling, bad luck or we know not what, that they struggle to keep body and soul together. Here, Cowley laments that Reuben J Dodd the solicitor and moneylender is hot on his case for outstanding payment and has apparently issued a writ. He proposes to seek the help of the Sub-Sheriff, Long John Fanning.

They meet Ben Dollard, a big man with a big bass voice. Music and, in particular, singing, is important for all three. There is some banter concerning Dollard's clothes. He's a large man and a bankrupt, so well-fitting clothes might be a challenge. Cowley repeats his lament for Dollard's benefit who, it transpires, is something of an expert on the law of debt and tenant's rights, as befits a man currently housed courtesy of a homeless charity. The good news for Fr Cowley, says Dollard, is that his landlord, who has also issued proceedings, has *qua* landlord, the prior claim over household items, so the nasty Jewish moneylender can, as Simon eloquently states, put it where Jacko put the nuts. The landlord, as it transpires, is that nice Reverend Love we just met in the crypt of St Mary's Abbey, so Fr Cowley will, after all, receive his calling from the church. To state the obvious: Jew and Christian are acting precisely the same, both have reverted to litigation for non-payment of money due. One is referred throughout as Barabbas, Judas Iscariot and Jewman, the other is welcomed, almost as a conquering hero.

Gear shift: 1: Cashel Boyle O'Connor Fitzmaurice Tisdall Farrell is on Kildare Street (we saw him in the library). 2: Rev Hugh C Love exits St Mary's Abbey.

No 15

Martin Cunningham and Jack Power, discuss in the vicinity of their workplace, Dublin Castle,[13] the precarious Dignam finances and, in particular, the funds raised for the widow at the funeral and school arrangements for one of the children. They are joined by John Wyse Nolan and shortly by Jimmy Henry. Compared to the three in the last vignette, these are men not only in gainful employment but of some responsibility, not to say influence, in the city and are greeted by the Sub-Sheriff, Long John Fanning, when they arrive at Kavanagh's winerooms.

Gear shift: 1: Miss Kennedy and Miss Douce look out of the window of The Ormond Hotel. 2: Blazes Boylan is outside la Maison Claire.

No 16

Haines and Buck Mulligan sit in the DBC, Dublin Bakery Company. Damn Bad Cakes as translated by the Buck for the furtherance of Haines' education. Over there, and playing chess, sits John Howard Parnell, brother of the great man. He, too, translates, in his case, a bishop which may be an allegorical hint of state triumphing over church. It's an odd use of the word. They discuss Stephen's off-kilter state of mind and, with some prescience, that it would take him ten years to produce a book.

Gear shift: 1: The beggar in Nelson Street. 2: 'The Elijah' crumpled throwaway amid an archipelago of corks by the three-masted schooner,

Rosevean. This was the schooner, with its cargo of bricks, that we and Stephen pondered may be significant at the end of Proteus.

No 17

Cashel Boyle O'Connor Fitzmaurice Tisdall Farrell, the eccentric lamp post-dodger who whizzed passed in Lestrygonians and was deep in studious thought at the National Library, is again on the move. Along Merrion Square, he is, as usual, in a rush and stops only briefly to frown at Rev Alexander J. Dowie on a billboard advertising 'Elijah is Coming'. As he speeds he is oblivious of all-comers including the Blind Stripling into whom, as a Wandering Rock, he bashes outside the Bloom dental practice (no relation) on Clare Street and, without a care or, seemingly, even a flicker of brain activity, continues on his way.

He receives a curse for his trouble: 'God's curse on you, he said sourly, whoever you are! You're blinder nor I am, you bitch's bastard!'[14]

This young blind man, whom Bloom earlier guided across the street, will appear further.

Gear shift: None.

No 18

A poignant segment as we spend a minute or so with Master Patrick Dignam, who we estimate to be around 12 years old. Coming to terms with the still very raw death of his father but irritated to sit among the mourners, he has been sent out for some pork chops. Master Dignam is another of the few honoured with an interior monologue. Passing a billboard, he's briefly elevated, excited at the prospect of attending a forthcoming boxing match, then deflated upon realisation that the match has been and gone: the poster advertises old news. Death through a child's eyes: it's good stuff.

Gear shift: None.

No 19

The episode ends with the Viceroy's cavalcade. It sets off from his Lordship's residence in Phoenix Park and will meander east through the city, east before heading south for the annual charity bazaar on behalf of Mercers Hospital. We shall see the concluding fireworks later that evening.

'To Caesar what is Caesar's, to God what is God's.'[15] This corruption of the biblical phrase that popped into Stephen's head in episode two seems to neatly sum up the gist of things; beginning in vignette No 1 with the church, we conclude the episode with a benign show of strength on behalf of the state. Each institution convincing itself, at least, that it runs the show. Let's see if London fares any better than Rome. In a short train of carriages, His Lordship, the Earl of Dudley, rides as does Lady Dudley, Lieutenant-Colonel Hesseltine and several aides of both sexes. In one of the most entertaining passages in the book, we are interested less in the cavalcade than the city's reaction to it. Some run with joy and excitement to see and to greet and others run from it. For the vast majority, the overwhelming sentiment is one of indifference.

Those in the excited camp, include the reluctant convert and 'West Briton' Tom Kernan, the allegedly mad Dennis Breen (UP:up), obsequious policeman, schoolboys and Master Patrick Dignam's over-starched shirt collar which repeatedly pops up in salute. Simon Dedalus brings his hat low in deference: apparently genuine. In the nay camp, the Englishman Haines who gazes gravely from the Dublin Bakery Company and John Wyse Nolan who smiles with unseen coldness from the doorway of Kavanagh's Winerooms. And let's not forget the Dublin sewer system which sluices a tongue of liquid effluent into the River Poddle in salute as the cavalcade sweeps by Wood Quay. But, generally, indifference: for Lenehan, for Dudley White, for Richie Goulding and Reuben J Dodd; for John Henry Menton, for Tom Rochford and Nosey Flynn. All of whom seem to just go about their business, even on this Thursday half-day for business. Gerty McDowell, of whom we shall see much more, around 8.30 this evening, is very excited it's true – excited to see the choice of latest fashions sported by their ladyships. Blazes Boylan has a winning smile but, again, only for the ladies. To even matters up, Miss Lydia Douce snares the Lieutenant-Colonel with a killer smile from the window of The Ormond Hotel. There is general cordiality. Politeness in the sense no-one shouts abuse or launches Molotov cocktails. But cordiality seems to be as emotive as it gets as few muster much beyond indifference Where there is interest, it's out of self-interest. The cavalcade, symbolic of the colonial regime, is endured and pretty painlessly.

We wish the Viceroy well and expect the charity bazaar to be a great success but we don't find out, for the last word in this piece (and indeed the episode) is left, unknowingly, to Mr Almidano Artifoni's trousers, which present their sturdy buttocks to the Viceroy as the Senor jumps to board a passing trolleybus.

This concludes our nineteen little stories that in the tradition of *Dubliners*, simply present themselves without ramming any message down the reader's throat. They are as they are and such lessons as exist lurk between the rocks in dangerous waters.

Anthony Burgess observed,[16] that, at 3.30 in the afternoon on a warm summer's day, blood is probably pumping around the body slower than at any other time. The rocks of Dublin's metaphorical labyrinth, the clashing aspirations of Dubliners not to mention the Ascot Gold Cup, raise pulses a little but only a little. It is churlish to suggest that church and state, the grandest of institutions, are not vital. Order is maintained, schools are run, church masses are well attended, the poor are fed, albeit meagrely, and hospitals function. Thus, the vital organs of our metropolitan patient are serviced but these snapshots hint that the soul of Dublin life, its *anima,* has its own independent life force.

LECTURE 12, 3 MARCH 2021: EPISODE 11

Sirens Turn Up, Tune In and Drop Out

Music: In the Shade of the Palm – Kevin McDermott & Ralph Richey

If Wandering Rocks is an *entr'acte*, Sirens is the beginning of part two of the book. After developments in Lestrygonians and Scylla & Charybdis, there are aspects of this episode that are, let's not say inevitable, far from that, but that, looking back, one can see their geneses in earlier episodes. What might be more of an inevitability is what flows from this episode to the next. The mythological Sirens lured sailors with their irresistible song until, too late to avoid, the ships were dashed on jagged rocks. Odysseus was advised[1] to plug his crew's ears with wax and have himself tied fast to the mast. He may then hear the delightfully tempting song of the mermaids, he may well scream at his crew to change course and head towards their island but, deaf to his pleas, they would maintain course. That was the plan.

The island inhabited by Dublin's sirens is The Ormond Hotel on the north bank of the Liffey in the city centre. Dublin menfolk gravitate towards it. Simon Dedalus, Lenehan, Bob Cowley, Ben Dollard, George Lidwell, Hugh (Blazes) Boylan, Leopold Bloom and several others. They may have reasons for alighting at that spot at that time, some such reasons shall be revealed, others will not. Perhaps some men, if asked, are not sure why that pub at that time; maybe they we just drawn to it. We call it an hotel, whether it caters for residents is not spelled out, for our purposes it is a pub. It has several salon areas, the main bar, where barmaids Lydia Douce and Mina Kennedy preside; an adjoining restaurant, attended to by Pat, bald Pat the deaf waiter, and, open to both, a concert room with its recently tuned piano. In those days, pre-home entertainment by way of television and even radio, social life centred on pubs and often around a piano. Fittingly, then, this is an episode of music.

Of music: the very narrative is underscored by music or it might be the other way around. Joyce writes music with words. We recall, after struggling with the Italian, that in Wandering Rocks, Stephen bumped into his old music teacher Almidano Artifoni, who mildly rebukes him for giving up his singing, for Stephen could have derived a pretty nice living. Stephen, we know, believes his calling to be for aesthetics beyond 'a nice living' which, having witnessed the deterioration of his father's financial state, is a bold move. Schopenhauer, he of episode three's *noumena* and phenomena considered music to be one of our few portals to the mysterious *noumena* and that, in this, it is alone among the arts. One can see that, reading a book or looking at a painting, no matter how emotional and uplifting, does not elevate beyond appreciation into uncontrolled bliss. Admiration, no matter how effusive, remains at an intellectual level. 'Wow, what a fine picture! That's so clever and beautiful how Van Gogh has suggested that emotional state with those brush strokes' – always an intellectual cognisance. It's almost unimaginable without, say, hypnosis, to move from appreciation of a painting into an out-of-body experience. More so, with a book. But music, occasionally, very occasionally, might turn insides to jelly as though something has been accessed that is other-worldly and beyond comprehension.

It's possible that Joyce may be attacking such sentiment head-on. He may be suggesting that there is nothing music can do that he cannot do with words. More likely though, he is using that as a gimmicky hook because, for reasons just stated, words may be capable of replication of some music but cannot reach the parts music reaches. All that said, we have here literary equivalents of chords, trills, arpeggios and more. Above all, the fugue. These are signs a non-musical person is ill-equipped to read but, for those adept, they are there to be seen, admired and provide a richness to the episode. A fugue, one understands, is a melody that is subject to repetition and characterised by question and answer whereby the melody is passed to different players, possibly in counterpoint, before all come together for the resounding climax. Even I, a musical dunce, can recognise the lilt of the hyena-like barmaids sneering and guffawing, to which Bloom responds in counterpoint, speaking perhaps for hounded middle-aged men everywhere and marching to his own tune near Essex Bridge. Or the cock, cock carracking of the door knocker, as rapped by randy impatient Blazes Boylan and the tap, tap, tapping of the blind stripling's white stick, returning for his forgotten tuning fork. For those with eyes to hear, such musical delights accrue through the episode and with a purpose. As well as Homeric resonance, it builds tension like a cat gut being stretched taught. Touching nerves and adding piquancy as we approach the agonising hour of four o'clock.

The episode begins in confused style but, when properly considered, is easily explained. We've had our interval of Wandering Rocks and now return to the auditorium for Act Two. Naturally, the orchestra is warming up and that is how we shall consider the jumble of words in the first couple of pages. Fragments of sentences and bits of phrases as snatches of arpeggios as instruments are warmed up and fine-tuned pending the return of the conductor. That it is dominated by Bloom reassures us that, although he is far away at Essex Bridge (now Grattan Bridge), and heading in the opposite direction, he is our conductor. Odysseus is in the house. It is he that taps his baton and announces: Begin.

Before we do, some noteworthy points that may aid comprehension:

- The dreaded hour of four in the afternoon will strike this episode. This is the crescendo of the tension that has been building since Bloom opened the post at just after 8 am.
- From the outset,[2] we marked sentimentality as being one the nets that traps the Irish and by the Irish we don't mean the well to do, the likes of Baron Ardilaun[3] and Lady Gregory, we mean the lower middle and working class, overwhelmingly Catholic men and women. Where in this episode and the next mud is slung, particularly in the direction of Irish nationalism, it is slung vicariously on behalf of James Joyce, he is the mud-slinger. We explored this to an extent by way of Stephen's salvos against the Irish Literary Revival and do so again here.
- Finally, we will sense in Leopold Bloom a change of attitude, making this episode something of an energising catalyst.

Wandering Rocks was a *tour de force* in terms of continuity: knitting together not only the vignettes within but also foregoing episodes and propelling the narrative onward in anticipation of those yet to come. So it is that we begin, as propelled by 'the Rocks', with two barmaids: flaxen-haired Mina Kennedy and the copper-toned-headed Lydia Douce as they gaze out of the window watching the Viceroy's cavalcade sweep past. We safely assume these to be two of our Sirens, though we will have a care not to allow our assumptions to run aground upon jagged rocks.

Bronze Lydia Douce quickly establishes her credentials as the more luscious and alluring of the two mermaids, catching the eye of one of the Viceroy's aides sat in the carriage, and he looks back at her with a charming smile: 'He's killed looking back. She laughed: O wept! Aren't men frightful idiots?'[4]

Fortunately for this one, he gets away, bound Odysseus-like to his vessel as he sails by and the mermaids return to the bar to prepare for customers and to savour the cup of tea served by Boots, the impertinent young factotum. Bronze and Gold wear a uniform of sorts, dark tight blouses, upon which rest a rose, that symbol of love and romance and a rose that, especially in the case of bronze Miss Douce, will rise and fall with the heaving of her embonpoint – all the better to tempt these men, the frightful idiots. We suspect the rose may be significant, being the flower of both Virgin Mary and of Venus, goddess of sensual lust, and we shall be careful, for Miss Douce in particular, will reel silly men into her Venus fly-trap. One also thinks of Lenehan's Rose of Castile joke[5] and of the aria 'The Last Rose of Summer' which will feature in the episode. In counterpoint, we have the red carnation in the buttonhole of Blazes Boylan.

The first customer of note is Simon Dedalus which is a little surprising because we left him in Wandering Rocks with barely a few pence to spare for his half-starved daughter Dilly. Miraculously he has struck lucky, for he now strolls into the bar, on exceedingly familiar terms with Miss Douce and orders a whiskey. It transpires that she has just returned from a two-week holiday, sunbathing on the beach up in the County Down in the shadow of the Mourne Mountains. Simon, in mock admonishment, accuses her of tempting poor men as they walk along the beach though she later admits she was with a gentleman friend so had got her tempting in early: holiday over, she's back at work but remains in Siren mode. She sings of the heroine, Idelores[6] as she fixes the drinks. Idelores, queen of the eastern sea, is courted by many men one of whom pleads with her to look to the west for him. This inversion of roles causes us, but only momentarily, to wonder if she is a Siren after all.

Simon fills his pipe with tobacco as he flirts with Miss Douce. At the same time, Leopold Bloom is walking by Moulang's, the pipe and tobacco products shop.[7] Thus, the two men are linked: one father in body, the other, incrementally, father in soul. Oh Stevie boy, the pipes, the pipes are calling. Simon, who, a few short hours earlier at Glasnevin Cemetery, was tearfully crying for the lord to take him to join his dead wife, now flirts outrageously with bronze Miss Douce. She tells him the piano was tuned earlier by a blind piano tuner and, so sad, for he was such a young man and the beauty of his playing only heightened the poignancy. Simon, talented musician himself, will after exchanging pleasantries with Lenehan, head toward the piano in the adjoining concert room.

In parallel, we watch Bloom as he makes his way along the quay around Essex Bridge, now, as said, Grattan Bridge. He enters the stationery shop and buys paper and envelope to compose a response to Martha Clifford. Both men, Simon and Bloom, are between two women with head-swivelling. In addition, Bloom counterpoints a conversation between Misses Bronze and Gold regarding sunburn treatment. They talk, nay giggle, splutter and guffaw, as they insult the greasy and ugly appearance of a local pharmacist, the interchange yodelled in duet. The intertwining with Bloom causes us to wonder if they speak of him? Is his appearance so off-putting? No, it is the pharmacist. But there are similarities and more besides. We note increasing sea references. 'Greaseaseabloom'[8]: 'By Cantwell's offices roved Greaseabloom.'[9]

Moments later, coinciding with Lenehan's arrival at The Ormond (you may recall that he arranged with Miss Dunne to meet Boylan there at 4 pm), Bloom crosses not Essex Bridge but Yessex Bridge, all of which requires some unpacking. These references to the sea: Bloom cannot see the Irish Sea either from here or Eccles Street, so our suspicion is that this is intended to hint at a closer association with the sailor Odysseus. This is confirmed by the play on words between greasy, the country Greece and sea. Bloom, far from comparison with an ailing pharmacist and figure of fun, is Odysseus, modern hero and, moreover, he may be beginning, just beginning, to live up to that name.

Let's start by his saying Yes to Sex as he crosses Yes sex Bridge. Odysseus is returning, he was spotted metaphorically in the form of *Rosevean* (another Rose) the three-masted schooner that Stephen first sensed and then saw as he walked along the beach.[10] Now the man that has said no to sex (leastways with his wife and we so far know of no others during his marriage) for 11 years, now crosses Yes Sex bridge. He's about to buy the stationery to write Martha's letter so might it just be that he feels frisky? No, he rejected earlier any notion of moving that 'relationship' beyond safe anonymity which shall shortly be confirmed in his latest letter. Besides, he holds *Sweets of Sin* tight to his breast which he procured for Molly, for whom 'Yes' is a word of some significance. Do we have a new Bloom and is he sweeping clean? We do not get ahead of ourselves but there's a whiff of something in the air.

Back in the pub, amidst Lenehan flirting in vain with Miss Kennedy, we hear out of nowhere 'Jingle' and then a little beyond: 'Jingle jaunty jingle.'[11]

We first heard something like around eight o'clock when Molly, set the brasses jingling as she leaned over in bed, her large soft bubs sloping within her nightdress. Then in Sandymount, as the creaky jingly funeral cortège commenced its sad journey. The sound now heard is, distressingly, a combination of both. It is the sound of Blazes Boylan's jingly cab en-route to The Ormond Hotel for a quick drink and appointment with Lenehan, all the while thinking of the subsequent cab ride to Molly's creaky jingly bed at 4 pm. Bloom not only hears this but, goodness me, he sees him:

> It is. Third time. Coincidence.
> Jingling on supple rubbers it jaunted from the bridge to Ormond quay. Follow. Risk it. Go quick. At four. Near now. Out.[12]

Well, here's a turnabout! Contrast with the Bloom at the end of Lestrygonians, the hunted fox, panic-stricken as he ran unseen from the horrible prospect of meeting Boylan to the safety of the library portico. Now he's on the hunt. Bloom, Bloom! Following Boylan to the Ormond. Even the syntactical rhythm as we ended Lestrygonians, has a familiar ring:

> Ah, soap there! Yes. Gate.
> Safe![13]

Spoiler alert, but it's not as if he's going to have it out with Boylan when he gets there, because you know, it's Bloom, cautious Bloom, cautious Odysseus. But hey, baby steps. One may take the view that those five words: 'Follow. Risk it. Go quick',[14] represent a serious departure in the book and, with them, the Wanderings of Ulysses reach a metaphorical if not geographical extremity.

In this musical episode, we return to Simon at the piano. He's tinkling and warbling. He fiddles with the tuning fork misplaced by the blind stripling. We hear it vibrate in the writing:

> That he now poised that it now throbbed. You hear? It throbbed, pure, purer, softley and softlier, its buzzing prongs. Longer in dying call.[15]

Also in dying call are Lenehan's amorous advances, each dashed on the rocks of Miss Kennedy. But, by way of temporary diversion, enter his idol, the conquering hero, Blazes Boylan – sharp suit, serge blue tie with socks to match, straw boater and new tan brogues. These are not wishy-washy, creaky, tentative, unobtrusive brogues as might be modelled by the Quaker Librarian: these are sure-footed, man about town, knock-em-dead brogues. If they squeak, they squeak authority and as smooth as sloe gin out of a pretty bottle. Yet not all swoon in his wake. Bloom, as yet unconquered, is on his trail. Cautious Odysseus, he enters the bar but then turns out of sight into the restaurant. With door ajar, he can hear what's going on without being seen. Added to which, he only had a light snack in Davy Byrne's and needs a proper meal that he may eat with relish.

He is greeted by Richie Goulding, also there for lunch. You remember him, Simon Dedalus' brother-in-law: 'Oh weeping God, the things I married into.'[16]

Alluded to before but let's spell it out, his joke, so we can enjoy it in all its well-worn glory. Goulding works for the solicitors Collis and Ward. He is not a solicitor or lawyer of any kind. So far as we can gather, he's a sort of costs clerk. Simon refers to him as 'the drunken little costdrawer' and, generally, an absent one, either off work with a bad back or a hangover. He carries a legal document bag on which is printed the name of the firm. His little joke, over-used by him or at least Joyce, is to have written Goulding at the beginning, promoting himself to founding partner. In this scene he is usefully employed, binding our Odysseus to the restaurant area, well away from temptation and danger next door. The restaurant is Pat's domain. Pat the waiter. Bald Pat, deaf Pat. Goulding will take steak and kidney pie and a pint of Power's bitter; for Bloom, liver and bacon and a glass of cider.

Back in the bar, Boylan is salivated over by barmaids Gold and Bronze and also by the obsequious Lenehan. Boylan orders a pint of bitter for Lenehan and takes a sloe gin for himself. He asks if the wire is in. Pre-radio, he's referring to the electric communication of the racing results that vibrates across airways to bookies and also to some of the larger pubs. He's a little premature with his request but then he is on a tight schedule. The Gold Cup usually gets going around 3.40 pm and is run over three miles, so will comfortably, take less than fifteen minutes. Allowing for Dunsink time, some fiddling about, and what with pub clocks being five minutes fast, we can see that Boylan will do well to get the result before he needs to head for Molly in Eccles Street. In fact he's already late but seems in no obvious hurry. So much so, that Bloom, from his safe distance, begins to raise a flicker of hope that he's forgotten or changed his mind.

At the magic moment of 4 o'clock Boylan is not knocking on Molly's door but is otherwise pre-occupied. Creepy Lenehan, rebuffed by Golden Miss Kennedy, is encouraging Bronze Miss Deuce to ring the bell: *sonnez la cloche*.[17] By which he means she should surreptitiously lift her skirt for her private audience of these two discreet gentlemen and twang her elasticated garter against her thigh. She feigns modesty but with her eyes fixed on Boylan and his eyes on the slowly rising hem of her skirt, she tenses the frilly elastic as the crescendo rises from the piano but that august percussive can't compete with its humble elastic rival on show at the bar. Twang! It rebounds. And thwack! The circle of thigh scarlets. Thus is marked our much anticipated hour of 4 pm or as close as pub clocks allow, in any event.

This is Boylan's cue to be on his way. If he disappointed Gold on entry, Bronze is devastated on his exit. Not her winning smile, not heaving rose upon heaving bosom, not even her smackable thigh is enough to tempt him onto her rocks. He's off to win his own personal Gold Cup (we have previously considered Molly as a Holy Grail). Is Molly the siren? Is Boylan a siren? He has, after all, drawn both Bloom and Lenehan to the Ormond. Is there any merit in trying to identify the Sirens? Probably, though we will see that sirens may not be confined to people.

More punters arrive: Ben Dollard and Bob 'Fr' Cowley. We were introduced last episode and, presumably, they have by now spoken to the Sub-Sheriff, Long John Fanning. They hear Simon Dedalus at the piano and head for the concert room. Simon's piano virtuosity is no match for his singing and Bob Cowley takes over the melody, fugue style, while Simon sings. Initially, we have a song of love and war, possibly foreshadowing Bloom's row with the citizen next episode and with tenor and bass roles for Simon and Ben Dollard, respectively. War reminds us that the Sirens tried to tempt Odysseus with big news concerning the Trojan wars which were started, if one believes the ancient Greek tabloids, for love.

There's much mirth and banter about Dollard's *basso profundo* voice and his male appendage to match. They recall the time, when he, as a late call-up for a concert, required an emergency dinner suit. Molly and Bloom, back in the day, ran a theatrical clothing business from their then house in Holles Street and supplied him with a penguin suit, albeit several sizes too small. Dollard it seems is a big man in every respect and the way-too-tight trousers displayed his charms for the ladies even several rows back. Ribald aspersions are cast in Molly's direction, described as both Daughter of the Regiment and then in reference to that clothing hire business: 'Ay, ay, Mr Dedalus nodded. Mrs Marion Bloom has left off clothes of all descriptions.'[18]

Poor Bloom has to listen to it. We shall discover (episode seventeen), that he suspects both Simon Dedalus and Ben Dollard of having tripped the light fantastic with his wife over the years. Intended or otherwise, coupled with Boylan's imminent touchdown in Eccles Street, it's an association between Molly and well-endowed men. Met him pike hoses. Molly will provide her account in graphic detail, in the final episode.

The piano boys run through their repertoire. Richie Goulding, remarks on Dedalus's lovely tenor voice and we have some amusing counterpoint as Simon's lyrics weave a game of conversational tag that may for the observant reader underline what Simon thinks of his brother-in-law. Bloom is on a different wavelength as he listens to the aria *'M'appari'* from the opera *Martha*. He thinks of Boylan making his jingly jangly way to Eccles Street which would appear to confirm Bloom's cuckold status. The line 'All is lost now'[19] adds especial piquancy: but at the same time, confusing. He's purchased the stationery for the surreptitious letter to Martha Clifford and here is Simon singing about Martha:

> Co-me, thou lost one!
> Co-me thou dear one![20]

A sign maybe? And a tempting one. Would we blame Bloom, as Blazes randy Boylan – Jingle-jaunty-got-the-horny[21] – winds his way towards Eccles Street? Bloom, staring into the abyss, imagines the knock 'knock knock Paul de Kock' on the door and Molly's 'wavayaveyavey' hair all tousled. The usurping suitor, conquering all, it now seems inevitable. Why shouldn't Bloom be tempted by the irresistible strains of Martha's aria? And yet, and yet . . .

Clever, cautious, Odysseus-Bloom remains calm, at a safe distance. He hears the tempting melody but has no need to draw closer for all his needs are catered for by Pat the waiter. Pat brings cider with liver and bacon. Pat, deaf Pat, waits as he waits. Pat hears as little as Odysseus' crew with wax in their ears. We might also say that Bloom is trapped in his sanctum: tied to the mast. Would he have been better rushing in and having it out with Boylan? Not his style and, besides, nothing has happened yet. What would he say and would it have changed anything? Would it have impressed Molly or would she simply resent him for ruining her tryst and the forthcoming trip to Belfast? He didn't do it, so we'll never know.

Bloom not only resists temptation, he remains on course. His thoughts turn from Martha to Molly and to her beautiful singing. He's taken back to that night in Terenure when they first met. More tag conversation with the singers. Bloom recalls her large Spanish eyes;

Simon sings 'Charmed my eye.' He recalls Molly's yellow and black lace dress and the game of musical chairs which thrust them together as the last pair. Why did she pick him? It's a good question. Those of us, by now, firmly in the Bloom camp, need no convincing but we'll have to await the final episode for Molly's considerations.

Meanwhile, in the bar from where one presumes one sees as well as hears the performance, resistance is futile and the patrons are swept up in the dreamy sentimentality of the love song. Bloom though continues to resist, his mind wanders to divers matters practical: how tenors get women by the score; how Simon, with that lovely voice, has wasted his life; whether an extra-marital affair is worth the aggravation. His body language reveals underlying angst. He idly plucks an elastic band, a bit of cat-gut and then winds it ever tighter across his fingers as Simon crescendos. Tension mounts as, all the while Boylan, horny Boylan, encourages the cabman to go faster and faster up the hill at Rutland Square. Simon really can sing. Notes soar on the Daedalus wings built by the ancestral artificer that he could have been. Instead, the actuality is that his feeble wings barely get him off of the ground. To steal his son's earlier phrase, he lapwinged.[22] Yet, as that final note soars in beauty, it, for a moment, entwines the three men: singer Simon, character Lionel and his real life counterpart, Leopold, all into one; Siopold.

It's an appropriate juncture to linger a moment on Simon Dedalus, who is clearly based, in whole or part, on John Joyce, the author's father. Joyce senior was talented and witty but, having inherited a modest income-producing property portfolio, was disinclined to work too hard. Life was generally spent as the charming and funny *bon viveur*, singing around the piano in the pub or at home but generally in the pub. With the passage of time and ten surviving children, the income became insufficient and, rather than work harder, property after property was mortgaged and then sold until nothing was left. He was generally resented by his children but his relationship with his eldest son James was more nuanced. James understood and pretty much agreed with the contempt felt by his siblings but, and perhaps partly because his early memories were shaped in John's better times, James had more in common with his father. He shared his moderate Parnellian and socialist politics, his wit and his love of music. James recognised himself in his father. Young Joyce could so easily have headed the same way as his father and, as so many of their talented contemporaries, just another drunk in Dublin. It's true that passion and longing for art tended the young Joyce more to brooding than the father's hail fellow well met but James remained more his father's son than his mother's. Her prudent home economics, reminding us of Bloom, found little purchase with James and it was generally his sisters and, most emphatically, his brother Stanislaus that tended in that direction.

In the book, written only partially as a retrospective arrangement (Joyce senior died in 1931), Simon Dedalus is largely unsympathetic and contemptible but the wit is there: so many funny lines. At his father's funeral, Joyce remarked that what wit there is in *Ulysses* was all his father's, sometimes lifted word for word.[23] The cast list is also largely his father's friends and contemporaries and, generally, as Dublin is portrayed, it is the Dublin of John Joyce.

Back to Bloom . . .

He's trying to compose the letter to his Martha which is not easy sat opposite the inquisitive Goulding and can only manage a few lines under the bogus guise of answering a job advert. We marvel at clever Odysseus's occasional idiocy. We recall from her letter, the offence taken by Martha Clifford that Bloom included a stamp with his previous reply and so, one wonders, what of that makes him think she'd welcome a postal order for 12s 6d? Yet this seems to be his ill-judged intention. Is it a double bluff to drive her away? If so, why reply at all? Perhaps Bloom likes keeping his dalliances on a professional basis.

In the midst of crafting the letter, he thinks of Shakespearean quotes and then an unrelated line of narrative: 'In Gerard's rosery of Fetter lane he walks, greyed-aubern. One life is all. One body. Do. But do.'[24]

Which sounds very odd and, apropos nothing, but somehow familiar. We dredge it up from Scylla and Charybdis[25] where Stephen had the same vision of Shakespeare in London worried about being cuckolded in Stratford – a tiny snippet of Stephen and Bloom thinking in tandem.

Meantime music wafts from the bar as well as concert room. Lidwell, the suave solicitor, is tempted by bronze Miss Douce and fancies his chances. But the bronze tabby cat is reeling-in the mouse with, we assume, the inevitable result. Her weapon of choice? A large conch shell, centrepiece of the mirrored glass display which sings of the sea.

Bloom resisted love's sweet call but now faces a new challenge as the concert room music turns political, indeed, back to war as Ben Dollard applies his barrel tones to 'The Croppy Boy'. This, depending on one's point of view, is either a stirring ballad to rouse the nationalist fervour, or a song wallowing in pointless sentiment. So it's a little out of character that it is encouraged by Tom Kernan whom we know is no man of Sin Fein, though we also know from Wandering Rocks that he can role play when it suits. To over-simplify, the gist is this: the Croppies[26] were a band of Catholic anti-British rebels in the 1790 uprisings. Powdered wigs were associated with the establishment and those without were, the opposite and liable to suspicion of sedition. Thus mark of Cain for one side was a badge of honour for the other and was taken up by these Catholic rebels who not only eschewed the wig but cropped their hair short. The boy of the song was the youngest son of a man, killed with all of his other sons by the British in the Wexford uprising.[27] This lad has missed confession and, on seeing a priest in an abandoned barn, seeks absolution and imparts not only that he failed at Easter to pray for his mother (sounds familiar) but that he's continuing the family fighting tradition and proud to be taking up arms against the British. Unfortunately, the priest is actually a disguised British captain and, having heard the confession, provides absolution by way of the hangman's noose. Thus, family tradition upheld, albeit sooner than the Croppy Boy expected.

It is very beguiling and conversation in all three rooms grinds to a halt as they listen to Ben Dollard's deep and emotional rendition: tears well up.

Now Bloom was actually readying to move on. He'd finished his meal, had a bit of a go at Martha's letter and Boylan was gone. So, nothing keeping him. He left a tuppence tip for Pat and was saying goodbye to Richie Goulding but then he hears Dollard's resonating timbre from the other room . . . 'Oh Leo Boy, the pipes, the pipes are calling', and he lingers. We've mentioned Joyce's concern with the Irish tendency to hark back in sentimental terms to Irish myth and that this was one of nets that Stephen, in Icarus mode, wanted to fly high to escape. Professor James A W Hefferman in his lecture series[28] on *Ulysses* speaks of this episode setting out that sentimentality and the next, Cyclops, pointing to some of the dangerous places it might lead.

As said, all are in thrall to Dollard's powerful voice, Cowley's sympathetic accompaniment and, above all, to the lump-in-the-throat theme of the song. Well, nearly all. Perhaps helped by lingering in the midst of going, Bloom is impervious to the emotional siren song. He listens intellectually but not emotionally. From the off, his mind wanders; he half-watches Miss Douce, as she watches Big Ben Dollard whilst absently stroking the phallic ivory beer pull. He considers whether Ben Dollard might be better off focusing on sorting out his mess of a life rather than entertaining the troops in the pub. And, prompted by the lyrics, he thinks of deeper issues. That how, just like 'The Croppy Boy', 'The Last Rose of Summer' and that lonely sardine under the glass bell, he is also the last of his race in that, having lost his son, the Bloom name will die with Leopold: 'I too, last my race. Milly young student. Well, my fault perhaps. No son. Rudy. Too late now. Or if not? If not? If still?'[29]

Is that another sign of the worm turning? That he thinks maybe it's not too late to create further offspring? Any moment Molly will surely cuckold him, yet Bloom is still mulling over re-kindling their sexual flame. As if to underline his ambivalence, Bloom does leave before Dollard concludes, he does so without absolution but at least not drawn in by the siren call of gushing sentimentality.

All the while, Boylan in his cab is making his impatient way to Eccles Street. The narrative is not over-kind to this conquering hero. What with egging on the cabby to go faster and him sitting there with the haw-haw horn. A fairly unflattering cartoon image is painted as he perches, slightly desperate in his straw boater, serge blue tie and with a tumescent bulge in his trousers, straining the stitched artistry of the suit's tailor George S Mesias. No pun.

The rhythm of the episode continues to beat. Interspersed with Boylan's knock on the door with a cock, with a cock with a carra carra cock, Paul de Kock, we become aware of a tap, tap, tapping: initially insignificant but increasingly intrusive. The blind stripling returns to retrieve his forgotten tuning fork.

This seemingly minor character is of interest but we are uncertain as to his significance. Bloom was kind to him in Lestrygonians but the chap wasn't expressly appreciative. Cashel Boyle O'Connell Fitzmaurice Tisdal Farrell bashes into him in Wandering Rocks and gets a curse for his trouble. Joyce, by this time in life, had good reason to fear losing sight in at least one of his eyes. His cane, carried with swagger for effect in younger years, had become far more of an essential aid. Let's not rule out a Joyce personal intrusion but perhaps Tiresias may be more likely. He is the seer with whom Odysseus consulted in Hades and who indeed guides much of the Homeric plot but features far more subtly in our book. He's cursed with blindness but blessed with the gift of foreseeing the future. One might, one supposes, consider that Bloom is wilfully blind to Molly's dalliance with Boylan but perhaps because he sees a bigger and brighter future. One also notes that, in the Hades episode, Joyce links Tiresias to Robert Emmet, an early nineteenth century Irish martyr. He, too, asks to be judged only by circumstances which are yet to arise.[30] But this, too, is downplayed and marked only by Bloom thinking in error that he spots his grave. So the end to this episode might be wrapped up with injustice and wrongful conviction because the goddess that cursed Tiresias with blindness reflected that it may have been too harsh a punishment: the injustice of British occupation? We add that Emmet apparently was unjustly executed and we have the natural injustice of the congenitally or otherwise blind. The link is strengthened by the blind stripling entering the pub just as Bloom reads, in a shop window, a framed reproduction of Emmet's dying speech.[31]

Where are we going with this? Is Joyce concluding the episode with a serious point on injustice? An injustice wrought upon Bloom? This episode, if anything, has been sceptical of the lauding of historic Irish heroes. Whatever he may have intended, Joyce does not allow easy conclusions (at least not yet) and this is confirmed by the coda to the episode's musical score. Accompanying the percussion of the piano and the timpani of bar glasses, today we guest feature in the wind section – Bloom's digestive system. Never mind dusty bones of the long since dead, Bloom's guts remind us that he's very much in the here and now. The episode rests as he reads Emmet's stirring scaffold speech while emitting a loud fart.

One in the Eye for the Cyclops

Music: The Harp That Once Through Tara's Halls – Eleanor McEvoy

This time we have a contender for a favourite episode. Joyce stipulates no colour but our location is the Pub, our symbol, appropriate for St Patrick's Day is Fenian, our bodily organ is Muscle and our art is Gigantism. That sounds like it might make for some interesting unpacking and better done in Homeric context.

The crew anchor at yet another island, well we are, after all, near an archipelago. The travellers do not know what to expect, is the island inhabited? If so, by whom? Well, this is the island of the Cyclopes, a race of one eyed giants.[1] They are a solitary, cave-dwelling people, rarely mixing with strangers other than to eat them and are hardly more engaging with each other. They care more for the sheep they tend than most bipeds. Odysseus and his men are exploring a cave when someone or something pushes a large boulder across the entrance to slam it shut. This is the living quarters of Polyphemus and they are now his captives. Odysseus, who can sweet talk his way out of most tight spots, explains their story and expresses the traditional expectation that guests will be treated hospitably and helped on their way. The giant hears him out before grabbing and eating two of the crew. The only travel help on offer, it would seem, is passage to that other world.

To wash down his meal, Polyphemus takes some of Odysseus's wine followed by quite a lot more. They talk a little and Odysseus, lying like a trooper, says his name is Noman. Before long the giant is lulled into a deep wine-addled sleep. Nearby on the floor are some olive branches, traditional symbols of peace. Odysseus selects one of the largest, sharpens it, sets it alight and, assisted by some crew, thrusts the fiery spear into the sleeping giant's only eye and blinds him. The giant rages and hollers in agony so alerting his clansmen. They gather outside the blocked cave and ask if he is all right, to which he replies 'Noman is killing me'. A little puzzled, they think that weird Polyphemus is being weird and disperse. All very clever, but there's a way to go. Whilst Odysseus has averted the immediate danger of being eaten by the giant they remain trapped in the cave and have just blinded the only animate object capable of moving the boulder. Fear not! The clever chap's *coup de grâce* is that he and his men tie themselves to the bellies of the sheep and when the blind giant moves the boulder, only sufficiently to let the flock out to graze the men escape and are free. But proud Odysseus can't resist gilding the lily and shouts back to gloat his success at which the giant hurls the boulder at them, or in their general direction. It misses but Odysseus thereby courted unnecessary danger.

Back in Dublin, our giant is a Fenian nationalist brute of a man called the citizen, Joyce denies him the respect of a capital C. There's an Homeric reversal with Bloom named and the giant anonymous, though we also remember that Bloom represents everyman. This chap sits astride a bar-stall in his cave, which is Barney Kiernan's pub, 8, 9 and 10 Little Britain Street. He is one-eyed in the sense that he sees the world only through the prism of Irish nationalism. Only this is good and everything else, especially anything British, is bad. He becomes increasingly drunk at the expense of his little coterie, for he buys no beer himself, rather expects others to pay for the pleasure of his company as he lords it over his little world. Or so he thinks, for there are small signs that reality is nuanced and he may be tolerated, even subtly mocked, more than respected. At his feet, sheep-like, is a mangy mongrel, Garryowen, which we assume belongs him. The pub (ironically in a Fenian episode) in Little Britain Street is not a natural destination for Leopold Bloom but he's on a charitable mission concerning a life policy which it is hoped will provide some funds for Mrs Dignam, Paddy's widow. A legal complication requires some business at the courthouse around the corner in Green Street and Bloom has arranged to meet those two decent gents, Martin Cunningham and Jack Power, in this pub before setting off.

It is now 5 pm, therefore, that afternoon's blood sports, the adulterous tryst up in Eccles Street and the Ascot Gold Cup are either run or well underway. The outcome of neither of those is yet known to the reader and this event in the pub is about to begin. We are guided by two narrators, both nameless, so let's consider them 'Noman'. The key to this episode is to succeed where the Cyclops failed and get to grips with Noman

The first narrator is a compadre of the citizen. From his dialogue and style, we deduce he is working class, a collector of doubtful debts, a bit of a layabout and certainly a member of the drinking class. We come to see that he shares many of the citizen's nationalist and anti-Semitic views and yet there are hints that his support for the citizen is not totally heartfelt. As well as natural resentment of the bully, this may also be due to his natural inclination to mock. Mockery of anyone and everyone is this man's stock in trade. Moreover, unsavoury as his views are, his humour is endearing and his cynicism of interest. This novel has many unappealing characters but very few are unremittingly awful. This chap flits in and out of shadows, on terms with both Fenians and Troy of the DMP (Dublin Metropolitan Police). His currency seems to be hearsay and gossip and he's prepared to criticise pretty much anyone for the price of a pint (though one notes, not to their face), including the citizen but especially Bloom. His allegiances flit to suit his roving agenda and that of the chap buying the next pint. We suspect he lives on snippets of information picked up on the QT and a prime source apparently, is Pisser Burke, the off-stage resident of the salubrious [*sic*] City Arms Hotel.

The timing of his tale maybe of note – he's both within the drama and reporting upon it for someone's benefit and we do not expect this to be live reporting. There are hints that he recounts events from another pub sometime later and, no doubt, in return for more pints of beer. So when, midway through his story, he steps out the back to painfully urinate, there is a chance (albeit a small one), that he may not be at Barney Kiernan's, notwithstanding mention of Joe and Terry. There are hints of another pub later that night because he mumbles that he's drunk about a gallon (which is eight pints) and one doubts that even he has done that by 5 pm.

So this narrator, available for hire to any given buyer of the pint, is hardly reliable but compares favourably with our alternative. The best we can say of our second narrator is that he/she/it is reliably unreliable. We'll plump for the male vernacular for convenience and, to distinguish from the other chap, we'll call him the Parodist. He intrudes thirty or so times with lampooning vignettes hung upon recent or anticipated events. Generally, he ridicules to make a point which Joyce calls Gigantism, the stated style of the episode. We take this to mean that the Parodist takes a kernel of fact and inflates it to cartoon fairy-tale impossibility.

For example, towards the end of the episode, having been bought a drink, Martin Cunningham, toasts the good health of the fellow drinkers and innocently adds:

> God bless all here is my prayer.
> Amen says the citizen.[2]

Which triggers several pages of a medieval religious procession, which seems to be a ritualistic inauguration of a new cathedral or, in this case, Barney Kiernan's public-house.

In an earlier instance, the citizen questions Bloom's true nationality. In response to Bloom's answer as Irish, he spits a large globule of phlegm onto the floor and then swabs his chin with his handkerchief. This grim and messy nose rag is inflated, again over several pages, into an ornate ancient embroidered Irish facecloth attributed to Solomon of Droma and Manus Tomaltach og MacDonogh, authors of the *Book of Ballymote*[3]which was paraded by all for their prolonged admiration. You get the gist.

What is the point of the parodies? A suggestion is this: tradition and mythology are all well and good. All cultures hark back to it and it is part of what defines us. This novel, of course, takes ancient myth and applies it to the modern world but, in doing so, takes universal and inter-racial characteristics which are migrated from Greece to Ireland via Hungary. But when the myth centres on fighting heroes such as Cuchulin or Siegfried and *in extremis* such heroics are taken to racially define, there is the danger that one believes, for example, that the Irish or the Germans are exclusivist superior races and, well, we know where that might lead.

We are in this territory with the second parody beginning 'In Inishfail the fair . . .',[4] which is a gushing, rose-tinted description of Ireland back in the time of Tara and the Kings. Guided by such untrustworthy narrators, how do we discern reality? First, the Narrator (as opposed to the Parodist) provides enough sturdy ground upon which to stake some belief and, secondly, that our information bank concerning characters and events in our story is, by now, sufficiently well-stocked to distinguish some fantasy from reality. One narrator is anti-Bloom and the other phantasmagorical. It's all part of Joyce's stated aim to examine his Odysseus from all angles.[5]

The broad synopsis is relatively simple. Men are in the pub pond-skating various subjects. It starts to get exciting when conversation moves from the death of Dignam to discussion of capital punishment which leads, via Bloom's input on the male erection, to Irish nationalism and then, more generally and via animal cruelty, to nationhood. Bloom becomes increasingly isolated when pressed on his nationality. He leaves for the courthouse wondering if Cunningham and Power have gone straight there but in his absence they arrive at the pub. Inebriation increases and conversation bounces around those public bar perennials:

nationalism and male virility when, significantly, Lenehan has a theory on Bloom's departure, which is to cash his winnings, having backed the horse 'Throwaway' at 20–1 (or 100 to five, as they say). We know Bloom didn't do this, indeed has no interest in betting, but Lenehan's account is readily accepted. The atmosphere thereby shifts from abstract argument to hard evidence of the crafty snideness of Jews who must have some secret information on what was assumed to be a no-hoper horse. So, when Bloom returns to the pub his pockets, as they think, weighed down with cash yet still not buying drinks all round, things turn nasty. Martin Cunningham and Jack Power shuffle Bloom outside just in time to the waiting cabbie[6] (locally called the Jarvey). Bloom, like Odysseus, can't resist shouting back but, fortunately, the worst the blind drunk citizen can now muster, is to chuck an empty biscuit tin. In a final comic parody, the cab elevates as a fiery chariot identifying Bloom with Elijah and, just as likely, Jesus Christ.

That's the gist. Let's now pick out some of the more interesting aspects.

The episode opens with our first narrator, whom we'll call the Narrator to distinguish from the Parodist. He is recounting to Joe Hynes, that poor excuse for a journalist, to whom, you may recall, Bloom has lent three shillings although readers of *Dubliners* will recall a more nuanced character,[7] and Joyce's selection of him at this point is noteworthy. The narrator accounts to Hynes how he was standing on the corner of Arbour Hill, talking to a policeman, when a chimney sweep passed by and nearly poked him in the eye with a broom. It transpires he was there on some sort of court business, trying to levy execution of a court order upon a local swindler. It's a confused account but we work out that, despite his anti-Semitic humour, he is actually working on behalf of the Jewish merchant and plaintiff in the case, for whom judgment has been awarded. We also note early on, the near-miss of the sharp stick in the eye; indicating that this isn't our Cyclops, no matter that he may be deserving of similar fate.

The first parody intrudes: an overly legal account of the court order after which we are back in reality as the narrator and Hynes walk toward Barney Kiernan's tavern because Hynes wants to update the citizen on some council meeting news concerning Irish sports and that running theme since episode two, foot and mouth disease. One senses that this simply dictates to which pub they head, for the impression gleaned is that at 5 pm on a Thursday afternoon, any afternoon, they will be heading for a pub.

The citizen, on his usual perch is introduced in Irish heroic parody:

> The figure seated on a large boulder at the foot of a round tower was that of a broadshouldered deepchested stronglimbed frankeyed redhaired freely freckled shaggybearded widemouthed largenosed longheaded deepvoiced barekneed brawnyhanded hairylegged ruddyfaced sinewyarmed hero. From shoulder to shoulder he measured several ells and his rocklike mountainous knees were covered, as was likewise the rest of his body wherever visible, with a strong growth of tawny prickly hair in hue and toughness, similar to the mountain gorse (Ulex Europeus). The widewinged nostrils, from which bristles of the same tawney hue projected, were of such capaciousness that within their cavernous obscurity the fieldlark might easily have lodged her nest. The eyes in which a tear and a smile strove ever for the mastery were of the dimensions of a good size cauliflower. A powerful current of warm breath issued at regular intervals from the profound cavity of his mouth while in rhythmic resonance the loud strong hail reverberations of his formidable heart thundered rumblingly causing the ground, the summit of the lofty tower and the still loftier walls of the cave to vibrate and tremble.[8]

It continues: several more paragraphs describe his clothes and a couple of pages on his necklace from which hang cameo images of various heroes. The predictable cast list of Irish mythical and historic names descends into absurdity with dozens of unrelated characters and then, even more bizarre, as several are 'shamrocked' so that we have: Patrick W Shakespeare, Brian Confucius and Murtagh Gutenberg.

This chap is a thinly disguised lampoon of a real person, Michael Cusack,[9] teacher and founder of the Gaelic Athletics Association. By no means a giant, he was of average height but a broad-shouldered muscular man. He was a shot-putter of some distinction and fond of announcing himself as Citizen Cusack. Very pro-Irish and, by all accounts, pretty bombastic but perhaps not the racist thug as portrayed in this episode, at least his Wikipedia page so denies. But again, the style and perhaps the point, of the episode are to take a kernel of truth or characteristic and blow it out of proportion to either emphasise or undermine a point. Also to lambast the likes of the Gaelic League and the Irish Literary Revival for doing something pretty similar, that is, taking a semblance of an event in Irish history or legend and expanding it to grandiose, heroic proportion: Gigantism, for example, 'The Croppy Boy' song of the last episode.

He's the central character in the episode and his simplistic racially pure world-view is pitted directly against Bloom, the Jew, preaching universal and inter-racial love and tolerance. One static and rooted to his land, the other representing a race rooted in their heads to a land in the Middle East but dispersed throughout the world. The citizen, of course, appears to miss the irony that the Irish by then had emigrated far and wide. But this is no David versus Goliath for, as we'll see in the next episode, Nausicaa, initial assumptions aren't always correct and, deflated to reality, the citizen is no fine specimen of a man, let alone a giant. Yes, Bloom finds himself at the centre of a racist maelstrom with an undercurrent of violence and much of the fun of the episode is watching him challenge this and overcome. But is his victory so heroic? Our answer lies towards the end of the episode when the citizen's rage against Bloom explodes as he chases him out of the pub. To this point, our vision of him has been one of strength, virility and vitality, so we believe that brave Bloom has been flirting with considerable danger. But consider this late narrative description:

> I saw the citizen getting up to waddle to the door, puffing and blowing with the dropsy and he cursing the curse of Cromwell[10] on him . . . [11]

It's easy to miss, caught up as we are in the hilarity of the moment, but, once aware, we must re-calibrate our impression to an ill and quite weak man whose frustration at his own pathetic inadequacy causes a belligerence that emits bark far worse than bite and whose stasis on that bar-stool accelerates and exacerbates his debilitating dropsy. An affliction that may well have been caused in the first place by the copious amounts of alcohol he consumes. One may now reinterpret Bloom's hovering outside the pub as impatience to get to the courthouse rather than fear of entering the cave and his fighting his corner less to abject bravery and more to the worthiness of the cause but also to Bloom's inability to resist debate. Basically he likes to display his intellectual dexterity. Phenomenology as the narrator calls it:

> I declare to my antimacassar if you took up a straw from the bloody floor and if you said to Bloom: Look at, Bloom, Do you see that straw? That's a straw. Declare to my aunt he'd talk about it for an hour so he would and talk steady.[12]

And love him as we do, we suspect this to be right.

It would also be a mistake to judge the cause by the protagonist: Fenian nationalism by the standards of the citizen. He's about as effective an advocate as is Kevin Egan out in Paris.[13] That the issue is more nuanced is further demonstrated when it transpires that Bloom, for all his lauding of the civilising effect of colonialism and respect for British civilisation, has advised Arthur Griffith's Sinn Fein on strategy based on his knowledge of Hungarian anti-Austrian resistance tactics. Whether this is true[14] (for our fictional purposes, Cunningham appears to confirm it) and whether such advice was sought or even noticed by Griffiths, we know not and it hardly matters. The thing is, it queers the pitch. It's easy to assume that Joyce was anti-Fenian. His family background was Parnellian home rule though we also know that some of the Fenian connections in Proteus were autobiographical.[15] It's a murky world where a little knowledge is more dangerous than usual but a guess would be that Joyce was pro-independence but with a larger agenda embroiling socialism and continental Europe.

Joe Hynes buys a round of drinks: indeed he will buy several rounds indicating that he heeded Bloom's advice to visit the cashiers at the *Freeman's Journal* and that it yielded a bumper return. The barman Terry pulls the pints and is lampooned as he brings:

> . . . a crystal cup full of the foaming ebon ale which the noble twin brothers Bungiveagh and Bungardilaun[16] brew ever in their divine alevats, cunning as the sons of deathless Leda. For they garner the succulent berries of the hop and mass and sift and bruise and brew them and they mix therewith sour juices and bring the must to the sacred fire and cease not night or day from their toil, those cunning brothers, lords of the vat.[17]

Thus the court presided over by the citizen is in session and likely to continue well into the evening with increasing inebriation. Conversation will ebb and flow as men arrive on the scene and contribute to the drama. All the while, as beer is imbibed, the atmosphere becomes, by degree, increasingly threatening and malevolent, with Bloom, unwittingly, in the eye of the storm. The setting itself is a sort of crime scene, for Barney Kiernan, proprietor, collects morbid criminal memorabilia which is strewn about the place, for example, the hangman correspondence we will see in a moment. So, the increasingly violent feel to the proceedings has a suitable backdrop.

An early topic is poor lamented Paddy Dignam. Alf Bergan can't believe it: he could have sworn he spotted him not a few minutes earlier and the general disbelief of the demise leads to a cracking one-liner entrusted to Joe Hynes to deliver, that, whether or not he's dead, Hynes was at Glasnevin cemetery that morning and saw them take the liberty of burying him, just in case.[18] Drunken Bob Doran of *Dubliners* fame,[19] lets himself down with an uncontrollable episode of blasphemous weepies.

The Parodist steps in with an inter-stellar theosophist[20] road map of the afterlife and, once we are beyond that tantric wisdom, he moves into direct communication with Paddy Dignam from beyond the grave:

> In reply to a question as to his first sensations in the Great Divide beyond he stated that previously he had seen as in a glass darkly but that those who had passed over had summit possibilities of atmic development opened up to them. Interrogated as to whether life there resembled our experience in the flesh he stated that he had heard from more favoured beings now in the spirit that their abodes were equipped with every modern home comfort such as tālāfānā, ālāvātār, hātākāldā, wātāklāsāt and that the highest adepts were steeped in ways of volupcy of the very purist nature ...
>
> Asked if he had any message for the living he exhorted all who were still at the wrong side of Maya to acknowledge the true path for it was reported in devanic circles that Mars and Jupiter were out for mischief on the eastern angle where the ram has power ...
>
> ... Before departing he requested that it should be told to his dear son Patsy that the other boot which he had been looking for was at present under the commode in the return room and that the pair should be sent to Cullen's to be soled only as the heels were still good. He stated that this had greatly perturbed his peace of mind in the other region and earnestly requested that his desire should be made known.[21]

Bloom arrives on the scene. Indeed, in contrast with Homeric parallel, the citizen invites him in. Bloom was hovering outside because you'll recall that the pub was just a meeting point for onward travel to the courthouse: 'Come in, come on, he won't eat you, says the citizen.'[22] Which is to state something of the obvious as snores rather than snarls emit from the mongrel.

Bloom asks if they've seen Cunningham and Power and, like Odysseus to Polyphemus, explains the context of his sojourn. He rejects Hynes' offer of a drink, which is up there with one of the worst etiquette *faux pas* one can commit in Dublin, and establishes Bloom as the outsider, though, when pressed, he accepts a cigar.[23]

Alf Bergan is mulling through a pile of dusty letters on the bar and morbid interest is piqued by the letter from H Rumbold, Master Barber, from The Wirral in Lancashire who is tendering for a job as a professional hangman. As said, Bernard Kiernan, proprietor, has an unsavoury interest in morbid memorabilia. A discussion on capital punishment ensues and Bloom weighs in, challenging its effectiveness as a deterrent against serious crime. Joe Hynes, again the comedian, quips that it is no deterrent against lusty thoughts because, when the Invincible Joe Brady,[24] was cut down from the scaffold, life extinguished, he had a huge erection.

The virility is somehow attributed to his Fenian nationalism:

> 'Ruling passion strong in death, says Joe, as someone said.'
>
> 'That can be explained by science, says Bloom. It's only a natural phenomenon, don't you see, because on account of the . . . '[25]

The Narrator amusingly lambasts Bloom's long-winded explanations on anything and everything, before the Parodist intrudes with a scientific account showing that, whilst Bloom is gigantist with his use of long and complex words, he turns out to be scientifically correct in this instance. Hanging by the neck will, like it or not, induce the male erection.

But the real significance here is the reference to Joe Brady because it's a trigger of Irish nationalism and enables the citizen to let rip on his favourite subject: how wonderful is everything Irish and how it would be the finest country in the world were it not for the terrible Brits. Any intimation by Bloom that aspects of the British Empire have been civilising, is swatted away by the citizen as 'Their syphilisation, you mean.'[26]

Conversation bounces around diverse matters but wherever it goes, the citizen is on the opposite side to Bloom and becoming increasingly bellicose. Lenehan enters looking like a fellow that had lost a shilling and found a tanner (half the value) and we learn why – a huge shock in the Gold Cup which was won by the 20–1 outsider, 'Throwaway'. Basically, all the punters in this pub and pretty much all over Dublin, have done their money.

The topic shifts to Molly's forthcoming musical tour and presents a repeat of the ribald banter that Bloom heard from the sanctuary of the restaurant in the Ormond Hotel but now the derision of his virility is up front and personal. It is also a foreshadowing of what will shortly be repeated with greater venom in his absence. The Narrator assumes that, whilst Blazes Boylan is not part of the official ensemble, he'll still be 'doing the tootle on the flute'. Their impression of Molly is parodied thus:

> Pride of Calpe's rocky mount,[27] the raven haired daughter of Tweedy. There grew she to peerless beauty where loquat and almond scent the air. The gardens of Alameda knew her step: the garths of olives knew and bowed. The chaste spouse of Leopold is she: Marion of the bountiful bosoms.[28]

Note the play on the word, 'chaste' for, at that very moment, she is being chased around the parlour and bedroom with 'left off clothes of all descriptions'.

J J O'Molloy arrives from the courthouse which prompts a heavily biased account of a case involving a Jewish moneylender, and the ubiquitous undercurrent of England's enslavement of the far greater Ireland is parodied in a boxing match. Bloom, all the while, preaches peace unto the nations. We then cut to the chase: 'What is your nation if I may ask, says the citizen.'[29]

When Bloom answers 'Ireland', for he was born there, the citizen rebuts by spitting a huge gob of phlegm (a Red Bank oyster) onto the sawdust floor. The thought occurs that this projectile is as near as he now gets to champion shot-putting. The likes of the citizen only understands Ireland in terms of white catholics and can never accept a Jew as Irish. His myopic division of the world between friends and enemies is displayed as he glares at Bloom: 'Sinn Fein! says the citizen. Sinn fein amhain! The friends we love are by our side and the foes we hate before us.'[30]

He identifies Bloom with Ahasuerus, the Wandering Jew, as have we throughout these lectures, though one doubts the citizen intends it as a compliment. He then unwittingly links him with Jesus Christ: 'A new apostle to the gentiles, says the citizen. Universal Love.'[31]

And a little later, with irony: 'That's the new Messiah for Ireland! says the citizen. Island of saints and sages!'[32] And, of course, right near the end of the episode will want to crucify him.

Bloom protests that, as well as belonging to the Irish nation, he also belongs to a race. A race that is hated and persecuted: 'Taking what belongs to us by right. This very moment, says he, putting up his fist . . .'[33]

He continues by referencing Moroccan slave markets and it's all somewhat confusing as we assume he must be talking about Jews but, were they sold as slaves in Morocco around 1904? We clearly haven't paid sufficient historical attention to 1904 Morocco for we do not know. Has he lost the plot?[34] Maybe the Narrator was right about Bloom and his phenomenology, after all, he does get carried away, for example, he will shortly claim the composer Giuseppe Mercadante to be a Jew and he was a devout Italian Catholic. No, wait up, maybe he's talking about the human race. We are by now all trained in Schopenhauer so we know we should be empathetic to all humans, indeed all things, because we are, according to that philosopher, all united into one entity. This is underscored when Bloom preaches as if from the Mount that we simply all need to love one another. He convinces John Wise Nolan at least, who in that moment, shows some decency.[35]

We are wary of jumping to conclusions. Bloom flatters himself on his logical thinking and with some, but not complete, justification for, sometimes, his logic becomes a little, well, illogical. Especially when stressed and now at around 5.30 pm as he assumes another man to be in his bed with his wife – why wouldn't he be stressed? 'This very moment, this very instant': why is he so particular? How does he know what's happening this instant in Morocco? Yes, Bloom is empathetic; yes, he believes in what he says about love not hate but what's really important to him, as we saw earlier on his way back from the butchers with his Zionist pamphlet, especially just now, this instant, is his Moorish Gibraltarian girl, Molly, and what she's getting up to in the master bedroom at 7 Eccles Street; or might that be the slave master bedroom?

So we are delighted to see Bloom stand up to the citizen and preach racial tolerance, pacifism and universal love and, metaphorically, stab him in his myopic eye with his 'knockmedown' cigar but one fears that the trigger for his outburst is less likely to be empathy for humanity of whatever creed or colour and more likely to be the anger and humiliation arising out of the cuckolding. The equanimity he has maintained over the previous hours has erupted.

We fast forward a little. Bloom has headed back to the courthouse but *in absentia* remains the topic of conversation. The air is drunk with rumour concerning Molly, Blazes Boylan and Bloom's virility with the citizen casting doubt on whether any of Bloom's children are his own. Then the penny drops with Lenehan who thinks he realises where Bloom has really disappeared to, this very instant. And he lights the metaphorical fuse concerning the racehorse 'Throwaway'.

You will recall that the seeds for this were sown back in the Lotus Eaters episode. Bloom leaves Sweny's pharmacy and bumps into

Bantam Lyons who asks to borrow Bloom's newspaper so he can check the runners for the Gold Cup, running that afternoon. Bloom, who is in a hurry, tells him he can keep it for he was just about to throw it away. When Lyons sees that the race includes a horse called 'Throwaway' he thinks Bloom has imparted insider knowledge[36] and, though it's a rank outsider, decides to risk backing it. Later in the Wandering Rocks episode Lenehan persuades him otherwise.[37] Lenehan's theory is readily accepted as fact and so the belief is that Bloom has made a fortune on the horse race, possibly the only man in Dublin that has, and has gone to collect his shekels. On the other hand, these fine upstanding citizens have all blown their money. Bloom is out defrauding widows and orphans, menaces Lenehan, which statement is a challenge to logic even if we didn't know that Bloom's actual mission was precisely the opposite.

By the time of Bloom's return, Martin Cunningham and Jack Power have arrived at the pub. All hell breaks loose in a chaotic pantomime scene. One has difficulty working out the greater crime. Is it keeping the horse racing tip to himself (to this Bloom is decidedly not guilty)? Is it being a Jew (not technically guilty – but that's a complicated one)? Or, and we feel this is the winner, is it not buying a round of drinks? This, it seems, is the cardinal sin in Dublin. Though, we observe, one that is shared this day by the citizen, Lenehan and our Narrator who, not recognising his own guilt, sums up his thoughts:

> 'Courthouse my eye and your pockets hanging down with gold and silver. Mean bloody scut. Stand us a drink itself. Devil a sweet fear! There's a jew for you! All for number one. Cute a shithouse rat. Hundred to five.'[38]

Martin Cunningham and Jack Power, our Homeric sheep, sense where this is headed and usher Bloom out of the pub as quickly as possible as the citizen shouts after them: 'Three cheers for Israel!'[39]

We end with a phantasmagorical scene to rival any in the upcoming episode, Circe. The horse-drawn cab is gigantisised into Elijah's fiery chariot[40] ascending, at a forty-five degree angle, to heaven. Bloom stood aloft upon it, looking back in Odysseus pose and provocatively claiming:

> 'Mendelssohn was a jew and Karl Marx and Mercadante and Spinoza. And the Saviour was a jew and his father was a jew. Your God.'[41]

Martin Cunningham tries to haul him down, reminding Bloom that the Saviour had no father. But Bloom is undeterred and unrepentant:

'. . . Your God was a jew. Christ was a jew like me.'[42]

It's all so good and so dramatic that we'll gloss over the subliminal consubstantiation and the Bloom equals Christ subliminal messages. Back to the story:

Incendiary stuff, the citizen, with no irony, swears he'll crucify Bloom but the only weapon available is the empty biscuit tin his dog has been slobbering over, which, as though it were a boulder, he launches, shot-put style. But blinded both by drink and (like that other racist Mr Deasy back in episode 2) by the sun in his eyes, the missile is well off target but, in our penultimate parody, its landing is so cataclysmic as to cause an earthquake of biblical proportions engulfing many surrounding buildings including the courthouse. The clouds part and God calls Bloom, Elijah, to his side. Bloom answers, *abba,* father, thereby proclaiming himself to be the son of God.[43] There's a lot happening as this amazing episode fades out, like a shot off a shovel.

LECTURE 14, 31 MARCH 2021: EPISODE 13

Nausicaa and the Coming of Elijah

Music: Girl, You'll Be A Women Soon – Neil Diamond

This is an important episode. It marks transition from day to night, from child to adult and, arguably, from masculine to feminine – a controversial episode and in its way wonderful. It infamously played into the hands of censors and burners of books for, not only do we have a voyeuristic sexual act on the beach, but, right there under the nose of, and in allegorical reference to, the Virgin Mary, at her church in Sandymount, St Mary's, Star of the Sea.

We left Leopold Bloom elevating into the heavens at a 45-degree angle over Green Street in celestial escape from the citizen. We can report that he will land in Sandymount, having sojourned off-stage, at the house of the recently widowed Mrs Dignam. On this beach he will find the company of a beautiful, fragile and graceful young lady named Gerty MacDowell and he will find a little relief and respite from the trials of the day. We will get to know something of Gerty, her friends and family as we go.

We become accustomed to a female voice which is a pleasant departure. Other than a little Molly, Mrs Breen and other minor cameos, we've inhabited a male world, an emphasis that will shift a little, beginning here. One might make a case that we remain in a womanly domain for the rest of the book, excepting the Eumaeus episode, but Eumaeus, almost by definition, is a trickster.

This journey to womanhood begins at the outset as though regressing into an enfolding womb:

> The summer evening had begun to fold the world in its mysterious embrace. Far away in the west the sun was setting and the last glow of all too fleeting day lingered lovingly on the sea and strand, on the proud promontory of dear old Howth guarding as ever the waters of the bay, on the weedgrown rocks along Sandymount shore and, last but not least, on the quiet church whence there streamed forth at times upon the stillness the voice of prayer to her who is in her pure radiance a beacon ever to the storm-tossed heart of man, Mary, star of the sea.[1]

Those opening words paint a pretty and inviting picture. Do we note more? We are reminded that midsummer day is just around the corner, we have Howth Head a place of supreme significance for Molly and Bloom, we have Dublin Bay, the waters of which bitter mystery Stephen is to brood upon no more and, of course, the church, naturally a beacon of Catholicism but also an homage to Mary which, in this blasphemous book, might also be to Marion, she of the bounteous bosoms.

It's around 8 pm. We have the last embers of a pretty acceptable early summer's day. Storm clouds have vaguely threatened and that levy will breach in around two hours' time but, for now, the air and the sun are gentle and the light soft and flattering. We have returned to the very beach along which Stephen strolled and then rested this morning, indeed, if the gods of serendipity smile, it's a fair bet that either Gerty or Bloom will recline on what we might term, Stephen's rock.

Our schematic Organ is both the eye and the nose; the Art is painting, the subject a Virgin and the Technic, tumescence and detumescence and that may hint at more gigantism from the last episode.

Bloom is tired. His experience in Barney Kiernan's took a toll, physically and mentally. Since then he's spent an hour or so in the apparent squalor of Mrs Dignam's house quite nearby in Newlands Avenue. He will expend further life-force here on the beach and it's no surprise that he ends the episode asleep on a bench or a rock. Odysseus is also tired. He washes up on the shore of Scheria more dead than alive.[2] General thinking is that this may be modern Corfu. If we also accept that Calypso's island of Ogygia is Gibraltar, then Odysseus has 'sailed' the greater chunk of the Mediterranean for much part, thanks to angry Poseidon, hanging onto a couple of planks of wood and, for the last days, hanging on to nothing. He arrives, to say the least, storm-tossed and lies bedraggled and naked among the foliage where the river meets the sea. Several hours later Princess Nausicaa appears at the same spot with nubile friends and servants to do the laundry: girls becoming women, learning adult responsibility. Their laughter, ball games and washing awaken Odysseus. Not knowing on what sort of island he has beached and having experienced cannibals and man-eating cyclopes, one may understand that he feels scared and vulnerable. His nakedness hardly helps. When a ball bounces close by, he emerges, tentatively, grabbing some leaves for modesty. He will find the Phaeacians more than hospitable. Whilst Nausicaa's less mature friends run off in horror, she's of royal lineage and lingers to hear Odysseus's story. Goddess Athena has intervened just in time and made Odysseus taller and sexier so as to appeal to Nausicaa. He does and she invites him back to the palace for dinner and to meet the royal parents but she's smart as well as beautiful and knows tongues will wag if they arrive together. Moreover, she advises that the key to a happy life round these parts is sweet-talking her mother, the queen. To cut a long story short, Odysseus regales all at dinner with tales of his adventures (such tales being a good chunk of Homer's book) and good King Alcinous agrees to supply him with a sturdy boat which will, and indeed does, enable his return to Ithaca. There is some mutual and quite profound electricity between Odysseus and the young Nausicaa but he has not come this far to be distracted from Penelope and so it remains, especially for Nausicaa, unrequited love.

We now join the modern beach party and three friends aged twenty or thereabouts. Two of them, Edy Boardman and Cissy Caffrey are, for this evening at least, surrogate mothers to younger siblings. Tommy and Jacky Caffrey, twins, are two curly headed boys dressed in sailor suits with caps to match. They are three or four years old and then there's baby Boardman,in the care of big sister Edy.

The episode falls into two halves: initially the interior monologue of Gerty MacDowell and then, after an explosive climax midway, Bloom takes over. The narrative, certainly for the first half, reflects Gerty's style of thinking. It's romantic, clichéd and rose-tinted. It would be wrong to say that this is typical of young teenage women because Gerty may no longer be a teenager and, moreover, it is not true so far we can tell, of either of her friends. Both Edy and Cissy seem far more brusque and hard-bitten, indeed both will be hanging around the red-light area in a few hours' time with the children still in tow. Life as cocooned within a romantic novel seems, in this company at least, to be something peculiar to Gerty.

After the complex style of some previous episodes and others yet to come it is a welcome relief to be able to read a normally written episode. It would, though, be a mistake to underestimate its subtle power. The fluency of the writing tempts one to dispense with too much commentary, for events, as narrated, are quite clear, but what the narrator sees isn't necessarily actuality and that is of interest to us, eager students of Joyce. The schematic style is painting and indeed our narrator falls in with Gerty-style cliché and describes her as pretty as a picture. Yet whilst Gerty is aware of her natural beauty and whilst her appearance is of utmost importance to her, she nevertheless feels it must be artificially enhanced. We sense self-doubt: that, to her mind, she is as she is, insufficient. Accordingly make-up, beauty tips and skin care products are not only highly prized but essential and Gerty is proud of her good taste in selection and dexterity in application. She is combined artist, muse and canvas; she paints, together with the narrator, a lovely self-portrait, adorned by her plumage of various hues but tending towards blue.

Her apparent purity, the paleness of skin and the blue of her various garments bring to mind the Virgin Mary and the adjacent church, the Star of the Sea, dedicated to the Blessed Virgin. The service we can hear is a retreat for reformed or reforming alcoholics. Gerty is also on a rescue mission. There's a man out there somewhere that needs the Gerty treatment. She'd make the perfect wife: she'd cook him a lovely breakfast and she'd hold him close while they stare dreamily into each other's eyes. She's not so sure about the baser aspects of marriage but does not dwell on those. Talking of base, she doesn't much like the baser aspects of anything, such as her menstrual cycle and coarse language, blushing rose-deep (rose being the Virgin Mother's flower) when Cissy says "beetoteetom" in reference to her little brother's backside. Her man would treasure her, worship her almost, and she'd save him, for her man straight out of the romantic magazine stories, would be a little older, would have had seen something of life and, above all, would have suffered. He'd need the comforting arms of a loving wife, not like that silly, no more than a child, Reggie Wylie, who rides his bicycle past her house but whose Protestant family has discouraged anything progressing. She's trying not to think of that, too.

The little Caffrey boys are playing sandcastles and ball games under the watchful eye of their elder sister, practising motherhood. Their reference to a sand Martello tower, ties us to Stephen and his walk along the same beach. A man, reclines upon nearby rocks until fate draws him into the proceedings. Across the millennia from ancient Greece, the ball over-bowls its way towards him and, in endeavouring to return it to the bowler, he succeeds only in nestling it beneath Gerty's skirts. She miskicks it back into play amidst a silent mutual acknowledgment.

Edy and Cissy barely record his presence beyond some banality. But for Gerty this man counts for something. She has noticed him and feels sure he notices her, particularly her. She attributes to this stranger all the qualities of her ideal man. He is tall, dark, handsome, with more than a touch of the exotic: especially as he is, suited and booted, top to toe in black. We'd better at this point consider Mr Leopold Bloom, for it is he. Do we know what he looks like? We learned in Aeolus that height wise, he's around five foot nine inches,[3] so more average than tall. But he appears tall to Gerty – perhaps due to her real or imagined perspective for that is how she expects her man to be. In Sirens, Miss Bronze and Miss Gold seemed to consider Bloom ugly until we caught on they were talking of the pharmacist. Nevertheless, some of that mud stuck. We assume him to be a touch swarthy with perhaps some heaviness around dark eyes and, in spite of or because of this (depending on taste), had enough going for him to attract Molly.

But here at last, we have genuine description:

> She could see at once by his dark eyes and his pale intellectual face that he was a foreigner, the image of the photo she had of Martin Harvey, the matinee idol, only for the moustache which she preferred because she wasn't stage struck like Winny Rippingham that wanted they two to always dress the same on account of a play but she could not see whether he had an aquiline nose or a slightly retrousse from where he was sitting.[4]

So there we have it. All we need do is find a picture of the matinee idol Martin Harvey to find our Bloom. We'll have to add in a moustache but that was ok because Gerty liked a 'tache – though this is to indulge Gerty as an accurate narrator. She's apt to idolise and romanticise but, nevertheless, do check out Martin Harvey for this link will be subsequently corroborated.

Like Odysseus with Nausicaa, some twenty years separates Bloom and Gerty and she, Gerty, could feel the intense hungry stare of those mysterious deep eyes, reaching into her, yearning for her. Was it to stretch a point to think, like those reforming sinners, that he was in supplication to her? And, all at the same time, she could smell the incense burning in the church and heard the beseeching of those men for the forgiveness of the Blessed Virgin. Gerty would forgive this man. She would redeem him, whoever he was, even if he were a Protestant or a Methodist. He had suffered, she could tell, and, if a sinner, then more sinned against than sinning.

As for the men inside the church, they needed rescuing. She knew all about the demon drink, her own father was in its thrall and so bad was he sometimes that she had witnessed violence in the family home; and where had it got him? He was now so afflicted with gout he couldn't even attend the funeral this morning of their close friend and neighbour Paddy Dignam nor could he attend his place of business, which we know because it was Gerty who earlier in Wandering Rocks, had to fetch the post and the cork lino samples from his office. Now that

Dignam is mentioned, we recall that Mrs MacDowell was one of those mourners at the Dignam house whose incessant jabbering and sighing Master Patrick Dignam was so desperate to escape. And here we are in Sandymount, close to the Dignam house at 9 Newbridge Avenue. One wouldn't be surprised if one of those drawn blinds belonged to the MacDowell residence and it may have even been Mrs MacDowell, back in episode six, her nose flattened against the window as the funeral cortège moved away. Bloom spent the early evening at that house, so our modern Odysseus did as Nausicaa advised his ancient counterpart: spend time with her mother, Mrs MacDowell; as for violent drunken Mr MacDowell, more shortly.

Leopold Bloom has struggled with the word parallax. As with other technical matters he has a pretty decent amateur grasp but, truth be told, is a little vague on some of the all-important finer detail. In Lestrygonians he pondered seeking answers from Professor Joly up at Dunsink Observatory but thought better of it. Parallax. The word has multi-applications. One concerns the intricate and difficult technicalities entailed in measuring the distance of planets from earth. It's a complex business, involving speed of orbital rotation and factoring in precisely from where and to where, on both planets, measurements are taken. We don't need to worry too much about it, notwithstanding the interstellar aspects of our book and the respective orbital trajectories of Stephen and Bloom.

A little closer to home, one is unreliably informed, it has come to describe a deficiency of the twin lens reflex camera. That is one of those slightly old-fashioned looking box cameras where the image is fixed by looking down into a viewfinder lens from above yet the picture is captured through a second front facing lens. A Hasselblad, apparently, was a fine example. What the photographer sees is not precisely the image captured and the difference between the two is . . . the parallax. In other words, one's impression is sculpted by one's perspective and that, in this episode of painting a picture, is portrayed before us. Gerty sees what she wants to see through a romantic, genteel soft-focus prism. Like the goddess Athena she paints the man better and shinier than he actually is. And so Bloom is her exotic foreign Prince Charming who will sweep her off of her feet and, Julia Roberts *Pretty Woman* style, be rescued right back in return. For his part, Leopold also does not see Gerty for what she is until just after the crux of the episode.

The crux of the episode

Several hours ago the Viceroy, the Earl of Dudley and his party headed in ceremonial cavalcade to the bazaar in the south of the city in aid of Mercers Hospital. That event is drawing to a close which will be marked by a crescendo of fireworks. Daytime has given way to twilight and suddenly, out of the violet-indigo sky a whoosh sound and an accompanying explosion: fireworks! The kids are running off to get a better vantage with elder sisters pushing baby close behind. Gerty however remains static on her rock:

> She had no intention being at their beck and call. If they could run like rossies she could sit so she could see from where she was. The eyes that were fastened upon her set her pulses tingling.[5]

The more she reclines to see the pyrotechnics, the more her charms are revealed to the voyeur. Still she leans back, so far that she must hold her bent leg at the knee for balance and to facilitate an even more lurid display, way up above her knees. He is looking and she knows it. And not just looking . . .

> . . . she seemed to hear the panting of his heart, his hoarse breathing, because she knew about the passion of men like that, hot-blooded, because Bertha Supple told her once in dead secret and made her swear she'd never about the gentleman lodger that was staying with them out of the Congested Districts Board that had pictures cut out of papers of those skirt-dancers and highkickers and she said he used to do something not very nice that you could imagine sometimes in the bed. But this was altogether different from a thing like that because there was all the difference because she could almost feel him draw her face to his and the first quick hot touch of his handsome lips. Besides there was absolution so long as you didn't do the other thing before being married . . . '[6]

As rockets fly and roman candles zig-zag across dark sky, a bat darts hither and thither with vampiric ambience, as though there to take by force, Gerty's innocence: reminding of Steven's poetic creation possibly on that very rock. Mouth to mouth's kiss.[7]

The tension builds until analogous with the exploding fireworks, Bloom orgasms, not quite as a seedy flasher (though let's face it, as close as dammit) but discreetly into his trouser pocket. Like Odysseus, he disguises his manhood, like Canon O'Hanlon in the nearby church he is veiled as he gives benediction with the Sacrament in his hand. One can understand that this did not go down too well with the Catholic hierarchy and shocks even in our supposed enlightened times. What is undisguised and obvious is that Bloom, who so misses his dead child, wastes his seed whilst Boylan before his own shrine to the Blessed Marion, thrusts his divine essence into Bloom's wife. Wasted seed and the crime against fecundity will be considered at length next episode.

From this moment narration, like her innocence, is extracted by Bloom from Gerty's grasp. It, an interior monologue, oozes and intermingles in the style with which we are by now accustomed:

> Then all melted away dewily in the grey air: all was silent. Ah! She glanced at him as she bent forward quickly, a pathetic little glance of piteous protest, of shy reproach under which he coloured like a girl. He was leaning back against the rock behind. Leopold Bloom (for it is he) stands silent, with bowed head before those young guileless eyes. What a brute he had been! At it again? A fair unsullied soul had called to him and, wretch that he was, how had he answered? An utter cad he had been! He of all men! But there was an infinite store of mercy in those eyes, for him too a word of pardon even though he had erred and sinned and wandered. Should a girl tell? No, a thousand times no. That was their secret, only theirs, alone in the hiding twilight and there was none to know or tell save the little bat that flew so softly through the evening to and fro and little bats don't tell.[8]

A sexual experience has occurred between them and engulfed them, though it seems only the man achieved total fulfilment. To de-tumesce to practical matters, it shows that Bloom remains sexually capable, in discharge as well as tumescence and so his rumination in Sirens that it's not too late for him to produce offspring, remains good, technically at least. We also learn that he did not masturbate in the Turkish bath that morning and that he is not circumcised. We are not surprised that the sexual act here was conducted without touch of other or any speech and with anonymity and disguise. In that sense, as gregarious as he might otherwise be, Bloom, like Stephen, represents the isolation of the human condition. They (Bloom, Stephen and perhaps Gerty, too), are kindred spirits.

And we learn more of Gerty as she stands tall to join the others. They share a final moment:

> Their souls met in a last lingering glance and the eyes that reached her heart, full of a strange shining, hung enraptured on her sweet flowerlike face. She half smiled at him wanly, a sweet forgiving smile, a smile that verged on tears, and then they parted.[9]

We can take a lofty moral view to all of this: that it was tacky, a little disgusting, obviously written by a man, a poor excuse for sexual intimacy . . . all of that. But, by the same token, a moment of intimacy occurred between two people, groping in the twilight for some sort of emotional salvation.

And off she goes, without a backward glance. Bloom mistakes her struggled step for tight boots before realising she is lame. This slender image of Irish perfection is flawed – she walks with a pronounced limp. Bloom feels even more guilty and is glad he was not aware 'while she was on show'. But then consoles himself as he quickly comes to terms with it: 'Hot little devil all the same.'[10]

So ends what one may argue is the most profound interaction between Bloom and another, aside from Stephen and aside from the kissing of a buttock some hours hence.

For most of the second half of the episode we have Bloom's rambling monologue. Various thoughts nip back and forth like the flying bat, many of which he considered earlier that day. Scent, for example; Gerty's scent, no doubt perfumed but he thinks of the essence of female scent and wonders if there's a male equivalent. Girls becoming women, Milly's burgeoning sexuality, her first period, morphing her into Molly. Naturally as ever, he thinks of Molly. It is by now around 8.30 pm and the worst may or may not be over. Boylan, he thinks, got the plums whilst he's left with the plum-stones, an accidental allusion both to Stephen's parable of the plums and Boylan's basket of fruit. The light in the sky is pretty much exhausted. The rainbow colours of the day have subsided to indigo, which leads by the circuitous route of Ponchielli's 'Dance of the Hours',[11] back to Molly. This music played the night Molly met Boylan a little while back. He thinks he will not join Molly on her tour: that is the week of the anniversary of his father's death which he will mark by his annual stay at the old hotel in Ennis. He acknowledges that this leaves the way clear for Boylan. Whether such resolve is formed by equanimity, cowardice or confused familial guilt we shall wait to see. We know it isn't lack of love.

Bloom doesn't seem terribly guilty over his semi-public display of lewdness and almost considers it an entitlement. Comfortable with bodily function he was sufficiently excited to climax and now reflects upon it with detachment worthy of the laboratory. We are supposed to consider our Odysseus from all sides but this really is a bit much and, at risk of being a prude, it is not Bloom's finest moment of the day. Yes, he's had an incredibly stressful time of it, what with the citizen and the constant reminder of Molly but, even so. Not that he needs a trigger scent of Molly for he's been carrying that citrus-scented soap around all day like a Moorish memento. Public indecency features in both *Finnegans Wake* and *Dubliners* and one assumes it carried some significance for Joyce.

Therapeutically de-stressed, Bloom reminisces on the trials and tribulations of the day: the funeral, the cannibalistic men in The Burton, Simon Dedalus's song in The Ormond, the citizen.

What goes up must come down. Beyond the fireworks and Bloom's tumescence this includes Elijah's fiery chariot. It ascended around 5.30 from Little Britain Street and landed, one may reasonably assume, in Sandymount, specifically Newbridge Avenue, to help Mrs Dignam with her finances. There are further links between the Cyclops episode and this. Gerty, for whom appearance is everything, talks about Grandpa Giltrap's lovely dog, Garryowen, and it being almost human with those noises he makes. Surely this cannot be the mangy mongrel slobbering over the biscuit crumbs in Barney Kiernan's? Yet it is one and the same: different narrator – different perspective. Does this make the citizen Gerty's grandfather? We think probably not which would mean that the citizen is the dog's carer, not owner A more intriguing notion is that the citizen is the gout- or dropsy-ridden, wife-beating Mr MacDowell. Smoking-gun proof is elusive but Vladimir Nabokov seems convinced:

> The citizen is there with a fierce mangy dog Garryowen, belonging to his father-in-law old Giltrap. Giltrap is the maternal grandfather of Gerty MacDowell, the leading young lady of the next chapter, where she thinks about her grandpapa's lovely dog. It would thus seem that the citizen is Gerty MacDowell's father.[12]

Which illuminates that he was too incapacitated that day to make it to either funeral or his place of business, yet coped with the journey we assume from Sandymount to Little Britain Street and return, so as to go drinking with his mates. If Nabokov is right then stasis runs in the family, the citizen on his bar stool, Gerty stranded on her rock.

Bloom finds a bit of a stick on the beach and plays with it idly. This might conceivably be a snapped part of Stephen's ashplant, he had it with him in the library and will need it at Bella Cohen's later tonight. Bloom also finds a scrap of paper which we conject may have been torn off by Stephen around these parts but that, too, is grasping at straws. In any event, Bloom is near enough walking in Stephen's footprints and uses the stick to write in the sand.

'Signatures of all things I am here to read, . . . ',[13] Stephen thought earlier on the same beach.

Bloom writes '*I AM A . . .* '[14] and then gives up. He questions the point of concluding the statement for it will disappear with the next tide. We have lived inside his head for most of the book but are denied his intended concluding word: I am a what? It remains a mystery. He contemplated writing a message to Gerty who may return to the same spot next day but we sense something deeper. It could be anything – I am a . . . Man, Jew, Father, Pacifist, Time-traveller, Pervert? Perhaps 'A' leads not to a noun but is part of a word: I Am Angry? All manner of possibilities have been posited. From 'AMA' being the derivation of Amare, the Italian for Love (what is that word known to all men?) to the biblical 'I am alpha to omega',[15] hinting that Bloom is God/Life/Nature: the writer in the sand on the beach of the universe, to be read by humanity or whatever.[16] In any event, he stops short of revealing the message, throws the stick and is amazed to see it land perpendicular in the sand: 'I am amazed?'. Does this mean he's a miracle worker or stick in the mud? We must draw our own conclusion.

After a long and exhausting day Bloom rests a while and drops off to sleep, thinking, like a good Odysseus, of Sinbad the Sailor and life at sea. Like a good Odysseus he has spent time with the daughter and the mother, the Virgin Mother.

The church service now finished, Gerty imagines Canon O'Hanlon and Father Conroy enjoying a spot of late dinner at Canon O'Hanlon's table. Gerty knows the little room well with its cuckoo clock on the wall. We know that cuckoos pitch-up in other men's homes for, example, 7 Eccles Street, and even into the bedroom. This automated cuckoo will pop out nine times at nine o'clock to say 'cuckoo, cuckoo, cuckoo'. In this episode of painting portraits, of the formation of impressions and image, we are thus left with the impression of Bloom: I AM A . . . Cuckold.

LECTURE 15, 21 APRIL 2021: EPISODE 14

Oxen, Suns and Mothers

Music: A Hard Rain's A-Gonna Fall – Bryan Ferry (out of Dylan)

The Ascot Gold Cup is run on the flat. Of course it is; it's in June. Were it run in colder and wetter months, when the going is softer, it would be over the jumps and we could then call this episode our Becher's Brook. Not the tallest fence of last week's Aintree Grand National, just as this episode is not the longest, but both are the most notoriously tricky on the course. Even Joyce's loyal supporter and benefactor Harriet Shaw Weaver, was shocked. Why not call this one Hades? she mocked, for in ploughing through it, she'd been to hell and back. It's a near impossible episode, sometimes a jumble of words and we need all the help we can get. Fortunately, whilst the gateways to comprehension are double-locked, two keys happen to have been left under the flowerpots, so let's use them.

First, Homer. What's with Joyce's suggested episode title, Oxen of the Sun? What oxen, why oxen and why the sun? In book twelve of *The Odyssey* the fleet approaches the island of Trinacria which is modern Sicily. Odysseus has been warned that the cattle that graze there cannot be harmed for they belong to the sun god Helios. But, after several days becalmed, the crew are hungry and fed up with eating fish. While Odysseus sleeps they slaughter and eat the cattle. Livid Odysseus fears the prophecy of Tiresias: harm the cattle and the crew will be killed as retribution for Helios and, further, Odysseus will have all manner of struggles on his return to Ithaca. So it comes to pass. That's the story but it's no real answer to our questions. Why oxen, why sun and what the hell has it got to do with our book?

Let's start with this: humans one way or another revere cattle. Back in ancient Greece, they were the optimum sacrifice, food for the gods rather than the staple diet of humans. So, these looing interlocutors between human and divine, warranted sacred status and still do in parts of the world. In post-industrial Ireland, and throughout western civilization, cattle have long lost such status but remain a prime source of sustenance and so are life-preserving. More so the sun which was, is and always will be a life-source and life-sustainer. So we double down with cattle that belong to the sun god. It's fitting then, that our episode setting is the Holles Street maternity hospital, the source of life round these parts.

Consider this in context: first, the concern over foot and mouth disease is being ignored: in episode two Mr Deasy was irate, his point being that there are doctors in Austria that can apparently easily cure it but the Irish politicians do nothing. Meantime, the best of the healthy beef is exported to England as contemplated by Bloom at various times and as tub-thumped by the heavy drinkers of Barney Kiernan's tavern. Thus, the perpetrators of the crime against the cattle are collectively punished by the sun, to wit Ireland has suffered a drought for some weeks. Bloom's contemplated trip to Mullingar or more likely to Ennis will take him not by lush green fields but parched yellow-brown countryside.

A second factor might be the great famine of the 1840s. This generation won't directly recall but their grandparents will and its shadow still looms large. In 1840 the population of Ireland was over eight million. By 1851 it was six and a half million and by the twentieth century four million.[1] The nation, as collective, had for decades been withering on the vine.

The key under the other flowerpot is in the form of a letter dated 20 March 1920 from James Joyce to Frank Budgen. This is cribbed (and bastardised) as follows:

> Am working hard at Oxen of the Sun, the idea being the crime committed against fecundity by sterilizing the act of coition. . . Technique: a nineparted episode without divisions introduced by a Sallustian-Tacitean prelude (the unfertilized ovum), then by way of earliest English alliterative and monosyllabic and Anglo-Saxon . . . then by way of Mandeville . . . then Malory's Morte d'Arthur . . . then the Elizabethan chronicle style . . . a choppy Latin-gossipy bit, style of Burton-Browne, then a passage Bunyanesque . . . after a diarystyle bit Pepys-Evelyn . . . and so on . . . until it ends in a frightful jumble of Pidgin English, . . . [patois],[2] Cockney, Irish, Bowery slang and broken doggerel. This progression is also linked back at each part subtly with some foregoing episode of the day and, besides this, with the natural stages of development in the embryo and the periods of faunal evolution in general. The double-thudding Anglo-Saxon motive recurs from time to time ('Loth to move from Horne's house') to give the sense of the hoofs of oxen. Bloom is the spermatozoon, the hospital the womb, the nurse the ovum, Stephen the embryo. How's that for high?[3]

J S Atherton comments that this presents Joyce with five challenges beyond the customary development of plot and portrayal of characters one expects of a novel:

1. A series of imitations showing the development of English.
2. A continuation of Joyce's Homeric parallels.
3. A treatment of the growth of the human foetus.
4. An outline of 'faunal evolution'.
5. A linking with earlier parts of Ulysses.[4]

As it's a nightmare to read and understand, it may be of some comfort to learn that writing it was no walk in the park.

Picking out the essential bones, there's a parallel between human gestation over the nine months of pregnancy and nine or so fairly arbitrary stages of the development of the English language, mixed in with the maturation of Stephen as artist and the re-birth of Ireland culturally and even its development geologically. In referencing the evolution of the language, we rely on various commentators, particularly, Stuart Gilbert because your humble lecturer is wholly ill-equipped for the task. Apparently, these parodies of style are not the gigantism of previous episodes; not lampoons but rather attempts at reproduction.

There is little precise linkage between style of prose and gestation for they run at different speeds. The prose evolves throughout the episode whereas Mrs Purefoy gives birth halfway through. Rather, there will be occasional crossovers in an episode concerned with birth in its widest sense. That Joyce attempts this Herculean task in the first place is, you may think, little more than a flaunting of his intelligence and that may be so, but it is also a valid exploration of the theme aired in the Scylla and Charybdis episode: that Stephen will be literary father of the nation. The general theme of fecundity also hints at the Fisher King, the Holy Grail notion of a well-intentioned but flawed leader, whose self-inflicted wound renders him unable to perform his leadership duties, which in turn causes his community, thirsting for leadership, to degrade and disintegrate. One thinks of Parnell, whose personal fallibility, an affair with a married woman,[5] led to his downfall and, with it, for a decade or two, the hopes and dreams of Irish independence. Ireland was left on its knees, restrained in the nets we have discussed several times. Let's not personalise it with Parnell, one feels that Joyce laments the paucity of any Irish leadership worthy of the name.

There is also more than a hint of T S Eliot's *The Waste Land* and Wagner's *Parsifal*, for which there was something of a mania in the first decade of the twentieth century. If Bloom might be the herald of the messiah, in the mould of say Elijah or John the Baptist, and Stephen cast as cultural saviour, then one might see Bloom, the flawed Bloom of the Nausicaa and Circe episodes, as the wounded, incapable Amfortas or, more likely, Kundry, the female Wandering Jew messenger. One might then see Stephen as the young Parsifal, innocent but destined to be the redeemer and saviour. Heavy stuff: we might glibly say that reading this episode is worse than childbirth, which is, of course, the very point and hits another major theme – the suffering of women. Generally in life but especially in childbirth and when families of ten or more kids were commonplace, childbirth was for many women, a life-long career.

Metaphorically, our sun-god Helios is played by Dr Andrew Horn who is not only named for a fertility symbol but is (and really was in 1904[6]) doctor-in-chief at the maternity hospital. The hospital building is the womb. Stephen, the unfertilised embryo, is inside in the company of a posse of young off-duty student doctors (these are Odysseus' crew), all getting drunk in an anteroom. The spark of life is Mr Leopold Bloom whose role is to be the sperm and he enters the womb (that is, the hospital) to check on Mrs Purefoy in her third day of labour. He is warmly greeted by Nurse Callan, whom the Blooms used to know when they lived in Holles Street and who now presides over midwifery proceedings in Dr Horn's absence. Bloom, virtually teetotal Bloom, will be tempted to join the drinking party where the action will take place and, crucially, where Bloom will meet Stephen. There will be much talk, medical and bawdy, of copulation, contraception, abortion, still-births and various mal and deformed births. This is the metaphoric slaughter of the cattle – 'the crime committed against fecundity by sterilizing the act of coition'.

It may help to bear in mind that the obscure language masks straightforward mundane events (if we may describe the miracle of childbirth as mundane). We summarise the entire episode thus:

Man enters hospital and joins off-duty student doctors for refreshments. Jocular discussion ensues. It rains. A man is scared of the thunder and lightning and is reassured by other man. Nurse advises that man's friend has eventually given birth. When the beer runs out, the party leave for nearby pub. At closing time, two men head for the train station with an older man following.

As an example of the obfuscation of language, below is the medieval English account, in the style of Mandeville, of a tin of sardines and a loaf of bread:

> And there was a vat of silver that was moved by craft to open in the which lay strange fishes withouten heads though misbelieving men nie that this be possible thing without they see it natheless they are so. And these fishes lie in an oily water brought there from Portugal land because of the fatness that therein is like to the juices of the olive press. And also it was a marvel to see in that castle how by magic they make a compost out of fecund wheat kidneys out of Chaldee that by aid of certain angry spirits that they do into it swells up wondrously like to a vast mountain.[7]

Let's get into it, beginning with the best opening passage of any episode in the novel:

> Deshil Holles Eamus. Deshil Holles Eamus. Deshil Holles Eamus
> Send us bright one, light one, Horhorn, quickening and wombfruit.
> Send us bright one, light one, Horhorn, quickening and wombfruit.
> Send us bright one, light one, Horhorn, quickening and wombfruit.
> Hoopsa, boyaboy, hoopsa! Hoopsa, boyaboy, hoopsa! Hoopsa, boyaboy, hoopsa![8]

This is a mixed bag of language from the off. 'Deshil', a slight corruption of the Gaelic meaning to go right, to head in the right direction, the good way. 'Holles', to Holles Street and '*Eamus*', the Latin for let us go. Taken with the next verse, it is suggestive of a fertility chant to a Pagan sun-god. Going right, or clockwise was the lucky direction – and, finishing with an exclamation of joy, as by a midwife, at a new-born baby boy. Repeat three times in traditional invocation and in recognition, commentators have said, of the three promontories of the triangular island of Trinacria. Watch out for phallic fertilising triangles later in the episode.

Our first few pages are a jumbled mess of words, almost anti-language. This represents the unfertilised egg, the universe pre-big bang, just a random mass of stuff. The gist is, isn't Ireland wonderful for treating its pregnant women in such fine hospitals, surely making it one of the most civilised nations on earth. Mrs Purefoy, we know, is in her third day of painful labour, so it hasn't done much for her.

With the linguistic Anglo-Saxon entry of Mr Bloom into the maternity hospital, the sperm is ejaculated into the womb. We note the wandering Jew/Odysseus motif as well as the natural empathy that underlines his visit:

> Some man that wayfaring was stood by housedoor at night's oncoming. Of Israel's folk was that man that on earth wandering far had fared. Stark ruth of man his errand that him lone led till that house.
>
> Of that house A. Horne is lord. Seventy beds keeps he there teeming mothers are wont that they lie for to thole and bring forth bairns hale so God's angel to Mary quoth. Watchers they there walk, white sisters in ward sleepless. Smarts they still sickness soothing: in twelve moons thrice an hundred. Truest bedthanes they twain are, for Horne holding wariest ward.[9]

Let's consider Bloom's empathy because it's important. He earlier asked Mrs Breen how Mrs Purefoy was doing and was quite upset to hear that she was still in labour after three days. It's one thing to enquire after another's health but quite another, at the end of a personally distressing day, to go to the hospital at 10.30 pm to see how she is getting on. This is behaviour one may expect say, of a priest, but not of a passing acquaintance. Dare one say, it demonstrates female sensibilities and this is the likely intention. Bloom is greeted by Nurse Callan whom, as said, he remembers. She is concerned, due to his black suit, that he is in mourning and he reassures. Bloom thought much earlier that this would happen all day, he was right. Upon entry, Bloom removes his hat. Polite etiquette, of course, but might also be seen as removing any contraceptive barrier to ejaculation.

The precise moment of ejaculation is likely marked by the risqué double entendre on the word 'thatch'.

Nurse Callan: ' . . . him drew that he would rathe infare under her thatch.'[10]

He's a little embarrassed because he recalls once ignoring her as they passed in the street and apologises. He enquires after two people: first, that nice Dr O'Hare, the head doctor back then and, of course, Mrs Purefoy. Bad news all round. O'Hare died three years earlier in Mona island[11] of the bellycrab (cancer) and, after three days' labour, poor Mrs Purefoy still suffers, though she is getting close. Bloom and Nurse Callan; two of life's carers:

> He heard her sad words, in held hat sad staring. So stood they there both awhile in wanhope, sorrowing one with other.[12]

Bloom, about to leave, is greeted by Dixon, a junior doctor who treated Bloom for a bee sting two weeks earlier in the house of misericord, the hospital in Eccles Street:

> '. . . the traveller Leopold came there to be healed for he was sore wounded in his breast by a spear wherewith a horrible and dreadful dragon was smitten him . . .'13

Dixon insists Bloom joins the merry bunch inside for a quick drink and, despite initial reluctance, he's been on his feet most of the day and could do with the rest. His little nap on the beach scuppered his plan to go to the theatre and, poignantly, we have a man determined to stay away from home even some six hours beyond the appointed hour. This time of night, the pubs are rocking The modern vernacular would be 'the craic' and although we are in a hospital, this junior common room is a handy equivalent for these men coming off duty at divers times and in need of some 'r&r'.

Month One – Headless bodies

Dixon guides Bloom into the junior common room. There's a bunch of rowdy half-cut student doctors, a couple of others, including Stephen Dedalus, all tucking into the beer and those tinned sardines. Dixon pours Bloom a beer, much of which he surreptitiously empties into his neighbour's glass. Discussion, fortified with Bass ale, and buoyed by headless sardines, centres unsurprisingly on childbirth from conception to evacuation with emphasis on conception. At this juncture, however, it's about how dangerous the whole thing seems to be for the poor mother whose chances of survival back then seem to be around fair to middling. If only one can be saved, should it be child or mother? Sympathies in the room tend to align with religious adherence and Catholic doctrine sides firmly with the child. Sorry mum.

Month Two – Formation of the Soul

The ribald conversation is in full flow. Stephen finds a pro-life ally in Bloom. This should not be interpreted in terms of a woman's right to choose rather, for Stephen, the reproductive/creative process concerns his art . . . 'In woman's womb word is made flesh . . . [14] and of he being the father of a thousand characters, as he hopes to evolve into the Irish Shakespeare. He notes the doctrinal view that the soul is formed at month two. Bloom, feeling the loss of his real child, simply cherishes life. No obscure style can disguise the touching sentiment of the narrative:

> . . . of his good lady Marion that had borne him an only manchild on which in his eleventh day on live had died and no man of art could save so dark is

> destiny. And she was wonderous stricken of heart for that evil hap and for his burial did him on fair coreslet of lamb's wool, the flower of the flock, lest he might perish utterly and lie akeled (for it was then about the midst of winter) . . . [15]

Nor, as it continues, can it disguise the paternal transference to Stephen and his disappointment that Stephen may be wasting his considerable talents in pubs and brothels:

> . . . and now Sir Leopold . . . looked upon his friend's son and was shut up in sorrow for his forepassed happiness and as sad as he was that him failed a son of such gentle courage . . . so grieved he also in no less measure for young Stephen that he lived riotously with those wastrels and murdered his goods with whores.[16]

Month Three –The first three months she was not well, Staboo

Stephen, filling and re-filling all glasses, is in his drunken element and lectures on hypostasis. How our mothers umbilically link us back to Eve and to the second Eve, the Virgin Mary, who, as mother of Jesus, either recognised him as God, rendering her both mother and daughter or, like St. Peter, failed to recognise and so denied him. This is a re-hashing of some of the heretical consubstantiation discussion we had in Proteus. Stephen sober is impossibly precocious, Stephen drunk is just plain impossible. His own mother, never far from guilty thoughts, is mixed up in this intellectual tumble: ' . . . and with a kiss of ashes hast though kissed my mouth.'[17]

Whilst Bloom and Stephen do not yet actively engage each other, it is an opportunity for Bloom to observe Stephen up close and understand or misunderstand a little of what makes him tick. He learns. for example. that Stephen was very close to accepting holy orders but ultimately, as we know, was tempted by the life of a sinner: 'obedience in the womb, chastity in the tomb but involuntary poverty all his days.'[18]

We get a feel for the other folk around the table. Crotthers, Dixon, Madden and Costello are the student doctors. Another is Vincent Lynch, Stephen's university chum and probably his host at the proceedings, and then there's Lenehan, of course, Lenehan, with his uncanny knack of sniffing out free booze. Buck Mulligan, another student medic, was expected a little later because, you will recall, he (and not Stephen) was invited to George Moore's party.[19] Lynch deserves a little more attention for he was the willing listener in *A*

Portrait to Stephen's theory on art and aesthetics[20] and it may be noteworthy that Joyce has placed him here to endure some of it again. Lynch proves to be a very poor friend and will, in a couple of hours, desert Stephen when most needed.

Month Four – the heart shook

The thunderclap – the turning point of the episode and arguably, the book.

In the midst of proceedings there's a flash of lightning and a great roar of thunder. Joseph Campbell considers the significance:

> Ulysses takes place mainly on a Thursday – Thor's day, . . . the Day of Thunder – and in the exact middle of the book, a thunderclap wakes Stephen's heart. In Sanskrit the word for 'thunderbolt' (vajra) also signifies 'diamond' and connotes transcendent illumination. As the lightning shatters phenomenal forms, so does transcendental illumination; and as the diamond can be neither cut nor marred, so neither can illumination by any cut of phenomenal experience. So, the thunder in the middle of Ulysses marks the instant of transition from Stephen's fixed and sterile pride to the commencement of a purgatorial process . . . [21]

Campbell then talks about how this links with *Finnegans Wake*, which is beyond our current exploration, but what we take is that, when Stephen hears the thunderclap, the shout in the street, for him it's the wrath of God. For all of Stephen's secular bravado with the religious Madden a few minutes earlier, he cannot escape the grip of Catholicism, crystallised and made personal in the maternity hospital of all places, by the death plea of his mother. What happens next is that Madden, the Catholic spokesman, tells him he should be scared because he's going to hell but there's a different reaction from elsewhere in the room. Bloom is a modern and secular voice and tries to comfort Stephen, explaining that thunder and lightning are all natural phenomena. Such logic may not pacify, for, whilst logical phenomenology might alleviate the prospect of hell, it nevertheless reinforces the inevitability of mortality. However, the compassion shown to Stephen by Bloom marks the start of the gradual disintegration of Stephen's psychological self-imprisonment. One might consider it a further moment of conception albeit out of step with episodic choreography.

It may also be a pivotal moment in the Vicoan historical cycle. We've talked before of this 17th-century Italian philosopher. In episode two, for instance, where we contrasted it with Mr Deasy's linear history, which was an unwavering road leading to heavenly light. Vico's version concerns Molly's initial question on the meaning of metempsychosis and is essentially that history is a repeating cycle of four ages which may very broadly be summarised as follows:

1. The age of those present to directly hear the voice of god. The age of the fathers. God need not mean the God of the Bible (though includes it) but something of a universally cataclysmic effect. These fathers create a god-fearing world
2. Next comes the age of the sons that did not hear the voice of God directly but expect to inherit the wealth and power of the fathers that did. This might be seen as the shift of power from divine right of kings and the priesthood to the aristocracy.
3. With education, comes an expectation from below of wider distribution of wealth and power: the age of democracy.
4. By the fourth stage, the voice of God is all but forgotten and reverence is instead vested in goods and chattels, the scramble for which descends into chaos. One may recognise elements of this in the modern era.

At the nadir of chaos, God intervenes to reset the cycle. A giant thunderclap, a tsunami or, dare one say it, global pandemic. For some this will be God of the Bible, for others, scientific phenomenon or something in between, perhaps akin to Spinoza's god in nature or the Virgin Mary's *Magnificat* which you may recall was suggested as part of that long word from Proteus:

Contransmagnificandjewbangtantiality.[22]

In any event, Joyce is telling Stephen and us all that a sea-change has occurred and a new era begun.

Let's think about what thunder meant when this episode was written in early 1920. First, obviously, the very raw memory of First World War bombs that had everyone running for cover. But peacetime heralded creative upheaval: Cubism, Stravinsky, *The Waste Land* and surely this episode influenced Eliot's seminal poem.[23] Thunder and lightning announces rain, buckets of it – an explosion of rain fertilising the fields and the towns. Back in Calypso, Bloom, like Elijah, sat atop Mount Carmel, saw a little cloud and predicted the end of the drought. So Bloom it is that provides the germinating seed here, with his comforting of Stephen. Let's also note the excavational uncovering of ancient cities that occurred around the turn of the century. Following Heinrich

Schliemann's discovery of Troy in 1886, Sir Arthur Evans uncovers the Palace of Knossos in Crete in 1900. Dead cities being brought to life.[24]

Conversation Bunyan-style,[25] has preceded the thunder and continues, a la Pepys and others, to bob around various attacks on fecundity, whether by contraception, abortion, prostitution or survival of the fittest. Bloom and Stephen remain on similar sides of the argument and in favour of fecundity and the preservation of life.

Month Five – hair, teeth and nails

The rain washes in Mulligan together with Bannon whom he met outside and who welcomes a respite from the deluge. It is he you will recall from conversation in the swimming area,[26] that has a girlfriend in Mullingar who we deduce to be Milly Bloom.

The ne'er do well Lenehan, bit between his teeth and taking the bull by the horns, mentions the letter he read in the evening paper concerning Foot and Mouth disease that is blighting Irish cattle. This we presume to be Deasy's letter that Stephen delivered for publication. Bloom, we know, cares for animals, his natural empathy sharpened by unpleasant memories of his days working near an abattoir for Joseph Cuffe, the cattle trader. He is shocked to hear how widespread the disease has become and yet most of the healthy cattle is still being exported to Liverpool. Stephen, bullock-befriending bard, airs Deasy's assertion that it can be cured if only the Irish politicians lifted their horizons to European medical science, but, Bloom aside, fails to gain traction in the room. Most are either impervious to the need for intervention or do not want to sully the Irish bull with anything foreign; there's been more than enough of that with the British. The suffering of the cattle becomes synonymous around the table with that of the people of Ireland. The nasty British bull impregnating and so corrupting the Irish cattle, starting with Pope Hadrian IV (Nicholas Breakspear)[27] who gave Henry II Papal licence to tilt at Ireland and continuing through Henry VIII until it is claimed that elements of the two races were 'as fast friends as an arse and a shirt'[28] while many others were fleeing the country.

Month Six – scrotum and sex organs

Mulligan, in the style of Pepys, tells his audience of his intended contribution to the effort to repopulate Ireland as well as providing Irish womenfolk with a sexual experience only the Buck can endow. He proposes to buy Lambay Island[29] on which he will locate his Omphalos, a purpose-built copulation and impregnation chamber; so much for his lofty ambition for the omphalos to be the centre of ancient Greek culture. Will he also be carrying coals to Newcastle?, he is ironically asked. We know better of Mulligan than to take him seriously; his only step in the venture, hitherto, is the printing of joke business cards.

The Final Trimester

Bannon, very happy to be out of the rain, talks of his lovely new girlfriend in Mullingar and that he's come to Dublin to buy some contraceptives. He's oblivious, until later, that her father sits opposite (fortunately beyond earshot, we think).

With the rain falling in sheets across the parched land, the boys are boasting of their own ejaculate, that, in the style of Laurence Sterne,[30] may or may not be restrained by a condom:

> But beshrew me, he cried, clapping hand to his forehead, tomorrow will be a new day and, thousand thunders, I know of a marchand de capotes, Monsieur Poyntz, from whom I can have for a livre as snug a cloak of the French fashion as ever kept a lady from wetting. Tut, tut! cries Le Fecondateur, tripping in, my friend Monsieur Moore, that most accomplished traveller (I have just cracked a half bottle avec lui in a circle of the best wits of the town), is my authority that in Cape Horn, ventre biche, they have a rain that will wet through any, even the stoutest cloak. A drenching of that violence, he tells me, sans blague, has sent more than one luckless fellow in good earnest posthaste to another world. Pooh! A livre! cries Monsieur Lynch. The clumsy things are dear at a sou. One umbrella, were it no bigger than a fairy mushroom, is worth ten such stopgaps. No woman of any wit would wear one. My dear Kitty told me today that she would dance in a deluge before ever she would starve in such an ark of salvation for, as she reminded me (blushing piquantly and whispering in my ear though there was none to snap her words but giddy butterflies), dame Nature, by the divine blessing, has implanted it in our hearts and it has become a household word that il y a deux choses for which the innocence of our original garb, in other circumstances a breach of the proprieties, is the fittest, nay, the only garment. The first, said she (and here my pretty philosopher, as I handed her to her tilbury, to fix my attention, gently tipped with her tongue the outer chamber of my ear), the first is a bath . . . but at this point a bell tinkling in the hall cut short a discourse which promised so bravely for the enrichment of our store of knowledge.[31]

Without too much effort, we can translate marchand de capotes – cloak merchant as the condom seller and an umbrella as a diaphragm. One of them tells how his girlfriend Kitty will have none of this contraception and puts her faith in mother nature and that other reason to get naked, a good bath.

Note also reference to the tongue and the outer chamber of the ear; pretty much the last piece of human anatomy to fall into place indicating the baby is full term, and sure enough . . .

Birth of Baby Purefoy (but not yet of baby Stephen)

Nurse Callan enters to whisper to Dixon that Mrs Purefoy has at long last given birth to a baby boy and he is needed on the ward. Bloom is very relieved that her suffering is at an end but the edge of that happy revelation is blunted a little by the low opinion he has of some around the table: as well as Mulligan, he is unimpressed by the schoolyard antics of Costello and Lenehan. He opines to himself upon the character of Punch Costello and pulls no punches:

> But the word of Mr Costello was an unwelcome language for him for he nauseated the wretch that seemed to him a cropeared creature of a misshapen gibbosity born out of wedlock and thrust like a crookback teethed and feet first into the world, which the dint of the surgeon's pliers in his skull lent indeed a colour to, so as it put him in thought of that missing link of creation's chain desiderated by the late ingenious Mr Darwin.[32]

However, our narrator questions Bloom's right to sanctimony in the matters of fecundity and good character, having attempted some years before to seduce a scullery maid with whom, we may presume, he did not intend to father a child. We don't know if that is true but we do know he just masturbated on the beach and has ignored the fertile Molly for ten years: 'It ill becomes him to preach that gospel. Has he not nearer home a seedfield that lies fallow for the want of a ploughshare?'[33]

You may find it an interesting aside, that, back in ancient Greece, it would have been oxen that pulled the ploughshare.

Despite the culmination of Mrs Purefoy's ordeal, Bloom does not leave for he has recalibrated his empathetic mission to focus upon Stephen's wellbeing. He has, though temporarily, drifted from the conversation. He is calm after the storm of the birth and stares absently at the bottles of Bass beer, lost in thought. This is an interesting passage and illuminated by of all people, Buck Mulligan, who perhaps after all is Malachi, messenger of God. Mulligan prevents another chap from breaking Bloom's 'druid silence',[34] recognising that any object can, when isolated, be a focus of meditation. In this case, it is the famous red triangle logo on a bottle of Bass beer. The triangle in this episode of fecundity, may represent the tantric symbols of *lingan* and *yoni*, *Shiva* and *Shakti*, combining feminine and masculine into the universal life force.[35] All this from a bottle of Bass ale: who knew? We touched the merging of the sexes in episode nine; in episode twelve, the citizen accused Bloom of being half-way between male and female[36] and we will explore this further next episode.

During this time, the others are talking of Stephen's schooldays and the hope that he will one day write the book on which, even back then, he staked his reputation. They also talk of how they lost money today on the horserace. The phallically named 'Sceptre' (Boylan) was surprisingly beaten by the dark horse named 'Throwaway' (Bloom) and which won the Holy Grail gold cup (Molly). We'll see by the end of the book if life replicates sport.

Bloom, all the while, is not meditating but rather day dreaming of certain past events in his life. His own schooldays, his first day at work, losing his virginity in a dirty alley with a young girl named Bridie Kelly. Which of these Blooms is the real Bloom? 'What is the age of the soul of man?'[37]

Linguistically speaking, we are now pretty modern. Mr Purefoy, father of many, is lauded without obvious irony in the style of Dickens. One recalls Stephen's earlier cynicism concerning the heroic contribution of the father, who after a moment's rutting,[38] can leave the next nine months, and well beyond, to the suffering mother. Stephen continues to preach from the pulpit and there is more than a hint of the Last Supper with Stephen as Jesus and Vincent Lynch as Judas, as he shall prove to be.

Stephen's outburst jolts Bloom's attention back to the here and now. He recalls Stephen as a six year old at a garden party sixteen years ago, thereby recalling both himself and Stephen at a similar age. Stephen may have fallen and needed his mother. This was the afternoon of the game of bowls recalled by Bloom and John Henry Menton at the end of the Hades episode. Coming shortly after Bloom's memory of Bridie Kelly, this recollection enhances Bloom's paternalistic sensibilities. He lost his virginity twenty-two years ago; Stephen is twenty-two. Whilst there is not a shred of supporting evidence, Bloom could be Stephen's father.

The Birth of Baby Stephen

The narration transports us back 2000 years, gathered around a crib in Bethlehem. The very atmosphere is heavily pregnant: ' . . . stormclouds, heavy with preponderant excess of moisture, in swollen masses turgidly distended, . . . '[39]

We are on the precipice of something outstanding, momentous. Not the birth, that has occurred, the levee has broken and the parched land is being replenished. But the gathered crowd awaits hearing what this means, awaiting the utterance of the Word. We await this word, presumably the word of God. Yet, when uttered, the word is . . . Burkes! Stephen announces that, as the beer has run out, they shall head to Burkes, the pub on the corner: and why not? We are, after all, at this point, drunk on the word of the Lord, so, in this modern representation, we shall be intoxicated by absinthe and beer. Led by Stephen, all the men spill out of the hospital and onto the street. Stephen, the metaphorical embryo, has evacuated the birth canal of the womb and, as fully formed human being, arrives.

After the rain the air is fresh and new. But a bill poster, pasted on the wall hints at further resurrection. Alexander J Dowie is advertising his forthcoming arrival in Dublin. Elijah is coming.

Burke's pub is packed with barely twenty minutes left until closing time. We hear snippets of myriad conversation. Language now whilst modern, is a confused mess of overlapping bits of slang and corrupted and guillotined speech as various groups compete to make themselves heard. The commentator Harry Blamires suggests they have been endowed with the gift of tongues.[40] At closing time, there's a general intent to head to Westland Row station for pastures new. Stephen and Lynch are heading to Nighttown, the red light area near Mabbot Street. Bloom, paternal antennae twitching, is concerned and resolves to follow. Buck Mulligan's direction of travel is unclear.

The last word goes to the evangelist preacher on the billboard poster. In crass Americanese preacher style, he warns that judgement day is coming and, indeed, a fire seems to have already broken out in a neighbouring street. He implores the men to rejoice in the salvation of the baby Jesus and makes himself heard above the ubiquitous language of the new born, belching and vomiting. With our hunch that we've not seen the last of this preacher, the episode closes.

Where does all this leave us? It is near impossible to follow the labyrinth of leads and clues but, as a shot in the dark, let us say that whether it be the Word of God or Word of Joyce, language has been integral to humanity's struggle to survive and progress and it has evolved through many traumas. Stephen has emerged. His metempsychosis or better, yet, metamorphosis, that began with thunder in this episode will bud further in the next. It will provoke change that we presume to grow and thrive and that language will be his tool as he forges away in the smithy of his soul.

Meantime, we mere mortals in our new world, a little blinded by the light, offer hearty congratulations to Mr and Mrs Purefoy and simply try to make some sense of it all.

See you in Nighttown.

LECTURE 16, 5 MAY 2021: EPISODE 15

Circe Part One – the Witching Hour

Music: Visions – Stevie Wonder

In the midst of life we find ourselves lost in a magical part of the book. You may recall[1] that Joyce's works have been paralleled with Dante's and that in that *Ulysses* correlates to *Inferno,* possibly due to the characters' isolated and competing interests which, as we saw last time, may have begun to thaw. Whilst Joyce did not confine hellish allusions to *Ulysses,* for example, 'The Boarding House' the episode closest of *Dubliners,* but in *Ulysses,* Circe is the closest visually to hell with a gothic horror ambience. It is magical both in wonder and weirdness, throw in hallucinogenic, drunk and surreal. The episode Joyce linked to the Circe book of *The Odyssey*[2] constitutes pretty much a quarter of our novel – too large a chunk to bite off in one lecture. Today Bloom will alight upon the threshold of Bella Cohen's at number 82 Lower Mecklenburgh Street (or possibly 81[3]) and next time, he'll enter the brothel.

The midst of life is often decision time. Dante, a middle-aged man, was given the unique opportunity to sample heaven and hell and yet return to mortality better off for the experience. Middle-aged Bloom has to decide if his marriage is worth saving. Stephen, is a younger man but one also at crossroads. Does he wind up another talented drunk like his father or make something of himself? Does he continue to cut the silhouette of solitary brooding intellectual or live among people slightly lower down the intelligentsia scale but in a more fulfilling social and humane way? Choices all round and here we are at the crossroads. Crossroads mean boundaries and it is the breaking down of personal psychological boundaries that will be the key to Stephen and Bloom's relationship and, to quite an extent, understanding the book.

We spent most of last episode in the sterile milieu of a maternity hospital. We now move to a very seedy part of town where the stock in trade is half a bob for a quickie up against an alley wall or, for the connoisseur, ten shillings down and into the back room where the lady will peel off.

An hour or so earlier, a huge thunderclap brought torrential rain and scared the bejesus out of Stephen. Dublin thirsted for that rain: it fertilised parched earth it saturated arid pavement and it heralded renewal. Now the storm has passed yet the air, leastways around here, is not cool and fresh, it is dank, murky and comes in misty swirls. So swirling, it reveals a pantomime street scene of surreal gothic horror. Stephen and Lynch exited the station and making their way to Mabbot Street,[4] arrived in Nighttown on the prowl for women of negotiable affection. Stephen chants, possibly absently, certainly drunkenly, the Pascal mass concerning the death and resurrection of Jesus. Bloom will arrive shortly, a little breathless. He's Odysseus following his advance guard onto Circe's island. He's seen sufficient of Stephen to justify his intended intervention to save Stephen from himself and he rightly senses that Lynch is no ally. Bloom, sober, exhausted, and something of an emotional wreck on this difficult day, will have a series of psychological episodes. Joseph Campbell cites the Jungian 'personal unconscious'[5] to explain the phenomenon. They are phantasmagorical and cannot possibly be real though, occasionally, it's harder to judge as reality and apparition blur. Stephen shall also have a significant vision of his mother towards the end of the episode but, with him, one must factor in his absinthe consumption.

The Circe episode has been explained by reference to Penelope's weaving.[6] You may recall that she has kept the Suitors at bay by proclaiming that she will select one of them when she has finished weaving a death shroud for Odysseus' father, the aged Laertes. Like a great tapestry, all the events and characters in our book have been carefully woven together. Some weaves are strong and sinuous, reinforced and repeated. These are the main themes. Others may be so minor as to be represented by single strands of cotton but they are all there. It all goes into the great tapestry: every strand plays a part and, were any lost, the overall effect is diminished. Yet Penelope was playing for time and at night unpicked that day's efforts. This episode might be the unpicking. Everything that has gone into our story thus far, at least into the Wanderings of Ulysses, is extracted and left in a great mess on the floor. All of Bloom's thoughts, every social interaction, every glance, every slight he suffered, has a role to play in this episode but there's no knowing how, when, or why, each may pop into his head – the same, to a far lesser extent, for Stephen. No matter how surreal the phantasmagoria, every last piece has antecedence earlier that day.

The Circe episode is structured as a play which is how our book began with Mulligan and his parody of a black mass atop the Martello tower. Several times he called Stephen a mummer, an antiquated word for an actor. In a chaotic episode, authorial stage direction is precise. Each scene is described in detail as are the appearance of characters, especially their clothing. This is stark contrast to the book hitherto: we may feel we know Martin Cunningham or Simon Dedalus or John Eglington, but try describing what they look like or wear. Try describing Essex Bridge or the school in Dalkey. Prior to this episode solid description is thin on the ground.

Yet consider this description of a vision of Molly appearing out of something like *1001 Arabian Nights*:

> Beside her mirage of datepalms a handsome woman in Turkish costume stands before him. Opulent curves fill out her scarlet trousers and jacket, slashed with gold. A wide yellow cummerbund girdles her. A white yashmak, violet in the night, covers her face, leaving free only her large dark eyes and raven hair . . . A coin gleams on her forehead. On her feet are jewelled toerings. Her ankles are linked by a slender fetterchain.[7]

One might say with some, but not utter, conviction, that in this book only imaginary entities are blessed with detailed description.

Bloom has been running, probably because he missed Stephen's train though he knew he and Lynch were headed for Nighttown and is a little breathless trying to catch up, though, apparently, he still found time to nip into a closing butcher's shop for tomorrow's breakfast. Indeed, part of the weird grotesqueness of the opening scene is that, close to midnight, several shops remain open and streets are full of unkempt and unsupervised children. It's an unsettling cameo of Edwardian horror. How desperate is Stephen for female company to venture to such an area and how paternal is Bloom to follow? Joseph Campbell alerts us[8] that Stephen and Bloom are in the same place but with different perspectives; one drunk, one sober, one several minutes ahead of the other, one has sex on his mind, the other paternal protection. It is the merging of these perspectives, Campbell maintains, the closing of the parallax that is the essence of the book and the lesson for us all.

The episode oozes symbolism: almost every line much, by and large, beyond the remit of this brief summary. An early example is the children surrounding and teasing Kithogue, the supposedly idiotic deaf mute, and asking of him where is the great light. This might echo the first Canto of Dante's *Inferno* with the great light far above the dark forest, though Dante's guide, Virgil, is as far as one gets from an idiot. Perhaps it's also a reinforcement of the *Parsifal* theme that the pure innocent fool will save the community. We need not dwell too much on Homer, the long and short of that is that Odysseus' advance guard are captured by the witch Circe who turns them into swine. Odysseus arrives and Circe applies the same spell, yet her magic is powerless against the protection of the Moly herb, given to Odysseus by Hermes. Circe is impressed, even turned on, by this power. She promises to reverse the men to swine spell provided Odysseus shares her bed. This he does and has such a lovely time he stays for a year. His men, restored, are finer versions than the pre-spell models.

Whilst the apparitions or visions permeate throughout, Bloom will have three main ones before he enters the brothel in which Stephen is tinkling at the piano and these will form the bulk of this lecture. Waking dream may be a better description, the very mention of which invokes Freud. The name Nighttown suggests a time to dream and that these visions occupy a space somewhere between awake and asleep is significant as we'll consider this lecture or next. The German for dream is *traum* and that seems to better fit their malevolent aura. Notwithstanding that they occupy several pages in space, they are, objectively, almost non-existent in time and occur in the blink of an eye. This elasticity alerts us that time is an unreliable charlatan and a trickster – one is reminded of Thomas Mann's novel *The Magic Mountain*.[9]

These waking dreams can be seen as extensions either of Bloom's guilt or ego: more so guilt; they have weighed on his brain and accumulated, perhaps since childhood. What makes them burst forth now? It might be the drama of the day as well as the dawning revelation that Stephen might occupy some of the great void left by Rudy and which may finally allow Bloom to move on with his life.

As Joseph Campbell summarises:

> So now vulnerable Bloom is in the mystic realm, in the lewd suggestive nightland, where he comes under enchantment. His own activated imagination begins to spew from beneath the floors of his mind the whole sewer of what Jung has termed the 'personal unconscious': the repressed, half-forgotten urgencies and memories of desire, shame, and libidinous fantasy that, throughout his life from infancy onwards, have been running off below decks, so to speak, and accumulating there in a timeless, sloshing, fetid bilge.[10]

The first one occurs when Bloom calms down a little after a series of shocks. He is nearly run down in the street, twice – initially by cyclists and then by a sand-strewer, the driver of which swears at Bloom for his trouble. Then the two little Caffrey boys, Tommy and Jackie, rush into him as they run past. Bloom, without a hint of recognition of meeting them earlier, is relieved they haven't picked his pocket. In times of stress and, without thinking, Bloom touches his potato. It's his lucky charm and more, as we shall consider shortly.

An apparition materialises: his long-dead father, Rudolph Virag, speaks to him. He is a vulture but with his recognisable face streaked with the yellow stain of the poison he took. He reprimands Bloom for being in such an unsavoury part of town and for wasting his money. Bloom discreetly holds the over-priced, non-kosher meat behind his back. Virag then hits deeper guilt: 'Are you not my dear son Leopold who left the house of his father and left the god of his fathers Abraham and Jacob?'[11]

Virag reminds his son of how he previously came a-cropper by associating with *goyim,*[12] a childhood incident when Bloom slipped in an impromptu running race and caked his clothes in mud. Bloom's mother Ellen appears, worried sick as though seeing, not adult Bloom, but the mud-caked child. She's dressed as a pantomime dame conflating her with Stephen's dead mother who was fond of the pantomime character Turko the Terrible.[13] Like Virag's over-egged Jewishness, so Ellen is a stereotypical Irish peasant and it does not escape our attention that the potato falls from her petticoats:

> Oh blessed Redeemer, what have they done to him! My smelling salts! (She hauls up a reef of skirt and ransacks the pouch of her striped blay petticoat. A phial, an Agnus Dei, a shrivelled potato and a celluloid doll fall out.) Sacred Heart of Mary, where were you at all, at all?[14]

As they fade, Molly appears in oriental garb, just as she appeared in Bloom's dream the previous night and as she might have been in his dream, when Stephen 'almosted' it.[15] For Bloom, Molly all the way from the rock of Gibraltar, always represents the exotic orient. This is domineering-mistress Molly, ordering her husband about, which is not so different to the reality we witnessed this morning, as she lay in bed with her breakfast while he cleared up her dirty garments, retrieved the dropped book and collected the post. But now articulated directly, though with interesting advice: that he should go off and see the world. What do we make of that? That she wants him out of the way or that he should be more like Odysseus? Besides, she's found a new whipping boy, her camel, and we wonder if this is Boylan.

Molly fades and before entry of our next main player, Mrs Breen, we have a brief but significant walk-on role for Gerty MacDowell, mixed with a street prostitute, possibly real:

(Leering, Gerty Macdowell limps forward. She draws from behind ogling, and shows coyly her bloodied clout.) [One wonders if the citizen has beaten her?]

GERTY

With all my worldly goods I thee and thou. (She murmurs) You did that. I hate you.

BLOOM

I? When? You're dreaming. I never saw you.

THE BAWD

Leave the gentleman alone, you cheat. Writing the gentleman false letters. Streetwalking and soliciting. Better for your mother take the strap to you at the bedpost, hussy like you.

GERTY

(To Bloom.) When you saw all the secrets of my bottom drawer. (She paws his sleeve, slobbering.) Dirty married man! I love you for doing that to me.

(She glides away crookedly. Mrs Breen in man's frieze overcoat with loose bellows pockets, stands in the causeway, her roguish eyes wideopen, smiling in all her herbivorous buckteeth.)[16]

Note the shift of emphasis, the guilt of the accusation coupled with the ego-inflator: 'I love you for doing that to me.' This adjustment continues with the far more significant love interest, Mrs Breen. Bloom is initially sheepish; she's spotted him in the red-light district for which he concocts various excuses. There's more than a hint of frisson, not only due to their mutual historic attraction, but also and, especially, the thrill of the guilt itself. Such theme will recur. There's a different aspect to Bloom in the company of youngish women: at least in their virtual company. Not only is he flirtatious he permits himself to be flirted and the object of desire. The Bloom is on the Rye.[17] We also note that he dresses for the part which adds vividness and insight as to his level of comfort in the particular role play. Here, as he and Josie Breen reminisce of a trip to the race track, he is the debonaire sporting gent with an easy nonchalance. A man at the top of his game:

(In an oatmeal sporting suit, a sprig of woodbine in the lapel, tony buff shirt, shepherd's plaid Saint Andrew's cross scarftie, white spats, fawn dustcoat on his arm, tawny red brogues, fieldglasses in bandolier and a grey billycock hat)18

He has at least three changes of clothes during this love-bird parley with Mrs Breen. Back then, of course, gentleman of genuine class may have changed several times a day but this is more likely the actor, the mummer Bloom, constantly changing character but unable to escape himself. Earlier in the library, Stephen cited Maurice Maeterlinck: wherever we go in life, no matter how far, we find only ourselves.[19]

This vision of Bloom is going terribly well for our hero. He has Josie Breen eating out of the palm of his hand with his easy turn of phrase and, as the vision fades, she is somewhere between earnest agreement and orgasm:

> MRS BREEN
> (Eagerly.) Yes, yes, yes, yes, yes, yes, yes.[20]

Yes: A word we shall see again before the book is up.

She fades to a dog and we snap back to reality. Commentators have noted the role of dogs in *Ulysses*, the word being God in reverse. This dog is especially interested in Bloom and it is quite some time before he realises this is due to him having a piece of raw meat in each pocket. The eventual cognisance leads to the second main vision. Bloom has come around to thinking these bits of meat are too much trouble and despite the echo of his father's words that he's wasted half a crown, he's better off throwing them for the dogs. He lets the meat slide to the floor but, as he does so, frets that two passing policeman may prosecute him for littering and this enlarges towards panic that they will mistake him for an anarchist bomber, dressed, as he is, all in black.

The vision that flows takes the form of a trial in which Bloom stands charged with unspecified offences but generally comprised of many of his guilty secrets (not all, he saves plenty for later visions). He is represented by J J O'Molloy, the lawyer and addicted gambler that we met in the Aeolus episode. In his advocacy, he adopts the various oratory styles depicted there including that of Seymour Bushe, KC, and John F Taylor. A string of character witnesses come forth for and against, but mainly against. First up is the writer Philip Beaufoy whom, as you may recall from Calypso, was the author of a short story featured in *Titbits* called 'Matcham's Masterstroke' and for which Bloom, as he sat on the toilet, calculated he was paid three pounds, thirteen and six.

So commences an hilarious passage where Bloom's guilty peccadilloes are given a public airing. Beaufoy's initial complaint is that Bloom's imaginary stories plagiarised his far superior published works (precisely what Bloom intends to do) but his real beef is that Bloom tore off a page to wipe his dirty backside. The irony of course is that *Titbits* hardly attracted high calibre writers.[21] He is followed by the scullery maid Mary Driscoll, with whom Bloom apparently tried it on and then by current pen-pal, Martha Clifford, but the hilarity really gathers pace with three upper-class, sadistic women each of whom Bloom has no doubt, lustily ogled. We presume one to be the cab passenger outside the Grosvenor Hotel that morning[22]:

MRS YELVERTON BARRY

(In lowcorsaged opal balldress and elbowlength ivory gloves, wearing a sabletrimmed brickquilted dolman, a comb of brilliants and panache of osprey in her hair.) Arrest him, constable. He wrote me an anonymous letter in prentice backhand when my husband was in the North Riding of Tipperary on the Munster circuit, signed James Lovebirch.[23] He said that he had seen from the gods my peerless globes as I sat in a box of the Theatre Royal at a command performance of La Cigale. I deeply inflamed him, he said. He made improper overtures to me to misconduct myself at half past four pm on the following Thursday, Dunsink time. He offered to send me through the post a work of fiction by Monsieur Paul de Kock, entitled The Girl with the Three Pairs of Stays.

. . .

THE HONOURABLE MRS MERVYN TALBOYS

(In amazon costume, hard hat, jackboots cockspurred, vermilion waistcoat, fawn musketeer gauntlets with braided drums, long train held up and hunting crop with which she strikes her welt constantly.) Also me. Because he saw me on the polo ground of the Phoenix park at the match All Ireland versus the Rest of Ireland. My eyes, I know, shone divinely as I watched Captain Slogger Dennehy of the Inniskillings win the final chukkar on his darling cob Centaur. This plebeian Don Juan observed me from behind a hackney car and sent me in double envelopes an obscene photograph, such as are sold after dark on Paris boulevards, insulting to any lady. I have it still. It represents a partially nude señorita, frail and lovely (his wife, as he solemnly assured me, taken by him from nature), practising illicit intercourse with a muscular torero, evidently a blackguard. He urged me to do likewise, to misbehave, to sin with officers of the garrison. He implored me to soil his letter in an unspeakable manner, to chastise him as he richly deserves, to bestride and ride him, to give him a most vicious horsewhipping.

MRS BELLINGHAM

Me too.

MRS YELVERTON BARRY

Me too.

(Several highly respectable Dublin ladies hold up improper letters received from Bloom.)

THE HONOURABLE MRS MERVYN TALBOYS

(Stamps her jingling spurs in a sudden paroxysm of fury.) I will, by the God above me. I'll scourge the pigeonlivered cur as long as I can stand over him. I'll flay him alive.

BLOOM

(His eyes closing, quails expectantly.) Here? (He squirms.) Again! (He pants cringing.) I love the danger.

THE HONOURABLE MRS MERVYN TALBOYS

Very much so! I'll make it hot for you. I'll make you dance Jack Latten for that.

MRS BELLINGHAM

Tan his breech well, the upstart! Write the stars and stripes on it!

MRS YELVERTON BARRY

Disgraceful! There's no excuse for him! A married man!

BLOOM

All these people. I meant only the spanking idea. A warm tingling glow without effusion. Refined birching to stimulate the circulation.

THE HONOURABLE MRS MERVYN TALBOYS

(Laughs derisively.) O, did you, my fine fellow? Well, by the living God, you'll get the surprise of your life now, believe me, the most unmerciful hiding a man ever bargained for. You have lashed the dormant tigress in my nature into fury.

MRS BELLINGHAM

(Shakes her muff and quizzing-glasses vindictively.) Make him smart, Hanna dear. Give him ginger. Thrash the mongrel within an inch of his life. The cat-o'-nine-tails. Geld him. Vivisect him.[24]

And so it continues – Bloom both quaking and revelling in his masochistic mess. He is being treated like an errant animal that will be brought to heel. This man into beast follows the Homeric men into swine theme which we see throughout, say: Virag as vulture, Paddy Dignam as beagle and, in the next lecture, Bloom thoroughly metamorphosed and what's more, in the carnalized setting of a brothel. The vision continues and the die seems cast. Even the jingly brass quoits on the marriage bed condemn him as a cuckold. The Recorder, Sir Frederick Falconer, he, who believed the perjurers in Cyclops, sentences Bloom to death by hanging and Rumbold the hangman from the Wirall steps forward at the ready. Paddy Dignam speaks briefly for Bloom from beyond the grave to confirm Bloom's alibi (for what, we are not sure) that he was indeed at his funeral and Bloom has a stay of execution.

Back in semi reality, Bloom is guided along the street by a group of kisses that, butterfly-like, orbit his head. We cannot tell if these are Bloom or authorial visuals, an important distinction to be explored next time. He is brought fully to reality by the sound of a piano: 'A man's touch. Sad music. Church music. Perhaps here.'[25]

It's a good call. He's outside Bella Cohen's brothel and that, indeed, is Stephen at the piano. A prostitute, Zoe Higgins, stands at the doorway and beckons him over. She caresses him provocatively and without shame, around his groin and she feels something hard: it is Bloom's potato. Zoe takes it and, when hearing of its significance, flirtatiously asks to keep it as a present. Amidst some verbal sparring, we struggle to separate reality from wishful thinking for, at one point, Bloom gropes her breast which seems out of character. Zoe puts the potato into a pocket which we assume to mean a pocket but, with all this symbolism, one cannot be sure. Anyway, the point is that the potato is lost which is pretty momentous, if indeed it signifies the loss of the Moly, the protective herb that shielded Odysseus from Circe's magic.

It's time to think about this potato and we draw some fascinating insights from a recent episode of the Blooms & Barnacles podcast.[26] It was a keepsake from his mother and an obvious allusion to the Irish famine that cast a giant shadow over hers and earlier generations. Potatoes are apparently endowed with amazing protective properties, packed with nutrients as well as an ability to absorb toxicity which might otherwise harm. It has, therefore, since pagan times, served as something of a talisman and, it transpires, particularly in Jewish tradition. What was very interesting was the allusion drawn on the podcast to the *mezuzah*. Being Jewish does not come naturally to Bloom. He has not been circumcised, had no *bar mitzvah* or, so far as we can tell, even set foot inside a synagogue, so falls well below the most rudimentary benchmarks of being Jewish. He feels Jewish, that much is clear, but, as for ritualistic detail, well he's picked up bits and pieces in passing, much from his father who himself converted to Christianity. He has a vague idea what a *mezuzah* is. He knows it is nailed to the doorpost of Jewish homes but it's unlikely he knows that the word refers to the extract of prayer inside the protective case. He mistakenly calls it a *tefillin,* also part of daily prayer ritual, but something else altogether. He may know that Jews out of habit, superstition or religious devotion touch the mezuzah as they enter or leave a Jewish house or even, sometimes, different rooms. And this is where it gets interesting because Bloom tends to touch his potato at such moments.

He did it when he left 7 Eccles Street that morning. He did it when about to enter the National Library, not of course a Jewish establishment, but that was a moment of extreme anxiety and perhaps subconsciously felt in need of its protection. Now, on the threshold of the brothel, it is Zoe who not only touches but appropriates the potato. And wouldn't you know it, Zoe, working after all at Bella Cohen's establishment, is Jewish (or is this Bloom's wishful thinking?). Okay so she's a Jewess whose lips are glossed with a little pig fat but, nevertheless, little wonder that on the threshold of a Jewish establishment, she touches the *mezuzah*/potato:

> ZOE
>
> (Murmuring singsong with the music, her odalisk lips lusciously smeared with salve of swinefat and rosewater)
>
> Schorach ani wenowach, benoith Hierushaloim.[27]
>
> BLOOM
>
> (Fascinated.) I thought you were of good stock by your accent.[28]

Mid-conversation with Zoe, Bloom evaporates into another vision, the final one for this lecture. The visual crutch for this seems to be the rising hallway into the body of the house. Bloom imagines the hall wall-lights are a torch born in procession in his honour. But he ventures forth without potato, so without protection of his mother and thousands of years of Jewish superstition. But he has Zoe as his guide (one might be tempted to think Beatrice[29]) and not only does she have the potato but let's not forget, her surname is Higgins, the maiden name of Ellen Bloom. Thus, in a sense, the potato falls from Ellen's petticoats in the first vision and is collected up by her modern counterpart in the second. Are both Bloom's guardian angels? Let's see.

In this next vision, Bloom will run the full gamut of the Messiah complex from adulation to crucifixion. He begins with a short account of the protective qualities of the potato before he is on a political soap box speaking to the eager crowd. In line with many heroes, he is initially utopian before coming a cropper. We sense a vaguely socialist manifesto intermixed with crowd-pleasing nonsense. It's hard to tell if it's naïveté or savvy politicking:

> I stand for the reform of municipal morals and the plain ten commandments. New worlds for old. Union of all, jew, moslem and gentile. Three acres and a cow for all children of nature. Saloon motor hearses. Compulsory manual labour for all. All parks open to the public day and night. Electric dishscrubbers. Tuberculosis, lunacy, war and mendicancy must now cease. General amnesty, weekly carnival, with masked licence, bonuses for all, esperanto the universal language with universal brotherhood. No more patriotism of barspongers and dropsical impostors.[NB undisguised reference to the citizen] Free money, free rent, free love and a free lay church in a free lay state.[30]

He starts as a local politician but quickly elevates to Lord Mayor of Dublin and adroitly champions both the Fenians ('there's the man that got away James Stephens') and the British Empire: basking in reflective glory of Ladysmith, Rorke's Drift and Plevna (the British didn't even fight at Plevna and it seems this may be one of several exaggerated claims of Bloom's father-in-law 'Major' Tweedy). Bloom is ultimately crowned King Leopold I, his kingdom replete with Irish and Jewish banners and iconography. Pride before a fall, he is in full megalomania mode with the creation of the New Bloomusalem, a vast kidney-shaped palace and new young replacement wife. But we sense matters may be getting out of hand when, heading towards Messiah status, he performs a series of miracles, arguably none greater than him explaining the meaning of the word parallax.

We know from those fireworks in Nausicaa that what goes up must come down and, indeed, the tide begins to turn. This starts with Father Farley objecting to Bloom's overwhelming secularism: 'He is an episcopalian, an agnostic, an anythingarian seeking to overthrow our holy faith.'[31]

Mrs Riordan then weighs in, in a similar vein. We take her to be 'Dante' Riordan, the long-dead Dedalus housekeeper who featured in *A Portrait of the Artist* but who also drifted into Bloom circles later in life.[32] At this sea change in the vision she has a foot in both Bloom and Stephen camps. Why she pops up here may be this: the Dedalus household, including Mrs Riordan, were firm Parnell supporters. But when rumour circulated of his affair with the married woman Kitty O'Shea, her Catholic convictions took priority, causing a resounding rejection of Parnell and a major rift in the Dedalus house. Here she again takes the holy biscuit, siding with Father Farley and setting in train a sequence that will see Bloom, like Parnell, and, ironically for Mrs Riordan, like Jesus, hung out to dry. It's interesting that an episode from Stephen's past, some twenty years earlier, should pop up in Bloom's fantasy.

With matters looking bleak, again with a judicial backdrop, Bloom appeals to Dr Malachi Mulligan. Now begins a process whereby masculine Bloom blurs into feminine Bloom, something that will really take hold once inside the brothel and is bound up with the merging or transubstantiation of *Shiva* and *Shakti* into a unified life force. Odysseus, you may recall, was advised by Circe to travel to Hades to consult with Tiresias, the blind prophet whose wisdom was all the greater for having been a woman for seven years. Mulligan tells the court that he has performed a pervaginal examination and that the court should judge Bloom leniently because he is both *'virgo intacta'* but also, according to his colleague Dr Dixon, pregnant. Sure enough, the virgin Bloom gives birth to eight male babies dressed in yellow and white. Having proven the Immaculate Conception, Bloom is indeed, for his followers, the Messiah. His biblical genealogy is recited in a parody of Matthew 1:1–16 but, instead of the generations ending with the begetting of Jesus, it culminates in Virag begetting Bloom. Unfortunately for Bloom, these followers are now vastly outnumbered by the majority calling for blood. The descent continues until, by public demand, the Dublin Fire Brigade are called to immolate Bloom. A group of followers, The Daughters of Erin, approach the pyre, replicating the Daughters of Jerusalem[33] that approached the crucified Jesus. But there, too, is 'Il Commendatore' from *Don Giovanni,* so Bloom's destination, either to heaven or hell, remains uncertain.

Bloom, in the way of Jesus on the cross, reassures them: 'Weep not for me, O daughters of Erin.'[34]

The Daughters fall before the immolating Bloom and recite a prayer in parody of the Litany of the Sacred Heart[35] which closely resembles an index of the Bloom episodes of our novel:

> THE DAUGHTERS OF ERIN:
> Kidney of Bloom, pray for us.
> Flower of the Bath, pray for us.
> Mentor of Menton, pray for us.
> Canvasser for the Freeman, pray for us.
> Charitable Mason, pray for us.
> Wandering Soap, pray for us.

Sweets of Sin, pray for us.
Music without Words, pray for us.
Reprover of the Citizen, pray for us.
Friend of all Frillies, pray for us.
Midwife Most Merciful, pray for us.
Potato Preservative against Plague and Pestilence, pray for us.36

The fire blazes and exhausts until we are left with the carbonised remains of Bloom. Zoe pulls us back to the reality of the building hallway. As far as she's concerned, they've had a normal conversation whilst walking through. Whilst she has no idea where Bloom has been in his head, by telling him he can talk until he's black in the face, she reveals that she is, at some level, of the vision. Further, although she deprived Bloom of his potato, she also imparts helpful information which we'll consider in due course.

We leave it there; Bloom one side of the door, Stephen the other and pick it up next time, using believe it or not, Mel Brooks' film *Blazing Saddles* as a study aid.

LECTURE 17, 19 MAY 2021: EPISODE 15

Circe Part Two – Potatoes and Chandeliers

Music: April in Paris – The Count Basie Orchestra

Leopold Bloom stands on the threshold of the brothel. Zoe Higgins, bearer of the potato, will guide him inside where Stephen sits at the piano.

This part of the episode is introduced by way of Mel Brooks' film *Blazing Saddles*. Back in the introductory lecture I doubted I would make any original contribution to the world of James Joyce but let's revise that because previous use of *Blazing Saddles* as an aid to understanding *Ulysses* will be hard to find. It's a 1970s zany spoof western written and directed by Mel Brooks and, in its modest way, may help us to consider these visions and thus an aspect, dare one say thrust, of the Circe episode.

Never mind Homer, *Blazing Saddles* is nineteenth-century wild west. The new sheriff is extremely smooth, extremely handsome and extremely black. Played by Cleavon Little, he rides towards the extremely racist town of Red Rock through the desert passing nothing bar an occasional cactus. But we gradually become aware of an incongruous jazzy soundtrack, almost as smooth as our Cleavon, and, hey presto, there's Count Basie and his orchestra, set up, right there in the desert, dinner jackets and all. This is obviously a surreal moment in a whacky film, there for a cheap joke which no-one expects to take seriously. But the question is this: Are we supposed to think this is Cleavon's personal vision? That Count Basie is not really there? Unlikely. We the viewer believe the Count Basie orchestra is really there in all its finery and would be seen by anyone else riding by. This is because we take it that the surrealist before us is not the character but rather the author, Mel Brooks, because, well, that's just what he's like. The relevance to our novel is that author-driven surrealism might live outside of one character's head and be shared by others.

Moreover, you may recall that, the end of *Blazing Saddles* descends into a chaotic time-space farce as a fight in a saloon bar crashes through a wall. We find ourselves not, as expected, in the next room but in another studio, which is filming a Fred Astaire type dance scene and, thence, the fight, now embroiling ostentatious dancers as well as cowboys, spills into the streets of modern Hollywood. This, too, is helpful. Up to now in our book the story has unfolded in an intelligible way: yes, some episodes are more complex than others but there is logical method and it flows naturally. Until now. Last time we talked about this episode as the unwoven mess of Penelope's tapestry and this is how we might consider cowboys fighting or dancing with Fred Astaires on Hollywood Boulevard; pieces of foregoing normality, simply jumbled together. Do not mistake this for nihilistic nonsense. These strands may look like a mess on the floor but all are catalogued and ready for action when James Aloysius Joyce comes a calling.

Back to Bloom, in the hallway, just outside the inner door to the brothel rooms. He's distracted by an antler framed mirror cum hat stand in the hall: antlers you recall being the sign of the cuckold. In the act of entering he stumbles on the last step and is helped across the threshold by Zoe. The parlour hosts two prostitutes, Florry and Kitty, who with Zoe are intended to complete the animal, vegetable, mineral triumvirate, in other words, all the world is here. And there's Stephen sat at the piano and Lynch relaxed on the floor. The piano is actually a pianola, one of those new, mechanical, self-playing pianos which must work in either mode because Stephen is sat there tinkling. The principal light is a gas-fired chandelier into which a moth relentlessly bumps.

Stephen idly plays empty fifths. The significance of this, according to Joseph Campbell,[1] is that the fifth is the furthest note in the scale before returning to base and so, suggestive of Stephen's semi-conscious realisation that he has travelled far enough in this strive for Bohemia and, like the earth vis the sun on next week's midsummer's day, it's time to be homeward-bound. As Bloom enters, so waft scratchy strains of music from a nearby gramophone: it's Jerusalem, the Holy City. Matters continue biblical as Florry, perhaps by way of idle conversation, airs that the newspapers say that the end of the world is coming and that some believe the anti-Christ to be due next week – we presume also on midsummer's day. Earlier than expected, but on hearing his name, the anti-Christ appears in the form of the moneylender, Reuben J Dodd, complete with half-drowned son over his shoulder.[2] We assume, with good reason, this to be Bloom's personal fantasy for, of those present, he alone heard the Reuben J story that morning and expect that it is unseen by anyone else: certainly no-one reacts. Then arrives the end of the world itself as a two-headed octopus in Scottish tartan (reminiscent of George Russell's snatch of theosophist conversation in Lestrygonians, again heard only by Bloom) and is ushered in by Elijah who, of course, predicted[3] the coming of the Messiah. In this phantasmagorical cacophony (still we think apparent only to Bloom) Elijah is performed by the evangelist American preacher Alexander J Dowie whose throwaway leaflet predicted it all: Elijah Is Coming:

> ELIJAH
>
> No yapping, if you please, in this booth. Jake Crane, Creole Sue, Dave Campbell, Abe Kirschner, do your coughing with your mouths shut. Say, I am operating all this trunk line. Boys, do it now. God's time is 12.25. Tell mother you'll be there. Rush your order and you play a slick ace. Join on right here! Book through to eternity junction, the nonstop run. Just one word more Are you a god or a doggone clod? If the second advent came to Coney Island are we ready? Florry Christ, Stephen Christ, Zoe Christ, Bloom Christ, Kitty Christ, Lynch Christ, it's up to you to sense that cosmic force. Have we cold feet about the cosmos? No. Be on the side of the angels. Be a prism. You have that something within, the higher self. You can rub shoulders with a Jesus, a Gautama, an Ingersoll. Are you all in this vibration? I say you are. You once nobble that, congregation, and a buck joyride to heaven becomes a back number. You got me? It's a lifebrightener, sure. The hottest stuff ever was. It's the whole pie with jam in. It's just the cutest snappiest line out. It is immense, supersumptuous. It restores. It vibrates. I know and I am some vibrator.[4]

This passage, as well as being great fun, is quoted as an example of the characters beginning to lose control over the fantasies, which harks back to *Blazing Saddles*. It was Bloom that was given the throwaway evangelical leaflet back in Lestrygonians although Stephen, as well as Bloom, may have seen the poster on the wall in Holles Street (episode 14). There is no evidence that Bloom has been introduced by name to Florry and Kitty yet they are mentioned in what we presumed to be his vision. Therefore, we are entitled to ponder whether this is a character vision or an authorial one which they can all see. Just who is privy to these visions remains vague and, especially, through this end-of-the-world experience. It seems unfettered by normal boundaries and we are in the realm of the supernatural.

The Day of Judgement has arrived. Elijah encourages the assembled to admit their sins before the Lord (addressed by the evangelical preacher as Mr President). The three prostitutes bare their souls under their real names (as opposed to their professional soubriquets) and Bloom definitely wasn't introduced to them by these. Thus Zoe is rendered Fanny Higgins which happened to have been Bloom's grandmother's name. Harry Blamires points to this alluding to the recurring theme of Grandmother Ireland prostituting herself before England.[5]

The eight beatitudes appear in the guise of the drunk doctors and bestow eight blessings by vague way of the Sermon on the Mount:'(Incoherently) Beer beef battledog buybull businum barnum buggerum bishop.'[6] Note the blasphemous buy bull for Bible.

The next intrusion harks back to the scene in the National Library, which Bloom did not witness though, at one point, was only a smoked window away. There's Lyster, the Quaker Librarian (who, one expects, has nothing to fear come Judgement Day), and the Under-Librarians, Richard Best and John Eglington. But where's George Russell? Our answer lies behind the coal scuttle next to the fireplace from where Mananaan MacLir, gradually arises. 'Ollave, holyeyed', precisely the description that introduced George Russell in the Scylla episode. MacLir, we recall, is the indestructible three-legged sea-god for which the Isle of Man was named and whose legs are depicted on its flag. He's a Celtic version of Poseidon and, further east, *Shiva* and Stephen thought of him both on the beach and in the Library. Again, no-one in the room appears to notice him and we remain unclear if this is a Bloom or Stephen fantasy; Bloom has not considered MacLir all day (he may have never heard of him) and one suspects that it is the disintegration of the psychological boundaries between them that is entirely the point of this experience. Like a Hindu god, Mananaan holds life in one hand and death in the other. Such are represented by a bicycle pump for life and the crab of cancer for death. George Russell once so depicted Mananaan in a play[7]:

> MANANAAN MACLIR
>
> (With a voice of waves.) Aum! Hek! Wal! Ak! Lub! Mor! Ma! White yoghin of the Gods. Occult pimander of Hermes Trismegistos. (With a voice of whistling seawind.) Punarjanam patsypunjaub! I won't have my leg pulled. It has been said by one: beware the left, the cult of Shakti. (With a cry of stormbirds.) Shakti, Shiva! Dark hidden Father! (He smites with his bicycle pump the crayfish in his left hand. [One supposes that this might represent the constant life cycle or metempsychosis] On its cooperative dial glow the twelve signs of the zodiac. He wails with the vehemence of the ocean.) Aum! Baum! Pyjaum! I am the light of the homestead, I am the dreamery creamery butter.[8]

This ends with the mischievous reference to George Russell, editor of the *Irish Homestead*. But, of greater significance, is that MacLir announces himself in the name of Hermes Trismegistus. This chap is believed to have been an ancient Egyptian philosopher-cum-shaman and teacher of the young Moses, though later academic thought casts doubt on whether he actually existed, that, instead, he represents a belief system. It is, though, a pretty significant belief system feeding into much eastern philosophy and thereby theosophy. Joyce has been pretty scathing of the theosophists thus far (we previously mentioned his poem 'The Holy Office'[9]), but this should be seen less as criticism of the thinking and more so of the privileged intelligentsia – W B Yeats, Lady Gregory, George Russell, the fictional Haines – who, as Joyce saw it, played at being ideological.

Forgive the liberty taken in producing a snappy and in all probability inaccurate summary of the Hermetic tradition,[10] which is that the universe is all one and indivisible and so not only are the barriers we set up between one and another artificial but that tiny actions here in this parlour on Mecklenburgh Street impact way out in the cosmos and vice-versa. This resonates with the Kantian/Schopenhauerian concept of *noumena* which we looked at back in Proteus. It resonates, too, in our novel where great mythic events are represented on the humdrum streets of little old Dublin and where respective father and son voids in Stephen's and Bloom's separate lives might be filled by them, respectively, opening up to each other.

'Aum', says Mananaan MacLir, the yogi chant to invoke the universal waking and dream consciousness and unite them. Then the word *Baum*, German for tree, which we take to be the tree of knowledge, the font of eternal wisdom and medium of temptation in the Garden of Eden, precipitating the great fall (thirty-two feet per second). Blamires is unconvinced[11] but Campbell considers it the crescendo of the book,[12] heralding both unification of masculine *Shiva* and feminine *Shakti* as well as the combined waking and sleeping consciousness into the universal life-force. Take your pick. It is of personal comfort that there exists a belief system that lays great store in visions vesting somewhere between awake and asleep, much as we've experienced this episode.

Bloom's grandfather, with detachable head, appears to guide Bloom, and this is clearly personal to Bloom, through the menu of the prostitutes on offer. He is immensely entertaining and merciless in his unveiling as to which female physical attributes appeal and do not appeal to Bloom. Lack of time prohibits further delving for we move to the grand entry of Bella Cohen, our Circe. Bloom has earlier (on several occasions) been identified as a womanly man, so Bella is a manly woman: either, thereby, might be combined *Shiva/Shakti* or wise Tiresias.[13]

(The door opens. Bella Cohen, a massive whoremistress, enters. She is dressed in a threequarter ivory gown, fringed round the hem with tasselled selvedge, and cools herself, flirting a black horn fan like Minnie Hauck in Carmen. On her left hand are wedding and keeper rings. Her eyes are deeply carboned. She has a sprouting moustache. Her olive face is heavy, slightly sweated and fullnosed, with orangetainted nostrils. She has large pendant beryl eardrops.)

BELLA
My word! I'm all of a mucksweat.[14]

Bloom catches her eye and he is of interest. To flag that we have entered another fantasy, this undoubtedly is Bloom's, the conversation is mediated through Bella's concertinaing fan, an instrument that can administer both pain and relief. It identifies 'petticoat government' in the Bloom house, where mistress is master. It commands Bloom to kneel, something he's done twice that day in Westland Row church and at Glasnevin Cemetery and it hurt his knees on both occasions. Now, humiliation and pain are the very point. Bella's foot has become a hoof and Bloom is invited to lace up her boot. Refusal is not an option though the idea never flickers, for Bloom finds this most exciting and is at her feet, eager to please.

Bloom becomes female as Bella takes the male form, Bello. Bloom's transubstantiation is necessary to achieve the *Shiva/Shakti – Lingan/Yoni* amalgamation. He also becomes a piglet who hides trembling under the couch. That transformation is so true to *The Odyssey*: when the spell is reversed, he shall return shinier and better than before. Under Bello's spell, Bloom suffers a host of indignities, including being sold at auction as a sex slave to one of Bello's more demanding clients and is given bedpan cleaning duty for the whorehouse residents. All resistance is useless and his nadir might be that, while bent over (as a piglet) and Bello checking if he even has residual male genitalia, Bello reminds him/her of the cuckolding at the hands of Blazes Boylan:

BELLO
What else are you good for, an impotent thing like you? (He stoops and, peering, pokes with his fan rudely under the fat suet folds of Bloom's haunches.) Up! Up! Manx cat! What have we here? Where's your curly teapot gone to or who docked it on you, cockyolly? Sing, birdy, sing. It's as

limp as a boy of six's doing his pooly behind a cart. Buy a bucket or sell your pump. (Loudly.) Can you do a man's job?

BLOOM
Eccles street...

BELLO
(Sarcastically.) I wouldn't hurt your feelings for the world but there's a man of brawn in possession there. The tables are turned, my gay young fellow! He is something like a fullgrown outdoor man. Well for you, you muff, if you had that weapon with knobs and lumps and warts all over it. He shot his bolt, I can tell you! Foot to foot, knee to knee, belly to belly, bubs to breast! He's no eunuch. A shock of red hair he has sticking out of him behind like a furzebush! Wait for nine months, my lad! Holy ginger, it's kicking and coughing up and down in her guts already! That makes you wild, don't it? Touches the spot? (He spits in contempt.) Spittoon!

BLOOM
I was indecently treated, I . . . inform the police. Hundred pounds. Unmentionable. I . . .

BELLO
Would if you could, lame duck. A downpour we want, not your drizzle.[15]

Bello visualises Bloom's foreseeable future with suitors ensconced in Eccles Street, modern day Ithaca, enjoying all of Bloom's worldly goods:

BELLO
(Cuttingly.) Their heelmarks will stamp the Brusselette carpet you bought at Wren's auction. In their horseplay with Moll the romp to find the buck flea in her breeches they will deface the little statue you carried home in the rain for art for art's sake. They will violate the secrets of your bottom drawer. Pages will be torn from your handbook of astronomy to make them pipespills. And they will spit in your ten shilling brass fender from Hampton Leedom's.

BLOOM
Ten and six. The act of low scoundrels. Let me go. I will return. I will prove . . .

A VOICE
Swear!

(Bloom clenches his fists and crawls forward, a bowieknife between his teeth)

BELLO

As a paying guest or a kept man? Too late. You have made your secondbest bed and others must lie in it. Your epitaph is written. You are down and out and don't you forget it, old bean.[16]

For the third time that evening, Bloom, cuckold epitaph signed and sealed, is sentenced to death, this time by fiery biblical sacrifice. From these flames, like the moth from the gas-lit chandelier, springs the Calypso nymph – she of the picture above the bed in Eccles Street. She stands amid a glade of yew trees, which is the parlour wallpaper pattern, and she's in accusatory mood. She admonishes Bloom for all the base activity she has had to witness in that bedroom over the years. The worm turns. Bloom can take no more and retorts, well that's because he's human and has human needs and fallibilities which will include lustful thoughts over reproduction pictures of immortal nymphs as well as abundant use of the chamber pot in the middle of the night. The chamber pot activity is depicted as the waterfall at the Irish beauty spot of Poulaphouca. Because, he continues, unlike nymph goddesses, humans do have anuses and drink real liquid, not electricity.

Such anger, his eventual standing up for himself, breaks Circe's spell and the bravado continues in full waking mode as Bloom, no longer a piglet, is sufficiently bolstered to ask Zoe to return the potato because it means a lot to him. He has simply appealed to her humanity and she is, after all, a decent sort and, we suspect, the spirit of his mother and grandmother. It is yielded up and Bloom is restored to full power. Nay, more than that: he is bigger and better than before, possibly suggesting that we might all improve for being in touch with our cohabiters of the planet. We notice his more confident aspect towards Bella (restored from Bello) and yes, it's time to present . . . Mr Leopold Bloom, superhero.

Bella demands money down for services to be rendered, its ten shillings a girl. Stephen, when sober, allows money to drain away and so we expect no less of him when drunk. He flings a couple of notes to cover Lynch, Bloom and himself and, when Bella claims that to be insufficient, he throws more into the game without any real idea what he's paying and has, in fact, substantially overpaid. Bloom observes and takes control, he grabs it back from Bella, pays her the correct fee and, in returning the balance to Stephen, suggests it is best if he, Bloom, looks after the remaining money, it is, after all, supposed to last a month. We continue to note that neither Stephen nor Bloom seem remotely interested in any sexual activity and Lynch perhaps only slightly more.

Stephen wants a cigarette which leads, it is contended, to a pivotal even goose-bump evoking passage as the novel begins to loosen its grip on the odd closely guarded secret:

> STEPHEN
> (Comes to the table.) Cigarette, please. (Lynch tosses a cigarette from the sofa to the table) And so Georgina Johnson is dead and married. (A cigarette appears on the table. Stephen looks at it.) Wonder. Parlour magic. Married. Hm. (He strikes a match and proceeds to light the cigarette with enigmatic melancholy)
>
> LYNCH
> (Watching him.) You would have a better chance of lighting it if you held the match nearer.
>
> STEPHEN
> (Brings the match nearer his eye.) Lynx eye. Must get glasses. Broke them yesterday. Sixteen years ago. Distance. The eye sees all flat. (He draws the match away. It goes out.) Brain thinks. Near: far. Ineluctable modality of the visible. (He frowns mysteriously) Hm. Sphinx. The beast that has two backs at midnight. Married.[17]

All fairly innocuous until pieced together with snippets from earlier that day. First, Stephen broke his glasses a day or two earlier and, with his awful eyesight, has struggled all day to see distances without squinting and, even then, poorly. He saw little beyond his frayed cuff in Telemachus as he tried to look out across Dublin Bay. On Sandymount Strand, he struggled with the ineluctable modality of the visible when trying to accurately identify pretty much anything and perspective, of course, can deceive brains served by good eyes. Sixteen years ago one assumes refers to the caning on his hand administered by Fr Dolan who did not believe the broken glasses excuse for young Stephen to have been excused study, an episode graphically set out in *A Portrait*.[18] But the match held close to light the cigarette, forces the squint and things are seen a little clearer. The married man in the room comes into focus and Stephen perceives Molly's adultery as he did earlier with Ann Hathaway. He will also be aware of Bloom's three acts of paternal kindness towards him: Bloom just helped him with the money, is now reprimanding him for smoking and asks Zoe if they have any food for the pale and gaunt Stephen (Bloom regrets giving his meat to the dogs).

Zoe manoeuvres Stephen back to the couch for some palm reading with Stephen warning her, by reference to Wagner's opera *Die Walküre*, not to be so inquisitive. One might see an oblique reference to Siegfried who, like Stephen, and Telemachus, is searching for a father figure and a true purpose in life but, in actual fact, the quote concerns Siegfried's father Sigmund. Clever Zoe in any event links it to parallels in *Hamlet*. But when she hints at something worrying on Stephen's palm, Bloom, concerned that Stephen might believe the mumbo jumbo, intervenes and offers his palm instead. Bloom's palm lines reveal him as a cuckold underlining the earlier observation by Bella's fan and this generates much hilarity at Bloom's expense. Bloom defends his honour, claiming a particular palm line to simply be an historic scar and not providential:

> BLOOM
>
> (Points to his hand) That weal there is an accident. Fell and cut it twentytwo years ago. I was sixteen.[19]

Zoe sarcastically retorts:

> ZOE
>
> I see, says the blind man. Tell us news.[20]

But this, as the cogs in Stephen's brain start whirring, notwithstanding Zoe's ironic scepticism, is indeed providential:

> STEPHEN
>
> See? Moves to one great goal. I am twentytwo. Sixteen years ago he was twentytwo too. Sixteen years ago I twentytwo tumbled, twentytwo years ago he sixteen fell off his hobbyhorse. (He winces.) Hurt my hand somewhere. Must see a dentist. Money?[21]

Stephen, here paraphrasing Mr Deasy's religious idea of history moving forward with designated purpose, is reviewing Leopold Bloom and, despite his dim sight, begins to see: links between he and Bloom gradually materialise. We are reminded of the higher consciousness achieved earlier by Bloom when staring trance-like into the Bass red triangle, namely, that as he lost his virginity twenty-two years ago: Stephen could be his son. Twenty-two and sixteen; the numbers keep repeating. Paternalistic Bloom recalls a garden party sixteen years ago at which six-year-old Stephen was distressed and calling for his mother:

the same garden party, mentioned in the Hades episode, where the racist solicitor John Henry Menton lost his game of bowls to Bloom.

So; where does this leave us and where are the goose bumps?

The answer to the first is that Stephen, selfish, self-centred Stephen, hardened even to his sister's abject poverty when they met in town earlier,[22] has an alien feeling. He has a pang in his heart for the cuckolded Bloom. He empathises that he suffers the cuckolding and is resentful on Bloom's behalf that it should be a source of such amusement for the others present. He rehearsed such thoughts earlier in the Library regarding Shakespeare and Ann Hathaway but that was intellectual and to support a theory he didn't believe – this time for real.

Wounded hand: Stephen's hand is wounded. Bloom's still bears the scar from twenty-two years ago. Stephen's wound may allude to Christ as we'll consider. It might also be noteworthy that Odysseus suffered a childhood accident that left his foot scarred and it was this that, despite his disguise, revealed his true identity[23] to Eurycleia, his old nursemaid.

Before we get to the goose bumps, the accusations of being cuckolded send Bloom into a final fantasy and, whilst deeply and excruciatingly humiliating, he is sexually stimulated. We are transported to a scene within *Sweets of Sin*, the book Bloom has rented for Molly but set in a phantasmagorical Eccles Street. The lover Raoul arrives and is greeted by manservant Bloom. Hat and coat are hung upon the antlered coat rack and the lover is ushered to Madam's salon where she is taking a bath. Blazes Boylan, for it is he, tips Bloom sixpence and allows him to watch through the keyhole, the private business Raoul-Boylan has with Bloom's wife.

As Bloom's personal vision reaches its darkest moment, Lynch points towards the antlered crested hallway mirror for it tickles him that with the angles just right, Bloom's face appears there, with antler horns. The three whores laugh uproariously. Stephen and Bloom both look towards the mirror: their angles are different, both from the others and from each other, yet they see the same image. Not Bloom but the face of Shakespeare, the cuckold to whom they have both earlier and independently alluded. Their planetary orbits aligned, they see the same image, indeed Burgess maintains[24] that the vision is only revealed at all if revealed to them together. Stephen has acknowledged Bloom's empathy by being empathetic in return. Schopenhauer would approve.

That flaming match held near his eye to light his cigarette, making him squint, helped him finally see Bloom as a fatherly type figure who would simply like to help. Whether that is entirely correct will be clarified a little later.

To the goose bumps: way, way back in the Aeolus, some 600 pages ago, we encountered a passage then inadequately explained. We might now review again without necessarily further explanation but with the new perspective of Stephen having struck the match:

> Messenger took out his matchbox thoughtfully and lit his cigar.
>
> I have often thought since on looking back over that strange time that it was that small act, trivial in itself, that striking of that match, that determined the whole of the course of both our lives. [25]

Moving on: someone has fired up the pianola and accompanied by it blared 'My Girl's A Yorkshire Girl' (Zoe hails from Yorkshire). Stephen, Lynch and the three girls dance with increasing and increasingly hypnotic vigour. This merges into a phantasmagorical version of the *Dance of the Hours*. Its significance is not only that it was the music played the night Molly and Boylan met but may be allegorical of this novel going from Day to Night, in contrast say to Dante's *Divine Comedy* which runs from the dark into the light.

It dawns on Stephen that his dream, 'almosted' the previous night, concerning an oriental street of harlots and Harun al Raschid ushering him inside with a creamy juicy melon, is this place and he recalls his dream of flying as Icarus. But he is suddenly stopped in his tracks. He's horror-struck at an apparition of his mother arisen from the dead. As macabre and complex as Bloom's fantasies were, they seemed to be private affairs in that, so far as we could tell, no-one was aware he endured them. Even in that shared glimpse of Shakespeare's face, it was not obvious that Stephen and Bloom knew the other shared it. Here whilst others do not see what Stephen sees, they can see that he's distressed and ashen-faced, indicating it is playing out in real time. Stephen finds no closure. His mother continues to implore him to repent and he, like Lucifer to the Lord, will not yield or serve: 'With me all or not at all. Non serviam!'[26]

With this he raises his ashplant and strikes the chandelier a fatal blow and it dies with a last mauve gasp of gas amid the toppling masonry of shattered glass.[27]

'*Nothung*!'[28] he cries. This means 'needed' and is the sword so named by Siegfried in the eponymous Wagnerian opera (being part of the 'Ring Cycle'). With it he cleaves in half the anvil upon which it was just forged. In that opera, this scene marks the threshold of boy to man and, no less, a man ready to reclaim his birthright and take on the world.[29] Has our Telemachus finally grown up? With this, Stephen runs out into the street. Hugh Kenner suggests that this act of violence may be redolent of an incident that may or may not have occurred an hour or so earlier at Westland Row station. We know from several references in this episode and the next that Stephen has hurt is hand. Kenner finds sufficient evidence that Stephen struck Buck Mulligan at the station, thus, if it happened, he dealt with his usurper in a very different way to the way Bloom, so far at least, has dealt with Boylan.[30]

Bella, seething at the broken chandelier demands ten shillings damages or the police will be called. Bloom, shiny, new, in control Bloom, inspects it and declares it to be fully functioning with simply the glass chimney broken. Sixpence will more than cover it which he deposits upon the table, but Bella remains in fighting mood. This brings us to the Moly, the herb that protected Odysseus. Earlier, we presumed this to be represented by the potato and, most likely, it is, but there is another candidate. In the initial banter with Bloom outside in the street Zoe inadvertently (or as Hermes[31]) provided Bloom with valuable information. Namely, that Bella Cohen, as well as house proprietor, was actually working that night, a treat she reserved for just a few, very special clients and, that night, the Vet was in the house. Apparently, the Vet is a veterinary surgeon who, in return for Bella's services, provides insider horseracing information and the winnings yielded from this illicit enterprise enable Bella to pay the tuition fees for her son at Oxford. In the course of Bella being bellicose and threatening to call the police, Bloom plays this card. She is flabbergasted that Bloom is privy to this intelligence and realises she has met her match. He has won this particular battle. Bloom Odysseus and Bella Circe part as equals and in mutual respect. Bloom exits to join the others who have rushed outside for there's a great commotion in the street.

We enter the last scene of the great Circe episode. Stephen is having a *contretemps* with two British soldiers, Privates Carr and Compton, named in honour of two functionaries at the British embassy in Zurich with whom Joyce had a run-in.[32] They, very briefly, met Stephen earlier but that is forgotten. Allegations fly, clashes of patriotism or, in Stephen's case the opposite, which the soldiers interpret as an insult to their King and Country. Even King Edward VII's walk-on part fails to placate. We cannot hope to do justice to a scene in which it seems half the book's characters re-appear and shall not try. One understands it is supposed to parody Christ's crucifixion[33] (apparently one can't have too much of this in one episode) and culminates in Stephen being punched to the ground, virtually unconscious. Stephen and Bloom differ in many respects but seem united by a subconscious martyrdom desire. Stephen's so-called friend Lynch has legged it at the first sign of trouble, confirming his Judas status.[34]

Bloom is again to the rescue. He retrieves Stephen's Hamlet hat which has rolled towards the wall, repeating the service, as we shall soon hear, he rendered many years before, to Charles Stuart Parnell.[35] With the help of Corny Kelleher, who just happens to be passing through the Red Light district, the police are dissuaded from prosecuting either puncher or punchee. Bloom suspects Corny of being a police informer[36] and, if true, then at least that unsavoury influence has been put to good use.

Stephen, now conscious but delirious is mumbling bits of the Yeats poem 'Who Goes With Fergus'[37] which, you may recall, was a favourite of his mother – indicating that the sword, *Nothung,* has not entirely excised his guilt. Bloom's poetry appreciation is not quite up to the mark, he thinks he caught the name Ferguson and presumes (as confirmed next episode) this to be a girl that Stephen was due to meet. Crouched by the prone Stephen, Bloom is distracted by a figure next to the wall. It is Bloom's son Rudy, aged eleven, as, had he lived, he would be:

> Against the dark wall a figure appears slowly, a fairy boy of eleven, a changeling, kidnapped, dressed in an Eton suit with glass shoes and a little bronze helmet, holding a book in his hand. He reads from right to left inaudibly, smiling, kissing the page.)
>
> BLOOM
> (Wonderstruck, calls inaudibly.) Rudy!
>
> RUDY
> (Gazes unseeing into Bloom's eyes and goes on reading, kissing, smiling. He has a delicate mauve[38] face. On his suit he has diamond and ruby buttons. In his free left hand he holds a slim ivory cane with a violet bowknot. A white lambkin peeps out of his waistcoat pocket.)[39]

That he is reading right to left and kissing the book, tells us that he has returned to Judaism and the god of his fathers. The white lambkin associates him with the pascal lamb in whose blood our sins are washed but, arguably of greater significance, he has kept the tiny woollen shawl woven by Molly to keep him warm in the grave ('lest he might perish utterly and lie akeled'[40]) and shows he carries the love and protection of his mother. We hope and dare to believe this gives Bloom closure.

And that is perhaps how both tarot card reader and psychiatrist might consider the episode and the many deaths or near-deaths in various fantasies. They are not actual deaths but death of aspects of character: Bloom's, Stephen's and increasingly shared. Bloom has re-lived his numerous guilty peccadilloes, whether with purgatorial effect one cannot say, nor would one wish to pronounce judgement as to several even being sins at all. But, as to his deepest guilt, his role in the death of his son, one hopes it has been a cathartic process.

Thus Circe ends. It is quite something; one is hard-pressed to find a character in the whole novel not resurrected somewhere within it. It also closes the great swathe of the book constituting the Wanderings of Ulysses which began at 8 am this morning in Eccles Street. Again, Dante is helpful. In the midst of that dark forest he looked up and saw the light at the top of the mountain. But the direct path to it was blocked by dangerous animals and so he had to find the true path, the one that plumbed all the circles of hell before he could rise up towards the light. Bloom has had a torrid day and whilst not yet home, he's on his way and, like Dante, has a travelling companion. Sometimes in life one just needs a companion.

PART III – THE HOMECOMING

LECTURE 18, 2 JUNE 2021: EPISODE 16

Trust Me, I'm Eumaeus

Music: Spanish Ladies – Jerry Bryant, Starboard Mess

Who you going to trust? That's the question for this episode.

Odysseus has at last arrived in Ithaca[1] but wary of what reception he'll receive, discreetly checks out the lie of the land disguised as an old beggar. Telemachus, too, has just returned to the island and is also most concerned that the Suitors are plotting to kill him. Both keep the cards close to their chest, the son unaware that the old beggar is his father.

Why would Odysseus be wary? Tiresias prophesised hard times if the cattle of Helios were harmed but in addition, Odysseus met Agamemnon, King of Mycenae or rather his ghost, in the kingdom of the dead and he heard his story. Odysseus and Agamemnon were friends and comrades-in-arms at Troy. Sometimes opposites attract and they were very different personalities. Odysseus we know to be cautious, practical and not above telling the odd lie where stratagem requires. Agamemnon, by contrast, was daring, emotional and over-trusting of his fellows. He returned from Troy in triumph and with pomp to meet Clytemnestra, his queen. Clytemnestra was the sister of Helen for whom the Trojan Wars were declared and Agamemnon was brother of Menelaus, husband of Helen, who pretty much declared them. So, all in all, Agamemnon and Clytemnestra were a power couple and big news in the wars. If *Hello Magazine* did a 'Trojan Wars Declared' special edition, they might have featured on the inside cover.

But in the king's absence, Clytemnestra has taken up with a new beau, Aegisthus, and they set a trap for the returning king and kill him. No need to fact check this too precisely, but it's the gist of what Odysseus is told and also as portrayed in Strauss's wonderful opera *Electra*, which depicts the subsequent revenge of the son. I, for one, tend to believe what I hear at the opera. It may also remind a little of *Hamlet*, never far beneath the surface of our book, in which the ghost of the king tells the prince that he was murdered by the Queen and her new chap.

Sensible Odysseus is cautious. He would not believe something just because the fat lady sang it and takes the precaution of checking out the lie of the land from a safe distance. The goddess Athena has disguised him as an old beggar and he arrives at the craggy end of the island near the hut belonging to Eumaeus, his loyal swine herder. Eumaeus, oblivious that the beggar before him is Odysseus, is hospitable and speaks in such glowing and loving terms of his long-awaited and much missed master that Odysseus considers he can be trusted and reveals his identity. He is told of the disgusting behaviour of the Suitors, of Penelope's valiant fidelity and that Telemachus has journeyed to seek his father.

Telemachus has been gone for far less time but we assume at least several months. Yet as serendipity would have it, he returns to Ithaca the very next day and to the same part of the island. As Odysseus spent the night in the hut and because in the best of fables life works like this, father and son meet at the shepherd's shelter. Odysseus, inwardly emotional at the sight of his son, keeps his true identity secret whilst learning more and still weighing up who to trust. Eventually he reveals his true self and together, father and son, with help from Eumaeus, plot their revenge on the Suitors.

In our twentieth century reflection of these events it's about one in the morning and Stephen and Bloom trudge from Tyrone Street Lower to a cabman's shelter near Butt Bridge They will take stock after Stephen's trauma and figure out what to do, especially concerning Stephen's immediate sleeping arrangements. Though, one should say, that Bloom seems far more concerned with such practicalities than Stephen. Like Odysseus and Telemachus, they are sounding each other out; shadow-boxing. Bloom more than Stephen, reflecting ancient counterparts. Bloom has aspirations for Stephen and not simply paternalistic. Stephen, still in something of a drunken stupor, is nevertheless on a different intellectual plane as he appraises or tries to learn a little of Bloom. They are both surrounded by characters whose cover stories are suspect. Can anyone be trusted?

Do you know the expression: 'After the Lord Mayor's Show'? It's when the grand procession has finished and all that is left is for the municipal street cleaners to sweep up the horse muck. That's a bit how we feel having summited the awesome peak of Circe and enter the first of three episodes that together comprise Part Three of the book, 'The Homecoming'. As befits small hours of the morning, reader, writer and main protagonists are all just a bit knackered. Yet in *The Odyssey*, this is the start of the build-up to the climax, so we dare not drop our guard. Knackered, yes – Stephen is beaten up, drunk and undernourished; Bloom has been wandering all day and must, by now, be emotionally washed out. Communication between them is, with the best will in the world, a little off-kilter and so, one might think, that building trust will be challenging.

In the interest of symmetry, we should mention that Joyce may have intended[2] the last three episodes to correlate, in order with the first three, pitting this against episode one, Telemachus. That Technique was Narrative Young[3] and we had three young men jousting witticisms and repartee. The older generation was championed with dubious success by the milk woman. The Technique of this episode is Narrative Old and Stephen, representing youth, is in the company of older men. Age and time of night has worn them all and blunted their edge. At this hour, life is slower and generally duller.

The book having a life of its own is also pretty knackered. Let's risk calling the kettle black and say that the writing style is laboured, which is to flatter. Sentences extend, deviate, contradict, repeat and generally meander for no apparent reason other than to nauseate and confuse. Beware: attempts to read aloud may induce shortness of breath. All in all it's a confusing episode and, like the corresponding books in *The Odyssey*, full of imposters, perhaps none more so than the narrator: sometimes, friendly, sometimes detached; sometimes advocating Stephen or Bloom, other times pronouncing judgement upon them. Generally, though, meandering and confused. We shall welcome the clarity of the next episode.

The Art of the episode is Navigation which applies to more than the sentence structure. Odysseus will arrive home via a circuitous route on the island. Likewise, taking (for this episode) Dublin to be the island of Ithaca, the detour to Butt Bridge is a substantial deviation from Eccles Street, the ultimate destination, though as yet unknown to Stephen.

In an episode of imposters, attempts to ascribe Homeric nomenclature to characters will yield slim pickings. Let's take the dominant character in the middle part of the episode, D P Murphy, a red-going-grey, hairy-bearded and pretty drunken sailor. He's fresh into port that day having disembarked from the schooner, *Rosevean*.[4] He regales all with his tales of a lifetime on the waves – a regular Sinbad the Sailor. They are so exotic and exciting that one is conflicted; this sounds very much like the adventures of Odysseus yet we've spent the book assuming Bloom was Odysseus. Has Joyce played a trick on us all along? No, the nature of the tales, some sounding very tall indeed, is the clue that he is no Odysseus, though he is likely to be symbolic of

Odysseus in disguise as the old beggar man, for he, too, told a bunch of tall tales so as to disguise his true identity.

What to extract from this episode of fabrication and concealed identity that might advance our understanding? At least, for time spent in the shelter, there are three paths which, whilst they may not reveal hidden truths, at least provide some sort of road-map in this forest of general disorder:

1. The travels of Murphy;
2. The identity of Skin-the-Goat; and
3. The return of Parnell.

Let's start with Murphy. A coarse, drunk sailor, equipped (in the abstinence shelter) with a bottle of rum in each pocket, who transfixes his audience of cabmen, waifs and strays with tales of far-flung adventure. When he learns that Stephen's name is Dedalus, he asks if Stephen knows Simon Dedalus: 'I've heard of him . . . ,'[5] replies nonchalant Stephen. Murphy then piques our interest with an account of Simon Dedalus, the gun-slinging sharpshooter who toured Scandinavia with a travelling circus.[6] This comes as something of a surprise, surely this must either be another man of the same name or just plain invented. An early example of Joyce tempting us to re-evaluate a character before concluding our witness is entirely unreliable. There follow tales of Peruvian cannibals, brought to heel with pieces of mirror. A man in a Trieste brothel is murdered by the plunging of a knife deep into his back. Another acquaintance of Murphy is eaten by sharks. Bloom the sceptic, smells a rat.

The sailor, having introduced himself, advises that he disembarked from the schooner *Rosevean* earlier that day with its cargo of bricks and that he has a wife down in County Cork and a son now old enough to have run off to sea himself. Murphy, so he says, has spent the last seven years at sea and both we and Bloom are reminded of The Flying Dutchman and, by extension, the wandering Jew motif. The legend has the ill-fated Dutchman, captain of the ghostly ship, destined to sail the seas for eternity unless he can find a woman to love him when allowed on-shore for one day every seven years. Our intrepid wanderer appears to have wasted his opportunity because his wife is in Cork and he has spent the day getting drunk. His ship, *Rosevean*, was the schooner the presence of which Stephen 'felt' over his shoulder some twelve hours earlier and sensed the return of the wanderer. The cargo of bricks might refer to the stoning of the martyr whom latter-day Stephen believes he is named for.[7] They might also represent the tools Bloom will metaphorically need to rebuild his home once the Suitors have been vanquished, for he, like Murphy, has, in his way, abandoned his wife. It is time, surely, that both wanderers returned home.

The sailor's fabricated tales of far-off exotica ignite Bloom's wanderlust. His horizons, by comparison, are modest: an operatic tour of seaside resorts along England's south coast, with an all-Irish cast and, naturally, featuring Molly. Yet it is the practical immediacy of this mundane ambition, by comparison with Murphy's exotica and the central role of his Penelope, that confirms our Mr Bloom as the reincarnated Odysseus.

The story of the stabbing in Trieste resonates with the Phoenix Park murders, which brings us to Skin-the-Goat, the proprietor of the shelter and, thereby, corresponding to Eumaeus. He is rumoured to be Fitzharris,[8] one of the gang of Invincibles that perpetrated the infamous knife murders.[9] Whether he really is we don't know, nor it seems do the patrons of the shelter but they enjoy the rumour. Bloom recalls that Fitzharris' role was simply as a decoy driver which is why he was spared the gallows, so, even if true, thinks Bloom, it's no big deal. What it is, however, is more smoke and mirrors disguising true identity. Nevertheless, as Skin the Goat is listening to the account, tales of stabbings in Trieste are probably not the best choice of table conversation and Bloom and Stephen are in silent agreement on this. Even if not the Fenian Fitzharris, the proprietor is fiercely nationalist and clashes with Murphy's pro-Empire outlook. Bloom silently contemplates that the British Empire is not about to crumble, it is rather like the sea, just there and we need to make the best of it. This brings us to Parnell. Not Fenian nationalism, not West Brit pro-Empire but the middle way, the mesial groove.[10]

Bloom suggests to Stephen that late night discussion among men inevitably comes around to the awaited return of that lost hero, Charles Stuart Parnell. Ireland, like Penelope, longs for the return of the 'king'. He actually died some twelve years before in one of those English south coast resorts of which Bloom was just daydreaming, yet, such was his popularity among sections of the electorate and such was the hope they invested in him, they clung now to the hope that he had faked his death and was secreted away, biding his time and awaiting the right moment for his glorious return to save Ireland.

Please forgive a little blind leading the blind and a moment or two on potted Parnellism. In the last decades of the nineteenth century, the two leading Irish political issues were land reform and Home Rule. The former was desperately needed in rural areas and, indeed, the young and then comparatively radical Bloom, was politically invested in such a cause. But for most townsfolk, Home Rule was the hot issue. This, essentially, was a devolution of power from London to Dublin save for crucial issues, say, relating to foreign policy. It was not full independence as required by the Fenians but was considered to be a great and potentially bloodless leap along that way. In hindsight, having seen, say, how Canada achieved full independence, who's to say it wouldn't have been the better way to go. The Fenian movement was disparate and disorganised and it was Home Rule, championed by the dashing and charismatic Parnell, that seemed the best bet for a great leap forward to freedom from the British yoke.

At the height of his powers news broke of his affair with Kitty O'Shea, a married woman. The Catholic, traditional and republican press smelled blood and led the charge with a campaign of salacious gossip, much unproven and self-serving, and through it Parnell was due to suffer the ignominy of being dragged through the courts as the third man in the very public 1889 O'Shea divorce proceedings. The party elders, previously in awe of Parnell, wasted no time but to turn on him in the infamous Committee Room 15 meeting.[11] His political career in tatters, within two years he would be dead of pneumonia in the arms of now wife, Kitty. His absence left a staggering void at the heart of Irish politics, one that reverberated still in 1904, that morning at Glasnevin Cemetery and that night in the cabman's shelter where the case was still being made for the coffin being full of stones (the *Rosevean* cargo?) and that he would yet return to save the nation. Part of the attraction, aside from the inevitable 'giganting' of a dead hero, was that, by 1904, the Fenian cause had been united into Sinn Fein[12] by Arthur Griffiths, the 'square headed' but rather sombre and studious character in comparison to the glamourous Parnell.

Stephen (we think still) and Bloom are in the Parnell camp. Stephen hails from a family of Parnell supporters and party activists and Mrs Riordan was considered in the first Circe lecture. Bloom's sympathies are also evident and he is proud of being part of the crowd that accompanied Parnell to the *United Ireland* newspaper printing presses, an aggressively anti-Parnell organ. Bloom even rescues his hat when he is jostled, just as he did for Stephen in Circe and Menton in Hades. Why would Bloom be sympathetic? Surely Parnell, tall handsome lover, plays the Blazes Boylan character – the usurper in the marriage. Bloom would be the cuckolded Captain O'Shea and Molly would be Kitty O'Shea. Yet life is not this simple. Parnell and Kitty didn't simply have a passionate fling, they had an enduring relationship which produced children and Kitty's marriage was long over, bar the paperwork, prior to Parnell entering stage left. Bloom seems unable to face relating Parnell's situation or failing marriages generally with his own situation with Molly. Perhaps because of this blind spot, he is less interested in Parnell the lover than Parnell the statesman. In that context, Parnell is the hounded fox, joining the several parallel allusions this novel – Jesus Christ, William Shakespeare, George Fox, founder of the Quakers, not to mention Stephen Dedalus and Leopold Bloom. Parnell's erstwhile party hacks wasted no time to gather in that committee room and metaphorically stab him in the back in a grubby power grab: as effective a stabbing as if he had been Lord Frederick Cavendish or that poor chap in Trieste. The political, and then earthly, demise of Parnell sent Irish politics spiralling into sectarianism, either pro-British or Irish nationalist. In his own quiet way, Bloom, Parnell supporter, still seeks the middle path, the compromiser that fully satisfies none but seeks to accommodate at least the basic demands of most. If he is in that sense a successor to Parnell, then the home rule sun or son may yet rise in the north-west, in Eccles Street.

This covers the essential themes as discussed by the men in the shelter.

Throughout Murphy's soliloquy, Bloom tries to engage Stephen with various asides. He encourages Stephen to drink the terrible coffee and eat the unappealing bun but with little or no success. Here they are, two souls in a vast universe, briefly entwined. They have little in common beyond a gradual sensing that there may be a pre-ordained purpose involving them both in each other's lives. Why else would Stephen head off into the night with Bloom, almost a total stranger? The answer of course is 'why not?' After all, he's inebriated, injured, homeless and has no other offer on the table. Moreover, for a man scared of water, dogs and thunder, he seems unfazed by any real or imagined night-threat and, one suspects, he is used to playing fast and loose with personal safety, especially in Paris and especially fuelled by alcohol. He also saw, whilst striking that match, that Bloom was a decent sort who, by small selfless acts, has been looking out for him, an impression that would have been augmented by Bloom's conduct during the fracas had Stephen been sufficiently *compos mentis* to notice. For his part, Bloom is mulling vague ideas of Stephen fulfilling a filial purpose that may kick-start his marriage.

Let's take a look at a few examples of Bloom reaching out to Stephen to see if they advance our understanding. Tipping our cap to mythical antecedence, Odysseus sounded out Telemachus before revealing his identity, not because he feared disloyalty of the son, but to gather intelligence and assess how his son might be of help in ousting the Suitors.

1. Tyrone Street to Butt Bridge

Barely conscious after his beating, Stephen requests a drink which Bloom takes to mean the non-alcoholic variety, though we are not so sure. At this hour Bloom can only think of one of the cabman shelters. Run by the temperance charity Coffee Palace,[13] these provide late-night, non-alcoholic, cheap refreshment for cabbies and others. The nearest is at Butt Bridge and, as Bloom fails to hail the only available cab which stands outside the aptly named North Star Hotel, they set off to walk. They cut a comical sight. Stephen tall, thin, drunk and broken, Bloom, stouter, exhausted and, as well as aiding his colleague, is trying to cope with misbehaving trousers, having lost a waist button.

The narrator informs that communication between them is stilted. Stephen is thinking of Ibsen while Bloom is tempted by the smell of a local bakery just firing up. But Bloom is on a mission to save his unofficial ward and tries to engage. He gently castigates Stephen for wasting his money on booze and in the brothels of Nighttown and that those men whose company he keeps are not helping; Bloom notices how one by one this evening they deserted him. This resonates with the Suitors' plot to kill Telemachus. Stephen is recognised by an old acquaintance, Corley, another from *Dubliners*. He's very much down at heel and asks if Stephen is aware of any gainful employment. Stephen attempts to offer him a few pence but finding only half-a-crown (has Bloom returned Stephen's money?), ends up making an expensive donation. Returning to Bloom, Stephen unknowingly twists the knife by passing on Corley's request for Bloom to ask Boylan if he has any jobs going.

Bloom questions where Stephen will sleep for they are a long way from the Dedalus family home and hears Stephen's sorry story. Bloom underlines his low opinion of Mulligan as a friend, guide in life and provider of accommodation and begins to feel some responsibility for Stephen's sleeping arrangements. They pass an ice cream car, it may be

Rabaiotti's gondola that we have seen twice before.[14] Four men shout passionately in Italian, Bloom, wishing to impress Stephen with his cultural appreciation, remarks on the beauty of the language and its suitability for song and poetry but Stephen brings him down to earth by advising that they are simply arguing over money. Two points arise: first, the intellectual mismatch, one hearing only the superficial melodic beauty of the language, the other, fluent in Italian, hears the intellectual truth and is not taken in. Secondly, this is significant intelligence for Bloom whose wife's repertoire calls for decent Italian and she lacks a little in both understanding and pronunciation. Hence Vorei and Voglio.[15]

2. In the shelter

Bloom tries to ingratiate himself with Murphy by asking him if he's been to Gibraltar. It is also for Stephen's benefit in an attempted display of sophistication. Bloom has never been to Gibraltar but it is a far-flung exotic place of which he can speak with authority. Murphy's reluctance to engage suggests an ignorance of Gibraltar and, if that is right, considering its strategic importance as the gateway to the Mediterranean, it casts serious doubt upon the veracity of his tales of further travel.

Bloom furtively slinks behind a raised newspaper as a middle-aged prostitute pops in, scans the room and then leaves. He saw her and avoided her earlier on Ormond Quay and is concerned she may recognise him from a previous dalliance. She is haggard and, from Bloom's comments to Stephen, may have syphilis. Bloom, the good burgher, years ahead of his time, remarks that her profession should not require that she jeopardises her health and that brothels ought to be properly sanitised both for the public good and the protection of the ladies or, as we would say these days, the sex workers. Stephen is less concerned with ravaged bodies than ravaged and stolen souls which we take to mean that he considers the control that the church has over people's lives to be a far more serious issue. Bloom, desperately trying to impress, engages Stephen in discussion on the nature of the soul but falls intellectually short and they barely engage at all.

Whilst their stars aligned in the brothel it may have been a fleeting moment of shared empathy as orbital trajectories appear to be diverging. One, the intellectual artist living in the clouds, the other the practical Everyman, delighting in life's simple physical pleasures and so he's shocked that Stephen has not eaten since the previous day. Bloom's initial double-take subsides as he assumes clever Stephen means just a few hours ago as it is now technically Friday, but no, Stephen reinforces the shock . . . he means since Wednesday. Stephen it seems, like the Greek gods, needs only intellectual stimulation not normal food. Bloom understands that he will resist the awful bun but might he at least try the terrible coffee.

Bloom quips to Stephen that he doubts the truth of Murphy's adventures, what with the cannibals and the murder in Trieste. Mind you, he continues, one cannot tell with those explosive Latin temperaments, 'washed in the blood of the sun',[16] and one could easily imagine a knife fight among Italians, witness the hot-blooded row by the ice cream cart. He recalls, incorrectly, that Kitty O'Shea had some Spanish blood. All of which returns him to his pet subject and half-Spanish wife, Molly. As well as her passionate nature she has, or at least had, that Mediterranean hourglass figure, like the statues outside the library, with so much more style and appeal than the typically undernourished, pasty Irish dame, complete with ruffled stockings nestled around her ankles. Bloom shows Stephen a posed and flattering photograph of Molly. The wheels in Bloom's brain begin to grind and an inkling of an idea develops as they walk to Eccles Street, which is that Stephen might join Bloom and Molly (and Milly) to form a symbiotic family triangle (or quadrangle).This is not as yet communicated to his companion.

Against the backdrop of the nationalistic ravings of Skin-the-Goat, Bloom tells Stephen of his earlier triumph over that other arch nationalist, the citizen, and, with admirable self-deprecation, rightly observes that defeat is all the more humiliating at the hand of the sheep than the wolf. He continues how nations would be better off with a little more tolerance of the other chap's point of view and by turning the other cheek. Now, without modesty, he re-enacts how the fatal blow was the charge that Christ the saviour was a Jew, just like Bloom. We are, one assumes, supposed to consider Bloom as Christ especially with Stephen's Latin mumblings to the effect that Christ, Bloom . . . 'all just names'. Bloom continues to build his case by saying that Jews are useful to the countries that welcome them for they inject vitality into various walks of life, artistic and commercial. We recall that Stephen heard precisely the opposite from Mr Deasy that morning: Jews '. . . the signs of a nation's decay. Wherever they gather they eat up the nation's vital strength.'[17]

This personal manifesto is bolstered by Bloom's advocacy of a somewhat socialist programme that looks after the needy and indicates he has read a little Marx but his attempts to impress Stephen again misfire. Stephen's manifesto is truth only to his Art and, if this helps his community, so be it but otherwise he isn't interested. He will lead from the front with his art, the hero detached from society, and in that detachment will save society.[18] He may forge in the smithy of his soul the uncreated conscience of his race but he will lead and they will have to follow and find him. If not, it's their loss but he expects they will. It's actually quite fascistic. Bloom, a little baffled, attributes it to the quirkiness of very intelligent people.

The discarded newspaper is an example of our story being both macro and micro as it contains stories of universal interest as well as those that have punctuated the Dublin wanderings of our Ulysses. The American ferry disaster, the Ascot Gold Cup, of broad appeal, alongside an account of the Dignam funeral. Bloom notes its many inaccuracies including the lauding of Dignam as a great citizen. In this episode of mismatch of faces and names the article credits Stephen Dedalus and C P McCoy with attending when they did not, yet denies Bloom's attendance by mis-reporting him as 'L Boom'. The anonymous mourner, as anticipated, appears as Mr Macintosh.

Bloom, deciding this lost soul be given a bed for the night, settles the four-penny bill and leads Stephen out. He's wary of Molly's reaction to him bringing a stranger home on this of all days when you'd think they'd need to have a bit of a heart-to-heart, suggesting that Bloom is still unable to face the issue. Nevertheless, compassion demands that he cannot leave Stephen resorting to a doss-house and offers a sofa at Eccles Street. Stephen commits at least to a decent cup of cocoa and off they go, elder supporting younger.

3. Towards Eccles Street.

Stephen hums and Bloom, sensing that music might be a point of convergence as well as an opportunity to display his profound knowledge, injects several musical nuggets, designed to impress. Unfortunately, basic errors convey the opposite to which Bloom is oblivious. His happy family scheme develops and, like Almidano Artifoni earlier that day, seeks to persuade Stephen that he could make a decent living as a professional tenor while residing in Eccles Street. He could accompany Mrs Bloom to local and touring performances and ensure her Italian pronunciation was on point. In return they would provide bed and board and, not to worry, he could write his bits of poetry in his spare time. A perfect triangle, Bloom thinks, a Holy Trinity with each consubstantially contributing to the whole. He even privately contemplates Stephen as Molly's young lover, which seems over-generous on his part and rather presumptive on behalf of his wife. Stephen, we note, does not reply though the horse we shall meet momentarily, surely does on his behalf. Bloom adds, for emphasis, that he considers Mulligan to be a very corrosive influence. Whether based on his personal observation in the hospital or the forceful opinion of Stephen's father in the funeral coach, we do not know. Nevertheless, as they near Eccles Street and with mythical Suitors to vanquish, Bloom has correctly identified Stephen's most obvious usurper. What he fails to realise is that he, too, seeks to trap Stephen, but in another net, that of domesticity

During the course of Bloom's sermon a cart has approached, led by a very old and exhausted horse. It may be symbolic of Argos, the dog trained by Odysseus in his youth, but some twenty years later can only muster a tail-wag in recognition of his disguised master and is unable to rise from the bed of dung on which it lies prone. Our modern equine equivalent also wags a tail but only to accommodate the dropping of three turds while its driver patiently allows the old animal to complete the toilet. We are indeed 'After the Lord Mayor's Show' and, whilst at the end of a very long day, not quite done yet. The travellers will shortly approach Eccles Street, Odysseus's home in the heart of Ithaca where Penelope awaits as do the demons of the day, yet to be vanquished. The Father and The Son approach. Have they forged the bond they will need for the battle ahead? If trust is built upon open communication then the answer must be a resounding 'No', for their attempts, largely Bloom's, have generally misfired. However, the father is bringing the son into the home of Penelope and the son, drunk as he is, appears not only friendly but willing to stand by the father. All of which we hope, in the battle to come, will count for something.

LECTURE 19, 16 JUNE 2021: EPISODE 17

Ithaca Part One, A Heaventree of Stars

Music: I'll Find My Way Home – Jon & Vangelis

16 June 2021: Happy Bloomsday! Today's lecture falls upon the anniversary of the day that Joyce first dated Nora Barnacle and, of course, of the day upon which the events depicted in our novel take place. It is also marks the 67th annual cultural celebration since the first Bloomsday in 1954, but now spread from Dublin to the universe. Sadly, in what one hopes is a very brief era of curtailed travel, today's celebration is generally virtual but, as Bloom says several times in the novel, 'next year in . . . '[1]

That lil' ol' Dublin has 'gone global' is pertinent to the Ithaca episode. The book as a whole takes small, everyday occurrences and reverberates them through unbounded time and space. A boomeranging of macro and micro, back and forth, through 'history', whatever that might be, and repeating *ad infinitum*. Moreover, in this episode in particular, the interrelationship between Stephen and Bloom, on the one hand, and the stars in the heavens on the other, is a hallmark. It's a sort of literary string theory which, if you don't know, seeks to find links between the unimaginable vastness of black holes and incomprehensible smallness of quantum mechanics. Just the sort of theory that, had he lived to hear of it, Bloom would have liked to have dropped into the conversation, even if, like me, he didn't quite grasp its meaning. We shall look out for this sort of stuff as well, perhaps, as other grandiose concepts such as the tension between destiny and chance. But at the end of the day, we have two blokes chatting and our main priority is the observation of the burgeoning relationship between Stephen, intellectual artist, and Bloom, practical Everyman.

We have bifurcated the episode, its length, density and complexity so demanded. This lecture shall consider the two new friends as they enter the house of the older host until they part and, next time, shall observe Bloom alone with his thoughts as he retires for the night. Odysseus and his son Telemachus stand at the gates of their estate where inside dwells Penelope, his wife unseen for twenty years. But there, too, dwell over one hundred men from all over Greece, each seeking to woo her and ascend to be the new King of Ithaca. They have occupied for years: they eat Odysseus' livestock at his table; they drink his wine and abuse the servants at will. Odysseus has, at long last, returned, but disguised as an old beggar, and Telemachus has pledged not to disclose his father's true identity until the right moment. With the help of the gods, these two men will kill all the Suitors and Odysseus will rescue Penelope. That's a lot of spilled blood and will make quite a mess of Bloom's living room, even in the extreme unlikelihood, at this hour, that Blazes Boylan is still there. Let's see what happens.

I for one, found the Eumaeus episode to be the hard-going slog Joyce intended. But, in the words of the Pythons, 'Now For Something Completely Different'. Joyce describes the Technique as Catechism (impersonal). A question is asked and it is answered: literally, accurately and totally. It is assumed that it replicates the style of the Catholic dogma that Joyce would have known in his youth; question and answer, learned by rote. Remember as well, however, that this penultimate episode resonates with episode two, Nestor, which begins with a teacher asking questions and the class, at least in theory, providing the answers. It is doubtful if this style would impress a creative writing teacher any more than Eumaeus. Totally factual, mechanical and formulaic, it seems more appropriate to a lab report than as a conveyer of an emotional denouement to a landmark work of fiction. Yet, despite the sterility of the format, humanity leaps unrestrained from several of its pages. The sheer wall of detail of some of the passages becomes so overwhelming as to be mantric and develops a beguiling aesthetic in and of itself. Consider, for example, Bloom's aspect towards water as he contemplates turning a tap to fill a kettle, to make two cups of cocoa.

> What in water did Bloom, waterlover, drawer of water, watercarrier returning to the range, admire?
>
> Its universality: its democratic equality and constancy to its nature in seeking its own level: its vastness in the ocean of Mercator's projection: its unplumbed profundity in the Sundam trench of the Pacific exceeding 8,000 fathoms: the restlessness of its waves and surface particles visiting in turn all points of its seaboard: the independence of its units: the variability of states of sea: its hydrostatic quiescence in calm: its hydrokinetic turgidity in neap and spring tides: its subsidence after devastation: its sterility in the circumpolar icecaps, arctic and antarctic: its climatic and commercial significance: its preponderance of 3 to 1 over the dry land of the globe: its indisputable hegemony extending in square leagues over all the region below the subequatorial tropic of Capricorn: the multisecular stability of its primeval basin: its luteofulvous bed: its capacity to dissolve and hold in

> solution all soluble substances including millions of tons of the most precious metals: its slow erosions of peninsulas and islands, its persistent formation of homothetic islands, peninsulas and downwardtending promontories: its alluvial deposits: its weight and volume and density: its imperturbability in lagoons and highland tarns: its gradation of colours in the torrid and temperate and frigid zones: its vehicular ramifications in continental lakecontained streams and confluent oceanflowing rivers with their tributaries and transoceanic currents, gulfstream, north and south equatorial courses: its violence in seaquakes, waterspouts, Artesian wells, eruptions, torrents, eddies, freshets, spates, groundswells, watersheds, waterpartings, geysers, cataracts, whirlpools, maelstroms, inundations, deluges, cloudbursts: its vast circumterrestrial ahorizontal curve: its secrecy in springs and latent humidity, revealed by rhabdomantic or hygrometric instruments and exemplified by the hole in the wall at Ashtown gate, saturation of air, distillation of dew: the simplicity of its composition, two constituent parts of hydrogen with one constituent part of oxygen: its healing virtues: its buoyancy in the waters of the Dead Sea: its persevering penetrativeness in runnels, gullies, inadequate dams, leaks on shipboard: its properties for cleansing, quenching thirst and fire, nourishing vegetation: its infallibility as paradigm and paragon: its metamorphoses as vapour, mist, cloud, rain, sleet, snow, hail: its strength in rigid hydrants: its variety of forms in loughs and bays and gulfs and bights and guts and lagoons and atolls and archipelagos and sounds and fjords and minches and tidal estuaries and arms of sea: its solidity in glaciers, icebergs, icefloes: its docility in working hydraulic millwheels, turbines, dynamos, electric power stations, bleachworks, tanneries, scutchmills: its utility in canals, rivers, if navigable, floating and graving docks: its potentiality derivable from harnessed tides or watercourses falling from level to level: its submarine fauna and flora (anacoustic, photophobe), numerically, if not literally, the inhabitants of the globe: its ubiquity as constituting 90% of the human body: the noxiousness of its effluvia in lacustrine marshes, pestilential fens, faded flowerwater, stagnant pools in the waning moon.[2]

We note the moon. We note Bloom's equal reverence of water in the humble faucet as in the mighty oceans. It mirrors Bloom, essence of ubiquity, liquid Everyman. We note the contrast with the hydrophobe Stephen. But in so noting, we may also query if we need such detail. What is the point of it all? Where does it take us?

Absent a definitive answer let us posit the following:

1. The style is aesthete of itself. We rejoice in the beauty of the mechanical detail just as we might a huge arithmetic formula in all its sprawling glory across multiple whiteboards. We may not understand it but its pretty patterns are hypnotic, compounded by the underlying comfort that there are people cleverer than us for whom it is meaningful.
2. It's a stylised swipe at Catholic dogma which, Joyce may be suggesting, does not in the great scheme of things, amount to a hill of beans
3. The statisticians have taken over the asylum. It's a swipe, ironic or otherwise, at boring Bloom and his scientific phenomenology.
4. We may question the relevance of the detail but should not doubt its accuracy and that is of comfort. When we turn a tap we expect water to flow: we care little for its journey in reaching that point but it has no doubt, journeyed. In a book in which we have struggled to find answers, here they are in abundance, all we need do is find the right questions. In contrast to Eumaeus, where people spoke the language of lies, here we have unadulterated truth which means that the answers to whatever mysteries this novel guards might be there, if only we can find them.

A case can be made for all four but surely it is the last that intrigues. The episode fractures into geographic segments:

1. Entering the house.
2. In the kitchen.
3. In the garden.

And for next time,

4. In the lounge.
5. In the bedroom.

1. Entering the house.

The scientific/mathematic tone is established in the very first line, by the parallel courses set as a pair of walking figures plot a graph on the page and also as they walk through the city. We learn of the various subjects discussed as Father and Son get to know each other. Both are sceptical of organised religion and dogma generally and both enjoy music and literature. They disagree as to the nourishing qualities of civic duty but re-align on the effect that gas-fired street lamps have upon the growth of nearby trees. They agree they have none. Bloom reflects that he used to discuss this and many subjects with friends and family but has socially regressed these last ten years and, with the Rudy effect, we think we know why.

His commentary on his withdrawal from society between the years 1884–1904 is of interest:

> He reflected that the progressive extension of the field of individual development and experience was regressively accompanied by a restriction of the converse domain of interindividual relations.
>
> As in what ways?
>
> From inexistence to existence he came to many and was as one received: existence with existence he was with any as any with any: from existence to nonexistence gone he would be by all as none perceived.[3]

Early in life, when one knows little and is eager to learn, one has many friends and much to discuss and learn. As one gains in knowledge and experience and so, arguably, has greater gifts to pass on to others, social circles reduce as we, and Bloom for his particular reasons, tend to retreat to the nuclear unit. Until death: when, like Paddy Dignam, most of our legacies are summed up in a few inaccurate words. Noteworthy for us, I think, is the sense that, as the individual matures, individuality reduces as personality disintegrates into pre-destined roles that absorb it into a much larger whole.

Bloom covets Stephen's attention whilst Stephen is a little blasé as to Bloom's. He is not particularly interested in Bloom's civic aspirations because they do not directly benefit Stephen or his Art (which is usually the same thing). They discuss the circumstances of Stephen's collapse (we assume this is immediately after he smashed the chandelier and not outside when he was simply punched). Bloom, practical man of science, believes it was all caused by an excess of alcohol accompanied by energetic spinning and dancing. Stephen, rather more cryptically, attributes it to the little cloud simultaneously seen by he and Bloom that morning. Both theories are reasonable. The coming of the thunder around 10.30 pm induced the seismic shift in Stephen's consciousness and we recall that Bloom's mood plummeted into deep depression in the shadow of that cloud as he returned to Eccles Street from Dlugacz, the butcher.

After a long day of travel, Bloom, back in Eccles Street, has a problem. The door key is in his other trousers and he cannot possibly wake Molly at this hour. He's especially annoyed because he's repeated the error made that morning when popping out for the kidney. The image of Bloom and Stephen both barred from home is replete with obvious significance and, like Odysseus, entry had to be effected without the knowledge of Penelope. Bloom, Odysseus-like, has a stratagem which is to jump down into the front vault and gain access via the normally unlocked pantry door. Writing this in Paris, much has been made of Joyce's detailed research, here writing to his Aunt Josephine in Dublin to enquire if a man of Bloom's height and weight could reasonably and safely perform such a feat at this property. She must have given her blessing because he does and, other than a mild momentary concussion caused by the jolt of landing, Bloom is fine and, from inside the house, is able to effect Stephen's ingress via the front door. Technically, in that jump, Stephen witnessed this father figure in flight, just as Icarus saw his father Daedalus and just as Stephen recalled dreaming of his real father, Simon. For Bloom it is also a momentous act as surely we cannot avoid the connection between the misplaced key and Bloom's sex-life and thence his marriage. That he has devised another means of entry looks encouraging.

Thus, having established aerobatic paternal credentials, Bloom lights a candle and guides the Son into the house – the Jew being a light unto the gentile.

2. In the Kitchen

Settled inside, Bloom kindles a fire, fills and boils the kettle and makes them each a cup of cocoa. Hospitality to the stranger is enhanced by serving to Stephen the breakfast cream reserved for Molly (Bloom also takes a soupçon for himself) and, foregoing his usual moustache-faux-Brown-Derby cup, so he and Stephen can have matching crockery: all kindly acts of a father looking after a child. The lighting of the fire reminds Stephen of various people that have done this for him throughout his life.

Each of these acts – the kindling, the water-drawing and the boiling – are described in minute detail running to several pages and no need to repeat the suggested reasoning for that, but we might also perhaps mischievously see it as Bloom, father of Stephen-Christ, and thereby God, panning out into the universe and seeing not only the tap but the pipes, the reservoir, the rainclouds, the solar system. Bloom the God, master of fire, air, earth and water. Note also, thinking back to Circe and Aeolus, the striking of yet another match: ' . . . one ignited Lucifer match . . .'[4] that determined the whole after course of both their lives?

Not sure: lucifer matches were very common but it's interesting that Joyce chooses to so name it here. Our story started with a black mass and the igniting of this flame is prelude to a further raising of chalices to drink the cocoa: 'Epps's massproduct'.[5]

Bloom returns to the sink to wash his hands but Stephen declines to follow suit. Bloom bathed that morning and, although we do not know if that is a daily, weekly or less regular ritual, we know he felt good for doing so. We also learn that he prefers to shave at night and that he 'waterlover' considers his ablution to be a pleasurable physical experience.[6] Stephen, however, generally eschews contact with water and so certainly bathing: Mulligan ridiculed him for this at the Forty Foot. We might attribute this to school-boy initiations[7] or, as commentators (Blamires) have remarked, to a rejection of baptism.[8] *Non servium*. In any event, their aspect to water is different, even unknowingly, for instance, Bloom has been baptised three times and Stephen once. Bloom refrains from lecturing Stephen over lack of hygiene, perhaps he feels he's lectured him enough already and if, as we think, the whole interaction is a courting of Stephen, the quirky brainbox, he may not want to blow his chance.

Bloom notices some torn raffle tickets upon the apron of the dresser and this naturally reminds him of Boylan's sojourn but also of his own gambling opportunities that day. This is revealing, and not only because we assumed, wrongly, that he was generally oblivious to his accidental tipstering:

> What reminiscences temporarily corrugated his brow?
>
> Reminiscences of coincidences, truth stranger than fiction, preindicative of the result of the Gold Cup flat handicap, the official and definitive result of which he had read in the Evening Telegraph, late pink edition, in the cabman's shelter, at Butt bridge.
>
> Where had previous intimations of the result, effected or projected, been received by him?
>
> In Bernard Kiernan's licensed premises 8, 9 and 10 Little Britain street: in David Byrne's licensed premises, 14 Duke street: in O'Connell street lower, outside Graham Lemon's when a dark man had placed in his hand a throwaway (subsequently thrown away), advertising Elijah, restorer of the church in Zion: in Lincoln place outside the premises of F. W. Sweny and Co (Limited) dispensing chemists, when, when Frederick M. (Bantam) Lyons had rapidly and successively requested, perused and restituted the copy of the current issue of the Freeman's Journal and National Press which he had been about to throw away (subsequently thrown away), he had proceeded

towards the oriental edifice of the Turkish and Warm Baths, 11 Leinster street, with the light of inspiration shining in his countenance and bearing in his arms the secret of the race, graven in the language of prediction.

What qualifying considerations allayed his perturbations?

The difficulties of interpretation since the significance of any event followed its occurrence as variably as the acoustic report followed the electrical discharge and of counterestimating against an actual loss by failure to interpret the total sum of possible losses proceeding originally from a successful interpretation.

His mood?

He had not risked, he did not expect, he had not been disappointed, he was satisfied.

What satisfied him?

To have sustained no positive loss. To have brought a positive gain to others. Light to the gentiles.[9]

That is a beautiful passage both to read and hear and warrants some picking apart.

First, Bloom joins the dots. He associates hearing about the 20–1 outsider 'Throwaway' winning the Gold Cup at Barney Kiernan's and elsewhere, with his innocent prediction to Bantam Lyons outside Sweny's the Chemist and also with the Evangelist pamphlet predicting the Coming of Elijah that he crumpled and threw away. This is surprising. We the reader knew it was information he objectively received but we did not know that he perceived it to be so, let alone understood the significance. He did so only in retrospect but even then it's quite remarkable. But join those dots he did, because, we are told, the information caused him anxiety, not as we might expect due to the betting slips belonging to Boylan, but due to the gambling coincidences above referred to.

Secondly, the reverberations we may feel are biblical – Bloom as both Elijah and Moses. Elijah heralding the Messiah is a well-trodden path that we have previously traversed, but Moses?

Let's contrast two passages, the first from Ithaca :

> . . . he had proceeded towards the oriental edifice of the Turkish and Warm Baths, 11 Leinster street, with the light of inspiration shining in his countenance and bearing in his arms the secret of the race, graven in the language of prediction.[10]

Then, an earlier passage from Aeolus and the paraphrasing of a speech about Moses by John F Taylor. The emphasis is mine:

> — But, ladies and gentlemen, had the youthful Moses listened to and accepted that view of life, had he bowed his head and bowed his will and bowed his spirit before that arrogant admonition he would never have brought the chosen people out of their house of bondage, nor followed the pillar of the cloud by day. He would never have spoken with the Eternal amid lightnings on Sinai's mountaintop nor ever have come down *with the light of inspiration shining in his countenance and bearing in his arms the tables of the law, graven in the language of the outlaw.*[11]

First point here is we have a merging with Stephen for it was he not Bloom that heard reference to John F Taylor's speech. Joseph Campbell refers to the disintegration of their individual personalities[12] in this episode and he would, one assumes, see this as an example. Secondly, in the Turkish bath extract, Bloom has received the message of the coming of the saviour and is heading for baptism in the public baths and now bestowed with a gift, the winner of the forthcoming race. Similarly Moses has been to the mountain-top and received his message – the Ten Commandments – and comes down bearing his (or the Lord's) gift to his people, the tablets of stone. Moses doesn't get to his promised land: we await Bloom's fate with interest. Either way, Bloom carries a message for the betterment of others: whether it is the winner of the horserace or the delivery of the message of the (literary) saviour to come. Bloom might have been momentarily upset that he didn't capitalise on the exceptional gambling opportunity but the equanimity of his personality shines through and he sees the positive side: he had not lost money and was able to present others with an opportunity. It is such traits that will enable him to deal with his Suitor-shaped demons.

Campbell's disintegration of individualism theory is borne out in the exploration of the gap in their ages, some 16 years, as Bloom is 38 and Stephen 22. Stephen, we recall, was mulling over this in Circe. The ratio of the age-gap is cast back and projected forward almost infinitely so that we imagine these human beings as mere dots and then a single dot somewhere on a distant horizon. Various topics of conversation and narrative catechism stress test the blurring or atomising of them as individuals. For example, in some theoretic experiment to see how each would have done in the other's education systems, they become Blephen and Stoom and, although this concertina of personality produced little obvious empathy for Bloom, they unintentionally find common ground. Bloom extols good advertising technique as against the not so good. The one he really dislikes is the ad he read in that day's paper for Plumtree's Potted Meat, its crassness made worse by its ignorant placement immediately above the obituaries, indicating cold storage department for dead meat of all description. But this disguises his true animosity, his sixth sense allusion (obviously unspoken), to Boylan potting his meat inside Molly's neglected and accommodating vessel – more on this next time.

Bloom concludes with his idea for an excellent advert but which, we recall from earlier,[13] was rejected by his employer, Hely. To encourage the purchase of stationery it entails a roving little display (drama is to stretch the point) of letter writing. One can imagine that Stephen is not over-impressed with advertising folklore but responds with his own dramatic vignette involving two people in an hotel room, one is writing a letter. Stephen's drama resonates with Bloom, especially as the imaginary establishment's name; is the Queens Hotel. That's quite a coincidence as Bloom's father killed himself in the Queens Hotel, Ennis, just after writing Bloom a letter and, moreover, Bloom is heading there shortly for the anniversary of that sad event.

Bloom recognises as further coincidence when Stephen recites his Parable of the Plums. We recall it concerned the two old ladies sat atop Nelson's Pillar spitting the stones down onto the unreceptive pavement below. We discussed[14] in Aeolus its allusion to Ireland's struggle and, generally, to unrealised dreams. Bloom, a little later in the day, ruminated that Boylan got the plums whilst he Bloom was left with the dry stones. The broader picture, however, is by its strap-line, A Pisgah Sight of Palestine, and might resonate that Bloom, as Moses, may look upon his promised land but is destined not to enter. Bloom needs to face these Suitors down or risk losing his personal Promised Land, Molly.

The parable naturally feeds into further comparison by the two men of the Irish and Jewish races with general accord that they have much in common – two peoples subjected and dispersed but possibly both on the verge of a return to their Promised Lands. Bloom and Stephen seem to be really connecting at this point, they write and compare the Hebrew and Irish alphabets; they compare respective revered philosophers and guides. Bloom sings the opening verse of the hymn we know today as the Israeli national anthem. But, when Stephen is invited to reciprocate, Stephen surprises us and Bloom by singing a grotesque and anti-Semitic ballad, an updated version based on the medieval tale of Hugh of Lincoln.[15] This was a boy whose premature death was falsely attributed to Jews and caused much blood-libellous violence against Jews in Lincoln. It is set out in full, demonstrating that Stephen knows and sings all verses. Why might he sing such a hurtful song? Possibly because his lack of social skills renders him blind or impassive to the hurt caused; this seems far-fetched. It might be a subtle reference that he knows Bloom is not technically Jewish. In fact the book confirms the answer, which concerns consensual execution:

> Condense Stephen's commentary.[16]
>
> One of all, the least of all, is the victim predestined. Once by inadvertence, twice by design he challenges his destiny. It comes when he is abandoned and challenges him reluctant and, as an apparition of hope and youth, holds him unresisting. It leads him to a strange habitation, to a secret infidel apartment, and there, implacable, immolates him, consenting.

Hugh allowed himself to be lured by the Jewess and, like Hugh, Stephen has, thus far, willingly accepted Bloom's hospitality as though, in both cases, it was pre-destined. Bloom does not intend to decapitate Stephen but he does have his destiny in mind and we shed some light on this by exploring a previous passage.

The narrator asked:

> Which domestic problem as much as, if not more than, any other frequently engaged his mind?
>
> What to do with our wives.[17]

There followed various examples of Bloom's condescension towards Molly. He wished he could improve her education not to say intelligence, a process in which he foresaw Stephen in a pivotal role. Stephen could reside with them, thereby solving his own immediate domestic issue, and could educate Molly by teaching her Italian. He would be a young intellectual presence in the house which would delight all residents, even possibly tempting the return of ex-resident Milly. So Bloom is busy making plans for Stephen and all of them domestic and economic. Together, they could improve on that terrible advert. Stephen would put the Plumtree into potted meat; with him, an abode of bliss.

Stephen may have earlier empathised with Bloom and one of the main thrusts of the book is that this day has for him been an epiphany in terms of future domesticity, but he will go down fighting. What would Icarus have done? Homemaking is not yet his destiny, far from it. He will not, like Hugh, walk willingly into a domestic abode of bliss which, as sure as decapitation, will kill off Stephen's artistic future.

And so...

> Was the proposal of asylum accepted?
> Promptly, inexplicably, with amicability, gratefully it was declined.[18]

Thus, they agree to part; before that, a further word on macro-micro aspects. At the macro level, we have Stephen carrying the weight of the Irish people: history, culture and the rest. With Bloom, the same for the Jewish people. It's as though it's a high level summit at which the destinies of the two races will be determined. That's all very well but we also simply have two blokes, sat across a table from each other, drinking cocoa and having a chat. They have differences, of course, but there is rapprochement as the elder rejoices in the vibrancy of youth and intellectualism, the younger recognising the worth of practical experience.

3. In the Garden

It's time for Stephen to depart. Bloom leads and lights the way, Stephen holding hat, crucifix/ashplant and reciting the 113th psalm which Blamires comments[19] celebrated the Israelites exiting the house of bondage and entering the Promised Land. Entering the garden they are greeted by a star-spangled night sky.

> What spectacle confronted them when they, first the host, then the guest, emerged silently, doubly dark, from obscurity by a passage from the rere of the house into the penumbra of the garden?
> The heaventree of stars hung with humid nightblue fruit.[20]

We are reminded of the allusion back in Nestor to Giordano Bruno:

> Gone too from the world, Averroes and Moses Maimonides, dark men in mien and movement, flashing in their mocking mirrors the obscure soul of the world, a darkness shining in brightness which brightness could not comprehend.[21]

We noted back then the stars which, in the day, blinded by the light of the sun, we do not see. But that is our affliction. They are there all along.

Blamires continues with the Christ symbolism. Stephen Christ figure (note he has torn the side of his jacket), will shortly leave our story and ascend to heaven, though we note that the 'shining in brightness' quote above is actually a blasphemous corruption.[22] The two men ponder the stars and the magnitude of the heavens, almost taking on planetary characteristics themselves as we pan out into super macro views of the world and beyond and then reverse to the billions of atoms on a pinhead. Bloom's horizons, unlike Stephen's dreams of flying, are a little more prosaic, there being no means of travel to it, space would simply have to exist on its own for the time being. However, like the ancient Greeks, who attributed human characteristics to the planets, Bloom considered a special affinity to exist between the moon and women:

> Her antiquity in preceding and surviving successive tellurian generations: her nocturnal predominance: her satellitic dependence: her luminary reflection: her constancy under all her phases, rising, and setting by her appointed times, waxing and waning: the forced invariability of her aspect: her indeterminate response to inaffirmative interrogation: her potency over effluent and refluent waters: her power to enamour, to mortify, to invest with beauty, to render insane, to incite to and aid delinquency: the tranquil inscrutability of her visage: the terribility of her isolated dominant implacable resplendent propinquity: her omens of tempest and of calm: the stimulation of her light, her motion and her presence: the admonition of her craters, her arid seas, her silence: her splendour, when visible: her attraction, when invisible.[23]

On such cue, Molly illuminates the garden proceedings, for it is her earthly light in the first floor window and we are supposed to perceive as significant that both Stephen and Bloom are attracted to it. The wording more than mimics Dante's *Inferno* as he and Virgil emerge from Hell.

Let's return momentarily to the opening of that garden door. As the two men exit, the cat enters. Cats have been symbolic (though not exclusively) of Bloom throughout and although Bloom will shortly re-enter in person, this crafty representative of the Odyssean soul may have here silently and stealthily made ingress.

In the final act before parting, Bloom and Stephen urinate against the garden wall. This is not to be scoffed at as an ironic comic parting, though it might also be that. Way back in Proteus we observed the symbolic and/or actual creativity in the act of picking one's nose or urinating and, even earlier in the 'Ballad of Joking Jesus',[24] and then in Calypso, as the thought flitted through Bloom's mind that he could fertilise his own garden. He is now so doing, so we ought to be a little reverential. The trajectories of respective jet streams are monitored. They appear not to coincide but remain parallel to each other as was their gait in the opening of the episode. To emphasise points of departure while urinating, Bloom thinks about his penis: its size, rigidity, tumescence and sanitation whereas Stephen contemplates the theological complexities associated with the circumcision of Christ. The reference to Bloom's schoolboy talent to attain the greatest altitude in micturition surely marks the moment of Odysseus passing Penelope's test. That is, she will marry the marksman that can fire his arrow through twelve pairs of crossed axes. Indeed . . .

> What celestial sign was by both simultaneously observed?
>
> A star precipitated with great apparent velocity across the firmament from Vega in the Lyre above the zenith beyond the stargroup of the Tress of Berenice towards the zodiacal sign of Leo.[25]

Blamires suggests this is Molly speeding away from Boylan and towards Bloom.[26] Others suggest[27] that it's a reminder to the reader that Stephen can do worse than to hitch his wagon to Bloom's.

At the moment of departure, a church bell peels. Stephen hears the prayer for the dead. Bloom hears heighho, heighho, heighho, heighho. They depart. We may have hoped for a moment of seismic significance but rather, the narrator describes the angle of their handshake and Stephen heads off into the night without a backward glance as he leaves our novel. Their meeting produced no great moment of clarity, no *kundalini* awakening to which we may have felt entitled. No as yet obvious disposing of the Suitors. But their exchange of views on various topics brought them close – a realisation that youth and experience both have value and virtue.

After a moment of introspection in which Bloom feels the searing chill of absolute zero, he heads back inside where we'll join him next time for his concluding thoughts upon the day.

LECTURE 20, 7 JULY 2021: EPISODE 17

Ithaca Part Two, Crumbs and Comfort

Music: Go To Sleep Little Baby – Angie C

Stephen and Bloom have parted. Bloom lingers a little in the garden before going inside. The lock he fumbled with to afford Stephen access to the street is emblematic of the fumbling out-of-practice sex act he and Molly have not performed together in many a year: a demon to be faced if they are to get back on track. With a chill in the air and the peeling of the bells still echoing, he thinks of that day's funeral and how the attendees will now all be asleep; then of passed friends and acquaintances. We wonder if this list of names represent the Suitors all now dead or living dead but dismiss that as unlikely. It does, though, serve to stress Bloom's isolation at this point. His world is asleep; he seems alone in a boundless universe.

4. In the Parlour

As Bloom enters the parlour in the dark he bumps his head on the upper reaches of a walnut sideboard. Kindling a light, he sees that the furniture has been shuffled around, someone has decided to rearrange the room with scant regard for the views of the master of the house. The decision was no doubt Molly's but would have needed muscular help. Stephen foreshadowed this with his question in the cabman's shelter as to why chairs are placed on tables in dining establishments at the end of the evening. We are reminded also that, in *The Odyssey,* a small stool is thrown at the old beggar and strikes a glancing blow but which only serves to galvanise the disguised Odysseus. The location of the piano, the full ashtrays and the music of 'Love's Old Sweet Song' alighted on the music rest, all point to jocular festivities.

The furniture, furnishings and other contents of the room are described, including mementos of the Bloom wedding and which presents like the marriage, have seen better days, the carriage clock having ceased performance years before. Twenty-two books are stacked on a bookshelf, several are dog-eared and book-marked indicating active perusal. We recognise some as inspiration for Bloom's musings that day, for example, *In The Track of the Sun* and *Thoughts from Spinoza*. Our impression of a pretty well-read man is reinforced, though had he paid even scant attention to Hozier's *History of the Russo-Turkish War*, he may have seen through his father-in-law's claim to have fought at the battle of Plevna, as British troops did not feature.[1]

Bloom sat at the table, loosened his collar and scratched his chest in the vicinity of the bee sting. He compiles profit and loss accounts for 16 June. Omitted items suggest his hand rather than our narrator of absolute truth. For example, there's no mention of the sixpence left with Bella Cohen to cover damage reparation nor of the train fare to Amiens Street. The whole Nighttown episode seems to be omitted save the sheep's trotter and pig's foot which could have been purchased anywhere. He might be rehearsing an anticipated interrogation from Molly yet he includes the 2s 6d postal order which we believe he sent to Martha Clifford. We are reminded of his generous 5s donation to the Dignam family. The balance sheet, like its author, is a little imperfect, a point reinforced in relation to the latter, by him removing boots and socks, picking a toenail and with satisfaction, smelling the detached chip. The satisfaction being due to odorous transportation back to schooldays where it seems this was a regular and pleasurable indulgence.

We learn in great detail, of Bloom's comfortable and moderately proportioned dream house and of how he might pay for it. Realistically it would be a combination of money down, mortgage and even some rent but whimsically and preposterously he ponders how he might come into serious money to buy it outright. Bloom, ever the urban planner, has a detailed vision of each room and the expansive gardens in which he can make dreams come true. He had bucolic daydreams earlier: we recall the fertilising of his Eccles Street garden and of making the desert bloom with enormous Jewish melon fields in Palestine through the co-operative movement of Agendath Netaim. Generally we may interpret this as him dreaming of improved domestic relations with his wife. He imagines his elevated status in society befitting of such a residence. The outsider finally inside, admitted and accepted as a pillar of the community whose vacation plans are of interest to the country at large. '(Mr and Mrs Leopold Bloom have left Kingstown for England).'[2]

He mulls over several means of efficiently passing the time in this abode of bliss, including upkeep of house and garden and finding time for indulgence of hobbies, some virtuous, others less seemly private concerns. His primary vocation would be to serve as a justice of the peace with powers, diligently enforced, to maintain civic equilibrium and social order.

> . . . against all traversers in covin and trespassers acting in contravention of bylaws and regulations, all resuscitators (by trespass and petty larceny of kindlings) of venville rights, obsolete by desuetude, all orotund instigators of international persecution, all perpetuators of international animosities, all menial molestors of domestic conviviality, all recalcitrant violators of domestic connubiality.[3]

We note, as should Mr Boylan, that Bloom will have no mercy for violators of domestic arrangements. Is this the killing of the Suitor? Possibly, but more likely a warning shot across the bows.

Of what help is this reverie, which includes his mulling over the perfect advert, to Bloom or for that matter, the reader? For Bloom, his habit of reflecting on various ideas before retiring to bed will he believes ease restful sleep for we learn that he fears sleepwalking and even unwitting homicide or suicide. We recall that in his deep sub-conscious he feels guilt for the death of Rudy. 'If it's healthy it's from the mother. If not the man. Better luck next time.'[4]

Bloom the killer. And for the reader it suggests the hidden Odysseus as warrior, revealed and restrained – a baring of teeth. We know Bloom considers his hand to be steady and dexterous with a blade but the talent is reserved for a clean evening shave as he eschews violence to all living things. But this fear of the devil inside, especially unrestrained during sleep, causes him concern. The crescendo to the slaying of the Suitors has begun.

In the parlour stands a sideboard with locked drawers. The narrator enquires as to the contents and we are all ears hoping for secrets revealed or, at least, a glimpse of Bloom dirty laundry. We think the sideboard key is the property of Mr B to the exclusion of Mrs B. Keys have eluded him all day but not to this particular sanctum.

The first drawer: assorted items and mementos from his childhood to near present. Selected items include: a drawing book belonging to the very young Millicent Bloom. Some photographs, a regal one of Queen Alexandra but of greater interest, are two of pornographic variety. These feature copulating couples including priest and nun and are, no doubt, for Bloom's personal arousal but they may also trigger underlying concerns regarding Milly whose first job is as a photographer's assistant and was described as 'Photogirl' back in Telemachus. She's in Mullingar, beyond his protective reach and the erotic photos lay in the drawer near her letter. There, too, are long expired Hungarian lottery tickets and three letters from Martha Clifford addressed to H Flower, esquire, allowing calculation of an approximate duration of the clandestine affair. Also a prospectus for Wonderworker, a treatment of rectal complaint addressed to 'Mrs L Bloom'. Finally, of interest is a pencilled record of measurement of Bloom's various muscled limbs, taken before and after use of Sandow-Whitley's Pulley Exerciser. We take this to be the equipment accompanying *Eugen Sandow's Physical Strength and How to Obtain It*, the book just seen on his parlour bookshelf. This might be no more revealing than a guy, Jew or gentile, wanting to develop his muscles but let's self-indulge by thinking of the Muscular Jew we considered back in Hades[5] then, in context of Father Coffey, Muscular Christian. On Bloom's micro level, the aspiration to body-build might be his reaction to characterisation as the physically weak and effeminate Jew, as we saw several times in Cyclops and Circe. At macro level, the Zionist political ideal of the strong Jew breaking free of the *Shtetl* to work the land and other physical labour in Palestine[6] – tasks historically denied to Jews by law in large parts of Russia and Europe.[7] Sandow, with Jewish connections himself, apparently coined the term body-builder and it was quite the *fin de siècle* vogue.[8] The body beautiful has preoccupied and impressed Bloom all day from the carpet-beating hip-swinger in the butchers to the statues of the Greek goddesses and including, inevitably, the photograph of his wife.

Bloom removes the latest and fourth letter from Martha Clifford from his pocket and adds it to the collection. In doing so he has two thoughts: one the pleasant reflection that three pretty attractive women have that day looked upon him with pleasure – Josie Breen, Nurse Callan and Gerty MacDowell (though Bloom is ignorant of her surname). The second, not so heroic, that he might in the coming days visit a prostitute.

The narrator enquires of the second drawer: the birth certificate of Leopold Paula Bloom. Paula is of interest. Bloom has been lambasted for his physical weakness and 'love-not-hate' outlook bordering on the feminine. 'A touch of the artist' as Lenehan remarked in Wandering Rocks.[9] Yet the reader appreciates androgyny as a quality – we men would improve for tapping into our feminine side. In actual fact this replicates a gender typographical error on the birth certificate of James Augustine Joyce.[10] The drawer also reveals life policy documents pledged for Millicent Bloom, various savings account booklets, deeds to the family plots at Glasnevin Cemetery and a change of name certificate of Rudolph Virag, subsequently Bloom. Inside a dog-eared *Haggadah*,[11] and alongside a photograph of Bloom's father, is Rudolph's suicide note addressed to his son. The mechanical style of the episode is an impotent restraint upon the emotional humanity that pours forth. As though the reader is judged ill-equipped to cope with the emotion, the passage is delivered partially redacted but the essential message is that Virag was unable to bear living after his wife's death, and it packs a punch.

The father's death left the son, aged twenty, bereft of parents yet Bloom bears no resentment, rather guilt of his teenage rejection of Jewish observance. This confirms the official abandonment of Judaism by the father to be simply cosmetic and that, in the privacy of the home, the son was raised a Jew. Why guilt? Does he now believe? No, but, on adult reflection, the rituals of Judaism are no more nonsensical than those of other religions. The guilt lies more with disappointing his father and is comparable with, but different from, Stephen's for disappointing his mother.

> How did these beliefs and practices now appear to him?
>
> Not more rational than they had then appeared, not less rational than other beliefs and practices now appeared.[12]

Bloom reflects on his father and his travels, his habits; the small individual oddities that define. He remains grateful, at least, for the financial security brought about by the untimely death and Bloom imagines various states of, and consequences of, the poverty that may have been suffered without it, including having to leave Ireland for both pastures and Odyssean adventures new. Noman[13] and Everyman, the freedom bestowed upon the anonymous traveller: the Wandering Jew.

> Assumed by any or known to none. Everyman or Noman.
>
> What tributes his?
>
> Honour and gifts of strangers, the friends of Everyman. A nymph immortal, beauty, the bride of Noman.[14]

Bloom is then catapulted, perhaps by the lateness of the hour, in dream-state through time and space, transformed as bigger than the stars, the unification not simply of male and female but of time, space and matter. Bloom becomes Schopenhauer's *Noumena*. Yet, by irrational contradiction, time, which does not exist, still manages to pass and Bloom returns in bodily form, immensely rich and powerful to avenge those that have done him harm. The Suitors of course. One thinks of Dumas' *The Count of Monte Christo*.

> Would the departed never nowhere nohow reappear?

Ever he would wander, selfcompelled, to the extreme limit of his cometary orbit, beyond the fixed stars and variable suns and telescopic planets, astronomical waifs and strays, to the extreme boundary of space, passing from land to land, among peoples, amid events. Somewhere imperceptibly he would hear and somehow reluctantly, suncompelled, obey the summons of recall. Whence, disappearing from the constellation of the Northern Crown he would somehow reappear reborn above delta in the constellation of Cassiopeia and after incalculable eons of peregrination return an estranged avenger, a wreaker of justice on malefactors, a dark crusader, a sleeper awakened, with financial resources (by supposition) surpassing those of Rothschild or the silver king.

What would render such return irrational?

An unsatisfactory equation between an exodus and return in time through reversible space and an exodus and return in space through irreversible time.[15]

Bloom, practical Bloom, puts the idea of further wandering to the back of his mind because, well, among other reasons, its late, he's tired and a bed, warmed with the warmth of a body, beckons him upstairs. He mulls over the events of the day and to emphasise their universal, biblical or, better yet, mystical significance, they are imbued with Jewish significance.

The preparation of breakfast (burnt offering): intestinal congestion and premeditative defecation (holy of holies): the bath (rite of John): the funeral (rite of Samuel): the advertisement of Alexander Keyes (Urim and Thummim): the unsubstantial lunch (rite of Melchizedek): the visit to museum and national library (holy place): the bookhunt along Bedford row, Merchants' Arch, Wellington Quay (Simchath Torah): the music in the Ormond Hotel (Shira Shirim): the altercation with a truculent troglodyte in Bernard Kiernan's premises (holocaust): a blank period of time including a cardrive, a visit to a house of mourning, a leavetaking (wilderness): the eroticism produced by feminine exhibitionism (rite of Onan): the prolonged delivery of Mrs Mina Purefoy (heave offering): the visit to the disorderly house of Mrs Bella Cohen, 82 Tyrone street, lower and subsequent brawl and chance medley in Beaver street (Armageddon): nocturnal perambulation to and from the cabman's shelter, Butt Bridge (atonement).[16]

Thus one might consider his day to be pre-destined, fettered by the chains of history and bereft of choice and independence of will. Yet chaos intervenes by dangling a tantalising loose end. Just who was MacIntosh? One might see this as the escape hatch, a portal through which to escape the Vicoan cycle and divert the course of history. So Bloom, travelling the universe in macro mode, retains the micro, the down to earth practicality and, specifically, the hope that he may secure that Keyes advertisement, pay for the soap, collect Molly's lotion and a quantity of tea from Tom Kernan, the tea merchant. That all sounds like a desire to improve his domestic status.

5. In the Bedroom

Bloom, father of Milly, father figure to Stephen, ascends the stairs to his bedroom , the holy of holies. Just as in the opening sentence of the book, Buck Mulligan, false father figure, Usurper, ascended the tower steps to the false altar. He enters the sacred bedroom. Ithaca, or as that might that be the bed itself, as close as dammit. Discarded female clothing adorns various items of furniture. Some chinaware, notably the chamber-pot, is orange keyed linking to Homer. Bloom undresses, then dresses in a night gown and enters the bed.

> How?
>
> With circumspection, as invariably when entering an abode (his own or not his own): with solicitude, the snakespiral springs of the mattress being old, the brass quoits and pendent viper radii loose and tremulous under stress and strain: prudently, as entering a lair or ambush of lust or adder: lightly, the less to disturb: reverently, the bed of conception and of birth, of consummation of marriage and of breach of marriage, of sleep and of death.
>
> What did his limbs, when gradually extended, encounter?
>
> New clean bedlinen, additional odours, the presence of a human form, female, hers, the imprint of a human form, male, not his, some crumbs, some flakes of potted meat, recooked, which he removed.[17]

He is confronted with definitive evidence of the adultery. His worst fear. Meat has been potted into his receptive wife and in this very bed where ambiguous dried meat-flakes remain to mock him. Ambiguous? Here they are, remnant crumbs of potted meat and not dried sperm, just as the opposite was presumed in the case of the flaky crumbs on the seat of the carriage headed for Glasnevin Cemetery. In both cases, a lovely picnic. Marion, wife, lover (of sorts), trusted ally and Holy Grail has deceived him in deplorable fashion. Yet, deception without duplicity, as she does little to hide the fact. Indeed, we shall learn that the sheets are also blessed with dried sperm. For Odysseus and Penelope the marital bed was the very essence of their mutual trust, so here, the opposite. The very bed itself deceives Bloom. He has always believed that father-in-law, Major Tweedy, purchased it from the Governor of Gibraltar himself [18] and whose personal bed it was. Whereas Molly knows[19] the true previous owner was an old man named Cohen. She lets Bloom enjoy this almost regal heirloom in ignorant bliss. Just as she also lets him believe her father was a Major.

We are in the final battleground. This is Mount Doom. The usurping Suitors have laid down the gauntlet to Bloom by marking their territory with imprints of male form and remnants of dried meat flakes. Bloom moves in for the kill.

> If he had smiled why would he have smiled?
>
> To reflect that each one who enters imagines himself to be the first to enter whereas he is always the last term of a preceding series even if the first term of a succeeding one, each imagining himself to be first, last, only and alone whereas he is neither first nor last nor only nor alone in a series originating in and repeated to infinity.
>
> What preceding series?
>
> Assuming Mulvey to be the first term of his series, Penrose, Bartell d'Arcy, professor Goodwin, Julius Mastiansky, John Henry Menton, Father Bernard Corrigan, a farmer at the Royal Dublin Society's Horse Show, Maggot O'Reilly, Matthew Dillon, Valentine Blake Dillon (Lord Mayor of Dublin), Christopher Callinan, Lenehan, an Italian organgrinder, an unknown gentleman in the Gaiety Theatre, Benjamin Dollard, Simon Dedalus, Andrew (Pisser) Burke, Joseph Cuffe, Wisdom Hely, Alderman John Hooper, Dr Francis Brady, Father Sebastian of Mount Argus, a bootblack at the General Post Office, Hugh E. (Blazes) Boylan and so each and so on to no last term.[20]

This is Odysseus surveying his great hall and weighing up the Suitors. Bloom suspects all of these men of having slept with Molly. Of such, only Lieutenant Mulvey preceded Bloom, for he was back in Gibraltar, though we cannot yet rule out subsequent assignation. Penrose is notable as the man that used to walk past their house and look through the ground floor window, especially at Molly's bath time. We have several familiar Dublin's drunks, Bloom's former employers, a Lord Mayor of Dublin and we learn that Pisser Burke, informant ally of the Cyclops narrator, has a first name, Andrew. We can well believe that all these men have lusted after Molly and have born witness to some of it. How many beyond Blazes Boylan elevated that to kissing or more salacious activity we do not know but shall discover more in the final episode. Many of these men have shown malicious intent towards

Bloom, again as we have witnessed this day: Menton at Glasnevin, Simon Dedalus in the coach, Lenehan speaking with McCoy, Dollard on the street and Pisser Burke's gossip-mongering. All shall pay.

After extracting Bloom's opinions on the morally bankrupt Boylan, the narrator draws him on his sentiments towards the series of Suitors. These are envy, jealousy, abnegation and equanimity. Envy we think is of the proportions of the Blazes phallus and its and his ability, or imagined ability and that of other men generally, to invoke female arousal culminating in complete satisfaction. Bloom recently contemplated his own organ during urination. His jealousy is of the natural fluctuation of action and reaction, the waves of chance and destiny that have drawn Molly and Boylan together. But he renounces such feelings, he abnegates. Why? Because he's the better man; because Boylan has been superficially decent to him; because he, smaller and meeker, quite likes being liked by the tall handsome gentile; and because now is the time for abnegation. Hostility, if it shall come, can wait at least until after the mutually beneficial tour of Belfast, profits divided.

And lastly equanimity. 'He's killed looking back.'[21]

We may recall Miss Douce's weapon of choice back in Sirens, illuminating more than one way to kill a Suitor. Bloom's equanimity is the comfort he feels. Comfortable that each of these men assumed at the time they would be the last of a preceding series, the man to sweep Molly off her feet, whereas they are just another in a line of shooting stars that briefly shone. He is the Siren's rock on which they all founder for it is he, Bloom, the Dark Horse 'Throwaway', outsider, that shares Molly's bed every night. They each have their moment whereas his is timeless. He is further assured because he can see a bigger picture. Adultery is not a happy state of affairs but there are worse eventualities; the collision of planets, murder, high treason, cruelty to children and various other misdemeanours that Bloom considers worse. He is, it seems, despite all, thankful for what he has. There will be those that oppose such an approach and they may be right but they may also not sleep the sleep into which Bloom will shortly lapse.

Thus, Bloom kills Molly's Suitors, his usurpers, without resorting to violence. The blade in his steady hand remains for the evening shave and not for plunging into a man's back right up to the hilt, as, legend has it, they do in Trieste.[22] But, for Bloom's purposes, they are disposed nonetheless. Of course, his calm and comparative comfort might be due to his simply biding his time. Little or nothing is to be gained by immediate action; besides it takes two to tango and Molly must be as culpable as Boylan and he, Bloom, likely as culpable as both. There are lots more Suitors in the world, he wisely concludes, and that rash action against Boylan will solve nothing and most likely exacerbate. For Boylan is not the problem here, the problem is Bloom, Molly and the void of incertitude that has lain between them for ten years.

Bloom rests top to tail with Molly. Ying and Yang,[23] the power of opposites[24] and, in a sort of back to front spoon, they are reminiscent of the earth spinning imperceptibly on its axis. As is his wont he kisses her bottom. She awakens. Whether she is caused to stir by the kiss or his erection in her face, we do not know.

> He kissed the plump mellow yellow smellow melons of her rump, on each plump melonous hemisphere, in their mellow yellow furrow, with obscure prolonged provocative melonsmellonous osculation.
>
> The visible signs of postsatisfaction?
>
> A silent contemplation: a tentative velation: a gradual abasement: a solicitous aversion: a proximate erection.
>
> What followed this silent action?
>
> Somnolent invocation, less somnolent recognition, incipient excitation, catechetical interrogation.[25]

Molly must consider the best form of defence to be attack for she interrogates her husband as to where he's been until this hour and why Stephen, whom she saw from the window, did not stay in one of the spare rooms. Bloom accounts for himself and his daily activity. Some truth, a little embellishment, significant omission and some downright lies. He omits the entire Nighttown episode, claiming to have been at the Gaiety Theatre watching Mrs Bandman Palmer play Leah.[26] Nor, understandably, does he volunteer masturbating at the beach. He sings Stephen's praises, he makes no enquiry of her day. After which he dozes and wafts towards sleep.

We are saying goodbye to our friend. He turned out to be far from perfect but no worse, and perhaps a little better, than many of us. He is weary, he has travelled. The two of them might be characters in a Chagall painting spinning, elevating in the marital bed and into dreamland way above the Dublin streets. Save that Molly is static. She has not left the house all day and barely left the bed. She is Gaia, mother earth, around whom Suitors will orbit before gravitating towards her timeless boundless womb. Her gravitational pull now draws Bloom. He drifts; nearer and nearer and, like his ancient Greek counterpart, thinks vaguely of the next adventure, until, finally, he is nowhere. Not just lost but extinct or even as never was, within the black hole of that oversized full stop[27] at the end of the episode. He's disappeared into the void of incertitude that is Molly Gaia Bloom. Gone as the auk's egg, never to return. Unless . . . met him pike hoses?

LECTURE 21, 21 JULY 2021: EPISODE 18

Lady Penelope and the Word Known to All

Music: Willow – Joan Armatrading

One might think that to call James Joyce a man and Molly Bloom a woman is not controversial, but in these gender sensitive times perhaps it is. Let us say that on the spectrum of humanity with male at one end and female the other, James leans decidedly one way and Molly the opposite. This is not to make a trite point. We have witnessed in our story the womanly man and the manly woman and, especially for the former, it was a positive experience. We have also seen the energising effect of *Shakti* indicating that Joyce felt much was to be gained by placing oneself in another sex or a mingling of the sexes for a while and to see how well those clothes fit.

In this final episode of the book, he, Joyce, for the sake of labels let's call him a man, puts himself into the head of what, for convenience, we shall call a woman. Authors have done this since stories were stories but Joyce not only narrates events via Molly, he invades her. He lives out her very soul, thinks as she thinks, feels every inner and outer bodily need – both adult Molly and reaching back to adolescence. It is hugely ambitious. He's perfected *monologue interieur* by this point in the book, but that was a walk in the park compared to what he now attempts. He knows Stephen intimately for obvious autobiographical reasons and honed that throughout *A Portrait* and *Ulysses*. Bloom is a greater challenge, far less familiar, and how Joyce, either through meticulous research or intuition, gets under Bloom's skin has been impressive bordering upon the astonishing. Yet Molly is in a different league again.

Gerty MacDowell provided a taste of female *monologue interieur* but it was romanticised cliché and Nausicaa was, for the most part, traditional male observation of the 'female form divine, undraped'.[1] In this episode, the world is seen through the eyes of a women with as little male filter as the author could manage: revolutionary in the 1920s and still shocking now.

As the denouement of a special book, Penelope bears a heavy responsibility. It must be a show-stopper in its own right and should resonate with Homer. But it is also obliged to draw together the many strings that inter-weave the book, it's the least we can expect having come this far. But we shall be left wanting, for this book – modernist novel par excellence – reflects the world as is and, in the real world, loose ends are not tied in a pretty bow: chromatic not diatonic, to borrow musical nomenclature. The standard Victorian novel may be diatonic with a nice wedding in the last scene but *Ulysses* is chromatic, the *Tristan und Isolde*[2] of novels where issues, as in life, are unresolved. Ironically this may have helped Joyce because it reduced the burden upon Molly to provide answers. Instead, she was allowed to roam free, given space to strut her stuff and the reader may interpret at will. Strut she does. In the vulgar, uncouth manner that we may all think inside our heads but which drove the few censors left in the Joyce camp way, way over the edge. So beware: profanity in language and subject-matter, both in the book and this lecture.

Joyce considered Molly unrestrained by petty detail such as space and time, so we risk the accusation of pettiness by placing her in bed next to Bloom, top to tail his face puckered against her buttocks as he drifts into sleep. She pond-skates a range of matters and puts the world to rights. The episode comprises a mere eight un-punctuated sentences each though constituting around several thousand words. This sounds a difficult read, and in places it is. It's not complicated, in the sense of episodes Proteus or Scylla, Molly is not grappling with intense intellectual issues, just the daily stuff of life. The trick is to take it slow and let it play aloud in your head. Better yet, have someone familiar with it read it to you: ideally someone at the female end of the spectrum.

In essence we have Molly's world, her version of events and point of view on aspects of life. About time, too, as we've heard pretty much everyone else's view on her. To Lenehan she's a gamey mare as, in poor taste, he mimes a nice handful. To Simon Dedalus, she's an Irish Molly, all the way from the rock of Gibraltar and who leaves off clothes of all description. To Boylan, she is one who can be kept waiting while he savours his sloe gin. To the Cyclops parodist she is Marion of the bountiful bosoms. For Stephen, she may be the route to the daughter or vice-versa. To most, she is Blazes' latest filly. As for Bloom: She's wife, soprano, adulteress, mother to Milly and briefly to Rudy; daughter of the Major and one who gets bloated after cabbage; attractor of dogs, human contact in bed. But when he's feeling rhapsodic, Molly is flower of the mountain and the world entire for whom the sun shines. So many opinionated men and, if we believe Bloom's list of Suitors,[3] many more besides that could contribute to the bank of knowledge of Mrs Marion Bloom.

The Molly view is long overdue.

For the final time, we consult Homer.[4] Penelope is awakened by a maid to be told Odysseus has returned and slain the Suitors, but she is sceptical that this man is truly her husband and so creates a test concerning their marriage bed, the very emblem of her fidelity and their trust. He passes: the family reunited, is happy and never mind that he is already thinking of his next adventure.

Joyce imbued Molly with the essence of mother-earth. He explains to Frank Budgen:

> It [her monologue] turns like the huge earth ball slowly surely and evenly round and round spinning, its four cardinal points being the female breasts, arse, womb and cunt expressed by the words because, bottom . . . woman, yes.[5,6]

It is as Gaia, mother earth, that she might be helpfully contemplated. Parental influence uncertain; there was a mother Lunita Laredo, a Gibraltarian Jewess, but whose absence, we might assume death, curtailed meaningful influence. Major Tweedy did what he could but was wedded to the army, rendering Molly indeed a daughter of the regiment. As Gaia, Molly is unfettered by normal rules of time and space. She just is: slowly revolving, existing. Men, believing they can know her, will be drawn into her orbit all the while assuming they can control but, ultimately, she is beyond control or comprehension. She is Kali, Hindu goddess, with a string of male heads around her neck. Sturdy and resolute, like the earth and as liquid, and as powerful as a river, she nourishes parched men with her inexhaustible vibrancy and energy. She foreshadows Anna-Livia Plurabelle of Joyce's novel to come – the river meandering lubricating, providing succour, energising, life-instilling and uncontrollable. The supernatural ambience is enhanced by this episode's astronomic metaphors and even the infinity of eight sentences.

However, such elevated interpretation must augment rather than detract from what is before us. Molly may be Gaia or Beatrice or representing womanhood, but, surely of greater interest, is the singular woman before us. We resist going all Notting Hill[7] with just a girl standing in front of a boy, etc, but that is the drift. We focus less on planetary constellations to emphasise the earthly one. She is base, brash, yet with some frailty and meeting the world head-on. Moreover, despite modernism, there are certain loose ends one cannot ignore and which ought to be tidied up before we close. Say,

1. What does Molly make of Bloom?
2. Where does that leave them?

And slightly out of left field,

3. What is, as Stephen asks in Proteus, the word known to all men?

These questions lead to others, such as, what does Molly make of Boylan, Stephen and Milly? Excavation of answers amid such an unstructured episode calls for structure. Let's take it a sentence at a time.

The First Sentence

> Yes because he never did a thing like that before as ask to get his breakfast in bed with a couple of eggs . . .[8]

The episode begins and ends with the word 'yes' and, at the start, is immediately followed by the word 'because'. Joyce has told us that this should be suggestive of vagina and womanly breasts. Bloom, apparently in the course of the nocturnal interrogation, has requested, perhaps demanded, breakfast, two eggs, in bed. It contrasts with Calypso where he waited upon Molly. Of course, eggs: finally, after the rain, there is fresh water in which to poach. Two eggs, not three, as were served (and burnt) by Buck Mulligan in the Martello tower, but two. Eggs: symbolic of fertility, suggestive of breasts and certainly new beginnings. Are they also redolent of Bloom having rediscovered his balls?

It is a new beginning of sorts because it's been many years since Bloom took such a stand. Not since they resided between houses in the City Arms Hotel and Bloom would suffer bouts of man-flu. This reminds Molly that Bloom would butter-up to their co-resident, the elderly Mrs Riordan, hoping, so Molly cynically thinks, for a bequest in her will. She may be right, we don't know. What is more interesting in terms of hypostatic symmetry is that the woman that ushered Stephen through his earliest years was ushered through her last by Bloom. Whilst Molly is critical of her husband, she also appreciates that he's kind to old women and generally receptive to those in need of help. This is a recurring theme: that she acknowledges Bloom's finer qualities in the very act of her admonition. Nevertheless, she thinks, better he be ill at home than in a hospital where she suspects he'd be trying it on with a nurse or a nun, which reminds her of Bloom's pornographic photograph that he believes is locked away beyond her prying eyes: '. . . shes as much a nun as Im not . . .'[9]

Molly suspects that Bloom has ejaculated that day and presumes he has been with a prostitute. She dismisses his cover story about meeting Hynes and Menton in an hotel and we get a little backstory as to his poor track record, allegedly re the household staff. She recently caught him furtively writing a letter and assumes he has some floozy or other. She convinces herself that she's not that bothered because it'll be just sex and not love. She bemoans that all he does with her is kiss her bottom and only occasionally ejaculate upon it so, she surmises, he is most likely discharging his seed somewhere else. She recalls that the last time he came on her bottom was the night she and Boylan first romantically connected. They walked along the River Tolker after a concert some yards ahead of Bloom. Two points confirmed: one, Bloom was right to suspect coded love messages passed between them and two, that Bloom was aroused as well as horrified by the prospect of Molly with another man.

Her denouncement of John Henry Menton as both solicitor and human being is the first hint that not all those Suitors on Bloom's list were as lucky with Molly as Bloom feared. There's a first allusion to Stephen as Molly considers seducing a young man and more love over sex sentiment as she belittles the sex act (is it the act of sex or is it adultery?) when she says

> . . . anyhow its done now once and for all with all the talk of the world about it people make its only the first time after that its just the ordinary do it and think no more about it why cant you kiss a man without going and marrying him first you sometimes love to wildly when you feel that way so nice all over you you cant help yourself I wish some man or other would take me sometime when hes there and kiss me in his arms theres nothing like a kiss long and hot down to your soul almost paralyses you . . . [10]

This feels noteworthy: her wanting to be unfaithful to Bloom but almost for Bloom's benefit. It will resonate shortly as she thinks back over her encounter with Boylan. Molly wants to be loved. She has been starved of sex but equally of passionate kissing and hugging and this, it seems, is what she misses the most. Snatches of adolescent petting here and there remind her of the subsequent embarrassing confession where a girl must reveal all to the strange priest. In this case Fr Corrigan, another Suitor on Bloom's list:

. . . I hate that confession when I used to go to Father Corrigan he touched me father and what harm if he did where and I said on the canal bank like a fool but whereabouts on your person my child on the leg behind high up was it yes rather high up was it where you sit down yes O Lord couldnt he say bottom right out and have done with it what has that got to do with it and did you whatever way he put it I forget no father and I always think of the real father what did he want to know for when I already confessed it to God . . . [11]

We note a little further on that her scepticism of the organised church does not preclude a little Fr Corrigan fantasy.

She flits back to Boylan and wonders if he was satisfied with her. He has a feisty sexual appetite and is very well endowed though the number of times he managed to orgasm increases with Molly's repeated wild recollection. But she didn't appreciate him slapping her behind and taking other liberties. He had little time for romance and expected to get right down to business, entirely for his own satisfaction. He is firmly in the sex not love category but, for all his great red brute of a thing, Molly considers Bloom to have more spunk in him, a remark possibly more interesting on its wider interpretation. Just as Bloom compared all women that day to Molly, so she matches Boylan to Bloom. We glean that, as a lover, admittedly a weird one, and generally in life Bloom is in his own way considerate to her and to most people and has decent manners which Molly holds in high regard. She considers it unfair that men enjoy the pleasure of *coitus* but suffer few of the consequences. Molly recalls the pain of breastfeeding and laments for all womenkind, casting Boylan, 'Mr Wham, Bam, Thank You Mam' in an even murkier light. In our first hint of Rudy, Molly resolved back then she would never have another child.

The first sentence concludes with Molly thinking back to earlier times when Josie Breen was a potential love rival, how handsome Bloom was back then and how poor Josie got stuck with Dennis and his UP: up postcard.[12]

The Second Sentence

The second sentence commences with Molly recalling when she first saw Boylan. It was at the Dublin Bakery Company where she went with Bloom for tea. Their eyes met, though he left all too soon. She lost a glove there and Bloom's fretting over it reminds her of his sexual enthusiasm for clothing accessories – gloves, boots, stockings and especially those dainty delicates. We recall Bloom's Circean confession of his dream to be a ladies shoe-fitter at Manfield's

> the darling joys of sweet buttonhooking, to lace up crisscrossed to kneelength the dressy kid footwear satinlined, so incredibly impossibly small, of Clyde Road ladies.[13]

Her thoughts turn to another Suitor on Bloom's list, the tenor Bartell d'Arcy,[14] whom, it transpires, she kissed passionately on the choir steps of St Francis Xavier, euphoric after singing Gounod's 'Ave Maria'. It is apparent, however, that she was unimpressed with him and his tinny voice and she stores the thought more for ammunition against Bloom, who thinks he knows everything that goes on.

She thinks of their courting days: of Bloom's courtesy, his persistence especially in his letter-writing and even of his duplicity. She recalls wondering if he were circumcised. They kissed and embraced but not, she notes, as well as she did with Lieutenant Gardner some time earlier and this leads to further thoughts of Boylan with whom she has arranged a repeat assignation on Monday. She cannot wait: she feared he had led her on today when he arrived several minutes late but seems more assured of next time. The week after will be the tour of Belfast which, fortunately for her, coincides with Bloom's annual memorial visit to the Ennis Hotel in County Clare. The thought of eloping momentarily flits. She's looking forward to the tour intensely, for the shopping as much as the sex and anticipates suffering no qualms in accepting several pretty gifts from the wealthy impresario. It's a two way street. After all, she does not expect to receive pretty clothes from her husband anytime soon (an ironic thought, as that is exactly what he's saving for and might have purchased today had he not given 5s to the Dignam welfare fund). She could do with a short break from Bloom, in any event, what with all his too clever conversation usually involving politics. She's distrustful of all the 'sinner fein' types he's been hanging around with and unimpressed with 'squareheaded' Arthur Griffiths (a phrase, one suspects, she heard from Bloom) who is always going on about the Boer War. The war that claimed her Lieutenant Gardner for whom she still laments and it remains an upsetting subject – what might have been. One assumes Molly means the first Boer War (1880–1881), the kiss thereby just preceding her meeting Bloom. In any event, Gardner is not in Bloom's Ithaca series of Suitors indicating he is Molly's little secret.

Molly laments the aging process but takes comfort that some women older than her still attract desirable men and she references Lily Langtry consort to the Prince of Wales (by now Edward VII), and how things might have been so different had Molly snared him on a royal visit to Gibraltar.[15] Not then a life at the mercy of Bloom's economic prudence. It might help if he held down a steady job and not this newspaper work with its occasional commissions. He's too outspoken though and it keeps getting him fired. Not even her low-cut blouse could persuade Joseph Cuffe[16] to reinstate him, though she recalls he took a good look at her chest while weighing his options.

The Third Sentence

Her thoughts meander around women's breasts as we move to the third sentence. How left and right are different, how Bloom worships them (is there any part of her anatomy that he does not?). How the female form is so much more beautiful than the male, a point emphasised by her recollection of dockers and soldiers exposing themselves to her in their drunken revelry. Back to her breasts, one is still a little tender from Boylan's over-enthusiasm. Bloom, by contrast, as she still remembers, was on hand to ease the pain when she was nursing Milly. He loved the taste so much he wanted to squirt it in his tea. He is a weird one:

> hes beyond everything I declare somebody ought to put him in the budget if I only could remember the one half of the things and write a book out of it the works of Master Poldy . . . [17]

Yes, he can come up with his big words like met him pike hoses and talk about repeating lives but can't make breakfast without burning the pan.

She counts the days until Boylan's return.

The Fourth Sentence

A train roars by belching its whistle and we may think of thrusting pistons, an image that would become an overused cliché by future risqué film directors. Molly thinks how hot it must be for the driver, ensconced with the adjacent coal furnace. This, and the heat of the recent drought, returns her to the Gibraltar of her youth: the sights, the smells (both encapsulating flowers) and, in particular, her friendship with Hester Stanhope. Mrs Stanhope was a little older but one of Molly's few friends, before or since. Military life it seems mitigates against lasting friendships and, indeed, Hester leaves when her husband 'Wogger' is posted elsewhere. It was a time of Molly's burgeoning sexuality, just as Milly's now. She enjoyed the attention and Wogger seemed very keen, especially for a newly married man, and we might point the same finger at Hester. Molly and Hester corresponded enthusiastically for a while but that dried up and Molly became lonely. Rather touchingly she recalls writing and posting a letter to herself. She is lonely still, stuck all day in the house. Milly has left and talking of correspondence, notes that Milly thanked her for the birthday present by way of a postcard but 'Papli' received a letter. Echoing Martha Clifford, she wishes Boylan would write more. She was thrilled to receive his letter this morning but it wasn't exactly gushing: ' . . . yours ever Hugh Boylan . . . '[18]

And for Molly, letters can make such a difference – a world of difference. We might consider this in the context of Joyce and Nora. What with Joyce's Irish commitments, hospitalisations, etc, they spent quite some time apart and Joyce's letters flowed both in number, heightened emotion and sexual transparency not to say obscenity.

The Fifth Sentence

Her first beau, Lieutenant Mulvey, now dominates her thoughts. All the while, she is silently rehearsing 'Love's Old Sweet Song'[19] which she will sing on tour along with 'La Ci Darem'.[20] We have previously considered both pieces of music but it's worth revisiting. 'La Ci Darem' from *Don Giovanni* is, for our purposes, the unsubtle wooing of an innocent girl by a nasty man who wants one thing and one thing only. Even if she's not so innocent (Zerlina is engaged) it concerns sex not love. 'Love's Old Sweet Song' is a different kettle of fish. The day may be long and full of hardship (or in Molly's case excitement!) but at the end of the day, all we have is love and it conquers all.

> Just a song at twilight, when the lights are low,
> When the flickering shadows softly come and go,
> Tho' the heart be weary, sad the day and long,
> Still to us at twilight comes Love's old song,
> Comes Love's old sweet song.

It was Boylan's letter this morning that notified her of the song list and it now triggers a letter from Mulvey, brought to her in bed in Gibraltar by the housekeeper Mrs Rubio. She thinks of her first kiss.

> . . . he was the first man kissed me under the Moorish wall my sweetheart when a boy it never entered my head what kissing meant till he put his

> tongue in my mouth his mouth was sweetlike young I put my knee up to him a few times to learn the way what did I tell him I was engaged for fun to the son of a Spanish nobleman named Don Miguel de la Flora and he believed me that I was to be married to him in 3 years time theres many a true word spoken in jest there is a flower that bloometh . . . [21]

Mulvey, the first in Bloom's series, is here confirmed as the first but so far just a kiss. Molly would have been around Milly's age as we assume from her budding breasts Also noteworthy is her prophetic alias, de la Flora. It's not quite clear how many times Molly saw Mulvey but she kept his more physical advances at bay though more out of a fear of pregnancy than any great moral dilemma. Nevertheless, her resolve is firm. She pretends to be engaged (which didn't stop Zerlina), and refuses to let him fondle her breasts until their last meeting nor inside her petticoat and most markedly, attack being the best defence, at that final tryst she unbuttons her blouse and brings him off into her handkerchief, pretending not to be excited. Just as, infamously, Nora is supposed to have done the same for James on 16 June 1904.[22] Mulvey is posted elsewhere and Molly *virgo intacta*, enters a pact with him to make love should they ever meet again. Molly assumes he's now long-since married (if still alive) and, mischievously, thinks of his pretty wife blissfully unaware of what young Marion Tweedy got up to with her husband back in Gibraltar. He leaves her with a memento, a ring which Molly subsequently gives to Gardner. This should not belittle her affection for Mulvey, after all, she kept the handkerchief under her pillow for weeks. But things move on. Thoughts of him married cause her to mull over the name Marion Mulvey. She is grateful to Bloom for a pretty acceptable and flowery surname. She feels very sorry for the Mrs Ramsbottoms of this world. She likes her mother's name, Lunita Laredo, and is grateful for having inherited her Spanish eyes and voluptuous figure. All her father left her was his working-class Dublin accent suggesting, further, that the Major in Major Tweedy may have been of the Sergeant or more likely Drum variety.[23]

Another train rushes by, another whistle. Molly determines to show her figure to best effect on stage in Belfast. Her vagina itches, we will shortly know why, and she has some wind which, frustratingly, she restrains for Bloom's face is on her bottom. But, by the sound of, or in mimic of, another train whistle, there it goes.

The Sixth Sentence

Having just farted in his face, this sentence starts with benevolent and concerned thoughts for Bloom. She hopes he's not falling in with those drunken medicos. Never mind breakfast in bed, she thinks of what he might like for his lunch or tea, maybe a nice piece of cod – by no means extraordinary thinking for a housewife, but a substantial improvement on recent thoughts of elopement. Sometimes, forgetting Milly has left, Molly will buy enough for three which may be a subconscious aspiration to entertain Stephen. Summer catering makes her think of a picnic which in her fantasy involves Boylan but reality intrudes with recollection of a picnic with Bloom and an incident in a rowing boat.

> . . . Whit Monday is a cursed day too no wonder that bee bit him better the seaside but Id never again in this life get into a boat with him after him at Bray telling the boatman he knew how to row if anyone asked could he ride the steeplechase for the gold cup hed say yes then it came on to get rough the old thing crookeding about and the weight all down my side telling me pull the right reins now pull the left and the tide all swamping in floods in through the bottom and his oar slipping out of the stirrup it's a mercy we werent all drowned . . . [24]

She's a bit harsh on Bloom. He means well but he's just not as accomplished a sailor as his 'metempsychosised' predecessor. And Molly bleats on again about the bad company he's keeping including 'that other beauty' Pisser Burke who lives in the City Arms Hotel:

> I dont know who he is with that other beauty Burke out of the City Arms hotel was there spying around as usual on the slip always where he wasnt wanted if there was a row on you'd vomit a better face there was no love lost between us . . . [25]

He's another one on Bloom's list of Suitors but we can safely say Molly wouldn't touch him with a barge pole, which places Bloom's list in the context of being, at best, fanciful. These chaps may well have had wicked designs on Molly and perhaps gave her a leery look. But here in the filter-free zone of Molly's head, had she had been unfaithful prior to Boylan she would surely have thought about it tonight just as she thought about kissing Gardner and masturbating Mulvey into a handkerchief. For all of the Dublin tittle-tattle, nothing suggests that, since marrying Bloom, she has done anything worse than have one quick snog with Bartell d'Arcy. And that was virtually in public.

Molly thinks of Bloom's various madcap business schemes which never amount to anything worth having, including plans to convert a previous house into something grand and income-producing. There are of course rooms to rent in Eccles Street and she feels the house is too big now that Milly has left. She wonders if Bloom encouraged her to leave because he sensed something between Molly and Boylan and didn't want to be shamed in front of his daughter. Molly is then quite critical of Milly, especially her increasingly casual attitude to men. Too many similarities to herself at that age and thinks she knows it all whereas Molly recalls these years being a bit of fumbling about and with real sexual fulfilment still several years hence. There's more than a hint of envy of mother for daughter. Even a soupçon of resentment at Milly's flirtation with Bloom, which in a way Molly understands because, despite all, she thinks her husband is or was pretty handsome. She married him after all. She likens him, as did Gerty McDowell, to the matinée idol Martin Harvey, only with a moustache.[26]

This brings her to a potential seduction of her own. He too, almost a minor well, twenty-two. She slags off Bloom generally but his finer points keep nudging back in, his delicate good looks, good manners and that he's not off getting drunk all the time. Even, bizarre though it is, that his father committed suicide rather than live on without his wife and that she, Molly, is the object of Bloom's love so that can't be too bad. That he's so kind to waifs and strays and she recalls him bringing home an injured dog. This brings her to Stephen and how embarrassing that he must have seen her old drawers hanging up in the kitchen. Him such an educated type as well, not that breeding shone through his father, that time they saw him at a cricket match proudly displaying a big hole in his sock. Mid-thought her menstrual period comes on. She clambers out of bed to get to the chamber pot and before she knows it, it is pouring out of her like the fertile river she represents. Her first thought though, and it's with relief, is that Boylan didn't impregnate her and her second is to worry about staining the bed linen, clean today. Then, how unfair it is that women have to go through this. As she's sat there on the pot she thinks again of that afternoon's sexual frenzy. Was she too heavy when she sat on his knee? How the bed was so noisy they put a quilt on the floor. She hoped her breath smelt sweet.

The Seventh Sentence

Molly wonders if her emissions are normal and if she should visit Dr Collins. Bloom used to send her ridiculous love letters adoring everything about her and, therefore, everything her body could produce, reminding the reader of Joyce's letters to Nora.[27] She thinks of the night they met at the Doyle's party and of him staring at her as though he knew her, an attraction Molly attributes to her Jewish mother. She thinks of how, during courtship, he used to use any excuse to see inside her bedroom. The pot makes her uncomfortable and thinks of Bloom as he squats to pee but then he's just weird, an opinion confirmed as he sometimes sleeps on the floor like a reclining Buddha. She recalls him taking her to a museum for an exhibition of Hinduism which she'd never heard of but which, apparently, in Asia, is a bigger religion than Christianity and Judaism put together. Although Molly resents the phenomenology almost as much as the Cyclops narrator she is also proud to have a husband with a natural curiosity of the world's workings. Back in suspicious mode, she is sure he's slept with a floozy that evening and is determined to go through his pockets tomorrow and find existence or absence of a condom, both equally damning. Perhaps he was with Josie Breen, who was always jealous of Molly snaring Bloom while she got lumbered with Dennis. Yet, when she compares him to most around Dublin and takes, for example, the list of Dignam mourners, as recorded in Boylan's newspaper, Bloom is pretty decent. Most others, as she observes, are either off of their faces, drunk or beating their wives or regularly impregnating them or keeping other women on the side.[28] As for that Tom Kernan, so drunk he fell down the stairs and bit off half of his tongue,[29] and Simon Dedalus maybe the worst of the lot. For all his faults, she's pretty lucky to have a well-mannered, respectful sort who, at the end of the day in this friendless world, is her friend. This repeats the pattern we have observed with Bloom all day. From Lotus Eaters onwards, however he tried to distract himself, he thought of Molly. Equally, however much she criticises Bloom and wants to do so with relish, this irritable fondness for her husband persists. But back to the drunks: thoughts of father Simon returns her to son Stephen who is also, she understands, frequently drunk. But apparently an intellectual one; she hears he's an author and a budding professor of Italian. She recalls him as a polite eleven year-old and is intrigued by the well-educated, cultured young man of twenty two recently returned from Paris. Moreover, it may be destiny:

> . . . wait by God yes wait yes hold on he was on the cards this morning when I laid out the deck union with a young stranger neither dark nor fair you met before I thought it meant him but hes no chicken nor a stranger either

> besides my face was turned the other way what was the 7th card after that the 10 of spades for a journey by land then there was a letter on its way and scandals too the 3 queens and the 8 of diamonds for a rise in society yes wait it all came out and 2 red 8s for new garments look at that and didnt I dream something too yes there was something about poetry in it I hope he hasnt long greasy hair hanging into his eyes or standing up like a red Indian what do they go about like that for only getting themselves and their poetry laughed at I always liked poetry . . . [30]

And Molly is really getting into the swing of the romantic possibilities:

> . . . I wonder is he too young hes about wait 88 I was married 88 Milly is 15 yesterday 89 what age was he then at Dillons 5 or 6 about 88 I suppose hes 20 or more Im not too old for him if hes 23 or 24 I hope hes not that stuckup university student sort no otherwise he wouldnt go sitting down in the old kitchen with him taking Eppss cocoa and talking of course he pretended to understand it all probably he told him he was out of Trinity college hes very young to be a professor . . . [31]

She thinks her exotic background and looks will fascinate him, especially as he yearns to travel. She the mature muse and lover will inspire his poetry and he will educate her so she understands all of Bloom's big words. There will be a scandal and photographs in the papers. She is becoming quite aroused, even sat there on the chamber-pot making Chamber Music[32] and has pretty obscene reverie as to what she might do to Stephen and even some other young male bathers she has seen. There seems to be an amalgamation of erotic visions merging Stephen with hard male ivory bodies and the cleanliness of bathing, which is ironic as we know Stephen hasn't taken a bath in over year.

She is awakened from this reverie with ' . . . O but then what am I going to do about him though'.[33] Does she mean the husband or the lover?

The Final Sentence

From the decency of Bloom and the supposed refinement of Stephen, Molly's thoughts return to Boylan and he's found wanting: 'the ignoramus that doesnt know poetry from a cabbage . . .'[34]

She really didn't appreciate his brusqueness and slapping her behind like she was his prize heifer. Removing his shoes and trousers right there in the parlour without so much as a by your leave and his erection stood up beneath his shirt like a hat stand. He was like a lion and she doesn't mean in a good way. (Hey! We thought Leo was the lion? He has been truly usurped!). Stallions and lions no doubt have their place in the bedroom but a little romance and chivalry wouldn't go amiss. She understands that men get excited by a woman's body as she does herself sometimes but, even so. It's interesting how her own animal passion has subsided, perhaps with her period. That doesn't mean Bloom has a clear run, far from it. Because, lord knows, she gets precious little affection from her husband. A woman just wants to be embraced and all Bloom can manage is an occasional grope of her bottom while asleep the wrong way around. And he expects breakfast in bed?

She reminisces how nothing has been the same since Rudy. She half blames herself (after watching the two dogs rutting[35]) and half regrets burying the mite in the knitted shroud when there were enough needy living babies that could have had it, but she could not think straight for crying. Once she stopped crying she knew they would not have another child – more than Rudy died that day. Molly snaps out of it, determined not to get too gloomy and wonders why Stephen didn't stay the night, especially against the prospect of wandering around a dangerous city at the prey of pickpockets or worse. He wouldn't be in this state, she thinks, if his poor mother were alive. We think back to Cyril Sargent[36] and Molly wants to surrogate mother Stephen but always with a hint of sex, as she imagines wearing translucent négligés around the house, distracting the writer.

Such thoughts morph towards Bloom as we head for the home straight of this Gold Cup. He needs to seriously buck up his ideas. She will get up early for him; she'll do it and put on a show. She'll throw his eggs at him in his moustache cup. She'll make sure he watches her as she dresses in the same sexy and now soiled underwear from the previous night and she'll give him a right eyeful of flesh so he knows that is how she'll be dressed for the day and maybe she'll go out and pick up god knows who. She'll make sure he sees the dried spunk on the linen. She's de-Kocking Poldy. He's driven her to adultery and he'll have it served back to him for breakfast. It'll either make him or break him and the same for their marriage. She's weaponising the adultery but we wonder why all the effort, if not to save rather than hurt the marriage? If he wants these perverted fantasies he can have them but he'll pay for it, no more rent-free. She'll expect nice lingerie and make-up and finery and if he won't cough up she'll take his cheque book that he thinks is safely locked away and write them herself (we suspect

Bloom will happily write the cheques for the clothes Molly has in mind). And flowers: she's going to buy lots of flowers and fill the house with them, perhaps Stephen will appreciate them. Molly adores flowers[37] because there's nothing like nature.

> . . . I love flowers Id love to have the whole place swimming in roses God of heaven theres nothing like nature the wild mountains then the sea and the waves rushing then the beautiful country with the fields of oats and wheat and all kinds of things and all the fine cattle going about that would do your heart good to see rivers and lakes and flowers all sorts of shapes and smells and colours springing up even out of the ditches primroses and violets . . .[38]

From the anger railed at Bloom, before we know it, she's back among the rhododendrons high up on Howth Head on the day of their first lovemaking and also of his marriage proposal and he's telling her she's a flower of the mountain and that the sun shines only for her and tumbling into that last wonderful passage. Her anger ebbs way as we float on a wave of love, possibly only nostalgic love, but there's a vestige of love nonetheless. Down to that final 'Yes'.

Which leaves us where?

Boylan

Let's start with Boylan. Molly is clearly very turned on. But if she's having doubts now, even in the after-glow of being 'fucked yes and damn well fucked too',[39] then it doesn't augur well. Notwithstanding her excitement for Monday and frustration that her period will still be underway, the affair smacks of a temporary sexual thrill. This is not to diminish its significance. We have established that Molly has not been unfaithful in fifteen years of marriage so this is seismic but in terms of Molly and Bloom, not Molly and Boylan. Had Joyce other intentions he would have bestowed Boylan with more than cartoon cut-out characteristics. It would be unfair to parallel this consummated affair with the Bloom/Clifford version, yet one expects Molly to tire of Boylan in short order as Bloom has with Martha. Moreover, this is just from Molly's perspective. There is nothing we have seen of Boylan to indicate any prospect of devotion beyond a Belfast fling and, as we get to know Molly, we wish her the strength to not be messed around anymore – so in all respects, a non-starter.

Stephen

For Stephen we are entitled and, without too much controversy, to assume James Joyce, and hence no mystery, for we know what becomes of him and the books he shall write. Stephen left Eccles Street as a released actor departs a soap opera: definitively. Yet we have his quote from Aeolus which resonated in Circe about the striking match changing the course of both of their lives, so we are obliged to delve further. He fascinates both Molly and Bloom who, for different but coinciding reasons, think they can use him and not altogether selfishly. Stephen, on 16 June, at least, appeared uninterested. If he anticipated Molly's aspirations, the parable of Willy Shakespeare and Ann Hathaway[40] in the cornfield (or rye field) probably resonated. We might read Marion-Mary-Mare-Mer into his fear of water. At times in this day we felt he may be inclined to shed insular arrogance and reach out to others and this is likely correct, but it is just the start of a long process. At same time, he is ditching or being ditched by so-called friends and is quite alone. Bloom, of course, is also the outsider and we've just read that Molly has no friends worthy of the name beyond her husband, so it's quite plausible that Stephen may become closer to the three Blooms but one expects, on his own terms. The two lives forever changed may well be Stephen the fictional character and Stephen the author. The character eventually joining the human race by reaching out to others and, as for Joyce, he realised that Stephen Dedalus had nothing more to teach. It was time rather, to learn, as Deasy recognised in episode two and Stephen agreed. The young artist has been portrayed and it's time for him to take leave and grow up. By his thirties, family was front and central in Joyce's life and much more could usefully be learned from Leopold Bloom, including all pitfalls – time to cast Stephen adrift.

Molly and her children

Molly is motherless. Lunita disappears from her life either at childbirth or when very young. That need not explain her apparent coldness towards Milly and hints of aloofness at losing Rudy, though, no doubt, literary psychiatrists have their opinions. Whatever it may mean, it should not be overlooked. Molly is aware of aging and appearing less desirable to her husband and others, just as her daughter is discovering sex. It's not so much jealousy of daughter as resentment of the aging process and this, especially in context of mixed messages from a husband that, on the one hand adores her, and, on the other, has not required intercourse for ten years. 'Not required'; an odd but intentional use of words that we'll get to. Meanwhile, there was a revealing comment in Ithaca:

> . . . inasmuch as complete mental intercourse between himself and the listener had not taken place since the consummation of puberty, indicated by catamenic hemorrhage, of the female issue of narrator and listener, 15 September 1903, . . . [41,42]

'Mental intercourse' we take that to be meaningful, satisfying conversation between two people, as opposed to the snatches of sentences we heard in Calypso. We also take 15 September to be the onset of Milly's first period and that this is connected to the drying up of social interaction. Rudy may have ended the physical relationship but Milly becoming a woman, it seems, has eroded the social aspect of the marriage relationship from a loving one to something more akin to functioning. This is very interesting and worthy of greater study than the short comment below.

The pain a parent must feel at the loss of a child is unimaginable though, in context, it was reported[43] that, for every eleven thousand babies born in Dublin in 1913, 660 did not survive a year, and four of Joyce's own siblings died in youth.[44] Nonetheless, despite her occasional quip, Rudy's death hit twenty-four-year-old Molly incredibly hard and she determined to have no further children.

Molly and Bloom

Here's the crux of the matter. Will they be ok? The starting point is bleak: no intercourse for ten years when they are both perfectly capable? Moses, we recall was denied his promised land in part at least because he has ceased sexual relations with his wife.[45] He, Bloom, not Moses, it would seem, has resorted to courtesans, she by all accounts has simply gone without, despite many an opportunity and is indeed a modern Penelope right up until that day. We do not judge. Rudy damaged them both – but ten years? On the one hand he's not wanted sex all these years so who can blame her for finally looking elsewhere, but it takes two to tango and it's hard to believe that, if she laid it on thick, he'd have it in him to refuse. What is arguably of even greater concern is that conversation has dried up these last nine months. One takes this to be pretty common. Milly's period marks her becoming a woman. What remains of a marriage once children can function independently? Fathers and mothers reverting simply to husband and wife, which may be insufficient. Molly recounts Bloom's faults in her mind as he sleeps next to her. They are manifold. Notwithstanding, she drifts to the day at Howth Head, mirroring his reverie of same event earlier that day in Davy Byrne's pub.[46] After ten years of hell it remains for both of them a vestige of pleasure though, sadly, one independently siloed. But all these Yeses. So many! We have to be positive among so many Yeses. Like all relationships they need to work on it and a lot harder than they've been doing. He needs to assert himself, maybe get a steady job, maybe keep a lid on some of the weirdness. She so values him. Does he still turn her on? One suspects he could if her reminiscences of Howth Head are persuasive. Yes, we vote 'Yes'. We nail our colours to the mast of that smellonous kiss of the buttock. He may have kissed it so often before as to be routine and *ersatz* but this time it is no ordinary kiss, nor ordinary buttock. This time, with such feeling that we hope and believe that it will open the silo door. Also that he will adjust his sleeping position so as to render *coitus* practical for the non-contortionist. Love is the word. It doesn't have to be fireworks over Dublin Bay, it might be a nice piece of cod on a Friday, though let's hope for the odd firework. Love is the word, the word known to all men, the word known to all.

LECTURE 22, 4 AUGUST 2021: EPILOGUE

In Our Ends are our Beginnings

Music: Finnegan's Wake – The Irish Rovers

There we have it. As we arrive, arm in arm, at the end of our journey, we are entitled to languish in the glow of a job well done. For many this confounded book has glared accusingly at its owner, smug, snug on its bookshelf perch. Such readers may now, in all good conscience, stare right back at it with a hint of self-righteousness and, possibly, if feeling ballsy, even give it the bird: as apparently, they say Stateside. Joyce would probably quite like it if you did. But here's trouble: what concluding thoughts after ten months of contemplation? It is one thing using Joyce's words as a crutch, as we did for the lectures but quite another to think for oneself, no stabilisers. We strap-lined this lecture series 'Normal Joyce for Normal People', which not only has the sort of Ad-man pizazz of which Bloom may have approved, but it's an escape valve for your intrepid lecturer with not so much as a literature 'A' level to his name. But after over twenty lectures at the coal face, there is expectation. We can only have been enriched by the experience so what have we learned? What have I learned?

Now that it lies conquered [*sic*] at our feet it occurs that there was little of which to be scared. Which is a crass statement because it cannot be conquered and Oxen of the Sun was downright impossible; yet I have formed a personal understanding of the book that is all mine and my hope is that you have yours. For the ordinary reader its bark is worse than its bite for we, indulged, may overlook canyons of impenetrability because they get in the way of the fun we are having in easier pastures. As Joyce famously said:

> I've put in so many enigmas and puzzles that it will keep the professors busy for centuries arguing over what I meant, and that's the only way of insuring one's immortality."[1]

One feels he speaks for us and at the expense of the professors. For the normal reader the abundance of salty humour, drama and pathos enables a glossing over of some of the denser passages without losing the essentials. In short it's a book to enjoy at all manner of levels and one hopes that these lecturesprovided an insight into some of the trickier elements and enhanced the pleasure. Of course I have no glib conclusion beyond what is already out there – no unique epiphany to unlock secret treasure. Instead in this last lecture, and from our lofty perch of accomplishment, I lob some random thoughts, fifteen of them, in the faint hope that someone somewhere will spot some cohesion.

Thought One: In what directions did listener and narrator lie?[2]

What happened and where are we? Well, nothing much, and we don't know. It's a modernist novel. In the last lecture, one of the ways we held Molly to account was via the musical terms diatonic and chromatic: the former being traditional, classical. This music behaves itself by heading off in the direction that it ought and all is well with the world. Good stuff; all the great composers wrote this way until the mid-nineteenth century, when Wagner shlepped up with his *Tristan* chord and inspired the likes of Mahler, Schoenberg and Richard Strauss. Suddenly there was squirming in the dress circle as music sparked out on frolics and, dare one say, jarred a little. So it was with literature. It would be as ludicrous to say the Victorian novel was formulaic as it would to say that of Beethoven but the *fin de siècle* modernists wanted something more and new: real life.

What happened 16 June? Not a great deal. I checked to see what I did last 16 June. A tremor of excitement for Bloomsday but tinged with whimsical disappointment at being unable to travel to Dublin. There were usual work commitments after which final touches on that evening's lecture. In the wider world, the Australian Prime Minister was received by the Queen and there was trouble in the Middle East, for a change. Neither of these events unduly impinged upon my day. It being summer, West Ham United news was patchy. Not the stuff of drama: no fights in the street, no earthquake in Muswell Hill. Why, therefore, should we expect more for Bloom and Stephen on their 16 June? Drama, as Joyce was fond of saying[3] and as writ large in Aeolus, is for the journalists; writers of quality should be concerned with the everyday minutiae of ordinary folk, for whom the queue-jumper at Sainsbury's will yield the same ire as the battlefield.

By same token, why should we be told what happened on and after 17 June 1904 when that knowledge would be denied in real time? For the most part, in *Ulysses*, the reader lives with the character and if she's not privy, then, neither are we. We can place our bets of course and we did so at the end of lecture 21. You may say, but there was an earthquake, it engulfed the courthouse[4] and, what's more, beached whales were delivered to frozen medieval Dubliners[5] and a fiery chariot ascended at a forty-five degree angle.[6] All true, but we are entitled to distinguish fantasy from reality and allow for the liberty Joyce takes in endowing this most modernist of books with phantasmagorical tendencies of equal brio.

Thought Two: The Mask.

We hide behind masks: donning this one for this person and that one for that person – trying to adopt a particular persona to make just the right impression: Tom Kernan, impeccably turned out to make that sale[7]; the citizen being all bluster and thunder; Stephen the morose bohemian intellectual. All worried lest guard be dropped to reveal imperfect reality. We're all Proteus at heart, schizophrenics with wardrobes of masks for various occasions and far more now than then with keyboard warriors on their anonymous crusades. Very few of us are sufficiently comfortable in our skins to face the world without superficial armour plating. Bloom is no different: he flirts outrageously with various women, which is most of them if they are young enough and pretty enough. Remember his metaphorical changes of clothes to suit his moods with Josie Breen in Circe?[8] Remember him yearning to join the anti-Semitic humour in the coach en-route to Glasnevin?[9] That was the price he was willing to pay for acceptance into the group. Molly gave the impression that she may rise above it. Her 'take me as I am' soliloquy suggested so, but we can all be king (or queen) with just our own thoughts for company; we didn't see her tested ringside. But one feels that the shedding of the masks, the baring of an honest soul to the world, may have been the direction of travel Joyce intended, as he, via Stephen, via Maurice Maeterlinck, pointed out in Scylla[10]: wherever we go in life we only meet ourselves. Joyce, of whom some have averred tended to the schizophrenic.[11]

Thought Three: The Fellowship.

Life is hard and harder still is facing it alone. So we approve of Stephen's eventual realisation that, no matter how much one deserves a personal ivory tower, it does no harm to descend to the ordinary folk every now and then. Aristotles aren't often found on street corners but some of the principles and conundrums that he deciphered and codified are not, when reduced to practicalities, so different from issues with which many of us grapple in the daily grind. Applied maths rather than pure maths was the point made in Ithaca.[12]

Thought Four: To Give is to Receive

From Aristotle to another philosopher, Arthur Schopenhauer, something of a personal favourite probably due to the attention paid to him as compared to others no doubt equally worthy – Nietzsche, for instance. Schopenhauer, much like Joyce in literary terms, took on the biggest, most complex issues but brought them right down to earth and into our everyday lives. He listened carefully to the terribly complicated things Kant and others had to say about reality, time and space and yet he formed uncomplicated conclusions, one of which concerned charity. It is a gross simplification, but an also heart-warming observation that, after seeking answers to the really huge questions, he concluded that we ought to be nicer to each other[13] – *Mitleid*, as they say in German. This comes naturally to Leopold Bloom who, throughout the day, wants to do the decent thing. Occasionally that coincides with serving his own agenda but he is only human. Such trait is hallmarked by the narrator in Ithaca:

> What satisfied him?
>
> To have sustained no positive loss. To have brought a positive gain to others. Light to the gentiles.[14]

Allied to which he's the thinly disguised wandering Jew, cursed to forever wander the earth for laughing at the wounded Jesus. A stranger wherever he travels yet, all the while, bestowing gifts upon others from which, so cursed, he derives no benefit. Again from Ithaca:

> Ever he would wander, selfcompelled, to the extreme limit of his cometary orbit, beyond the fixed stars and variable suns and telescopic planets, astronomical waifs and strays, to the extreme boundary of space, passing from land to land, among peoples, amid events . . . [15]

Some suggest that Bloom's wanderings, if tracked around Dublin, might form the shape of a question mark[16] – possibly. In terms of bestowing gifts, one thinks of him feeding the gulls, bringing breakfast in bed, the racing tip and, of course, helping Stephen. Yet he derives benefit for to give is to receive.

Thought Five: Can't Get No

On to another of Bloom's finer qualities: to be satisfied. Joyce wrote him drifting into peaceful sleep in the very epicentre of his wife's adultery. We know this must be fiction because Joyce could only watch in awe at such ability. The author was a jealous guy. There were times when it consumed him and we discussed in Calypso how Joyce's choice of 7 Eccles Street emanated from alleviation of jealous rage.[17] So, this is not a case of author writing from experience; yet Bloom, without undermining the profound sadness of the event, seemed to take it in his stride. One wonders if, like many of us, he felt that after ten years without full intercourse, Molly was, frankly, entitled to seek pleasure elsewhere. Bloom is as calm as Buddha. There is no evidence on his bookshelf that he studied eastern philosophy, it was Stephen that alluded to the Upanishads,[18] nor, despite contents of his bookshelf,[19] does Bloom take the New Testament seriously and there is little by way of Jewish tradition, of turning the other cheek. Yet Bloom is sanguine in the face of breach of marriage. Considering his own activity, to act otherwise might be gross hypocrisy. Does he forgive? Sanguinity is not absolution. He does not discount revenge either against Molly or Boylan but that's not for now. He lives in the moment and, for now, he has found the buttock of satisfaction and given it a kiss.

Thought Six: I've Got a Little List or Zen and the Art of Motor Neural James Patience

A common criticism of the book, even among devotees, is to bemoan the infernal lists. Why, readers plea, does Joyce have to go on and on with his interminable lists. The parodies in Circe or the description of his ideal home in Ithaca. Such frustration may stem from an impatient expectation that the book should go somewhere: a logical conclusion for instance. We recall the Deasy view of history, an unswerving progression towards the light, in contrast, say, to the Vicoan or the akashic records. The final of these three is that moments do not fade into history, they remain, all of them forever and are, depending on what occurred, to be permanently enjoyed or forever avoided. At least that's how it works on the planet Tralfamador as Kurt Vonnegut fans will appreciate[20] and it may be a helpful way to consider these terribly long passages in *Ulysses*. Because Joyce was a clever chap they do tend to have a point and probably are leading somewhere significant but they are also there to be enjoyed as they are for their own sake and in their own rhythm. Let us wallow in the lists for the sheer joy of wallowing. In this sense, the book foreshadows *Finnegans Wake* (ah, so that was where it was going!) As they say on the planet Tralfamador: 'so it goes'.

Thought Seven: I've Got a Little Review

Before Sylvia Beach published *Ulysses* in February 1922, parts were serialised in a modest New York literary periodical called *The Little Review* which had previously, and in the teeth of opposition, also serialised *A Portrait*. Edited by Margaret Anderson and energised from Great Britain by another American, Ezra Pound, it was via this periodical that *Ulysses* came to be convicted of and banned for obscenity well before it saw light of day as a book. One understands Nausicaa to have been the final straw. Joyce only ever intended *Ulysses* as a complete book but was grateful for whatever publicity and income the poorly circulated periodical could muster and so owed a debt of gratitude to a small band of libertarians, not to say anarchists, both sides of the pond. Not all liberals appreciated Joyce's talents; Virginia Wolf didn't until persuaded, belatedly, by T S Eliot. Whilst the book was banned in Britain and no-one would touch it in Ireland, the main drama unfolded in the US. There, one Anthony Comstock and his New York Society for the Suppression of Vice, arbitrated as to what constituted good taste and decency and, notwithstanding the constitutional right to free expression, was not about to permit the US Postal Service to be a conduit of smut. He and his successors effectively snuffed out distribution and sales for ten years until 1933, some fifteen years after the first serialisation. In this year the book was finally liberated by the wonderful landmark judgment of the Hon John M Woolsey.[21] Excellent accounts of Joyce's struggle to publish can be found in the Ellman biography and in Kevin Birmingham's *The Most Dangerous Book*.

Thought Eight: Forging in the Smithy

Just what is the point of Stephen? As authorial persona, he serves to keep us posted on Joyce's personal development aged twenty-two. He's also the artist in this tale, or at least the main one, as according to Lenehan 'There's a touch of the artist about old Bloom'.[22] Without diminishing Bloom's artistry, it is just one of his many turns whereas for Stephen it is vocational. This begs the question, 'what is the role of the artist in society?' A question asked many times before, notably by Dante in *The Divine Comedy* and by Wagner in several of his operas. Back in Telemachus, we have the passage:

Laughing again, he brought the mirror away from Stephen's peering eyes.

The rage of Caliban at not seeing his face in a mirror, he said. If Wilde were only alive to see you.

Drawing back and pointing, Stephen said with bitterness:

It is a symbol of Irish art. The cracked lookingglass of a servant.[23]

Oscar Wilde thought the artist's task was to reflect society back upon itself and, in the case of Victorian society, its hypocrisy. Stephen flippantly remarks that a broken mirror is appropriate for the Irish whose society was imposed by the coloniser. Dante took a broader view. He travelled from the darkness of hell, through purgatory and into the unimaginable white light of heaven and, clever chap, all during his mortal life. Having been afforded that opportunity he felt compelled to set out his experiences in a fourteen-thousand-line poem in which we hear and learn from those that have passed: From Adam and Eve to his own great-great grandfather who died much closer to Dante's own death in 1300. He hoped the reader might be improved by the experience and so, also, his Florentine society. Stephen, like Wagner, hoped through his art to change society. Wagner's apostles ranged from socialist revolutionaries through Christian evangelists to racial supremacists, which may only go to show that an opera may not be the best place in which to conceal a manifesto. Is a book any better?[24] Will reading *Ulysses* forge the Irish consciousness? Joyce hoped that *Ulysses* would be a mirror reflecting the soul of the Irish and Dubliners in particular. One assumes that he hoped it would elevate the collective consciousness until it could break free of the four nets we discussed right back in the introductory lecture: colonialism, Catholicism, middle-class self-protection and sentimentality, too often, drunken sentimentality. So freed, the Irish might reach for something more modern, more socialist, more European. When one looks at modern Ireland one may say that it has broken free to a great extent though this can hardly be attributable to Joyce whose book, whilst never technically banned in his homeland, was barely read for several decades.

A further consideration is the Dedalus factor. Stephen is asked in *A Portrait*,[25] what kind of name is Dedalus? Mulligan stated something similar in *Ulysses*.[26] This is a huge topic that has no place being raised in concluding remarks but it resonates with the creator/inventor Daedalus and his son Icarus. The son may have struggled with the burden of a creative father because he strove to fly higher on those man-made wings, so high that, as every schoolkid knows, the sun melted the wax and he fell to his watery death. But he died shooting for the moon, as it were,and surely that is the role of the artist; to be out there, pushing the boundaries. It occurs[27] that there are parallels, albeit imperfect, between the broken wings of Icarus and the broken pieces of Sigmund's Wagnerian sword. Both owned by men who died trying, and left the remnants to be forged into something stronger, enabling future generations to take up the baton. That Stephen's surname is Dedalus, that he shouts '*Nothung*' at the denouement of the Wanderings[28] and plans to forge in the smithy, suggests Joyce saw something in this, too.

Thought Nine: That's funny, you don't look Jewish

There's an apocryphal tale, recorded by Ellmann and others, concerning one Alfred H Hunter.[29] Sometime prior to meeting Nora, a very drunk James Joyce, made advances to an accompanied women in St Stephen's Green. Her male companion took this as badly as one may expect and gave Joyce a beating. He was left wounded on the ground while his companion, Cosgrave, fled the scene. It was a passing stranger, Hunter, that came to Joyce's aid, dusted him down and walked him home just as Bloom did for Stephen outside of Bella Cohen's. For Cosgrave, read Lynch. If one is to believe the account, it was something of a Joycean epiphany and it seems he was quite affected by this stranger's act of kindness, especially when abandoned by so-called friends. Hunter again came to Joyce's attention when going through a publicly reported divorce. His wife was rumoured to be unfaithful and Hunter was assumed wrongly, to be a Jew. One can see how this chap may have provided a basis for Bloom.

We've had Bloom as Moses and Elijah, both with crucial messages to convey and lessons to teach, but a Jewish factor which frankly I've shied away from a little is the whole business of *Kabbalah*, the teachings of Hebrew mysticism. It's just too deep a foxhole for NJs, (Normal Joyceans). But it is amazing and revealing as to parts of the narrative. We touched on some of its concepts with the various coincidences that have arisen and the power of words. We may recall the *shin* and *resh* business in Wandering Rocks.[29] Most relevant though, maybe what it has to say concerning the evaporation of boundaries in space and time[30] and so we have the different concepts of history and, especially, experiences and memories shared by people that conventionally should not have done so. For example, Bloom's and Stephen's shared dreams, thoughts and the shared view of Shakespeare in the brothel mirror before culminating in the Blephen/Stoom scene at Eccles Street. The following from Ithaca might embody the teacher Bloom as he oozes across time and space and is absorbed by Stephen.

> He heard in a profound ancient male unfamiliar melody the accumulation of the past.[31,32]

Here's a thought: the man in the Macintosh might be a human manifestation of the Zohar.

Thought Ten: Character forming

What do we know of Bloom, Stephen and Molly? If having spent twelve episodes in Bloom's company we do not know him, *Ulysses* as literature would be long forgotten. We know him as much as one can know a fictional character. He is a man of many turns and we have pretty much seen them all. We understand him. We feel his sense of alienation heightened by his natural inclination to join in. We plumbed the depths of despair with him over both Molly and Rudy, the latter less raw with the passage of years. We note, with dismay, how a passionate person allows a marriage to become devoid of passion. We observe it, we feel it and we feel for him. We are annoyed at his futile attempts at distraction. Above all, we like Bloom. We like his kindness his curiosity and his enthusiasms and wish he'd apply the same to his marriage. We also know Stephen, notwithstanding his enigma aspirations. How could we not? His life from aged two to twenty-two is written before us. Most of us, including Bloom, were once Stephens. The arrogance of youth and, with duller brains than Stephen, we thought we knew it all. One has some sympathy for Stephen because, compared to the average bear, he does. Nevertheless, with passing years comes maturity and one learns that crucial missing piece of knowledge: how even the cleverest among us are pretty ignorant. Stephen, like his author, will learn.

Despite the transparency of her monologue, it is Molly that most remains beyond the 'limits of the diaphane'.[33] We assemble pieces of her jigsaw from snatches of overheard conversation plus what she happened to think about in her soliloquy. This is insufficient. Few of us, as we fight somnolence or in-somnolence cast over significant aspects of our character, and modernist Joyce is not going to give it to us on a plate. We know bits, some really juicy bits and enough to form opinion but insufficient to be definitive. She's best left to the professors.

Thought Eleven: Ooo, 'er, Mrs

Those of us brought up on British 70s sitcoms, Frankie Howerd and *Carry On* films, enjoy an innuendo and *entendres* at the double. We are quite at home in bawdy hospitals where buxom nurses get out their jugs or in the department store with Mrs Slocombe's pussy. One suspects Joyce would have been a fan for part of the charm of our book, is that he oscillates between ultra-high-brow theorems that struggle to break through their pretensions and down and dirty earthy puns. The former sometimes distilled through the latter. For example, who can forget the real life Oliver Gogarty song 'Medical Dick and Medical Davy'[34] and also, from Scylla, a 'Honeymoon in the Hand'?[35] How we laughed in Telemachus at The Ballad of Joking Jesus.[36] Yet these, as crude and as blasphemous as they are, often tackled highbrow issues. The first, dealing with syphilis among the poor; and the last, the absurdity of transubstantiation. When it comes to smut, the Buck is never far from our thoughts. Generally Joyce relished the language, wit and ditties of the pub or brothel and the filthier the better. From Mary losing the pin of her drawers[37] to Lenehan's lascivious account of groping Molly in the back of a cab.[38] Not to lose sight of the non-smutty humour: the Cyclops narrator being teetotal between drinks[39] and later, same episode, taking the liberty of burying Dignam in case he might be dead.[40] And from Lotus Eaters: 'Come forth, Lazarus! And he came fifth and lost the job.'[41]

Thought Twelve: He Who Shouts Loudest

The book features several loudmouths: Buck Mulligan, Simon Dedalus and the citizen, to name three – people who impose their views by force of personality, wit and denigration and humiliation of others. We all know such people: they seem to proliferate on the right wing of the Tory Party and the left wing of the Labour Party. More often than not they are bullies with little to say of substance. Social media has bred a whole generation of anonymous bile-filled warriors. A lesson Joyce may have absorbed from Dante's *Paradiso*, is that, ultimately, what counts is the quality of the message not how forcibly it is delivered. Bloom was not immune from inflation of his own ego and one thinks of his self-promoting hero-worship reverie in Circe. Pride before the fall.[42]

Thought Thirteen: A Painful Case

Ulysses is a fun and uplifting book but imbued with pain. How could it be otherwise? Joyce felt intensely the senseless waste of life, human and animal, caused by the Great War. Even more acute and personal was the pain of countless operations suffered as he tried to retain his failing eyesight and, with it, the ability to write. The citizen's metaphorical blindness was an all-too-real prospect for James Joyce. We cannot underestimate the effect of the mental anguish and physical suffering.[43] 'Pain, that was not yet the pain of love, fretted his heart.'[44]

Joyce endured several familial deaths, but that was not unique. Equally painful may have been the genius artist unappreciated and, of course, the self-imposed torture of imagined Nora infidelity[45] which, in diluted form, may be reflected in Bloom's feelings for Molly and possibly also in Bloom's sometimes confused feelings around Milly, centred on his inability to protect her from the travails of womanhood. Lastly, the pain of exile: he and Nora left Ireland in 1904 never to meaningfully return. Like his favourite author Dante, Joyce dies in exile[46] having thought all the while of his homeland.

Thought Fourteen: It's the whole pie with jam in[47]

Is it, after all, just a religious book? A call to prayer? So much time has been spent on trying to square the circle of the triangle of the Holy Trinity. How are the Father, Son and Holy Spirit both, and at same time, three separate entities and one indivisible whole? How do Stephen, Bloom and Molly fit into the holy triangle? How is Jesus God and Man? Is Dog, God reversed? And, if so, so what? And so what that Stephen is afraid of dogs? All valid questions and why on earth should I have the answers? It may, though, be meaningful that, towards the end of Ithaca and, therefore, at the end of the book narrative, the following image is described:

> What moved visibly above the listener's and the narrator's invisible thoughts?
>
> The upcast reflection of a lamp and shade, an inconstant series of concentric circles of varying gradations of light and shadow.[48]

We compare this to Dante's beatific vision at the conclusion of *Paradiso*:

> In that high flame's deep and unblemished field
> Three circles of three colours were arranged,
> All of the same extent. One seemed to yield
> Its lustre – as a pair of rainbows may –
> To the other, and the third was made of fire
> Breathed forth by the first two. What can I say?
> Was this the trinity of my desire
> Or was it not? [49]

Three circles. In Dante's case representing the final and omnipotent sphere of heaven and the holy trinity within. For Joyce, the circles are imperfect. Does he mean heaven on imperfect earth? Does he mean we're not there yet but we're on our way? Elijah is coming? Perhaps that we are all sinners but have the chance to repent? One should also bear in mind the theory, wild or otherwise, that, following Dantean tradition and as previously mentioned, Joyce planned a fourth book corresponding to *Paradiso*. Yet I say No. *Non-servium*. Not for me and not for the man that refused to pray if not actually at his mother's deathbed, then in the vicinity.[50] His rejection of Catholicism and the Church was utter and irreversible and whilst that's not at all the same as rejection of God, and Joyce might be leaving that door ajar,[51] my personal view is that this is not the intention of the book. I prefer to think that those imperfect circles represent the prospect of the earthly heaven of Mr and Mrs Bloom, in bed with each other, the right way around and happy. The series of circles, an unspecified number, might allow room for others, say Milly or Stephen. Not quite at the pearly gates but, as with the deathbed, in the vicinity.

Even if the book is not conventionally religious, it is most certainly spiritual and one feels that a Joycean criticism of the established church is that it suppressed spirituality. His description of the formulaic 'Dringdring' and the going through the motions splashing of the coffin with holy water seems to drain the church of its transformative power. Joyce is big on epiphanies but they are spiritual not religious. They are for seeing life as it really is and living it, dragging it beyond the diaphane. This man who as a youth dallied with piety, saw the church as a layer of simonaic fog shrouding the human spirit.

Thought Fifteen: In Our Ends are Our Beginnings

We've had a birth, we've had a death or at least a dead man buried and a dead dog washed up. A man has reflected on how life begins, how it ends and the stream of life that passes. We've had the recycling of Odysseus into Bloom, the potential recycling of Simon Dedalus, if Stephen is not careful, into Stephen Dedalus and of Molly into Milly. Milly herself might be our next recycled Odysseus looking for far-flung adventure for as know from the Erin's King ferry trip, Milly has her sea-legs.

> On the Erin's King that day round the Kish. Damned old tub pitching about. Not a bit funky. Her pale blue scarf loose in the wind with her hair.[52]

If there's something in a name, Rudolph re-cycled to Rudy, both of whose days were eclipsed all too soon, but who may yet rise again. Stephen initially, and perhaps glibly, felt that history was a nightmare from which he wished to awake – one wonders, whether at the end of the day, having absorbed life from Shakespeare to frozen medieval Dubliners and now that he has an inkling of the teachings of the time-traveller Bloom, if he still feels the same.

Our Ulyssean adventure draws to a close and it's been a pleasure to have your company as we travelled. My Ulyssean adventure began a couple of years ago. The book had moved with us, barely touched in anger, through several house moves. This time I determined to read it and was helped on my way by the late and so lamented Frank Delaney and his 'Re-Joyce' podcast. And here we are together, concluding a lecture series. It's not the end though, I'm sure of that, just as I'm sure that, like both Bloom and Stephen, I'll be 'a learner rather'[53] and realise how much of what I've said requires correction, addition, gentle omission or obliteration. For this book is a journey and a fun one at that.

∞

> An ambition to squint
> At my verses in print
> Makes me hope that for these you'll find room
> If you so condescend
> Then please place at the end
> The name of yours truly, L Bloom.

Notes

For further information, see the Bibliogrphy, page 328.

Abbreviation	**Title**
AP	*A Portrait of the Artist as a Young Man*
B&B	*Blooms & Barnacles*
Birmingham	*The Most Dangerous Book*
Blake	William Blake, *Selected Poems*
Blamires	*The New Bloomsday Book*
Budgen	*James Joyce and the Making of Ulysses*
Cities	*Joyce's Cities*
Dub	*Dubliners*
Ellmann	*James Joyce*
Essays	*James Joyce's Ulysses Critical Essays*
FW	*Finnegans Wake*
Gabler	*Ulysses*
Gifford	*Ulysses: Annotated Notes for James Joyce's Ulysses*
Gilbert	*James Joyce's Ulysses*
Hamlet	*Hamlet*
HCE	*Here Comes Everybody*
JJQ	*James Joyce Quarterly*
L	Lecture
Mythic Worlds	*Mythic Worlds, Modern Words*
Nabokov	*Lectures on Literature*
Penguin	*Ulysses*
Poetics	*The Poetics of Aristotle*
Selected Letters	*Selected Letters of James Joyce*
Swin	Algernon Charles Swinburne, *Selected Poems*
WN	*Wagner Nights*
WW&R	*The World as Will and Representation*, vols I and II
Yates	*Girodano Bruno and the Hermetic Tradition*
Yeats	W B Yeats, *Selected Poems*

Lecture 1, 23 September 2020: Introduction

1. Penguin, p 1, Gabler p 3. **2.** Penguin, p 1, Gabler p 3.
3. Penguin, p 908, Gabler p 629. **4.** Budgen, p 16. **5.** *Cities*, p 30.
6. Penguin, p 77, Gabler p 52. **7.** Penguin, p 540. Gabler p 337.
8. Penguin, p 42, Gabler p 28. **9.** Penguin, p 933, Gabler p 644.
10. Penguin, p 183, Gabler p 119. **11.** AP, p 175. **12.** AP, p 184.
13. Penguin, p 906, Gabler p 628. **14.**Penguin, p 877, Gabler p 611.

PART I – THE TELEMECHIAD

Lecture 2, 7 October 2020: Episode 1, Telemachus and the Shan Van Vocht

1. Ellmann, p 519. **2.** Appendix 1. **3.** Penguin, p 15, Gabler, p 12.
4. Penguin, p 3, Gabler, p 4. **5.** Ellmann, p 117. **6.** Ellmann, p 131–132
7. Gogarty left for the United States in September 1939 for a lecture tour and applied for permanent residence.
8. James Joyce Museum. https://joycetower.ie/. **9.** L17, p 236.
10. *Mythic Worlds*, Editor's Foreword, p xvii. **11.** Ellmann, p 129.

12. Penguin, p 1, Gabler, p 3. **13.** Penguin, p 5, Gabler, p 6.
14. Penguin, p 6, Gabler, p 6. **15.** AP, p 269.
16. Joyce implies that Stephen paid the rent but evidence points to Gogarty having done so. Ellmann, p 172.
17. *Hamlet*: 1,4 Horatio. **18.** Penguin, p 7, Gabler, p 7. **19.** AP p 276.
20. West Brit or West Briton. The colloquial and derogatory notion to describe an Irish person that looks to London for governance. A 'Brit' located west of Britain.
21. For an account of the Dedalus/Joyce early family politics see AP, pp 30-39, Ellmann, pp 33–34.
22. Ellmann, pp 23–41. **23.** Penguin, p 826, Gabler, p 578.
24. Yeats, p 14. **25.** Penguin, p 4, Gabler, p 5.
26. Penguin, p 11, Gabler, p 9. **27.** L 22, p 303, **28.** Note 2.16 ibid.
29. Worth approximately £500 today, though Stephen in fact is paid a little less for his month's work.
30. 1904 was the third year of the reign of Edward VII.
31. As stated in the Gilbert schema. **32.** Penguin, p 13, Gabler, p 11.
33. *Nom de plume* of George Russell. See L 9, p 116.
34. See L 8, p 110 and L 15, p197.
35. Birmingham, p 142. '*Ulysses* was for Nora. The book he was writing – the novel that tried to say everything – was a monument to their first evening together. The day Joyce was immortalising in *Ulysses* was the day he walked with Nora beyond the docks, where they were alone for the first time. June 16, 1904. The ink of each word in his manuscript made those fugitive moments incrementally more indelible. *Ulysses* was his final love letter.'
36. Contrasting symmetrically with Bloom's overpayment in The Ormond Hotel, L 12, p 168.
37. Penguin, p 20, Gabler, p 15. **38.** Penguin, p 21, Gabler, p 15.
39. Penguin, p 22, Gabler, p 16.
40. For the full Gogarty version see Ellmann p 206.
41. A W Litz, *Essays*, p 401. **42.** *Hamlet*, Act 3, scene 2.
43. Penguin, p 24, Gabler, p 17. **44.** L 22, p 291.
45. Penguin, p 28, Gabler, p 19.

Lecture 3, 21 October 2020: Episode 2, Ancient Nestor and the Disappointed Bridge

1. L 2, p 33. **2.** Penguin, p 28, Gabler, p 20. **3.** Penguin, p 29, Gabler, p 20.
4. Stephen's sojourn to Paris takes place in the fictional gap between the end of AP and the commencement of Ulysses and reflects Joyce's experience. Ellmann, p 128.
5. Penguin, p 29, Gabler, p 20. **6.** Penguin, p 29, Gabler, p 21.
7. See for example, Blake's views on the power of imagination over reality.
8. *Das Kapital* (1867). Put extremely simply, the alienation of humanity intrinsic within capitalist society, by virtue of the separation of the means of production

and its value, will inevitably it is supposed, lead to the natural development of communist consciousness.

9. Penguin, p 30, Gabler, p 21. **10.** *Sliding Doors* (1998), Miramax.

11. P W. Joyce (no relation). Riddle me, riddle me right: What did I see last night? The wind blew, The cock crew, The bells of heaven Struck eleven. 'Tis time for my poor sowl to go to heaven" (B&B: https://www.bloomsandbarnacles.com/blog/2018/10/22/stephens-riddle).

12. Penguin, p 32, Gabler, p 22. **13.** L 7, p 85.

14. Penguin, p 33, Gabler, p 23.

15. Penguin, p 33, Gabler, p 23. **16.** Penguin, p 33, Gabler, p 23.

17. Averroès (1126–1198), Cordoba, Spain.

18. Moses Maimonides (1138–1204) Cordoba, Spain, Morocco, Egypt.

19. Giordano Bruno (1548–1600) Nola, Italy. **20.** Yates, p 384. **21.** L 1, p 17.

22. Colonel Blimp is a pompous jingoistic cartoon character that appeared in the London *Evening Standard* during and after the 1930s.

23. These are associated with the succession in 1603 to the English throne of James VI of Scotland (becoming James I of England) and with it in general terms, the proselytising of Ireland. **24.** Gifford, p 34, (2.201).

25. A farthing was one quarter of an old penny and so worth approximately one tenth of a modern penny. **26.** Penguin, p 36, Gabler, p 25.

27. The Wandering Jew is a mythical anti-Semitic trope thought to have arisen around the thirteenth century and concerning a man, sometimes Ahasuerus, that taunted Jesus on the cross and thus condemned to wander the earth until the second coming of Christ. The legend was widespread geographically and differs accordingly.

28. Penguin, p 42, Gabler, p 28. **29.** Penguin, p 42, Gabler, p 28.

30. Penguin, p 30, Gabler, p 21. **31.** Penguin, p 31, Gabler, p 22.

32. Penguin, p 34, Gabler, p 23. **33.** Newman pp 263–266.

34. Penguin, p 12, Gabler, p 10. **35.** L 15, p 196.

36. Penguin, p 45, Gabler, p 30.

Lecture 4, 4 November 2020: Episode 3, Proteus and the Third Eye

1. L 3, p 37. **2.** Bram Stoker, *Dracula*, 1897.

3. Something not confirmed until episode 15.

4. Homer, *Odyssey*, Book Four, p 41.

5. The conversion of the elements of the Eucharist, bread and wine, into the body and blood of Christ.

6. L 2, p 29. **7.** L 2, p 32. **8.** Penguin, p 45, Gabler, p 31. **9.** L 1, p 9.

10. Immanuel Kant, *Critique of Pure Reason* (1781).

11. George Berkeley (1685–1753), Ireland.

12. Immanuel Kant (1724–1804), Konigsberg, Germany.

13. Arthur Schopenhauer (1788–1860), Danzig, Polish-Lithuanian Commonwealth.

14. Penguin, p 45, Gabler, p 31. **15.** L 9, p 121.

16. An ashplant is an ash sapling cut and shaped to form a cheap or free walking stick. **17.** Penguin, p 45, Gabler, p 31.
18. Penguin, p 54, Gabler, 36. This appears later in the context of a Fenian bombing but it also serves to illustrate the entropic molecular structure over time.
19. Penguin, p 46, Gabler, p 32. **20.** Penguin, p 45, Gabler, p 32.
21. Penguin, p 47, Gabler, p 32. **22.** *Mythic Worlds*, p 72.
3. A canticle taken from the Gospel of Luke and in turn based on elements of the Torah.
24. Penguin, p 47, Gabler, p 32. **25.** Penguin, p 49, Gabler, p 33.
26. See for instance, *Mythic Worlds*, p 193. **27.** Penguin, p 50, Gabler, p 34.
28. Leo Taxil; born Marie Joseph Gabriel Antoine Jogand-Pagès (1854–1907), Marseille, France.
29. The quote in French found at: Penguin, p 51, Gabler, p 34.
30. 'Remembering thee, O Sion'. Penguin, p 55, Gabler, p 37.
31. Penguin, p 53, Gabler, p 36. **32.** Penguin, p 59, Gabler, p 39.
33. Harun al Raschid (766–809), Tehran region, Iran.
34. Penguin, p 58, Gabler, p 38. **35.** Penguin, p 57, Gabler, p 38.
36. Penguin, p 60, Gabler, p 40. **37.** Penguin, p 61, Gabler, p 41.
38. L 2, p 42.

PART II – THE WANDERINGS OF ULYSSES

Lecture 5, 18 November 2020: Episode 4, Calypso and the Dude

1. *The Big Lebowski* (1998), Working Title Films.
2. This is suggested by: 'He liked to read at stool. Hope no ape comes knocking just as I'm.' Penguin, p 82, Gabler, p 55. **3.** *Selected Letters*, pp 157–159.
4. Ellmann, p 281. **5.** Penguin, p 798, Gabler, p 558. **6.** L 20, p 267.
7. Penguin, p 196, Gabler,p 128. **8.** Penguin, p 67, Gabler, p 46.
9. *The New Bloomsday Book* (Third Edition, Routledge, 1996).
10. L 1, p 17. **11.** Penguin, p 833, Gabler, p 582.
12. Penguin, p 693, Gabler, p 486. **13.** Penguin, p 10, Gabler, p 9.
14. Re-Joyce ep 165.
15. For origins of the kibbutz movement, see, for example, Martin Buber, *Paths in Utopia* (1950).
16. Penguin, p 72, Gabler, p 49. **17.** Nabokov, p 304.
18. Penguin, p 72, Gabler, p 49. **19.** Penguin, p 73, Gabler, p 50.
20. Penguin, p 74, Gabler, p 50. **21.** Penguin, p 75, Gabler, p 51.
22. Penguin, p 76, Gabler, p 51. **23.** Penguin, p 72, Gabler, p 49.
24. L 1, p 16. **25.** Penguin, p 78, Gabler, p 53. **26.** Penguin, p 78, Gabler, p 53.
27. Penguin, p 26, Gabler, p 18. **28.** The Blooms were married 1888.
29. Penguin, p 358, Gabler, p 228. **30.** Penguin, p 120, Gabler, p 79.
31. Penguin, p 536, Gabler, p 334. **32.** Penguin, p 4, Gabler, p 5.
33. Gifford p 70 (Intro).

34. *Titbits* was a periodical of modest literary integrity, populated with short stories submitted by readers in return for payment. It was founded in 1881 and continued to 1984.
35. A colloquialism for an outside toilet. 36. Gifford p 81 (4.502–503)

Lecture 6, 2 December 2020: Episode 5, Lotus Eaters and the High Grade Ha
1. Source unclear but Bloom has on his shelf '*Thoughts from Spinoza* (maroon leather)', Penguin, p 832, Gabler, p 582, so there might be something in it.
2. Homer, *Odyssey*, Book Nine. **3.** Penguin, p 86, Gabler, p 58.
4. Gifford, p 85, (5.44).
5. Westland Row is about a mile and a quarter from Eccles Street.
6. Dub p 149. **7.** Penguin, p 301, Gabler, p 193. **8.** Penguin, p 92, Gabler, p 62.
9. Ellmann, p 375. **10.** Penguin, p 751, Gabler, p 529.
11. Respectively The Boarding House, Dub, p 56, and Ivy Day in the Committee Room, Dub, p 115.
12. Penguin, p 91, Gabler, p 61. **13.** Penguin, p 91, Gabler, p 61.
14. Gifford p 88 (5.194). **15.** Penguin, p 93, Gabler, p 62.
16. *Hamlet*, Act Five, Scene One.
17. Rudolph dies when Bloom is aged twenty, Blamires, p xvii.
18. Penguin, p 853, Gabler, p 595. **19.** Penguin, p 94, Gabler, p 63.
20. Rubens: 'Christ at the House of Martha and Mary'. Gifford, p 90 (5.289).
21. Penguin, p 98, Gabler, p 66. **22.** Penguin, p 98, Gabler, p 65.
23. Penguin, p 99, Gabler, p 66. **24.** Penguin, p 102, Gabler, p 68.
25. Penguin, p 102, Gabler, p 68. **26.** Penguin, p 93, Gabler, p 62.
27. Penguin, p 105, Gabler, p 69.

Lecture 7, 16 December 2020: Episode 6, Hades and the Dignified Send-off
1. L 3, p 42. **2.** R M Adams, *Essays*, p 97. **3.** Penguin, p 108, Gabler, p 72.
4. Penguin, p 111, Gabler, p 74. **5.** L 20, p 273. **6.** Gifford, p 106 (6.79).
7. Penguin, p 110, Gabler, p 73. **8.** Penguin, p 120, Gabler, p 79.
9. Penguin, p 112, Gabler, p 75. **10.** King James Bible, Kings 1,18:16.
11. Ovid, *Metamorphoses*. The Danaides were the 50 daughters of Danaus
12. Ellmann, p 37. **13.** Penguin, p 118, Gabler, p 78.
14. *Selected Letters*, p 270. 21 September 1920. **15.** L 15, p 196.
16. Gifford, p 115 (6.469). **17.** Daniel O'Connell (1775–1847).
18. L 18, p 241. **19.** Penguin, p 317, Gabler, p 202. **20.** L 20, p 270.
21. Penguin, p 57, Gabler, p 38. **22.** Penguin, p 131, Gabler, p 86.
23. Ajax rebuffs Odysseus in Hades. Homer, *Odyssey*, Book Nine.
24. Penguin, p 63, Gabler, p 41. **25.** L 5, p 69.
26. https://en.wikipedia.org/wiki/History_of_Dublin#Early_20th_Century_Dublin.
27. Traditionally a quorum of ten adult males is required for certain rituals including funeral prayers.
28. Penguin, p 143, Gabler, p 93. **29.** Robert Emmett (1778–1803). **30.** L 6, p 78.

Lecture 8, 6 January 2021: Episode 7, Aeolus in the Windy City

1. Russo-Japanese war, 1904–5.
2. George and Weedon Grossmith, *The Diary of a Nobody* (1892).
3. Homer *Odyssey*, Book Ten. **4.** *The 12 Chairs* (1970) Dir. Mel Brooks.
5. The future Lord Mayor of Dublin,(1906 and 1908). By 1904 Nannetti was no longer a Councillor, Joyce plays a little loose with the timeline and possibly conflates Nannetti with his son.
6. Gifford, p 113 (6.373). **7.** Penguin, p 157, Gabler, p 102. **8.** Ellmann p 289.
9. Penguin, p 164, Gabler, p 107. **10.** Penguin, p 171, Gabler, p 111.
11. Penguin, p 171, Gabler, p 111. **12.** Gifford, p 36 (2.272).
13. Dub, p 65. A Little Cloud. **14.** Penguin, p 176, Gabler, p 114.
15. Penguin, p 177, Gabler, p 115. **16.** Gifford, p 146. (7.763).
17. Nabokov and Burgess gloss over it altogether which gives credence to the Gifford view. **18.** Penguin, p 177, Gabler, p 115. **19.** L 17, p 236.
20. Gifford, p 147 (7.793). **21.** *James Joyce Reads* (Harper Collins, 1924).
22. Penguin, p 179, Gabler, p 116. **23.** Penguin, p 118, Gabler, p 78.
24. AP, pp 221–227. **25.** L 3, p 44.

Lecture 9, 20 January 2021: Episode 8, Lestrygonians and the Bottomless Buffet

1. Penguin, p 222, Gabler, p 143. **2.** M J Friedman, *Essays*, p 132.
3. Homer, *Odyssey*, Book Ten. **4.** King James Bible, 1 Kings 17:6–7.
5. King James Bible, Exodus 16:4. **6.** Penguin, p 193, Gabler, p 126.
7. L15, p 196. **8.** Gifford, p 163 (8.258). **9.** Gifford, p 160 (8.126).
10. Gifford, p 172 (8.500). **11.** Penguin, p 209, Gabler, p 135.
12. Gifford, p 35 (2.257).
13. Penguin, p 202, Gabler, p 131. 'Resp girl (R.C.) wishes to hear of post in fruit or pork shop.' **14.** Gifford, p 146 (7.784).
15. For Theosophy, G Russell and vegetarianism, see Gifford, p 173–174.
16. Gifford, p 81 (4.526) and as familiarised in Hello Muddah, Hello Fadduh (1963) Allan Sherman. **17.** *The Young May Moon* by Thomas Moore.
18. Then as now, Grafton Street was an upmarket retail area.
19. Penguin, p 214, Gabler, p 138. **20.** 21 Duke Street Dublin.
21. Dub (Counterparts) p 82. **22.** Penguin, p 222, Gabler, p 143.
23. Penguin, p 222, Gabler, p 143. **24.** Penguin, p 224, Gabler, p 144.
25. The National Library is 7–9 Kildare Street. **26.** Penguin, p 27, Gabler, p 19.
27. *Don Giovanni*, 'a cenar teco', Act Two.

Lecture 10, 2 February 2021: Episode 9, Scylla, Charybdis and the Cuckolded Bard

1. L 6, p 78. **2.** Homer, *Odyssey*, Book Twelve. **3.** Gifford, p 40 (2.412).
4. L 9, p 120. **5.** L 2, p 33. **6.** Ellmann p 147. **7.** L 9, p 116.
8. By use of the tick, 'don't you know'. **9.** Penguin, p 235, Gabler, p 151.
10. L 8, p 109. **11.** L 8, p 107. **12.** L 2, p 31. **13.** Douglas Hyde (1860–1949).

14. Penguin, p 16, Gabler, p 12. Note that no Gaelic appears, one has to read between the lines.
15. Penguin, p 157, Gabler, p 102. **16.** The Holy Office. Ellmann, pp 165–167.
17. Penguin, p 236, Gabler, p 152. **18.** Penguin, p 242, Gabler, p 155.
19. Venus and Adonis. **20.** Penguin, p 244, Gabler, p 156.
21. Penguin, p 251, Gabler, p 161. **22.** Penguin, p 192, Gabler, p 125.
23. Richard Burbage (1567–1619). **24.** Penguin, p 241, Gabler, p 155.
25. L 2, p 29.
26. Dante's guide through the Inferno and Purgatorio parts of *The Divine Comedy*.
27. The comic character appearing in *Henry IV*, parts one and two and *The Merry Wives of Windsor*.
28. Gifford, p 223 (9.473). **29.** Gifford, p 223 (9.474).
30. John Shakespeare died 7 September 1601.
31. Gilbert (1566–1612), Richard (1574–1613) and Edmond (1580–1607).
32. *Othello*, Act one, Scene one. **33.** Gifford, p 235 (9.748).
34. Penguin, p 272, Gabler, p 174. **35.** Penguin, p 48, Gabler, p 33.
36. Perdita (*The Winter's Tale*), Miranda (*The Tempest*), Marina (*Pericles*).
37. Penguin, p 249, Gabler, p 160. **38.** Penguin, p 243, Gabler, p 156.
39. L 3, p 42. **40.** Gifford, p 216 (9.332). **41.** Homer, *Odyssey*, p 8 (210).
42. AP, p 263. **43.** Gifford, p 241 (9.839). **44.** Penguin, p 252, Gabler, p 162.
45. Penguin, p 257, Gabler, p 165. **46.** Penguin, p 4, Gabler, p 5.
47. 'Poets and Dreamers', Ellmann, p 121. **48.** Penguin, p 278, Gabler, p 178.
49. George Moore (1852–1933). Irish novelist, poet and art critic.
50. Ellmann (footnote), p 174. **51.** Penguin, p 272, Gabler, p 174.
52. Penguin, p 273, Gabler, p 175. **53.** Penguin, p 278, Gabler, p 178.
54. Ellmann, p 117. **55.** Penguin, p 257, Gabler, p 165.
56. Yeats, p 20, 'The Song of Wandering Aengus' and Gifford, p 252 (9.1093).
57. Gifford, p 256 (9.1218).

Lecture 11, 16 February 2021: Episode 10, Wandering Rocks Gather No Moss
1. Penguin, p 281, Gabler, p 181. **2.** C Hart, *Essays*, pp 188–190.
3. Gifford, p 108 (6.184). **4.** Gifford, p 186 (8.1146). **5.** Ellmann, p 35.
6. Penguin, p 288, Gabler, p 184. **7.** L 8, p 109.
8. Artifoni was actually modelled on the Rev Charles J Ghezzi, an Italian Jesuit teacher under whom Joyce studied Italian. Ellmann, p 59.
9. L 15, p 207. **10.** Gifford, p 277 (10.850). **11.** Penguin, p 312, Gabler, p 199.
12. Gifford, p 22 (1.481) (Agenbite of inwit). The quote from Proteus when Stephen questions his ability to save a hypothetically drowning man. The point is he is still too self-centred to give sufficient of himself to help others, even his own family. The allusion to drowning extends to his family and emphasises the hydrophobe Icarus theme. **13.** Gifford, p 166 (8.362).
14. Penguin, p 322, Gabler, p 206. **15.** L 1, p 19. **16.** HCE, p 134.

Lecture 12, 3 March 2021: Episode 11, Sirens Turn Up, Tune In and Drop Out
1. Advised by Circe, Homer, *Odyssey*, Book Twelve. **2.** L 1, p 19.
3. Sir Arthur Guinness. Gifford, p 91 (5.306). **4.** Penguin, p 331, Gabler, p 211.
5. Penguin, p 170, Gabler, p 111. **6.** Gifford, p 291 (11.9).
7. Gifford, p 295 (11.86). **8.** Penguin, p 335, Gabler, p 214.
9. Penguin, p 335, Gabler, p 214. **10.** L 4, p 59.
11. Penguin, p 337, Gabler, p 215. **12.** Penguin, p 339, Gabler, p 217.
13. Penguin, p 234, Gabler, p 150. **14.** Penguin, p 339, Gabler, p 217.
15. Penguin, p 340, Gabler, p 217. **16.** L 4, p 54.
17. Penguin, p 343, Gabler, p 219.
18. Penguin, p 346, Gabler, p 221. **19.** Penguin, p 351, Gabler, p 224.
20. Penguin, p 355, Gabler, p 226. **21.** Penguin, p 347, Gabler, p 222.
22. Penguin, p 270, Gabler, p 173. **23.** Ellmann, p 22.
24. Penguin, p 362, Gabler, p 230. **25.** Penguin, p 259, Gabler, p 166.
26. Gifford, p 293 (11.39). The false priest of the song may remind of Fr Cowley, whom notwithstanding L 11, p 152, Gifford suggests may have been a priest. Gifford, p 88 (5.180).
27. Wexford Rebellion, 1798. **28.** See Bibliography, p 328.
29. Penguin, p 367, Gabler, p 234. **30.** Gifford, p 310 (11.1275). **31.** Ditto.

Lecture 13, 17 March 2021: Episode 12, One in the Eye for the Cyclops
1. Homer, *Odyssey*, Book Nine. **2.** Penguin, p 440, Gabler, p 277.
3. Gifford, p 361 (12.1439). **4.** Penguin, p 378, Gabler, p 241. **5.** L 1, p 12.
6. Indicating that Cunningham and Power have without Bloom dealt with the Courthouse business because they would not need a cab for that, it being in the adjacent street. They must be going to the Dignam residence in Sandymount.
7. Dub (Ivy Day in the Committee Room), p 115. **8.** Penguin, p 382, Gabler, p 243.
9. Ellmann, p 61. **10.** Gifford, p 365 (12.1507). **11.** Penguin, p 444, Gabler, p 280.
12. Penguin, p 410, Gabler, p 260. **13.** L 4, p 56. **14.** Gifford, p 366 (12.1574).
15. Joseph Casey. Gifford, p 52 (3.163), Ellmann, p 125.
16. Guinness brothers. **17.** Penguin, p 386, Gabler, p 246.
18. Penguin, p 388, Gabler, p 247. A quip attributed by Joyce to his father. Ellmann p 44.
19. Dub (The Boarding House), p 56. **20.** L 9, p 116.
21. Penguin, p 389, Gabler, p 247. **22.** Penguin, p 391, Gabler, p 249.
23. The flaming olive branch. **24.** Gifford, p 141 (7.639).
25. Penguin, p 393, Gabler, p 250. **26.** Penguin, p 421, Gabler, p 266.
27. Calpe being an ancient name for Gibraltar and hence the link with Calypso.
28. Penguin, p 414, Gabler, p 262.
29. Penguin, p 430, Gabler, p 272. This begs an interesting question as to the nature of the 'Irish' nation and whether nationalism becomes a meaningless concept in any event. Joyce picked up on potential genealogical links between the Irish and the Phoenicians (Calpe might have been Ireland, see note 27.

above), thereby Semitic and suggesting Bloom as the most 'Irish' person there! James Joyce lecture: 'Ireland, Island of Saints and Sages', 1907 (Trieste).
30. Glares at Bloom. Some artistic licence is taken, as this occurs earlier in the episode. Penguin, p 396, Gabler, p 251. **31.** Penguin, p 432, Gabler, p 273.
32. Penguin, p 438, Gabler, p 277. **33.** Penguin, p 432, Gabler, p 273.
34. Possibly Bloom was being generally orientalist, though see also Gifford, p 364 (12.1471). **35.** Penguin, p 432, Gabler, p 273.
36. There is a suspicion, with some justification, that Bloom is a freemason.
37. Penguin, p 299, Gabler, p 192. **38.** Penguin, p 443, Gabler, p 279.
39. Penguin, p 444, Gabler, p 280. **40.** King James Bible. Kings 2:11–12.
41. Penguin, p 444, Gabler, p 280. **42.** Penguin, p 445, Gabler, p 280.
43. In the Bible, 'father' is aimed *at* Elijah by his disciple Elisha, just to add to the Stephen/Bloom/Jesus/God consubstantial confusion.

Lecture 14, 31 March 2021: Episode 13, Nausicaa and the Coming of Elijah

1. Penguin, p 449, Gabler, p 284. **2.** Homer, *Odyssey,* Book Five. **3.** L 8, p 103.
4. Penguin, p 465, Gabler, p 293. **5.** Penguin, p 475, Gabler, p 299.
6. Penguin, p 465, Gabler, p 293. **7.** L 4, p 58.
8. Penguin, p 477, Gabler, p 300. **9.** Penguin, p 478, Gabler, p 301.
10. Penguin, p 479, Gabler, p 301. **11.** L 9, p 117.
12. Nabokov, p 342. **13.** L 4, p 49. **14.** Penguin, p 498, Gabler, p 312.
15. F Senn, *Essays,* p 294. **16.** L 4, p 49.

Lecture 15, 21 April 2021: Episode 14, Oxen, Suns and Mothers

1. https://www.mapspictures.com/ireland/history/ireland_population.php.
2. 'Patois' is author insertion to replace unacceptable language.
3. *Selected Letters,* p 251. **4.** J S Atherton, *Essays,* p 315.
5. Kitty O'Shea. Ellmann, p 32. **6.** Gifford, p 410 (14.74).
7. Penguin, p 505, Gabler, p 317. **8.** Penguin, p 499, Gabler, p 314.
9. Penguin, p 502, Gabler, p 315. **10.** Penguin, p 503, Gabler, p 316.
11. Mona island was the medieval name for the island of Anglesey in north Wales.
12. Penguin, p 503, Gabler, p 316. **13.** Penguin, p 504, Gabler, p 317.
14. Penguin, p 511, Gabler, p 320. **15.** Penguin, p 510, Gabler, p 320.
16. Penguin, p 510, Gabler, p 320. **17.** Penguin, p 514, Gabler, p 322.
18. Penguin, p 512, Gabler, p 321. **19.** L 10, p 138.
20. AP, pp 221–227. **21.** *Mythic Worlds,* p 48. **22.** L 4, p 53.
23. *The Waste Land* was published in 1922 and likely written over 1920 and 1921. As well as Eliot being independently acquainted with Joyce, they shared a mentor, Ezra Pound, to whom Joyce was sending episode manuscripts for serialisation in *The Little Review* and for general comment.
24. *Cities,* p 48. **25.** Gilbert, pp 296–297. **26.** L 2, p 34.
27. The only English pope (1100–1169). **28.** Penguin, p 524, Gabler, p 328.
29. Lambay Island is off of the coast of Dublin to the north. **30.** Gilbert, p 298.

31. Penguin, p 529, Gabler, p 331. **32.** Penguin, p 533, Gabler, p 333.
33. Penguin, p 535, Gabler, p 334. **34.** Penguin, p 545, Gabler, p 340.
35. *Mythic Worlds*, pp 153–154. **36.** Penguin, p 416, Gabler, p 263.
37. Penguin, p 540, Gabler, p 337. **38.** L 10, p 136.
39. Penguin, p 553, Gabler, p 345. **40.** Blamires, p 157.

Lecture 16, 5 May 2021: Episode 15. Circe Part One – the Witching Hour.
1. L 2, p 27. **2.** Homer, *Odyssey*, Book Ten. **3.** 81/82 Mecklenburgh.
4. Mabbot Street is now Corporation Street. **5.** L 16, p 215, below.
6. Source not found, though I thought it was Anthony Burgess. Apologies to whoever wrote it if not. The allusion is good.
7. Penguin, p 570, Gabler, p 359. **8.** *Mythic Worlds*, p 133.
9. Thomas Mann, 1924. **10.** *Mythic Worlds*, p 136.
11. Penguin, p 569, Gabler, p 357.
12. An unflattering term for non-Jews. **13.** Penguin, p 10, Gabler, p 9.
14. Penguin, p 570, Gabler, p 358. **15.** L 4, p 56.
16. Penguin, p 572, Gabler, p 361.
17. 'The Bloom is on the Rye', a popular music hall song also known as 'My Pretty Jane'. Music: Sir Henry Bishop, words, Edward Fitzball.
18. Penguin, p 577, Gabler, p 366. **19.** L 10, p 138.
20. Penguin, p 578, Gabler, p 367.
21. Whilst at Belvedere School, Joyce wrote a story intended for *Titbits* and subsequent payment. It is not known if it was submitted. Ellmann, p 50.
22. L 6, p 77. **23.** L 11, p 150. **24.** Penguin, p 591, Gabler, p 379.
25. Penguin, p 599, Gabler, p 387. **26.** B&B ep 66, Potato I Have.
27. Hebrew, from the Song of Solomon (1:5): 'I am black, but comely, O ye daughters of Jerusalem'.
28. Penguin, p 600, Gabler, p 389. **29.** *Divine Comedy* (Paradiso).
30. Penguin, p 610, Gabler, p 399. **31.** Penguin, p 611, Gabler, p 400.
32. L 21, p 281. **33.** King James Bible, Luke 23:28.
34. Penguin, p 617, Gabler, p 406.
35. https://en.wikipedia.org/wiki/Sacred_Heart.
36. Penguin, p 618, Gabler, p 407.

Lecture 17, 19 May 2021: Episode 15, Circe, Part Two – Potatoes and Chandeliers
1. *Mythic Worlds*, p 148. **2.** L 7, p 90. **3.** King James Bible, Malachi 4:5.
4. Penguin, p 625, Gabler, p 414. **5.** Blamires, p 177.
6. Penguin, p 626, Gabler, p 415. **7.** *Mythic Worlds*, p 151.
8. Penguin, p 627, Gabler, p 416. **9.** L 10, p 128.
10. For deeper analysis see Yates, Chapters 13, 14, etc.
11. Blamires, p 178. **12.** *Mythic Worlds*, pp 151–155. **13.** L 7, p 85.
14. Penguin, p 641, Gabler, p 430. **15.** Penguin, p 652, Gabler, p 441.
16. Penguin, p 654, Gabler, p 443. **17.** Penguin, p 666, Gabler, p 456.

18. AP, p 49. **19.** Penguin, p 668, Gabler, p 459.
20. Penguin, p 668, Gabler, p 459.
21. Penguin, p 668, Gabler, p 459. **22.** L11, p 152.
23. Homer, *Odyssey*, Book Nineteen. **24.** HCE, p 164.
25. Penguin, p 177, Gabler, p 115. **26.** Penguin, p 682, Gabler, p 475.
27. This phrase borrowed from Stephen's musings in Proteus in reference to a Fenian bombing but might equally imply the entropic reassembling of matter over time.
28. Penguin, p 683, Gabler, p 475. **29.** Newman, p 594.
30. H Kenner, *Essays*, p 353. **31.** Gifford p 452 (6.Intro).
32. Ellmann, p 459. **33.** H Kenner, *Essays*, pp 360–362.
34. L 15, p 209 and elsewhere. **35.** L 18, p 246.
36. In Lestrygonians, Bloom likens him to Harvey Duff. Gifford, p 169 (8.441).
37. Yeats, 'Who Goes With Fergus', p 14. **38.** H Kenner, *Essays*, p 359.
39. Penguin, p 702, Gabler, p 497. **40.** L 15, p 203.

PART III – THE HOMECOMING

Lecture 18, 2 June 2021: Episode 16, Trust Me, I'm Eumaeus

1. Homer, *Odyssey*, Book Thirteen.
2. Note and compare Technics of Part I and Part III (Appendix One).
3. As above. **4.** Per end Proteus. **5.** Penguin, p 718, Gabler, p 509.
6. Travelling sharp-shooter shows emulating those of Bill Cody ('Buffalo Bill') had been quite the rage in the late Victorian and Edwardian eras.
7. St Stephen, died 36 CE, the first Christian martyr.
8. James Fitzharris (1843–1910). **9.** L 8, p 104. **10.** L 10, p 137.
11. Gifford, p 553 (16.1301).
12. Joyce takes a little licence here as Sinn Fein was founded 28 November 1905.
13. Gifford, p 299 (11.486).
14. At MacConnell's corner in Wandering Rocks and in near Mabbot Street in Circe.
15. On the evidence before us in Calypso, it is Bloom's not Molly's confusion.
16. Penguin, p 737, Gabler, p 521. **17.** Penguin, p 41, Gabler, p 28.
18. For further consideration, see Williams, Simon, *Wagner and the Romantic Hero* (Cambridge University Press).

Lecture 19, 16 June 2021: Episode 17, Ithaca 1, A Heaventree of Stars

1. Penguin, p 498, Gabler, p 312. **2.** Penguin, p 783, Gabler, p 549.
3. Penguin, p 778, Gabler, p 545. **4.** Penguin, p 780, Gabler, p 547.
5. Penguin, p 791, Gabler, p 553. **6.** Penguin, p 84, Gabler, p 56.
7. Or rather Stephen reminisces on those days at Clongowes Wood: Penguin, p 57, Gabler, p 38.
8. Blamires, p 216. **9.** Penguin, p 789, Gabler, p 552.
10. Penguin, p 789, Gabler, p 552.
11. Penguin, p 181, Gabler, p 117. **12.** *Mythic Worlds*, p 179.

13. Penguin, p 195, Gabler, p 127. **14.** L 8, p 110. **15.** Gifford, p 579 (17.802).
16. Penguin, p 810, Gabler, p 567. **17.** Penguin, p 802, Gabler, p 561.
18. Penguin, p 815, Gabler, p 570. **19.** Blamires, p 225.
20. Penguin, p 819, Gabler, p 573. **21.** Penguin, p 34, Gabler, p 23.
22. King James Bible. John 1:5. **23.** Penguin, p 823, Gabler, p 576.
24. A W Litz, *Essays*, p 401, referencing Clive Hart.
25. Penguin, p 826, Gabler, p 577. **26.** Blamires, p 226.
27. A W Litz, *Essays*, p 401.

Lecture 20, 7 July 2021: Episode 17, Ithaca 2, Crumbs and Comfort

1. Gifford, p 71 (4.63). **2.** Penguin, p 842, Gabler, p 588.
3. Penguin, p 843, Gabler, p 58. **4.** Penguin, p 120, Gabler, p 79.
5. L 7, p 92. **6.** Note 5.15.
7. From the Middle Ages to the Age of Enlightenment, Jews in various European communities and city states were denied memberships of guilds and craft societies which was necessary to work in many fields and often barred from owning land. Even later across the Russian Empire which included much of modern Eastern Europe, Jews were restricted to living in the Pale of Settlement, where restrictions applied. Sources: various.
8. R Hernandez, 'Physical Culture and the Aesthetics of Jewish Regeneration in Ulysses', JJQ, vol 58, No 3, p 275. **9.** Penguin, p 302, Gabler, p 193.
10. It said 'Augusta' as per Ellmann, p 21. A photo available online of Certificate No 896 shows 'Augustine' (after his grandfather) and this stated to be 'Given' some years later on 22 March 1904, indicating it was subsequently corrected. https://crossrefit.info/files/images/James_Joyce_birth_and_baptismal_certificate.jpg.
11. The Jewish prayer book and narration of the story of the exodus from Egypt, which reading forms the crux of the Passover festival.
12. Penguin, p 853, Gabler, p 595. **13.** L 13, p 171.
14. Penguin, p 858, Gabler, p 598. **15.** Penguin, p 858, Gabler, p 598.
16. Penguin, p 859, Gabler, p 599. **17.** Penguin, p 862, Gabler, p 601.
18. Penguin, p 67, Gabler, p 46. **19.** Penguin, p 928, Gabler, p 641.
20. Penguin, p 863, Gabler, p 601. **21.** Penguin, p 331, Gabler, p 211.
22. L 18, p 244. **23.** Sources, various but see also, *Mythic Worlds*, p 272.
24. L 10, above. **25.** Penguin, p 867, Gabler, p 604. **26.** Gifford, p 88 (5.194).
27. Publishers of many editions assume this is an error and omit it, even modern editions. Gabler includes it, Penguin does not.

Lecture 21, 21 July 2021: Episode 18, Lady Penelope and the Word Known to All

1. Budgen, p 212. **2.** Newman, p 220. **3.** Penguin, p 863, Gabler, p 601.
4. Homer, *Odyssey*, Book Twenty-three. **5.** *Selected Letters*, p 285.
6. Author emphasis.
7. 1999, Roger Michell, Richard Curtis, Duncan Kenworthy.

8. Penguin, p 871, Gabler, p 608. **9.** Penguin, p 872, Gabler, p 608.
10. Penguin, p 875, Gabler, p 610. **11.** Penguin, p 875, Gabler, p 610.
12. L 9, p 114. **13.** Penguin, p 643, Gabler, p 432. **14.** Dub, (The Dead), p 175.
15. Verification of the visit not found. **16.** L 7, p 91.
17. Penguin, p 893, Gabler, p 621. **18.** Penguin, p 899, Gabler, p 624.
19. 1884. Composer, James L Molloy, lyrics G Clifton Bingham.
20. *Don Giovanni,* Act One, W A Mozart.
21. Penguin, p 900, Gabler, p 625. **22.** Birmingham, p 30.
23. For further exploration of the point, consider B&B, ep 65, Old Tweedy's Big Moustaches.
24. Penguin, p 907, Gabler, p 629. **25.** Penguin, p 908, Gabler, p 629.
26. L 14, p 189. **27.** *Selected Letters,* December 1909 for example.
28. We think, Mr MacDowell, Theodore Purefoy and Jack Power.
29. Dub.(Grace), p 149. **30.** Penguin, p 921, Gabler, p 637.
31. Penguin, p 922, Gabler, p 637.
32. L 17, p 233. Also an early Joyce poetry collection, 1907.
33. Penguin, p 923, Gabler, p 638. **34.** Penguin, p 924, Gabler, p 638.
35. L 7, p 88. See also *Cities,* p 82. **36.** L 3, p 40.
37. One may interpret as subliminal adoration of Bloom.
38. Penguin, p 931, Gabler, p 642. **39.** Penguin, p 929, Gabler, p 641.
40. L 10, p 130. **41.** Penguin, p 869, Gabler, p 605. **42.** Author emphasis.
43. *Irish Times,* 21 January 2019. https://www.irishtimes.com/culture/heritage/healthcare-in-the-war-of-independence-st-ultan-s-children-s-hospital-1.3750321.
44. Ellmann, p 21, but note that this includes three mis-births.
45. *Cities,* p 85 and, of course, Stephen's 'Parable of the Plums'. **46.** L 9, p 120.

Lecture 22, 4 August 2021: Epilogue, In Our Ends are Our Beginnings

1. Ellmann, p 521. **2.** Penguin, p 870, Gabler, p 606.
3. For example, Re-Joyce, ep 300 – Falling Winds.
4. Penguin, p 447, Gabler, p 281. **5.** Penguin, p 56, Gabler, p 38.
6. Penguin, p 449, Gabler, p 283. **7.** Penguin, p 308, Gabler, p 197.
8. Penguin, pp 574–577, Gabler, pp 363–366. **9.** Penguin, p 117, Gabler, p 78.
10. Penguin, p 273, Gabler, p 175.
11. *Mythic Worlds,* p 4 and again p 193. To say that Campbell thought Joyce a schizophrenic is undoubtedly to stretch a point. However, he indicates that he finds certain consistency between Joyce imagery and schizophrenic imagery especially archetypal or mythical.
12. Penguin, p 799, Gabler, p 559.
13. B Magee, *The Philosophy of Schopenhauer,* p 196, in turn quoting from A Schopenhauer, *On the Basis of Morality,* p 166: 'To a certain extent I have identified myself with the other man, and in consequence the barrier between the ego and non-ego is for the moment abolished; only then do the other man's affairs, his need, distress, and suffering, directly become my own. I no longer look at him as if he were something given to me by empirical intuitive

perception, as something strange and foreign, as a matter of indifference, as something entirely different from me. On the contrary, I share the suffering in *him,* in spite of the fact that his skin does not enclose my nerves. Only in this way can *his* woe, *his* distress become a motive *for me*; otherwise it could be absolutely only my own. I repeat that this *occurrence is mysterious,* for it is something our faculty of reason can give no direct account of, and its grounds cannot be discovered on the path of experience. And yet it happens every day; everyone has often experienced it within himself; even to the most hard hearted and selfish it is not unknown. Every day it comes before our eyes, in single acts on a small scale . . . '

14. Penguin, p 790, Gabler, p 553. **15.** Penguin, p 858, Gabler, p 598.

16. As variously reported. Clearly this must exclude the likely tram ride to Sir John Rogersons Quay, the trip to Glasnevin, flying chariot/taxi ride to Sandymount, the return trip to Holles Street and the train to Amiens Street. This leaves generally a northern area between Abbey Street, Ormond Quay and Little Britain Street and a southern area between Weston Row and Grafton Street with Temple Bar in the middle and Holles Street out on a limb. It's all a bit of a stretch to make a doubtful point. The same goes for claims of an infinity sign.

17. L 5, p 61. **18.** Penguin, p 14, Gabler, p 11.

19. *The Hidden Life of Christ*. Penguin, p 833, Gabler, p 582.

20. Kurt Vonnegut, *Slaughterhouse Five* (1969).

21. Ellmann, pp 666–667. **22.** Penguin, p 302, Gabler, p 193.

23. Penguin, p 6, Gabler, p 6.

24. *The Ragged Trousered Philanthropists* (by Robert Tresell) is a novel first published 1914 but said to have been a factor in the Labour victory in the 1945 general election in Great Britain.

25. AP, p 5. Nasty Roche asks this of six year old Stephen on one of his first days at school. **26.** Penguin, p 2, Gabler, p 3.

27. The thought for this point occurred after conclusion of the lecture series.

28. Penguin, p 683, Gabler, p 475. **29.** L 11, p 145.

30. *Cities,* p 81; IV. *Ulysses*: Joyce's Kabbalah. Additionally, we of course considered that most practical of mystics, Arthur Schopenhauer.

31. Penguin, p 807, Gabler, p 565. **32.** Added post lecture series as was this paragraph on Kabbalah. **33.** Penguin, p 45, Gabler, p 31.

34. 1903. Included in the script of the play *Blight: The Tragedy of Dublin* (1917).

35. Penguin, p 278, Gabler, p 178. **36.** Penguin, p 22, Gabler, p 16.

37. Penguin, p 96, Gabler, p 64. **38.** Penguin, p 300, Gabler, p 192.

39. Penguin, p 378, Gabler, p 241. **40.** Penguin, p 388, Gabler, p 247. Joyce attributed this joke to his father, see Ellmann, p 44.

41. Penguin, p 133, Gabler, p 87. **42.** Penguin, pp 601–610, Gabler, p 390–399.

43. Birmingham, at various points but for example, p 101.

44. Penguin, p 4, Gabler, p 5. **45.** *Selected Letters,* 7 August 1909, p 158.

46. 13 January 1941, Zurich. **47.** Penguin, p 625, Gabler, p 414.

48. Penguin, p 870, Gabler, p 606.

49. *Divine Comedy,* p 525. *Paradiso,* Canto 33:130.
50. Mulligan's deathbed account in Telemachus is fictional. For the actual circumstances, see Ellmann, p 136.
51. Particularly in context of Joyce and Kabbalah as touched upon above.
52. Penguin, p 81, Gabler, p 54. **53.** Penguin, p 43, Gabler, p 29.

APPENDIX 1

Gilbert Schema

Title	*Scene*	*Hour*	*Organ*	*Colour*	*Symbol*	*Art*	*Technic*
Tele-machus	The Tower	8am	-	White/ gold	Heir	Theology	Narrative (young)
Nestor	The School	10am	-	Brown	Horse	History	Catechism (personal)
Proteus	The Strand	11am	-	Green	Tide	Philology	Monologue (male)
Calypso	The House	8am	Kidney	Orange	Nymph	Economics	Narrative (mature)
Lotus Eaters	The Bath	10am	Genitals	-	Eucharist	Botany/ chemistry	Narciss-ism
Hades	The Grave-yard	11am	Heart	White/ black	Caretaker	Religion	Incubism
Aeolus	The News-paper	12 noon	Lungs	Red	Editor	Rhetoric	Enthy-memic
Lestry-gonians	The Lunch	1pm	Oeso-phagus	-	Constables	Architec-ture	Peristaltic
Scylla and Charybdis	The Library	2pm	Brain	-	Stratford/ London	Literature	Dialectic
Wandering Rocks	The Streets	3pm	Blood	-	Citizens	Mechanics	Labyrinth
Sirens	The Con-cert Room	4pm	Ear	-	Barmaids	Music	Fuga per canonem
Cyclops	The Tavern	5pm	Muscle	-	Fenian	Politics	Gigantism
Nausicaa	The Rocks	8pm	Eye, nose	Grey/ blue	Virgin	Painting	Tumes-cence/ Detumes-cence

Title	*Scene*	*Hour*	*Organ*	*Colour*	*Symbol*	*Art*	*Technic*
Oxen of the Sun	The Hos-pital	10pm	Womb	White	Mothers	Medicine	Embryonic develop-ment
Circe	The Brothel	12am	Loco-motor appara-tus	-	Whore	Magic	Hallucina-tion
Eumaeus	The Shelter	1am	Nerves	-	Sailors	Navigation	Narrative (old)
Ithaca	The House	2am	Skeleton	-	Comets	Science	Catechism (imperson-al)
Penelope	The Bed	-	Flesh	-	Earth	-	Monologue (female)

APPENDIX 2

Music Playlist

The list set out below shows the lecture number followed by the music chosen and then the artists involved.

1, Prologue, 'To Cut a Long Story Short', Spandau Ballet.
2, Telemechus and the Shan Van Vocht, 'The Shan Van Vocht', Ron Kavana & The Alias Acoustic Band.
3, Nestor and the Disappointed Bridge, 'I Am the Very Model of a Modern Major General', *The Pirates of Penzance,* The D'Oyly Carte Opera Company (W S Gilbert, A Sullivan).
4, Proteus and the Third Eye, 'Those Lovely Seaside Girls', Kevin McDermott & Ralph Richey.
5, Calypso and the Dude, 'La Ci Darem la Mano' (*Don Giovanni* – k.527, Act 1. Scene 3), Suzanne Mentzer,William Shimell, Wiener Philharmoniker (W A Mozart).
6, Lotus Eaters, 'The Last Rose of Summer' (*Martha*/Act Two), Renee Flemming, English Chamber Orchestra (F v Flotow).
7, Hades and the Dignified Send-off, 'Staying Alive', The Bee Gees.
8, Aeolus and the Windy City, 'The Air That I Breathe', The Hollies.
9, Lestygonians and the Bottomless Buffet, 'Food For Thought', UB40.
10, Scylla, Charybdis and the Cuckolded Bard, 'Sigh No More Ladies', David Snell.
11, Wandering Rocks Gather No Moss, The Wanderer, Dion and the Belmonts.
12, Sirens Tune In and Drop Out, 'In the Shade of the Palm', Kevin McDermott & Ralph Richey.
13, One in the Eye for Cyclops, 'The Harp that Once Through Tara's Halls', Eleanor McEvoy, Ruadhri Cushnan.
14, Nausicaa and the Coming of Elijah, 'Girl, You'll Be A Woman Soon', Neil Diamond.
15, Oxen Suns and Mothers, 'A Hard Rain's A-Gonna Fall', Bryan Ferry (B Dylan)
16, Circe 1. The Witching Hour, 'Visions', Stevie Wonder.
17, Circe 2. Potatoes and Chandeliers, 'April in Paris', The Count Basie Orchestra.
18, Trust Me I'm Eaumeus, 'Spanish Ladies', Jerry Bryant, Starboard Mess.
19, Ithaca 1, A Heaventree of Stars, 'I'll Find My Way Home', Jon & Vangelis.
20, Ithaca 2, Crumbs & Comfort, 'Go to Sleep Little Baby', Angie C.
21, Lady Penelope and the Word Known to All, 'Willow', Joan Armatrading.
22, Epilogue, 'Finnegan's Wake', The Irish Rovers.

Bibliography

Alighieri, Dante, James, Clive, Ed: *The Divine Comedy* (Picador Poetry, 2015).

Birmingham, Kevin: *The Most Dangerous Book* (Head of Zeus, 2015).

Blake, W: *William Blake Selected Poems* (Wordsworth , 2000).

Blamires, Harry: *The New Bloomsday Book* (Routledge, 1996).

Budgen, Frank: *James Joyce and the Making of Ulysses* (Oxford University Press, 1972).

Burgess, Anthony: *Here Comes Everybody* (Faber & Faber, 1982).

Butcher, S T: *The Poetics of Aristotle* (Martino Publishing , 2011).

Campbell, Joseph: *Mythic Worlds, Modern Words* (New World Library, 2016).

Cope, Jackson L: *Joyce's Cities* (Johns Hopkins University Press, 1981).

Delaney, Frank: *Re-Joyce*, www.blog.frankdelaney.com (podcast).

Ellmann, Richard, Ed: *Selected Letters of James Joyce* (Faber & Faber, 2003).

Ellmann, Richard: *James Joyce* (Oxford University Press, 1983).

Gifford, Don and Seidman, Robert J, Eds: *Ulysses, Annotated Notes for James Joyce's Ulysses* (University of California Press, 1974).

Gilbert, Stuart: *James Joyce's Ulysses* (Faber & Faber, 1930).

Hart, Clive and Hayman, David, Eds: *James Joyce's Ulysses: Critical Essays* (University of California Press, 1977).

Hefferman, Professor James A W: *Joyce's Ulysses – Lecture Series* (The Great Courses, e-book).

Homer: *The Odyssey* (Penguin Classics, 2003).

Joyce, James: *A Portrait of the Artist as a Young Man* (Penguin Modern Classics, 1992).

Joyce, James: *Dubliners* (Penguin Modern Classics, 1992).

Joyce, James: *Ulysses*, Joyce (Penguin Modern Classics, 1992).

Joyce, James, Gabler, Hans Walter, Ed: *Ulysses* (The Bodley Head, 2008).

Joyce, James: *Finnegans Wake* (Wordsworth, 2012).

Kelly, Brian and O'Connor, Dermot: *Blooms & Barnacles*, www.bloomsandbarnacles.com (podcast).

King James Bible

Nabokov, Vladimir, Bowers, Fredson, Ed: *Lectures on Literature* (Harcourt, 1980).

Newman, Ernest: *Wagner Nights* (Putnam, 1968).

Schopenhauer, Arthur, Payne, E F J, Ed: *The World as Will and Representation*, vols I and II (Dover Publications, 1966).

Shakespeare, William, Watts, Cedric, Ed: *Hamlet* (Wordsworth Classics, 1992).

Swinburn, Algernon Charles: *Algernon Charles Swinburne Selected Poems* (Everyman, 1977).

The Joyce Project, www.m.joyceproject.com.

Yates, Frances: *Girodano Bruno and the Hermetic Tradition* (Routledge, 2002).

Yeats, W B, Heaney, Seamus, Ed: *W B Yeats Selected Poems*, (Faber Poetry, 2004).

University of Tulsa: *James Joyce Quarterly*.